Great Yarmouth's School
One Hundred Years at Salisbury Road

Great Yarmouth Grammar School 1910-1981

Great Yarmouth High School 1981-2010

Michael Boon

The Owl Service

First published in Great Britain in 2010 by the Owl Service. ©

ISBN 978-0-9567512-0-1

Printed by Blackwell Print & Marketing, Charles Street, Great Yarmouth NR30 3LA

Michael Boon

Michael Boon is a Chartered Accountant and after reading English at Nottingham University had a long career in the ports industry, retiring as Chief Executive of the Great Yarmouth Port Authority after twenty-five years service with the port in his home town. He served on numerous national, regional and local organisations in his capacity as Port Chief Executive. He retired to return to an academic career in 1999 and since that time has written a Son et Lumiere Millennium project for performance at St. Nicholas Parish Church, *Yarmouth! Chronicles of Sea and Sand* (2000) and a play about Nelson's life *Now Nelson was a Norfolk Man* (2001) to celebrate a National Bi-Centenary. He followed this with his work with Frank Meeres on the revised edition of *Yarmouth is an Antient Town* (2001). He was awarded an Advanced Diploma in Local History from Cambridge University for his work on late 18th and early 19th Theatre Studies in 2001. He received a Diploma in Theatre History from Cambridge University for his work on *Shakespearean Performance in the Circuit Theatres of East Norfolk and North Suffolk c.1750-c.1830* in 2005. He has directed plays for the Masquers, the local town Theatre Company for many years specialising in the plays of Shakespeare. In 2005 he was awarded a Master of Studies Research Degree in Local History by the University of Cambridge, while at Corpus Christi College, his subject being *The Role of the Gentry in Yarmouth c.1450-c.1509*. He is currently a post-graduate 15th century research historian at Royal Holloway, University of London, studying for a PhD in *The Port and Town of Yarmouth c.1450-c.1509*.

By the same Author:
Yarmouth is an Antient Town, with Frank Meeres 2000

Dedication

This book is dedicated to the memory of Jack Boon my father who was at the Great Yarmouth Grammar School from 1928-1932 and was active in the Old Boys Association from the time he left school.

We were members of the Old Boys Association together. He was an influential member of the Grammar School Foundation for many years of which I am now Deputy Chairman.

When I gave the toast to the School at the Old Boys Dinner in April 2010, The Mayor, Tony Smith himself an Old Boy, responded by noting that my father Jack had given the same toast to the School which I was giving sixty years earlier at the Annual Dinner then.

His and my contemporaries will remember how proud he was of the Grammar School. I share that pride. He was supportive both of the Old Boys Association and was its Secretary for many years before handing over to George Skipper. As Secretary he assisted in the Annual Dinner for so many years first having assisted in organising it when George Skipper, then Ray Packard and John Cory did so much. In the last quarter of century and more the dinner organisation has fallen to David Rich, the late David Harrup and myself, latterly assisted by David Cooke, and he had the pleasure of seeing the Dinner continuing each year as it did in his own time of organising. He was an active member of the Committee which saw the War Memorial established after World War Two. He donated prizes at the School for a period. He kept the Old Boys Association Loving Cup from which we toast the School annually for many years and passed it on to my care. Father was born in the first decade of the Raven Tower's operation and went to the Grammar School, after transferring from Bridport Grammar School, in the second decade of the Tower, I write this book at the beginning of the decade when the Tower's life enters its second century and when the School is celebrating its centenary on the Salisbury Road Site and restoring both Tower and Clock and re-recording its history.. The School is very much made by its pupils.

Jack Boon and I have been part of it. This book is dedicated to him.

Jack Boon 1914-2002

Acknowledgments

When I was commissioned to write this book by Andy Toone, the Head Teacher of the Great Yarmouth High School, in March 2010 I felt it could be a very interesting project. The School Building on the site at Salisbury Road is 100 years old, the Head Teacher wished to commemorate that fact to coincide with the launching of his designated Humanities College.

I, of course, had known John Whitehead's Book, *The History of the Grammar School 1551-1951*, which was published on the Grammar School's 400th Anniversary. My book is totally different in so far as I have concentrated on the events which took place in the School and the students who made the School what it was over the period of 71 years as a Grammar School and 29 years as a High School. I decided to try and trace the development of the School by researching certain key individuals who had made their mark. The choice of this approach is mine and there could have been many books written out of the amount of material available. Inevitably with a project of this size – even with careful checking, there may be some small errors which have slipped through. My apologies in advance for any such problems. I would have liked to have provided an index to individuals and events in this book but the timing of its delivery made this impractical.

There are certain inconsistencies both within *The Chronicle* and *The Standard* and I have done my best to eliminate these. In the interest of brevity I have referred to the *Great Yarmouth Grammar School Chronicle* as *The Chronicle* throughout and the *Great Yarmouth High School High Standard* as *The High Standard*. I remain very grateful to those Old Grammar School pupils and staff who have provided me with their own information which I feel has enhanced this book. I acknowledge their contribution and name them below.

Ken Applegate, Lionel Balls, E. Barron, Bob Boardley, Michael Boice, Chris Bowles, Mike Bullock, Roger Canwell, Colin Cheshire, John Clare, Rodney Clayton, Peter Davey, Jane Ditcham, Russell Edwards, John English, Brian Fiddes, Richard Fuller, Adrian Gardiner, Rhoda Grimmer, Terry Grimmer, Mike Harvey, Brian Johnson, Brian Joice, David Kelf, Henry Kelf, Russell Leggett, Dorothy Maddison, Peter Phillips, Nick Pownall, William Rayner, David Rich, John Russel, Bernard Ryder, Roger Sandall, John Scott, Janice Stowers, Grace Swanston, Peter Swanston, Peter Tadman, Sir William Utting, Raymond Walpole, Michael Wood, Peter Woods, Tony Young.

I would like to thank the Head Teacher and the Staff of the Great Yarmouth High School, particularly Emma Mason and her Gifted and Talented team of History Students and also the Staff at the Norfolk Record Office for their assistance.

I would like to thank my Research Assistant Bill Rayner, my efficient Amanuensis Barbara Smith and my Proof Reader Enid Hunt.

Finally I must thank my wife Pamela for all the support she has given me throughout.

Michael Boon

Contents

List of Illustrations

Chapter 1
The New Building at Salisbury Road

The plans for the move from Trafalgar Road, where the Grammar School had been housed since 1872, were well advanced by 1909. The new School had been designed by two Old Boys then in practice in the town as architects in the firm of Bottle and Olley. H. Olley and F.R.B. Haward were both Old Grammarians and had been part of the Old Boy membership who had subscribed for the Olds Boys Loving Cup in the Jubilee Year of 1897 when Dr. Raven the former Headmaster had donated a base for the cup.

1. Coronation Medal presented to the School Children of the Borough in 1902

Already while the School was still at Trafalgar Road, Edward VII, who opened the Trafalgar Road School while Prince of Wales had been crowned in 1902 and at that time the Mayor of Great Yarmouth presented a Coronation Medal to the school children of the Borough.

It had been planned to open the School in 1909 and the Foundation Stone had indeed been laid by the Mayor Councillor C.A. Campling on May 5th of the year. The ceremony planned for the new venture was elaborate and the forerunner to the Grammar School Chronicle "The Yare" records that the morning was beautiful and that a distinguished company from the town representing both the Municipal and Educational forces of the town attended.[1] The Mayor and Deputy Mayor rode down to Salisbury Road from the Town Hall in carriages in state accompanied by the Town Clerk and proceeded by the town Maces and Insignia such as the Oars of the ancient Borough. The party was dressed formally as required and the Chairman Mr. R.H. Inglis Palgrave, the Chief Inspector for Secondary Education in the Country, W.C. Fletcher, were present as were also the Architects and the Head Master Mr. W. G. "Billy" Williams and the staff of the School. The prayers for the occasion were spoken by the Vicar and the Chairman of the Governors requested the Mayor to lay the Foundation Stone for the new building which the Governors proposed to erect on the Salisbury Road site. Mr Inglis Palgrave said that there was competition throughout the country for all vocations in which men were expected to forge their careers and the Governors were most determined that the ancient foundation of their own

Grammar School would not fall behindhand. He said that the Governors would be able to equip the boys with the set of knowledge which would enable them to make their mark as old Yarmouthians in their chosen careers. He went on to say that although this School was for boys, boys also had sisters and it was the Governors' intention to see that their charge in providing for the education of girls who would do the Borough equal credit was also fulfilled. The Governors had therefore to deal with the establishment of two school buildings and after careful consideration they had decided to place the girls' school in Trafalgar Road in the premises which the boys would be vacating.[2] These premises were at the sea end of Trafalgar Road which was centrally situated in the town and were easy of access. The boys would then be housed on the North Denes in a building which could be more extended site outside the core of the old town. The School had been funded out of the Foundation Funds with the support of Old Boys and family and friends of the present scholars. The advice given to the Governors by their Clerk, Mr. T.A. Rising, from the Yarmouth firm of solicitors of Worship and Rising and from Mr.H.Olley, himself an Old Boy and the architect of the new School had been invaluable. He was pleased to say that Mr. Olley's partner Mr. F.R.B. Haward, also an Old Boy, had been most supportive and he noted that the income from the Foundation Trust had doubled to £2,400 per annum from the period when he had first joined the Trust. He said that Governors were determined to provide the best education they could

---

[1] *The Yare*, Vol. 16 No.2, July 1909, p.3
[2] The Girls High School remained in the Trafalgar Road premises until it was relocated in new premises across the river at Lynn Grove in Gorleston in the mid 1950's.

for the boys and now also the girls. The lettering on the Foundation Stone read as follows

> *"This stone was laid by C. A. Campling, Esq., Mayor of the*
> *Borough 5th May 1909, R. H. Inglis Palgrave, Esq. FRS.*
> *Chairman of the School Governors, T.A. Rising, Esq., Clerk,*
> *Messrs Olley & Haward, Architects. Mr. J. D.Harman, Builder."*

The stone was laid in position by a chain and into the cavity was placed a copy of the current edition of the *Daily Press* together with the last week's *Yarmouth Mercury* and *Yarmouth Independent*. The Mayor completed the laying ceremony by tapping each corner into position with a mallet presented to him by the Architect and in a workmanlike manner tested the levels with a spirit level on each corner before declaring the stone well and truly laid. The Mayor was presented with the silver and ivory trowel with which he had laid the Stone. It carried the Borough Arms of The Borough and was inscribed:

> *"Presented to the Mayor, Councilor C. A. Campling Esq.,*
> *on his laying of the Foundation Stone of the Great Yarmouth Grammar School.*
> *May 5th 1909."*

The Mayor spoke of the history of the Grammar School in the town and noted that in 1553, two years after the Foundation of the School each member of the Four and Twenty, as the town Aldermen were then called, had contributed one shilling and six pence and each member of the Eight and Forty as Councilors were then called, had contributed eight pence. The history of the School had been largely been dealt with elsewhere but he recalled that following the housing of the School in temporary premises in the centre of Trafalgar Road, which were soon outgrown, the present School nearer to the Sea Front Parade was opened in 1872 by the King, then Prince of Wales. The speeches went on culminating in a vote of thanks given by the Headmaster, Mr. W. G. "Billy" Williams, on behalf of the Staff, Boys and Parents. He said he hoped that Parents, Friends and Old Boys would come forward and add to the School facilities by providing equipment for the Gymnasium, the pavilion and together with a suitable building on the beach at the top of Salisbury Road to enable the whole school to be taught swimming in the North Sea. The Head seconding the vote of thanks was greeted with cheers and the Mayor asked Mr. Williams to mark the occasion by declaring a half holiday.

The "Yare" goes on to describe the new School and the description can be matched with the surviving drawings, photographs and illustrations shown in the next Chapter. It had been necessary to secure as large a playground as possible so the buildings were established at the north end of the site with the main frontage leading on to Salisbury Road.

The main building was placed centrally on the site and covered a space, which seems very small now, of 134 x 90 feet. On the ground floor there were two entrances situated as now, the Senior Entrance to the east while that for the Junior School was on the west. Adjoining the entrances was a series of individual cloakroom lockers and lavatories. A central Hall remembered by many Old Grammarians and now classed as the Small Hall as time has gone on, with subsequent alterations, was 57 feet long by 32 feet wide with an arrangement by which the two adjoining classrooms, still present in the School,[3] could be added into the Hall by removing a folding partition which would then have given a Hall with an area of 2,556 square feet. Eight classrooms were grouped around the Hall some accommodating up to 24 boys while others held 20. Running parallel with the Hall were arrangements which many Old Grammarians will remember with the Headmaster's Room, the Library, the Masters' Room and the School Store having south facing entrances which were provided to directly face on to the School playing field.

A wide staircase on the north side of the building led to the first floor with a wide landing and corridor which gave access to the Lecture Room, and the Laboratory, with its Store. The School was to be heated by low pressure radiators powered by a boiler in the basement where there was also a Games Store. In the north

---

[3] In my time, in the 1950's, known as rooms 4 and 5 and to-day still present off a corridor which goes through what was the western end of the Hall

east block of the School, adjacent to the School entrance was the Caretaker's House with a large School Dining Room and Kitchen attached for Day Boys with a full sized Handicraft Room adjoining it. The School gymnasium had yet to be provided for in the plans at this juncture but a space had been reserved for it on the north side of the site. A wall on the north side of the site gave shelter to the playground.

In terms of material the building was of dark brick with grey-toned terracotta while the roof were covered with good hard wearing slates. Most of the floors would be of wood block and there would be reinforced concrete arching to support the first floor. The Hall would have an open timbered roof but the majority of the classrooms would have flat ceilings. Over the Senior Boys entrance there would be a Bell Tower to be called the "Raven Memorial Tower" since a considerable amount of the funding for the School had been subscribed for by the Old Boys of the School in memory of the late Dr. Raven who had been a notable predecessor of Mr. Willliams.

All seemed to be going well and the building of the School which had proceeded apace for 1909 and its opening for the students seemed set but an unexpected event occurred. Edward V11, the King who had opened the Trafalgar Road School while Prince of Wales was seriously ill and the Governors felt that in the circumstances they had no option but to postpone their long planned opening of the School and thus the opening of the School was delayed by a year to 1910. The awarding of the Freedom of the Town to the Governors' Chairman now Sir Inglis Palgrave was also postponed.

Edward VII died on the 6th May 1910 and was succeeded by his eldest son George. In the summer term edition of the "Yare" the editorial wished a happy and prosperous reign to King George V and Queen Mary. During the delays on the formal opening the School was fortunate in finding a former Headmaster of Wellington College to take the control in the revised opening procedures whose speech specifically addressed the boys from a viewpoint of a career rich in experience and in sympathy with school life.

2. Sir Inglis Palgrave
Chairman of the Governors

The Inauguration took place on July 16th 1910. The Lord Bishop of Norwich performed the Opening Ceremony after having been approached by the Chairman of Governors Sir R. H. Inglis Palgrave.

Sir Inglis had been presented with the Freedom of the Town earlier in the day and had then given a luncheon at the Town Hall where eighty ladies and gentlemen, who were his guests, had been present. He presided over a large gathering in the Big School as the main building was termed. Many dignitaries were present with the Chairman on the Platform at the School in a party which included the Bishop, the Mayor and the Member of Parliament, Sir Arthur Fell. Sir Inglis invited the Bishop to perform the opening ceremony for the new buildings which were to be for the boys of Yarmouth. He repeated the acknowledgements to which the Governors owed their success and

3. The Opening of the Great Yarmouth Grammar School in 1910 by the Bishop of Norwich

remarked in particular that the School was honoured since this was the Bishop's first engagement since he had been appointed to the Diocese of Norwich. The Chairman said that the School had been established in the reign of King Edward VI in 1551 and had been intended for the higher education of the boys of the town. He referred to the time when his great-great grandfather, the Reverend Francis Turner was Master. He commented that a great teacher was something more than the lesson he gave. This was something which was felt particularly by later generations of Old Boys of the School. The Headmaster then was Dr. Raven who was credited for having brought the School into a period of great efficiency. The Chairman said that the late King had opened the School at Trafalgar Road in 1872 in his first public appearance after a bout of serious illness and that the Tower at the present School at Salisbury Road bore Dr. Raven's name. Dr Raven's name was also on the Bell in the turret which was appropriate, considering his expertise on bells and bell ringing.[4] The Bell had been cast at the Loughborough Foundry. Sir Inglis said that the former Grammar School had now become the Girls' High School and it was the Governors' earnest hope that the two schools would provide for the Higher Education of the town. He said that while some of the students would make their way from these two schools to the Universities others would use their talents and education to serve the Town. The Bishop, responding, spoke of his time at Wellington College and said he was comfortable with the ranks of boys at the back of the Hall and felt on familiar ground. He said that he might have been regarded as a substitute for Lord Claud Hamilton who had been prevented by illness in performing the opening ceremony. However he said he had been both upstairs and downstairs in the School and had looked into every corner with a somewhat professional eye. The Bishop remarked upon the circumstances which had caused the delay in proceedings. He said that no part of the late King's work had been more appreciated than the fact that he was in the eyes of all Edward the Peacemaker.

The Bishop then declared the School formally open and the hymn "Now thank we all our God" was sung and prayers were offered by the Vicar. The Mayor, in proposing a vote of thanks to the Vicar, recalled the affection of all who came under the influence of the late Dr. Raven who had extorted such an influence on old Grammarians. He said that Dr. Raven's influence had been carried on by other Masters. Local dignitaries spoke including the Town's Member of Parliament, Mr. Arthur Fell.

The Headmaster, after giving a short speech, invited those present to an inspection of the building and the arrangements of the School. The National Anthem was sung to bring proceedings to a close and Tea was served in the Art Room.

Some of the Plans for the School building as designed by Olley and Haward have survived.

4. Plans for the Headmaster's House, Olley and Haward 1910

---

4 Dr. Raven was a great expert on Bells and Campanology. One of his interesting books was Raven J.J., The Church Bells of Suffolk, Jarrold and Sons, Norwich, 1890.

Chapter 2
The First Decade at Salisbury Road

Perhaps it could be said that the first decade for the School at Salisbury Road bore the stamp of its Headmaster W.G. "Billy" Williams. In 1911 he had a Second Master John Backhouse and a teaching staff of five plus two ladies who served in the Preparatory Department. Williams was not a direct successor of Dr. Raven but he must have felt the formative presence of his predecessor with the Raven Tower dominating the School building but he set about making the School his own at Salisbury Road. He had been appointed to the School in 1896 as Second Master and had been at Brasenose College, Oxford and then Senior Master at Crewkerne School. He was to become the longest serving Headmaster of the Grammar School and during his reign the School made considerable progress in both academic achievement and growth in size.

5. The Science Laboratory in The School in 1910

The Grammar School advanced with the strengths of academic and administrative continuity and the vision of its leaders.

The fact that John Backhouse, his able Deputy, served with him almost throughout the whole period of his Headmastership enabled Williams to have continuity of leadership. Williams started as Headmaster with a School Roll of 128 scholars with the hope expressed by Sir Inglis Palgrave the Chairman of Governors that a roll of 200 scholars might be achieved.

At this time the possibility that the School might grow to house 300 pupils had not been envisaged but already individual distinctions were being achieved and the case study of one noteworthy individual in 1912 E.J. Bevan, Bevan Major, who left his mark on the school in a number of fields said much of the influence of the Grammar School on a generation.[1] He was School Captain for three consecutive years from 1912 to 1914.[2] After this other members of the Bevan family E.G. Bevan and K.G. Bevan occupied the Captaincy from 1915-1917.[3] E.J. Bevan won an Exhibition Scholarship to St. Johns' College, Cambridge in 1912 and was Sizar at St. Johns in 1914.[4] After war service he resumed his career at St. Johns achieved First Class Honours in both Parts One and Two of the Cambridge Tripos and graduated in 1921. The war had meant a deferral of his studies

---

[1] *The Yare*, Vol. XVII, No.3, December 1910, p2
[2] See Appendix 2
[3] *Ibid.*
[4] *The Yare*, Vol. XX, March 1914, p.5

but he was one of the fortunate Grammarians who survived the First World War and returned to resume his academic career which had taken him almost ten years from his first triumphs of School. The Bevan Story is symptomatic of a generation of Grammarians who went to war during the period 1914-1918.

The outbreak of war with Germany in 1914 slowed the School from developing its growing reputation in both the academic field and also that of games and athletics. School Societies had been formed and the newly formed Dramatic Society presented its first play in the Easter Term 1913.[5] The comedy *"The New Boy"* by Arthur Law was staged at the Britannia Pier Pavilion for two nights on the 2nd and 3rd of April. The cast included a mixture of staff and boys,[6] as in John Whitehead's era 25 years later,[7] was led by Gomer Williams the Latin Master in the role of the New Boy while his wife also played in the cast.

Archibald Rennick (The New Boy) ...	Mr. Gomer Williams.
Dr. Candy, LL.D.	... Mr. T. H. Rowe.
Felix Roach	... Mr. T. Ayres.
M. de Brisac	... H. F. Rushmer.
Bullock major	... H. J. D. Day.
Farmer Stubber	... F. L. Loftus.
Policeman	... F. G. E. Cheyney.
Mrs. Rennick	... W. B. Diver.
Nancy Roach	Mrs. Gomer Williams.
Susan	... A. Chedlow.

6. Cast of "The New Boy" staged by the School Dramatic Society in 1913

The School performance in the Britannia Pier Pavilion had been a notable success but had there been thoughts of another production in the same venue in the Easter Term of the following year some disruption might have occurred. The Pavilion was destroyed by fire, thought to be started by Suffragettes on the 14th April 1914 and did not open again until the eve of the First World War in August of the same year.[8]

It is a sobering thought to know that this generation of Grammar School boys passed from School into the trenches of France in noting the Table of Former Grammar School Boys serving in the forces at the outbreak of war 1914.

The photograph taken of the School Boys and the Masters in 1920 showed that although the war had ended, the great preponderance of khaki uniforms of the School Cadet Force[9] show how quickly schooldays must have shaded into a willingness to join past members of the school already in the services and fighting for their country.

The Yare records in December 1910 the first Speech Day in the new School as being well attended with the scholars' dramatic presentation being well received. The Mayor in that year was Alderman T. A. Rising

The headline from the Yarmouth Local Independent was "Brilliant Success of the Grammar School Dramatic Society". Part of the Review is set out below.

The Yare.

"THE NEW BOY."

BRILLIANT SUCCESS OF THE GRAMMAR SCHOOL DRAMATIC SOCIETY.

The Grammar School Dramatic Society made a happy choice when it selected Arthur Law's "The New Boy" for its performance this year, for it is a delightful little comedy, simply abounding in ludicrous situations, the new boy himself supplying the majority of them. The little company of ten took to their respective characters with as much ease as the pro-verbial duck to the equally proverbial water, and the result was excellent in every way. The play was given on Wednesday and Thursday evenings in the Britannia Pier Pavilion, and the only regret one can possibly associate with the production is that more people did not turn up to witness the performance, which certainly ranked higher than many given by pro-fessionals. On Wednesday night the company was certainly a distinguished one, but one could have wished to have seen the rear part of the hall as well filled as the front seats were. The loss, however, belongs to those who stayed away, for those who came were more than repaid.

The title rôle requires a real actor to sustain it anything like well and the Society possesses the ideal for the part in Mr. Gomer Williams. He was simply splendid and from first to last there was never a flaw in his performance. There was an infectious whole-heartedness about his playing which took the audience by storm, and the way he carried through the ridiculous position in which he found himself kept the audience in a perpetual state of merriment. He was the life and soul of the piece and he sustained the difficult and exacting part of the New Boy in a manner deserving of nothing but praise. He had to be on the stage nearly all the time, and when he was away one always found oneself following the plot to the point when Mr. Williams would return.

His efforts were ably seconded by W. B. Diver, who was responsible for the part of Mrs. Rennick. Diver made up splendidly as a lady, though somewhat tall for a feminine rôle. The part did not afford the same opportunities as that of the new boy, but Diver made the most of them and was equally as successful as Mr. Williams. His affection for the latter and his concern for Archibald's welfare were so apparently genuine as to evoke many expressions of admiration from the audience, as well as considerable mirth. Mr. T. H. Rowe appeared as Dr. Candy, the wealthy relative, and he made an excellent and stately old school-master, whose only fault was that he did not make his voice travel far enough. Mr. T. Ayres had the unthankful part of Felix Roach, the company promoter and all-round swindler, to sustain, and while much of his playing was quite good he was a little inclined to overdo it at times. Generally speaking, however, he was a success. Mrs. Gomer Williams made a charming

7. Review of "The New Boy" from the "Yarmouth Independent"

5 *Ibid.* Vol. XIX, No.3, July 1913, p.1
6 *Ibid.* p.5
7 From 1930 onwards
8 Ecclestone A..W., *Great Yarmouth 1886-1936*, Great Yarmouth. 1977, p.129
9 The School Cadet Force had been formed in 1915. See p.17

OLD BOYS

SERVING IN HIS MAJESTY'S FORCES AT HOME AND ABROAD.

[This list is not by any means complete. The Head Master would welcome any further information about Old Boys serving.]

Alexander, D. C., Assistant-Paymaster, R.N. (1897-02).
Ames, A. V., Second Lieut., 14th Batt. Royal Fusiliers (1905 11).
Ames, A. J., 7th Batt. Middlesex Regiment (1900-04).
Archer, B. W., Norfolk Yeomanry (1900-01).
Arnott, G. J., 6th (Cyclist) Batt. Norfolk Regiment (1905-07).
Bagge, W. J., 2nd (Public Schools) Batt. Royal Fusiliers (1905-11).
Baines, K. J. M., 5th South African Mounted Rifles (1903-07).
Bales, J. B., Norfolk Yeomanry (1906-12).
Barnby, J. E., 5th Batt. Queen's Regiment (1894-99).
Baxter, A., 10th Batt. Norfolk Regiment (1904-5).
Beales, W. L., 6th (Cyclist) Batt. Suffolk Regiment (1903-08).
Beckett, H. V., 6th (Cyclist) Batt. Norfolk Regiment (1909-11).
Beeching, L. L., 10th Batt. Middlesex Regiment (1907-12).
Bell, S. H., A.O.C. (1905-08).
Blake, D. H., Lieutenant, Bedford Regiment (1903-06).
Bleakley, R. H. P., West Kent (Q.O) Yeomanry (1900-01).
Boake, B. F., 6th (Cyclist) Batt. Norfolk Regiment (1904-13).
Bond, C. E., Captain, 10th Batt. Welsh Regiment (1879-84).
Boning, A. K., Second Lieut., 6th (Cyclist) Batt. Norfolk Regiment (1906-08).
Boning, W., 5th Batt. Norfolk Regiment (1888-90).
Boulton, H. C. F., 9th Batt. Gloucester Regiment (1905-07).
Brown, F. J., 5th Batt. Norfolk Regiment (1906-10).
Brown, T. C., South African Mounted Rifles (1887-94).
Bunn, W., Second Lieut., 6th (Cyclist) Batt. Norfolk Regiment (1898-01).
Cann, W. B., 2nd Batt. Royal Fusiliers (1904-07).
Case, H. K., Lieutenant, H.M.S. Albion (1895-01).
Cheyney, F. G. E., 6th (Cyclist) Batt. Norfolk Regiment (1912-13).
Christian, R. F., A.O.C. (1905-08).
Clarke, A., R.A.M.C. (1904-07).
Clifford, E. R., 6th (Cyclist) Batt. Norfolk Regiment (1902-11).
Collier, Rev. H. F. S., Chaplain, 7th Batt. Liverpool Rifles (1894-01).
Collier, L. G. S., 9th Batt. London Regiment (Queen Victoria's Rifles) (1895-04).
Collins, G. R., 5th Batt. Norfolk Regiment (1910-12).
Cowl, C. H. H., Artists' Rifles (1894-98).
Cowles, R. P., 10th Batt. Middlesex Regiment (1905-08).
Cooper, S. A., 5th Batt. Norfolk Regiment (1903-05).

Cooper, C. S. B., 5th Batt. Norfolk Regiment (1912).
Curra, P. P., London Irish Rifles (1905).
Day, H. J. D., Public Schools Batt. Royal Fusiliers.
Deuce, H. E., 7th Field Ambulance, R.A.M.C. (1908-10).
Diver, W. B., 6th (Cyclist) Batt. Suffolk Regiment (1903-12).
England, E. A., 8th Batt. Norfolk Regiment (1904-08).
Fagg, C. G., R.A.M.C. (1905-07).
Falcioni, L. C., Captain, Royal Flying Corps (1904-06).
Fields, J. W., R.A.M.C. (1907-11).
Fitch, F. T., 5th Batt. Norfolk Regiment (1903-06).
Fletcher, A. B. W., A.O.C. (1910-11).
Glanfield, F. G., Lieutenant, Dorsetshire Regiment (1888-90).
Glanfield, B. J., Lieutenant, 4th Batt. Suffolk Regiment (1888-98).
Glanfield, S. J., Lieutenant, 106th Winnipeg Light Infantry (1888-97).
Glanfield, G., Second Lieut., 9th Batt. Norfolk Regiment (1900-06).
Grand, R., Second Lieut., 8th Batt. Norfolk Regiment (1899-06).
Grand, H. S, Second Lieut., 10th Batt. Norfolk Regiment (1904-08).
Green, L. G., E.R.A., H.M.S. Fairy (1905-08).
Harwood, C. B., Middlesex Regiment (1908-11).
Hall, T. B., Captain, 5th Batt. Norfolk Regiment (1891-00).
Haward, F. R. B., Captain, 6th (Cyclist) Batt. Norfolk Regiment (1894-97).
Hewitt, C. K, 6th (Cyclist) Batt. Norfolk Regiment (1902-10).
Hewitt, A. K., 6th (Cyclist) Batt. Norfolk Regiment (1904-11).
High, G. C., 6th (Cyclist) Batt. Huntingdonshire Regiment (1903-06).
Holsworth, H. S., 6th (Cyclist) Batt. Norfolk Regiment (1904-07).
Hoult, J. L., 6th (Cyclist) Batt. Norfolk Regiment (1902-05).
Hyde, S. F., 6th (Cyclist) Batt. Norfolk Regiment (1911-12).
Kendrick, E. H., Second Lieut., Royal Inniskilling Fusiliers (1898-00).
Kerrison, H. W., 10th Batt. Middlesex Regiment (1905-08).
King, V. R., Second Lieut., 3rd Batt. Northamptonshire Regiment (1905-08).
Knapp, F. G., Lieutenant, A.O.C. (1894-01).
Lark, G. A. P., 6th (Cyclist) Batt. Norfolk Regiment (1903-08).
Lawn, E. J., Royal Garrison Artillery (1899-02).
Lawn, C., 6th Batt. Norfolk Regiment (1899-02).
Le Grice, S. W., A.O.C., (1905-08).
Lewis, H., 12th Batt. London Regiment (London Rangers) (1903-06).
Lund, R., 6th (Cyclist) Batt. Norfolk Regiment (1906-12).
Lupton, W. M., I.M.S., B.E.F., East Africa (1896-02).
Martin, H. S., Captain, East Anglian Brigade, R.F.A. (1901-09).
Matthes, S. G., Norfolk Yeomanry (1906-07).
May, S. E., Royal Warwickshire Regiment (1902-12).
McJannet, M. F., 5th Batt. Norfolk Regiment (1903-07).
Miles, J. G., Captain, 6th (Cyclist) Batt. Norfolk Regiment (1895-01).
Miles, O., Lieutenant, East Anglian Brigade, R.F.A. (1900-05).

8. Old Boys serving in the Forces at home and abroad in 1914

who had been the Clerk to the Governors for over 36 years having been appointed in 1874 in Dr. Raven's time and he distributed the prizes. Sir Inglis Palgrave the Chairman of Governors in welcoming the Mayor paid tribute to his service and noted how the Governors' had determined to plan the School on the site.

The Prizes were then distributed many of which survive[10] to-day and it is notable that the Bevan family[11] were prominent in Academic Awards on the first Prize Day at Salisbury Road. E.J. Bevan was even one of the joint editors of *The Yare*.

The School celebrated Coronation Day on June 22nd 1911 with a whole holiday. The King had requested also that an extra week's holiday should be given at the end of the summer term.

School House was decorated with flags and steamers and with over one hundred and fifty bucket lamps which in the event could not be lit properly because of the high wind.

In looking at what the School was given as holiday work, the Sixth and Fifth forms were given *The Virginians* by Thackeray, the Fourth Form the *Legend of Montrose* by Walter Scott, and 3a *Quentin Durward* by Scott while 3b was asked to read *Tom Brown's Schooldays* by Hughes. A good grounding in English Classics was obviously given by the School.[12] The School in an initiative by the Headmaster decided to provide a commemoration of King George's Coronation. Subscriptions were raised to fund a Clock on the southward face of the Raven Tower which would be seen by most of the boys while in the School. Those installing it felt that the Clock would be seen in the undeveloped state of that part of Newtown, from the parade north of Britannia Pier, could be consulted from the school playing fields during cricket and football games, from

---

[10] The Senior and Junior Reading Prizes for example
[11] E.J. Bevan Members Prize for an English Essay, Senior Reading Prize. E.G. Bevan the Latin and Greek Fifth Form Prize and K.G. Bevan the Junior Reading Prize and the Lower Third Form Latin and French Prizes.
[12] *The Yare* Vol. XVIII, No.2., July 1911, p.3

Mortished, L. R., Second Lieut., Northumberland Fusiliers (1905-06).
Murrell, G., Norfolk Yeomanry (1898-99).
Nicholls, J. F., 6th (Cyclist) Batt. Norfolk Regiment (1907-11).
Nicholson, W. I., 6th (Cyclist) Batt. Norfolk Regiment (1904-08).
Page, F., 5th Batt. Norfolk Regiment (1903-06).
Palmer-Kerrison, C. K. D., Second Lieut., Norfolk Regiment (1897-99).
Pattern, J. A., 2nd (Public Schools) Batt. Royal Fusiliers (1907-11).
Peart, V. H., 6th (Cyclist) Batt. Norfolk Regiment (1902-03).
Perrett, C., Royal Australian Naval Reserve (1907-08).
Pertwee, H. G., Assistant Paymaster, R.N. (1904-06).
Phillips, C. B., 5th Batt. Norfolk Regiment (1904-11).
Pitcher, R. P., A.O.C. (1904-06)
Porter, H. C, 5th Batt. Norfolk Regiment (1905-11).
Porter, S. C., 6th (Cyclist) Batt. Norfolk Regiment (1907-14).
Read, F. R., R.A.M.C. (1907-11).
Reeder, P. G. E., East Anglian Brigade, R.F.A. (1906-09).
Rogers, C. H., Assistant-Paymaster, R.N. (1898-03).
Ruddock, H. G., Captain, East Anglian Brigade, R.F.A. (1892-98).
Rushmer, J. D., 8th Batt. Norfolk Regiment (1897-01).
Rushmer, H. F., Second Lieut., 10th Batt. Norfolk Regiment (1904-08 ; 11-13).
Seaman, W. J., 5th Batt. Norfolk Regiment (1906-10).
Spencer, F. H., A.O.C. (1904-05).
Squire, M. E., A.O.C. (1904-07).
Staden, C. G., 6th Batt. Suffolk Regiment (1905-07).
Staden, C. C. F., Royal Engineers (1905-08).
Starling, F. O., 5th Section R.A.V.C. (1906-10).
Stuart, G. M., 6th (Cyclist) Batt. Norfolk Regiment (1905-06).
Sutherland, P. V. C., South African Light Horse (1899-02).
Tacon, E. J. B., Second Lieut., R.F.A. (1908-09).
Tunbridge, S. T., Captain, 6th (Cyclist) Batt. Norfolk Regiment (1895).
Turton, R. D., Second Lieut., 7th Batt. Norfolk Regiment (1905-12).
Turton, Z. A, Lieut, 3rd Batt. Norfolk Regiment (1895-01).
Veale, W. H., A S C. (1895-96).
Ward, A. F., Suffolk Yeomanry (1911).
Ward, W. W., Suffolk Yeomanry (1911-13).
Wharton, H., Norfolk Yeomanry (1903-11).
White, G. G. G., City of London Yeomanry (1898-04).
White, L. A. G., Second Lieut., 9th Batt. Norfolk Regiment (1903-08).
Wilkinson, H. E., 10th Batt. R.F.A. (1906-10).
Woodcock, G. T, 6th (Cyclist) Batt. Norfolk Regiment (1902-10).
Wroughton, H., Suffolk Yeomanry (1899-08).
Wyness, C. J. L., 15th Batt. Royal Welsh Fusiliers (London Welsh) (1901-03).

9. More Old Boys serving in the Forces at home and abroad in 1914

THE TOWER CLOCK WAS ERECTED BY PAST AND PRESENT BOYS AND FRIENDS OF THE SCHOOL TO COMMEMORATE THE CORONATION OF KING GEORGE V JUNE 22ND 1911

10. The Plate commemorating the provision of the School Clock in the Raven Tower to mark the Coronation of King George V

13 *The Yare* Vol. XIX, No.9 July 1913, p.17

the Beaconsfield Recreation Ground and would also be seen from Nelson Road and the North part of the cemetery. This shows what a landmark the Raven Tower was in the first years of the establishment of the School. The plate which was found in the Tower marks King George's Coronation.

Records of some of the sports matches held in the early years of the School at Salisbury Road and a regular pattern of playing available opponents emerged prior to the commencement of the First World War. Masters were part of the team with the school boys with John Backhouse from 1909 and Gomer Williams the Latin Master who was a useful opening bat with the Head batting further down the[13] order. A. W. Rouse who joined the School in July 1911 and T.H Rowe (History, Latin and English) who was already on the staff in 1911 also played for the School team. Both the Head and Gomer Williams were useful bowlers as the match records as also was Rouse. The photograph of the School Cricket Team for 1913 shows a playing record of played 12, won 9 and lost 3.

What was also interesting is that apart from Paston Grammar School and the Norwich School and occasionally hosting Schools as far away as Woodbridge many matches are against local town teams. These included the Royal Naval Hospital, *The Mechanics* and a team from the County Asylum from Thorpe with many home games being played on the Beaconsfield playing field.

The Yare provide pen portraits of the team members which were actually recorded in the match section. Thus Bevan E.J., who gained his cricket colours in April 1910, captained the School Team topped the bowling averages as an effective slow bowler in that summer was a useful bat.

His critique recorded in the First Eleven Review for 1913 after holding the captaincy for four summers reads:

Bevan E.J. Captain (with old School Colours)
"Has greatly improved as a batsman. has some excellent driving and cutting strokes and is also sound on the leg. He is still rather slow in coming down to the stroke; in consequence of this his defence is not as good as it might be. Bowls with good leg break, but his pitch, though improved, is still uncertain. Good field. Has been a good, keen and painstaking Captain"

MATCHES PLAYED—12   WON 9 : LOST 3.

THE SCHOOL CRICKET TEAM,—1913.

Back Row—W. J. HINDES, R. H. MONTGOMERY, F. L. LOFTUS, S. E. MAY, THE HEAD MASTER, Mr. ROUSE, Mr. BACKHOUSE, Mr. WILLIAMS, Mr. ROWE.
Middle Row—†F. G. CHEYNEY, †E. G. BEVAN, †E. J. BEVAN Capt.), †H. F. RUSHMER, †O. H. BEEVOR.
†A. P. GODDARD, R. C. STARKINGS.
Front Row—S. C. PORTER, †H. E. HUKE.

11. The School Cricket Team 1913

Not all critiques of School team's performances were as generous. Bevan was also Captain of the School Football team in March 1914 where he is recorded in his critique as being

> *"Captain and mainspring of the team. Clever and "brainy"*
> *feeding continually in evidence, the ball invariably travelling on the ground.*

He was also a formidable athlete becoming Victor Ludorum in the School Sports on the 29th June 1915 coming second to his brother E.G. Bevan in the 100 yards who won in 10.8 seconds in what was described as a very close finish. This was a time which can be compared with that of Derek Farman for those of us who saw it when he flew past the opposition and won by yards in 10.0 seconds 43 years later in 1958, outstripping the rest of the field by yards in a wonderful race. I don't think Farman's time has been lowered by any boy of the School in the succeeding half century. In the sports of 1915 E.J. Bevan went on to win the Half Mile and the Long Jump by 4" on the last jump.

12. W. G. Williams Headmaster

E.J. Bevan's School career has been examined as an example in the first ten years of the School at Salisbury Road. It has been chosen to try and find the sort of Grammarian who was an all rounder and tried hard at everything he did and was just the sort of school boy that Williams and Backhouse hoped to encourage as an example in their School.

E.J. Bevan's all round achievement gives us a measure of Bevan the man looking back through a telescope almost one hundred years ago. A high achiever, an all round Sportsman, a Leader and an Academic in his chosen career. In each of the decades following at both the Grammar and the High School students have emerged as examples to their own generations. Such men and later women, after co-education occurred in the last quarter of a century, have been key figures to their own cohorts of students. Within the town during the last century such Grammarians have left their mark and looking back to the first decade of the School in 1910 such men have lifted the spirits of younger pupils at the School.

The war started to take its toll close to home and in the Yare Volume 2 of March 1915 the Editors recorded that naturally the war had affected the School. The Yare went on to mention some Old Yarmouthians who had distinguished themselves on the field. Captain L.G.Lawrence of the Essex Regiment who had been attached to the Royal Army Flying Corps had been killed in France in an aeroplane accident. Second Lieutenant E.H. Kendrick of the Royal Inniskilling Fusiliers having twice been wounded had been commissioned for Distinguished Service in the field. Second Lieutenant L. R. Mortished of the Northumberland Fusiliers and P. V. Sutherland of the South African Light Horse had been wounded. Mention was also made of K.J.M. Baines of the South African Mounted Rifles who had pulled down the rebel flag at the capture of Zandfontein. The diversity of the units in which old Grammarians served can be seen from the service list recorded in the Yare in 1915.

The lists of Old Grammarians serving in the forces continued to be published in the "Yare" annually up to the end of the war and the lists grew in size reflecting locally the size of a generation under arms.

The lists of service were important to their current pupils so that they could keep track of those who were their slightly older contemporaries. Many of the Old Boys who served lived to return, others suffered wounds and a number gave their lives for their country as can be seen in the War Memorial Roll of 1914-1918. The School remembered those who were killed in its annual service and the Memorial Tablet which commemorates the names of those who died is still in the School. The last Zeppelin raid on the country on the 6th August 1918 was on Yarmouth. On the 15th April 1913 the Royal Naval Air Station was commissioned with a runway and base on the South Denes.

On November 3rd 1914 a German Naval squadron tried to bombard the town from a position below the horizon at sea from a long distance but mistook the range.

The war came closer to Great Yarmouth on the 19th January 1915 when the first Zeppelin raid on Great Britain killed two people. The Gas works at Gorleston was hit and St. Peter's Church was also damaged in the raid when eleven bombs were dropped on the town but with comparatively slight damage. The raids had little effect on the running of the School and the first day of term in March 1915 resumed in its normal course with its work and games which proceeded in their customary fashion.

The original excuse used by some boys "please Sir, I could not do my work last night because I thought I heard a Zeppelin" no longer washed with the Masters. An unofficial rumour circulating in the School that a boy called Carter had actually seen a Zeppelin in fog in school hours. The editors of Yare recorded, that when questioned, Carter was unable to substantiate the report. However the Zeppelin raids did have some effect on the School as the German intrusions over the town had resulted in a blackout and the School was unable to use its electric lighting.

The curtailment of Concerts and the abandonment by the Debating Society of its meetings through the blackout was an effect of hostilities felt in the School which brought a remote war in France closer to the east coast in the same way as the large guns of either side could be heard across the Channel.

Bevan was awarded a Sizarship in Classics in addition to that Exhibition he had already gained to St. John's College Cambridge. The Governors also elected him to the Worship Leaving Exhibition Scholarship for three years.

In March 1915 *The Yare*, the school magazine, recorded that an effort had been made in the spring term to establish a uniformed Cadet Corps in the School. Parents had been circulated and in every case answers had been received. The report states that at that date 37 boys had joined the Corps, but to obtain recognition by the County Reserves, the Corps numbers should never fall below 30 members. The report states that to allow for natural leakage the Corps ought to have 45 members on the roll. It was hoped that this number would be reached prior to the end of term. The cost to members was 24 shillings for uniform and a terminal subscription of 2 shillings. All other costs such as instruction, ammunition, rifles, bayonets and badge would be borne by the School. The Yare article appealed to boys to get some definite form of patriotism by joining the Corps and giving it a sound healthy start.

Chapter 3
Into the 1920's – A Post War Decade of Recovery

The cessation of the publication of the "Yare"which recorded the everyday life of the School as Whitehead noted[1] resulted in a loss of a rich primary source which provided a picture of School life. No longer after 1915 was there a surviving record in the School recording which of the old Grammarians had joined which units in the forces, and for those who failed to return, the War Memorial was a record of their passing.

13. Prince Henry unveils the War Memorial in St. George's Park in 1922 which was dedicated by the Bishop of Norwich (by kind permission of Frank Meeres)

Prince Henry of Gloucester (1900-1974) was the third son of King George V and Queen Mary. The War Memorial was originally to be designed by Sir Edward Lutyens but the Town found this far too expensive and the final scheme was prepared by Mr. F.R.B. Haward an Old Boy of the School who was involved in the design of the new premises at Salisbury Road in 1910.

There were 773 names on the War Memorial listed as having died in action or by enemy action in the Borough and of these 229 were in the Norfolk Regiment.[2] Looking back to "The Yare" however I mention three soldiers who were recorded as Old Boys at the Prize Day in October 1915 as having joined His Majesty's Forces. Arthur James Ames (1900-1904)[3] of the 7th Battalion the Middlesex Regiment, Hugh Stevenson Grand (1904-1908)[4] Second Lieutenant in the 10th Battalion of the Suffolk Regiment and Thomas Ruddock (1904-1906 and 1909-1911)[5] Second Lieutenant in the 13th Battalion gave their lives. There were many others who were killed from this 1915 list of entry. These men were in their twenties when they were killed and provided a loss of those who could have contributed to the town. David McCowan the Mayor who presented the prizes in 1915 was both an Old Boy of the School and a School Governor.[6]

1 When he started *The Chronicle* in 1930
2 Meeres Frank, Norfolk in the First World War, Chichester 2004, p.190
3 *The Yare*, Vol. XX No2., March 15, p 32
4 *Ibid*. p.33
5 *Ibid*. p.34
6 *The Yare* Vol. XX no 2 p.5 March 1915

In 1920 a grand Boxing Evening arranged by Mr. A. A Cash of the Wellington Pier took place in which the chief bout was between Bandsman Jack Blake, the Ex-Middleweight Champion of England and Bill Hayward of Lowestoft. Blake won in 50 seconds and for years afterwards following, his retirement from the Ring, he taught generations of Grammar School boys to swim in the Yarmouth Sea Front pool.[7]

Times were not easy for the Grammar School in the post war period. The Governors, faced with a large deficiency caused a complete re-organisation of the Grammar and High Schools. Numbers of teachers were cut down and the Kindergarten was closed in September 1921 saving £1200.[8]

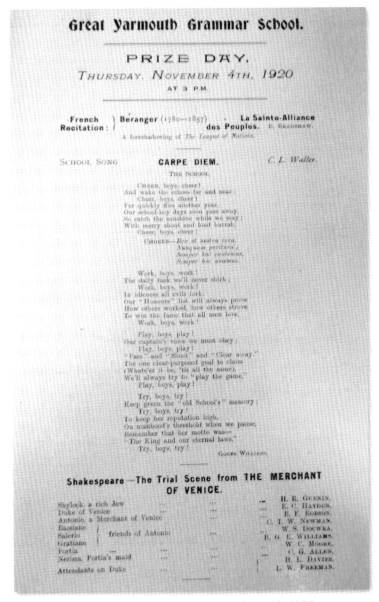

14. Prize Day cover programme November 4th 1920

Prize Day programmes from 1920-1923 have survived and these show both Honours won by old boys together with awards made to present pupils and the programme of entertainment for the assembled company.

Gomer Williams was the mainspring of the Dramatic Society and A.W. Rouse the Cricket, Athletic and Football enthusiast and the other members of staff had joined the forces leaving Headmaster Williams and Deputy Head Backhouse, supported by female staff (still addressed as "Sir"), striving to maintain the School's record. When the war ended it was some time before all the staff returned from War Service and then only T.H. Rowe of the staff at the School in 1911 was on the staff list in 1921. Billy Williams was still the Headmaster but the upheaval of the war had taken its toll from a School roll which had risen in 1919 to 240 Boys.

Until the end of the 1920s the Sixth Form was entirely Science based but just before 1930 a new but small Sixth Form also began to take History and English. For a time the Debating Society, having been firmly founded was the only Society is existence but the School Concerts continued to play a very important part in the School Year. Both boys and Masters participated and the Easter Entertainment was still a high point of the year. The Cadet Corps had been founded in 1915 with Captain W.G, Williams and Lieutenant T. H. Rouse as Commanding Officer and Deputy and the many members of the School serving in the Corps in khaki can be seen in the School photography in 1920. The Cadet Force was originally affiliated to the Royal Artillery but became affiliated later to the Norfolk Regiment and was well supported by School members joining it. In the post war years Captain A. W Rouse was in command and he was keen to see good skills on the miniature range located on the north side of School House within the School site.

[7] Ecclestone A. W., *Great Yarmouth 1886-1936*, Great Yarmouth, 1977, p.151
[8] *Ibid.* p.155-156

J. B. Whitehead who serving with A.W. Rouse on the staff list of 1931 recalled Rouse's keenness as a sportsman who enjoyed with enthusiasm his instruction and encouragement in Football, Cricket and Athletics. J.B. Whitehead who joined the School in the 1920's founded a Historical and Geographical Society and was responsible for the revival of the Dramatic Society which had ceased to function after the School's successful production of *The New Boy* at the Brittania Pier Theatre in 1913. Whitehead went on to launch a new series of School Magazine for the Grammar School called *The Chronicle* in 1930 and with the encouragement of the Headmaster W.G. Williams managed to stage Swimming Sports in the pool on Marine Parade. The pool had opened on 22nd July 1922 and had cost £14,000. At this stage it contained 600,000 gallons of sea water.

The School formed a Historical and Geographical Society with the aim of presenting interesting topics of History and local Geography to the school pupils. The President was established as the Headmaster with a Secretary and Committee. After several meetings in late 1926 a programme was established for 1926-27 with Mr. Whitehead opening the Society's meeting with a lecture on Social History in late November 1926. He spoke on the Archaeological History of the County from Old Stone Age times concentrating on this and the Iron Age. The second lecture on February 1st 1927 was on Canada by the Rev. R. Talbot who described

15. Honours Awarded Prize Day programme 1920-1921

how he had crossed by sea to Canada and travelled down the St. Lawrence Seaway including a visit to the Heights of Abraham, the scene of the famous battle between Wolfe and Montcalm. He finally crossed to British Columbia by the Canadian Pacific railway and his lecture was illustrated by numerous slides. Visits by the Society to St. Nicholas Church and the Norwich Guildhall followed and also a visit to the courtroom in Norwich where a Judge, Jury and Council sat at the Assizes. The visit to Norwich included a trip to the Castle Battlements and to Strangers Hall rounding off a very exciting first year for the Society.

In the Society's second season in 1927-28 another series of visits were arranged. The Society visited the Grey Friars Cloisters and the Tolhouse Museum. The second meeting was a lecture given by Mr. Rouse illustrated by lantern slides at which the whole school attended. He gave account of the countries he had visited, took in the Great War and described his visits to the Hague and Vienna where he had the opportunity to visit Museums, Churches, the Houses of Parliament and in Vienna the Empress Palace and Art Gallery. He returned via Munich where he showed slides of the Maximillian Museum and famous Art Gallery.

In December two historical debates took place in a joint meeting with the Debating Society. The first proposition was that "that the greatest days of English History were the spacious days of Queen Elizabeth". The motion was proposed by Mr. Page and opposed by Mr. Whitehead. The motion was defeated by 39 votes to 12.

The second subject was that "the execution of Charles 1st was neither justifiable nor lawful". This was proposed by Mr. Claxton and opposed by Mr. Rook, and the motion was carried by 31 votes to 11. Several members not voting.

On February 10th 1928, Mr. H. Johnson delivered a lecture on the Gateways and Defences of a 13th Century Walled Town, with an imaginary walk around its wall. In June of the same year a visit took place to the Town Walls and Towers, commencing at the North West Tower on the river bank, followed by an instructive walk narrated by Mr. Johnson.

The last visit of the year took place when 30 boys from the lower forms, under Mr. Whitehead, visited the ruins of Caister Castle. It was explained that the ruins were not the Roman Encampment at Caister, but the private Castle of a Hundred Years War hero, Sir John Fastolf.

16. Prize Day programme 1928

The Society continued to go from strength to strength in 1928-29 with lectures from Mr. Whitehead on local history. A lecture on silk by Percy Elton of Grout and Company followed, then the members of the Society were invited to a lantern lecture at the Town Hall on the antiquity of man in East Anglia.

In November 1928 there was a lecture on the dawn of Geography followed by a successful spring term programme. This included lectures on Oxford by Felix Crawshaw, who spoke on his days in College in Oxford prior to the first World War, Switzerland, a dramatic presentation night and Mr. Whitehead's third lecture on local history which was on Old Yarmouth. Visits were to Herringfleet and Fritton and to Trinity House.

The Yarmouth Independent of the 22nd June 1929 and the Eastern Daily Press of the 25th record the fact that the Historical and Geographical Society had launched its own magazine.

In the final year of the decade 1929-30 the programme included a visit to the Fish Wharf and Barrel Factory, a lecture on the making of a modern Newspaper and a further one on Bristol, concluding with a surprise night which involved a series of complicated competitions to win a book presented by the Secretary. The questions were challenging with a time limit being fixed.

Although the record of the 1920s at the Great Yarmouth Grammar School are sparse at least the notes of the active Historical and Geographical Society run by Mr. Whitehead have survived to illustrate the wide ranging interests of the Masters in presenting interesting programmes for the School Society members.

Amongst the few other surviving records, two programmes from the 1928 and 1930 Prize Days survive.

There is also an interesting outline of the curriculum for the school signed off by Mr. Williams the Headmaster, on the 25th September 1925. This shows what each form is expected to do during the year and it makes interesting reading when compared with later years. The outlines for individual subjects define in terms of the scope what each form is expected to cover.

The topics meant to be covered by the curriculum were interesting and some examples are set out below.

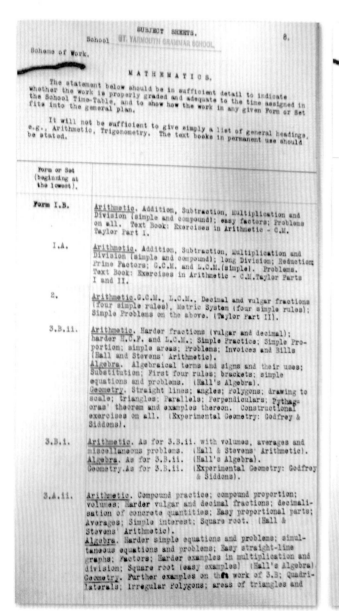

17. Curriculum Topics Mathematics

18. Curriculum Topics English

In the late 1920s the Cadet Force was quite active in parading, training and in field exercises. The latter involved full scale field plans and activities to assault several of the surrounding villages which were quite exciting for the School Cadets.

There is an interesting copy of a report of a General Inspection of the Cadet Force on the 1st October 1930. It records the following:

Squad Drill Good

Company Drill Very Good

Extended Order Drill Very Good

Compass Bearings Good

Physical Training Very Good

Weapon Training Very Good

The report also had general remarks from the Major Commanding the Norfolk Regiment, who was the Inspecting Officer. He said that the Corps was very well turned out and the Cadets were keen and very much "alive". He said he only one remark to make and he made it in the interest of the Officer commanding the Cadet Corps. The remark was in connection with Range Discipline, accidents could easily happen and the Inspecting Officer said that one could not be too careful. He was concerned that accidents might occur if the Cadets were forward of the firing points.

Chapter 4
1930'S Change and Progression

In the period ending in 1930 there are not many old Grammar School pupils who remain alive to contribute to the memories of the School. My father who went to the School in the 1920's passed away aged 88 in 2002. Across the world there may be some and I hope they have pleasure in recalling memories as they read this book.

As the History of the School on the Salisbury Road site moves into the 1930's Old Grammarians remember their own stories first hand and will be able to supplement the detailed records in *The Chronicle* with first hand experience. It is to record the History of the School and those within it that I am now able to turn to surviving photographs and memories to supplement what I have been able to glean from the official records of the Grammar School and those within it at this time.

The first major shift in the 1930's started with a change of leadership early in the decade. Second Master John Backhouse, able lieutenant to Williams since the School moved to Salisbury Road in 1911 retired in 1931. Williams' own retirement followed two years later in 1933. It was the end of an era moving forward almost from the influence of Dr. Raven into a developing School which had by the 1930's become in need of further facilities.

Williams had been Headmaster for thirty years and the Chronicle of December 1933, now to be published termly, recorded his retirement which had taken place on the 31st July at the close of morning school.[1] Many tributes were paid to the retiring Headmaster and Williams in his response said when he had first been appointed in 1908 that he had been the first lay Headmaster succeeding four clerical Headmasters whom had been in charge since the reconstruction of the early years of the 1860's and 1870's. He felt that the outstanding events in his reign as Headmaster had been moving to the new School in Salisbury Road in 1910, the staffing difficulties during the war caused by staff leaving for active service together with the more recent enlargement and modification of the School Buildings. He said he had seen the institution of Foundation Scholarships, Town Scholarships, the Worledge Memorial Scholarship, the Harrison Prize and the Inglis Palgrave and T.A. Rising Memorial prizes.[2]

Williams', own words on his retirement recorded in the Chronicle say much about the man for those who remember him

> *"What I set out to do he said and my main idea has been to put before*
> *the boys the importance of character, of responsibility and of having a*
> *job to do and doing it . . . .I believe that no real happiness can come to*
> *anyone who does not put his whole force into the job he is out to do.*
> *I have been perhaps rather strict in my dealings, bur that strictness has*
> *been deliberately tempered with fair mindedness and justice. I have never*
> *made any attempt to gain a popularity which arises from a sentimental*
> *leniency, a popularity that achieves really nothing in the long run and*
> *cannot be founded on real respect."* [3]

Stern and purposeful to the end yet Williams was remembered with affection by many boys who were taught under his care.

His successor was E.A. Seaborne, chosen unanimously by the Governors from a short list of four. Mr. Seaborne was selected for both his Administrative and Academic abilities as a man well equipped to move the School, into a new era. He had been educated at Bristol Grammar School and then at Magdalen College Oxford where he held a Demiship[4] and where he first studied Mathematics and then English Language and Literature.[5] In the reign of King Henry VI, William of Wayneflete, Bishop of Winchester, the founder of Magdalen College, ordained that in addition to forty poor scholars, or Fellows, there should be thirty Poor Scholars, commonly called Demies, of good morals and dispositions fully equipped for study. Interesting enough the connection

---

[1]   *Chronicle*, No. 5. New series, December 1933, p. 16
[2]   *Ibid*. pp. 17-18
[3]   *Ibid*.p.18
[4]   A Demy or Demyship is a form of Scholarship particularly at Magdalen College in Oxford being derived from demi socii or half-fellows.
[5]   *Ibid*.

of Yarmouth with Magdalen College Oxford is great because lands in Gorleston were lost to the town after a contest over Sir John Fastolfe of Caister Castle's will in the mid fifteenth century. The lands at Gorleston were only bought back by the Borough after the Second World War to provide new homes for those in Yarmouth who had been driven out of their houses in the core of the town by war damage and subsequent clearance to be rehoused on the new Magdalen College estate.

19. Poster for the Grammar School production of "Journey's End" by R. C. Sherriff

Mr. Seaborne had taught at University College School in London from 1925 where he was responsible for the school's magazine and where he became keenly interested in the school's dramatic work. His own interest in Art had already been felt by members of the School and his wide interests and made him an appointment well fitted to maintain both the high tradition of the school and to encourage many aspects of School life.

J.B. Whitehead, the Editor of the Chronicle, recalls that Seaborne introduced German on to the Curriculum as an alternative to Latin and that the Arts Sixth Form was developed to a wide choice of subjects.

Out of school activities received the new Headmaster's widest possible support while the old Societies flourished and new Societies were formed. The Dramatic Society flourished again and Whitehead directed R.C. Sherriff's *Journey's End*, its first full-length play since *The New Boy* in 1913, on March 8th, 9th and 10th 1934.[6] The School produced the play out of its own resources. Whitehead played Stanhope, the father figure, in this tense drama about inter-relationships war in the trenches in the First World War The play was uncomfortably relevant in portraying events in a scenario which could be recognized from the recent past and which some of the staff and audience would remember.

A.A. McNaughton's Osborne was recorded as one of the notable pieces of character drawing the School had ever achieved[7] and Neville Prouting who played the batman was a familiar figure in the town for many years as his long strides took him along Southtown Road to his work in the Treasurer's Department at the Town Hall. The production was a highpoint in the revitalization of the Dramatic Society led by J. B. Whitehead who continued to direct and perform in school plays until his early death while Second Master in 1951.

The Cadet Corps flourished. A.W. Rouse who had taken over command of the Corps in the 1920's as Captain now

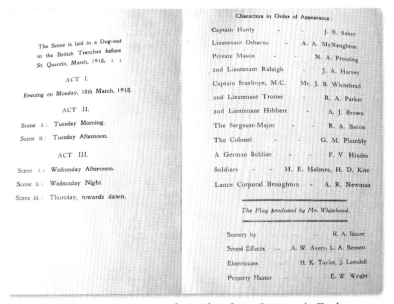

20. The programme and cast list from Journey's End

6   *Chronicle*, New Series No. 6., March 1934, pp.9-12
7   Report by W.J .Sayers, Old Yarmouthian, *Ibid*. 10

led it as Major with J.B. Whitehead and W. Way, the Science and Mathematics Master as Lieutenants. G. G. Jeary was Sergeant-Major while three prefects, F.L. 'Frank' Nunn, G. M. Plumbly and R.A. Bacon were Sergeants. Frank Nunn became a Headmaster in Yarmouth in the years after World War Two. Sergeant Majors tended to be promoted from the Sergeants. Thus when Jeary left the School G.M. Plumbly, who was also Chairman of the Debating Society became Sergeant Major on Jeary's retirement. In 1934 W.G. Way resigned as Lieutenant from the Cadet Corps to take command on the School's newly formed Scout Troop

By courtesy of]   [*The Yarmouth Mercury*
A SCENE FROM " JOURNEY'S END."

21. A scene from Journey's End from the Great Yarmouth Mercury

In the early years of the 1930's there were excursions for the Grammar School boys to Swanston's Fish Curing works, to Sutton's Barrel Making Factory and to the gardens of Koolunga in Gorleston the home of Commander Addison Williamson.[8] In 1934 the Sixth Form visited the Power Station on Southgates Road,[9] the predecessor of both the Oil Fired Station and the present Gas Fired Station which stands to-day further down the peninsular. Such excursions gave the Grammar School Boys insights into many aspects of their town.

The Old Boys who left the School often turned their skills into the Old Yarmouthians Association who were very active in sporting matches against the School and others in Football, Table Tennis, Tennis, Cricket where I see that my uncle J.P.F. "Jim" Boon had built on one his school talents at throwing the cricket ball into that of an effective bowler for the Old Boys.[10] J.P.F. Boon Captained the Old Boys team, to a notable victory over the School in 1937. He shared an unbroken partnership with Jack Baker who hit a century before he declared for the Old Boys. The School team still had two wickets to fall, and were 89 runs short when stumps were drawn on a wicket very wet after heavy showers.[11]

22. The School Scout Troop in 1938

8 *Chronicle,* December 1933 No.5, New Series, pp.19-20
9 South of the Fishwharf on the east side of the Road
10 *Chronicle* December 1936 New Series No.16 pp.18-19
11 *Chronicle* July 1937 New Series No.13 p.13

THE GAMES CLUB.

Chairman: Mr. Rouse.   *Secretary*: P. G. Lincoln.

FOOTBALL.

Scoring 80 goals against 24 goals, and all matches won, would seem to indicate a high degree of skill in the 1st, 2nd and Colts' XI's. We cannot claim all this, however; it is rather due to the fact that of last year's teams only the 1st XI has left, and the remainder have been keen to profit by the coaching under the F.A. scheme. A contributory factor is probably found in the competitive House system, under which budding talent very rapidly comes to the fore.

Dye is again captain of the XI and has lately led the forward line in good style, but the greatest advance on last year's form has been forthcoming from Vickery, who has not forgotten that a centre-half has a duty to his forwards in addition to assisting in the defence.

The term's football will be completed by the game against the Old Boys. The XI are very confident that last year's result will be reversed.

The half-way stage in the House Competition has not yet been reached, but it is evident that South are becoming strong candidates for the leadership, West having lost ground in the Junior teams. North seem likely to escape from the bottom position, whilst Centre are evidently quite content to receive the wooden spoon. It will need a strong pull and a long pull next term if the lost ground is to be recovered.   A.W.R.

1st XI Matches.

SCHOOL v. BUNGAY GRAMMAR SCHOOL.

The first match of the season took place on Wednesday, October 21st. The School team was identical with that of last season with the exception of the goalkeeper. The School attacked for the major part of the first half, but the forwards lacked finishing power. A good volley from Collins, however, near the interval, put the School ahead.

Half-time: School 1, Bungay 0.

The second half was a repetition of the first, with the School attacking but failing to score. The Bungay goalkeeper played very well, but was eventually beaten by Hammond. The School defence was sound, and although the forwards combined well, their finishing was lamentably weak.

Result: School 2, Bungay 0.   J. B. Dye.

---

the slips. The remaining batsmen mixed stubborn defence with good attack, and there were still two wickets to fall when stumps were drawn at 7.30. Their total of 133 was very creditable, as the wicket was very wet after heavy showers.

OLD BOYS.

Rev. H. F. Rushmer, b Lane	16
A. G. Ellis, c Heron, b Bowman	28
J. E. Baker, not out	104
B. J. T. Lawrence, c Fairclough, b Lane	9
J. W. E. Green, run out	1
E. A. H. Collins, c Lane, b Vickery	5
H. J. Guyton, lbw, b Lane	25
J. P. F. Boon, not out	21
W. R. Keeler, W. Plummer and J. M. Boon did not bat.	
Extras	13
Total (for 6 wickets, declared)	222

SCHOOL.

E. W. J. Gant, c J. P. F. Boon, b Ellis	24
D. J. Bowman, c Collins, b Green	14
K. Smith, c Lawrence, b Keeler	16
N. H. Fairclough, c Lawrence, b Keeler	18
M. E. Vickery, b Boon	2
A. R. Lane, b Ellis	12
J. S. Cook, b Ellis	2
F. H. Collins, c Green, b Keeler	22
A. G. Heron, not out	1
E. J. Lewis, not out	4
R. H. Platford did not bat.	
Extras	18
Total (for 8 wickets)	133

BOWLING ANALYSIS.

A. R. Lane, 3 for 52.	W. R. Keeler, 8 for 17.
D. J. Bowman, 1 for 28.	A. G. Ellis, 3 for 28.
M. E. Vickery, 1 for 70.	J. P. Boon, 1 for 18.

23. School versus Old Boys Cricket from the Chronicle July 1935

24. School Football team report from the Chronicle

An outstanding school sportsmen J.E. 'Jack' Baker was Captain of Football and Hockey in 1933 and in Cricket topped both the Batting averages and Bowling averages in 1934.[12] I remember Jack Baker as an all round sportsman even though he was much older and I used to enjoy my tennis matches with him at the Gorleston Club in the 1970's and early 1980's where we were both members. He became a School Teacher at the Technical High School now the Oriel High School. Jack Baker played in the Grammar School Football team which he captained and the team's success was built upon by later captains such as Jack Dye.

The Christmas Concert of 1933 showed a variety of talents and was directed by Mr. Rouse. Both the Choir and Forms 3ai and 3aii gave fine singing performances, the former including a series of carols and the latter nautical songs. The Junior School presented a play *"The Luck of Troy"*, while items by Miss Beevor from the School's Preparatory Department and from the Science Masters Mr. Fisher and Mr. Way were very popular. Mr. Macro who had arrived as Mathematics Master in December 1933[13] played the organ. He left the school in July 1936 so his tenure was a short one.

The School sometimes suffered the loss of a pupil from unexpected causes and a life lost before it could run its school course was always one of regret. J. Woods of the 2nd Form died of Septicemia on July 1st 1934 and the School Flag flew at half mast for him on the Raven Tower.

---

12 *Chronicle*, December 1933, New Series No.5, pp.13-14
13 *Chronicle*, December 1933, New Series No.5, p.5

THE GT. YARMOUTH GRAMMAR SCHOOL CHRONICLE. 5

THE CHRISTMAS CONCERT, 1933.

Mr. Rouse had again chosen his songs and carols well, and under his direction the Choir and Forms 3Ai and 3Aii gave excellent renderings. The Junior School's play was well presented and delightfully acted in a realistic stage-setting of a Greek temple. Items by Miss Beevor, Mr. Fisher and Mr. Way were once again deservedly popular.

The programme was as follows :—

PART I.

1—Carol, " O Little Town of Bethlehem "
(*Walford Davies*) ... The Choir
2—Song, " Take a pair of sparkling eyes " (*Sullivan*) ...
Mr. Fisher
3—Play, " The Luck of Troy " (*Oakden & Sturt*) ...
Junior School
Diomede: Applegate ii Odysseus: Bartlett
Antilochus: Almond i A Beggar: Almond ii
A Priestess: Swanston A Stranger: Lowther
4—Nautical Songs, (*a*) " Stormalong " (*Traditional*)
(*b*) " The Sailor Boy "
(*c*) " The Drunken Sailor "
Forms 3Ai & 3Aii
5—Dialect Reading (Selected) (*Jan Stewer*) ...... Mr. Way
6—Carols, (*a*) " The Angel Gabriel " (*Terry*)
(*b*) " Carol of the Little King " (*Fogg*)
The Choir

PART II.

7—Choral Fantasy, " Christmas Day " (*Holst*) . The Choir
8—Song, " Roadways " (*Löhr*) .... Miss Beevor
9—'Cello Solo, " The Swan " (*Saint-Saëns*) .... Mayes i
10—Songs, (*a*) " Haiden-Röslein " (*Schubert*)
(*b*) " Hark, the Lark " (*Schubert*)
(*c*) " Cherry Ripe " (*Horn*) ... Forms 3Ai & 3Aii
11—Lullabies, (*a*) Schubert, (*b*) Brahms, (*c*) Elgar ...
The Choir
12—School Song, " Carpe diem " (*Waller*) ...... The School

Mr. Rouse was Conductor, Miss Beevor accompanied on the piano, and Mr. Macro on the organ.

25. Programme of the School Christmas Concert for 1933

An unusual document came into the hands of the School in November 1934 from Mr. Ketton Cremer of Felbrigg Hall in North Norfolk. He had a book in his collection which was a Latin Primer written especially for use in the Great Yarmouth Grammar School by Mr. R. Pate Headmaster of the School 1691-1705. The book was found in the library of Felbrigg Hall and was returned to the School via the Norfolk and Norwich Archeological Society Great Yarmouth Branch.[14]

Death comes but mercifully seldom into the young life of a School; but this term our flag flew at half-mast during the early days of Carnival Week as the outward sign of the School's genuine regret at its loss in the death of J. Woods, of Form 2, who died of septicæmia in a Norwich Nursing Home on Sunday afternoon, July 1st.

A pleasant, unobtrusive personality, he worked amongst us steadily and well. It is difficult for us, even with our knowledge of the promise that was his, fully to realise how great must be the sense of loss to his father and mother.

He was buried in Potter Heigham Churchyard on the following Wednesday. Wreaths were sent by the School and by the Second Form, and among the large gathering of mourners were the Head Master and the Captain of the School.

26. Death Notice from the Chronicle of July 1964

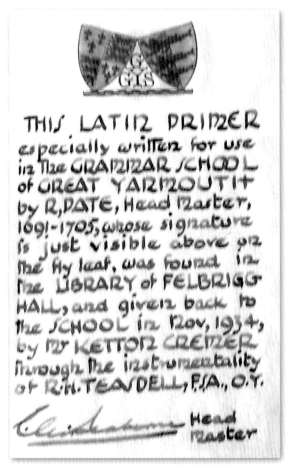

27. Latin Primer of the late seventeenth century returned to the School in 1934

14 NRO Deposit

22

28. *The School Cadet Force at Hunstanton at Camp in 1935.*

By 1935 the School Societies were effectively in full swing.

There are House Note records in the Chronicles showing how the Houses competed against each other with the star athletes and sportsman being a major factor in winning the competitions when they played for their Houses. Thus the Deanes in West House more often than not were instrumental in taking the Swimming Cup for their House and the new House points system made competition keen. Sports matches are refered in detail with Cricket in the summer term being recorded in the July Chronicle as well as Swimming and Athletics. In 1935 Jack Baker had topped the batting averages and was second in the bowling and in the match against the Old Boys he scored more runs than the rest of the team put together.[15]

In the Swimming Sports Deane Major won the swimming championships but sympathy was extended to Jimmy Masterson who was unable to compete against him because of a strain. The photograph from the Eastern Daily Press of 1937 shows the Deane brothers Kenneth H. (Major) aged 15 and brother William (Minor) aged 12 with the great variety of trophies they had won for swimming at that time.[16]

---

15 *Chronicle,* July 1935, New Series No.10., pp.19-21
16 Source, Old Yarmouthian E. Barron from Norwich

29. The Deane Brothers with their swimming trophies

A feature of the Chronicles through the 1930s was the woodcuts of Gilbert Sayer the Arts and Crafts Master who joined the School in 1934. His first woodcut in the Chronicle of December in that year shows the Raven Tower with another view repeated a year later in 1935. Another very attractive illustration in April 1936 shows, what many of us will remember, an impression of the old study of the Headmaster.

30. Three Woodcuts December 1935 to April 1936

ORDER OF PROCEEDINGS.

Arrival and Reception of The Mayor and Mayoress, by The Chairman of Governors, The Head Master and The Captain of The School.

The Architect will present The Key, and the Chairman of The Governors will request The Mayor to open the New Wing.

The Mayoress will unveil The Commemorative Tablet.

(The Mayoral Party will then retire for a short while to give other guests the opportunity of reaching their seats in The Hall.)

The Mayoral Party will then proceed to The Platform in The Hall.

GOD SAVE THE KING.

The Chairman of The Governors will then ask The Vicar of Great Yarmouth to dedicate The New Buildings.

DEDICATORY PRAYERS.

THE LORD'S PRAYER.

Psalm 127. Except The Lord build the house; their labour is but lost that build it.

2. Except The Lord keep the city; the watchman waketh but in vain.

3. It is but lost labour that ye haste to rise up early, and so late to take rest, and eat the bread of carefulness: for so he giveth his beloved sleep.

4. Lo, children and the fruit of the womb: are an heritage and gift that cometh from The Lord.

5. Like as the arrows in the hand of the giant: even so are the young children.

6. Happy is the man that hath his quiver full of them: they shall not be ashamed when they speak with their enemies in the gate.

Glory be to The Father, and to The Son, and to The Holy Ghost: As it was in the beginning, is now, and ever shall be; world without end. Amen.

THE GRACE.

The Chairman of The Governors will call upon The Head Master for his report.

THE HEAD MASTER'S REPORT.

The Chairman of The Governors will request The Mayor to distribute the prizes.

THE DISTRIBUTION OF PRIZES.

HIS WORSHIP THE MAYOR OF GREAT YARMOUTH
(Alderman H. T. Greenacre, J.P.)

A Vote of Thanks will be proposed to The Mayor by J. C. Miles, Esq., J.P., O.Y. (Governor and Old Boy), and will be seconded by Dr. Valentine Blake, O.Y., President of The Old Boys' Association.

The SCHOOL SONG, in which all present are invited to join.

Souvenir Programme of the Opening of the New Wing

31. Order of Proceedings for opening of the New Wing

The Chronicle of 1936 also described a service of mourning in Assembly in January 21st to mark the death of King George V.[17] The Chronicle records that the National Anthem at the end of the service was sung with perhaps less gusto in the knowledge that the King was lying, although not yet in State, at Sandringham where he had spent so many happy holidays in Norfolk. The School gathered for a Service in the School Hall on January 28th which was the day of the King's funeral in London. The Headmaster led the service in the School Hall and after the Two Minutes Silence of Remembrance the School sang the National Anthem and the chorus of the School Song and proceeded to listen to the radio broadcast of the funeral procession.

In April 1936 another significant change took place. One of the key figures in the School, unsung but remembered by all Grammarians when their time corresponded with his at Salisbury Road. Carter, the School Caretaker, who had been a traditional figure at the School for more than half his life, through 38 years, under three Headmasters and four Reigns retired.[18] Carter had seen the School grow to more than three times its size from the time when he joined the Grammar School from Maidstone in 1898 and more than 1500 pupils had spent their schooldays listening to him ringing the School Bell in the Raven Tower. He had often met the parents of present boys and recognized them on occasions as the boys he had once threatened with his broom. Carter retired to Blake Road where he could still hear the Bell in the School Tower being rung by his successor.

One of the major innovations of Mr. Seaborne's reign was the extension of the School, with architect's plans being available before the new buildings were opened on March 18th 1937, on Prize Day held at the School.[19] The Souvenir of the Opening shows the Order of Proceedings on the day.

The Mayor unveiled the Tablet in the new wing recording the fact that new classrooms, new laboratories, a new dining hall and a gymnasium had been built and opened in the Headmastership of Mr. Seaborne.[20] The tablet is still on the wall of the corridor on the south side of Tower Yard.

Mr. Seaborne was not to see how the new extension to the School which he had planned performing in operation because he had resigned to take up another appointment which was the Headmastership of Bablake School Coventry, one of the largest schools in the country.

---

17 *Chronicle,* New Series No.12, April 1936, pp.4-5
18 *Ibid.* P.6
19 N.R.O. D/ED9/65 (a) 1
20 *Chronicle,* New Series No.15, April 1937, p.7

32. *The Mayor, Alderman Harry Greenacre, arrives in Tower Yard at the School to open the New School Block. (acknowledgment to the Great Yarmouth Mercury)*

33. *The tablet in the corridor of the New Wing of 1937*

At the opening of the new wing in the School F. R. B. Haward the Architect, partner of H. Olley who has designed the Salisbury Road School and the Raven Tower presented the key to the building to the School. The new wing (already in use for some time) was officially opened by the Mayor. Major Haward had been an Old Boy of the School (1894-1897), had served throughout World War One and had returned to Yarmouth to resume his architectural practice. Two holidays were then granted to the School to mark the occasion and the proceedings were closed with the singing of the School Song and the Mayoral Party and Governors inspected the new classrooms and gymnasium followed by the Parents. The Chronicle records[21] that it was pleasing to see so many Old Boys present at both the afternoon session and that in the evening which followed for those who were unable to attend in the afternoon. J.B. Whitehead remarked that it was especially pleasing to see representatives from the newly formed London Branch of the Old Boys Association. This Society was kept in being for so many years by E.W. "Tusky" Fousler its first Honorary Secretary/ Treasurer.

34. The Old Boys' London Association Dinner and A. G. M 1937.

The School Prospectus published in 1936 records that Religious Instruction was part of the normal School Curriculum. The Homework was set to occupy the normal boy for the following times with regulation times being overseen by the Headmaster.

Maximum time every night:-:

Firsts 40 minutes

Seconds 60 Minutes

Thirds 90 Minutes

Fourth 120 Minutes

Fifth 120 Minutes

Sixths 150 Minutes.

Reports were issued to parents three times a term.[22]

J.B. Whitehead by now Second Master and editor of the Chronicle wrote that the School felt a sense of loss during Mr. Seaborne's short period of his Headmastership reign. He had seen the development of they Library, had positively encouraged the School Societies, the School Plays, the trips abroad, the Cadet Corps and the Scout Troop. He had only been with the School for four years but had lived his Headmastership to the full and left the school extension as a physical memory of his energy. The extension enabled the School to cope with the teaching of its pupils until a further extension became necessary in the early 1960's. The School Societies, which were active during Mr. Seaborne's Headmastership were the Dramatic Society, the Debating Society, the Art Guild, the Mermaid Society (a Literary Society), the Historical and Geographical Society and the League of Nations Union.

[21] *Ibid*. pp.9-10
[22] N.R.O. D/ED9/58

35. The New Headmaster
Mr. A. H. G. Palmer

Seaborne's retirement ushered in a new Headmaster who was to serve through the years of evacuation at Retford and to bring the School back to Salisbury Road again. Alan Henry Gill Palmer the Senior Mathematics Master at the Whitgift School Croydon had assumed the Headmastership from the beginning of the summer term in 1937. Mr. Palmer had been educated at Christ's Hospital Horsham and Trinity College Cambridge where he had been Senior Wrangler and had had a distinguished academic career.

The Old Boys Association in Yarmouth was thriving and invited Mr. Seaborne and past Headmaster W.G. "Billy" Williams to the Annual Dinner on January 9th 1937. Mr. Seaborne in speaking said that his successor and the school staff had the opportunity of making the Grammar School one of the best in the country.[23] Alderman P.C. Ellis, Chairman of the Governors, toasted the school and with it coupled the names of the Joint Secretaries of the Association Mr. G. Baker and Mr. J.M. Boon. Mr. Boon had announced his retirement as co-secretary and Mr. Baker paid tribute to the amount of work he had carried out. Mr. Boon in responding thanked both Mr. Baker and the Chairman of the Governors for their interest in the Association since such interest enabled the Association to carry on. Continuing Mr. Boon said present at the dinner were Old Boys from India, Africa and Abadan. He went on to say that in his opinion the success of the Association was the fellowship that was obtained from it. It was this point which I echoed in proposing the toast to the School at the Old Students Dinner in 2010 when I said that the strength of the Association was the commonality of interest and the members' common bond with the School.

Arnolds Department Store's illustrated advertisement in *The Chronicle* shows a raincoat for new boys and prices for many other items with Grammar School caps at 2 shillings and nine pence each.

In the December 1937 edition of *The Chronicle* congratulations were offered to K.R.H. Deane for being chosen to represent Britain at swimming in the Empire Games in Australia and also to Mr., Pereira who was shortly to be married.[24]

However the threat of storm clouds was on the European horizon and at a meeting of the Old Boys Association it was suggested that an Anti-Aircraft Battery be formed in Yarmouth. It was agreed that old Grammarians would form the core and all other Old Students Associations in the town should be asked to assist in forming the Battery. A meeting was held at the Jetty Dining Rooms which resulted in enthusiasm for the idea and a representative then had a meeting with the Director of Recruiting at the War Office only to be told that it would be three years before the War Office could think of any means of anti-aircraft defence at Yarmouth. In hindsight the Old Boys were wise to think of defending their town. The War Office comment in the phony war period was short sighted. In looking at the members of the Association who formulated the idea several of those Old Boys joined up together, before being conscripted, at the outbreak of war and J.M. Boon joined the Royal Artillery in anti aircraft defence. Hindsight is a great thing.

36. Advertisement in the Chronicle for School Uniforms.

---

23 *Chronicle*, New Series No.16, July 1937, p.39
24 *Chronicle*, New Series No.17, December 1937, p.5

Chapter 5
Evacuation to Retford and Return to Great Yarmouth

The last *Chronicle* of May 1939 finished abruptly as the country moved swiftly into War. When *The Chronicle* appeared again in May 1941 the School had been evacuated to Retford in Nottingham to avoid the risk to life in a front line town. The editor of *The Chronicle* recalled the two years intervening period and sought to bridge the gap in the narrative of the School's life in the period the absence of a Chronicle to tell the news.[1] He seeks to bridge the gap of twenty months of war in speaking from a town of whose existence most of those moving to it were unaware. He tried to make the historical records of the School complete something for which I am grateful since both Mr. Whitehead and I have been, in our respective times of writing, frustrated by the lack of any extant primary source material for the Schools life in the 1920's.

The School Officers for 1939-40 are recorded as they were in 1941. Of course there was a complete change of personal in those years and those senior boys in 1939-40 had left the School by 1941 mostly to serve in the forces. Ray Walpole recalls that Cadet Sergeant Major Kenny Chittleborough was killed at Arnhem. The First term of the war back at Salisbury Road was recalled as School Shelters had been constructed on the west side of the School field. Many practices took place but during the first nine months of the war no siren necessitated the school to seek shelter underground. The School adapted itself to war time strictures such as the black outs which curtailed any thought of a production of a School Play. The Headmaster persuaded the School to adopt a minesweeper crew as a local war charity and fund raising and voluntary contributions resulted in a number of "comforts" as the Chronicle put it being sent.

The second Term of the War in spring was marked by a major cold and flu epidemic and a German raider dropping some bombs near a ship in Yarmouth Roads. Jack Grice records that it was customary to watch German aircraft shooting up Marine Parade before ever a siren sounded. It was recalled as the hardest winter in living memory with snow lying on the ground for many weeks, the thermometers remained at a very low level, few sports could be played and even the Cross Country had to be cancelled. The School worked with the blackout and ignoring the enemy had several evening meetings of School Societies Mr. Angwin's lecture on Perthshire for the Historical and Geographical Society being notable.[2] The Debating Society returned to full swing and there was also a mixed play reading with the High School. A highpoint of the School 1940 Concert with the staff in good form was a Schuman Concerto played on two pianos with the Headmaster and Mr. Angwin followed by two Quartets in which they were joined by Mr, Fisher and Mr. Pereria.[3] At the Athletic Sports in the summer A.H.G. Rouse was Victor Ludorum for the second year running winning the 100 yards, the Hurdles the 220 yards, the Long Jump and Throwing the Cricket Ball with a new record of over 100 yards.[4]

Alan Hillyer the French Master wrote of the evacuation in June to Retford for which the School had only a week to prepare.

Dunkirk brought new drama to the School and the evacuation took place on Sunday June 2nd by train on a day which grew oppressive as the train moved inland away from the sea air. On arrival at Retford the boys were taken to various billets with labels round their necks and the School assembled on the following morning at Retford Grammar School to

COUNTY BOROUGH OF GREAT YARMOUTH
EDUCATION COMMITTEE.

GOVERNMENT EVACUATION SCHEME.

28th May, 1940.

Dear Sir, Madam,

The Government have decided that the school children of Great Yarmouth shall he evacuated to places of safety in the Midlands or in Wales. Exact information concerning destinations will not be available until Saturday next , 1st June.

The Government strongly urge that every parent shall take advantage of the evacuation scheme now being prepared. You are free to make up your mind, **BUT YOU MUST MAKE UP YOUR MIND AT ONCE.** It is your duty to do so for the sake of your children. The Authorities cannot make their plans at all if they do not know the number for whom they must provide.

Parents who desire their children to be evacuated should complete the form of consent which will be issued by the Head Teacher. **THIS FORM MUST BE RETURNED TO THE SCHOOL BY 9 O'CLOCK ON WEDNESDAY MORNING, 29th MAY.**

It is expected that the parties will leave Great Yarmouth by train on Sunday, 2nd June, and will be accompanied by their teachers.-

If you want any help, or there is anything you do not understand, go to your child's school where you will get full information of the arrangements.

Yours faithfully,

G. J. WROUGHTON,

Clerk to the Committee

Education Offices,
28, South Quay,
Great Yarmouth

37. Town Evacuation Notice for Schoolchildren 1940

1   *Chronicle*, New Series No.22, May 1941, pp.1-9
2   *Ibid*. p.5
3   *Ibid*. p.6
4   *Ibid*. pp.6-7

make arrangements for its future. The School settled in sharing its facilities on a timed base programme with the Retford Grammar School. A shift system operated recalls Lionel Balls, the Great Yarmouth School worked from 8.00 to 10.30am and 15.30 to 17.30 while the local Retford boys had the middle period. Retford was only about one third of the size of Yarmouth but had some good amenities. There was a fine library with up to date books, a heated indoor swimming pool and a park with tennis courts. The Girls High School form Yarmouth had also been evacuated to Retford and efforts had been made to keep the schools apart. On Sundays there was a compulsory Church Parade in the Parish Church which both schools attended recalled Grace Swanston a former High School girl. Although the two central aisles of the church were reserved for the usual town attendees and the Grammar School boys were on the north side and the High School girls on the south side, signals for meetings were often discreetly made across a crowded room and thee was also considerable mingling of boys and girls from both Yarmouth and Retford in the park after school.

However staff changes took place in 1940. Mr Burwell the Second Master way unable to travel to Retford and was given leave of absence and Mr. Whitehead way appointed as Second Master. In the Autumn Term of 1940 Mr. Rasmussen, the German Master, Mr Pereira and Mr Stafford were called up and in April Mr. Hillyer to the RAF. Mrs Pereira took over her husband's work in French and Mr. Fisher was given a commission in the RAF Educational Service. Both posts were replaced by female graduate teachers. The inevitably effect of war was reported with nine deaths of Old Boys including Harry and Douglas Sutton as a result of enemy action when the Ferry Inn at Horning was bombed by a German raider. A.H.G "young Nagger" Rouse, lately Victor Ludorum had gained his wings and was flying Hurricanes at a Fighter Training Station. He was reported as only receiving minor injuries when his Hurricane finished up after a 400 m.p.h dive in a ploughed field![5]

By 1942 most senior boys were attached to some form of junior service. Four were in the Home Guard, Ten in the local Air Training Corps and Sixty in the School Cadet Corps. It was anticipated that many of these would have attended camps during the summer. The Athletic Sports day arrangements were now different from those at the school in its Yarmouth days the meeting took place in the morning and not on the Wellesley in the afternoon. No times were given in the results as competition for the school records made and recorded at the school's own track. at the Wellesley in Great Yarmouth, now took place in Retfod. The School of course competed against the Retford Grammar School with whom they shared facilities so in addition to the School's own internal House contests an athletic match against Retford resulted in a loss by 8 points (88 to 80 points).[6] Old rivalries were also renewed and the last match of the football season saw the School defeat an hitherto undefeated Lowestoft Team by 2 goals to 1 in a plucky win and a successfully end to the season.[7]

The School had won itself friends amongst the dramatic critics of the Retford Times and the staging of *"I killed the Count"* a comedy thriller directed by J.B. Whitehead in difficult circumstances that meant that rehearsal space was constricted and access to the main stage was very late in the rehearsal period, The report in the Retford Times opened as follows:

> *"An endearing characteristic of Yarmouth Grammar School had been the*
> *Way in which it has made itself at home in its new surroundings and*
> *the enthusiasm with which it carried on its own activities and participates*
> *In ours. Members of the School have made notable contributions in*
> *Little Theatre productions and on Wednesday last it was only the first time*
> *that we have had the pleasure of seeing a play produced by the School*
> *Dramatic Society itself."*[8]

The School Concert had great variety opening with the School Song and concluding with the National Anthem and produced a satisfying and well balanced programme which satisfied the interest of the audience throughout. It was a good example of success supporting the Headmaster's declared desire "to maintain in these days the activities of the School unimpaired."[9]

---

5 *Ibid.* p.22
6 *Chronicle*, New Series no.23, June 1942, p.6
7 *Ibid.* p.8
8 *Ibid.* p.10
9 *Ibid.* p.11

The Cadet Corps all over the country had become a vital part of the Government's new Cadet Training Scheme which added to the enthusiasm for the Cadet Movement itself and formed a foundation for the training of the majority who would find themselves in the forces commented former Retford Cadet. John Scott. The cadets wore khaki uniform, short trousers with puttees for the rankers and the officers knee britches. In the early days ancient cavalry carbines, neutered, were used for arms drill and expected to be maintained as if they were useable. Existing Companies in recognition of their participation has been issued with new battledress type uniforms and were given weapons training by Army instructors who demonstrated the method of assembly and disassembly of guns like the Bren with a series of colourful mnemonics so that the cadets remembered the correct procedure.

Major Whitehead commanded the force which had suffered slightly numerically and then recovered with the formation of a Retford Town ATC Unit which he also commanded. The training requirements to enable cadets to obtain the award of War Certificate "A" where special classes had been organised to take place in addition to the weekly parades.

The Debating Society still had joint events with the Girl's High School The final debate of the 1942 Season involved the reading of three short paper. Victor "Pickles" Stowers read a paper on the motion that "The Arts have done more for Civilisation than Science." He was opposed by Miss Beryl Oakley of the High School with a very sound and logical speech but Stowers carried the motion with a narrow margin.

Deaths of Old Boys in action were now recorded in increasing numbers in all the theatres of the war, including James Tunbridge in Greece and Norman Butterworth in the disastrous explosion on *H.M.S. Hood*. Other news was encouraging and in which the school could take pride. Leonard "Lenny" Howes later a headmaster at Peterhouse School in Gorleston was commissioned in the Royal Artillery, Paddy Roche was commanding a minesweeper near Tobruk, Aldwyn Rouse was still living dangerously as a fighter pilot and Ralph Dye younger brother of Jack (whose marriage he reported) and later in Canada and the Barking Fishery in Gorleston was hoping to enter an O.C.T.U. Ralph survived the war became a Professor Emeritus in History in Canada and was a regular at the Old Boys diner until his death a few yeas ago.

1942

Glenesk House Retford

Glenesk House Purchased.

The Great Yarmouth girls now had their own building, so more normal hours could be resumed. Although for the previous two years the hours had been restricted, the work of the school had not deteriorated as the good examination results demonstrated

38. Glenesk House, Retford. Great Yarmouth High School building.

In 1942 W.W. Harpley was School Cricket Captain and was recorded as a "good field and a stylish bat who didn't "come off" except once." He was a popular captain and holder of Full School Colours. There was a joint play reading group with the Yarmouth Girls High School in "Glenesk" as the High School took over the house opposite the Retford Girls Grammar School. Glenesk provided a gain in the more intimate atmosphere in the limited accommodation The Group met twelve times during 1943 reading Shaw (two) Galsworthy, Sheridan, Stanley Houghton, Ian Hay, Arnold Ridley, Rudolph Basier, Noel Coward and A.A. Milne. Some of the dramatists have survived the test of time others have not. The highlight of the year was a reading of Basier's *The Barretts of Wimpole Street*. The group was reported as being highly successful with an increasing number of boys in membership.[10] A joint Choral Society between the Grammar School boys and High Schools girls was also formed with the choir trained by Mr. Angwin practising *Hiawatha's Wedding.*

[10] *Ibid*. p.15

A Recorded Music Club had been commenced with the Headmaster being President and Mr. Taylor the Chemistry and Physics Master as Chairman. The July 1943 *Chronicle* records the fortnightly meetings of the Recorded Music Club had continued even on the wettest nights and attendance never flagged and that many outside the Sixth Form attended the club.[11]

The School was also involved in the war effort and in the summer of 1943 the boys helped with farming. Two farmers were assisted and in total 83 boys worked for three weeks between 1.00pm and 5.00pm with no break as was the custom in the previous year. Mr. Way, the Chemistry Master commented that schooldays were meant to train the boys for good citizenship and part of that experience meant working for a wage while giving value for it. It was noted that the School's services were especially valuable in the war effort as no soldiers were available during the summer of 1943 to assist with farming.[12] Nick Pownall recalled large RAF trailers carrying wrecked war planes of all types often parked in the Retford town square while their drivers lodged locally overnight. He said that these were irresistible to the Grammar School boys who plundered bits of perspex, aluminium, bolts and bullets.[13]

It was noted that F.R.B. Haward, partner in the design of the Raven Tower in 1910, Major in the First World War, designer of the School New Block in 1936 now commanded the Yarmouth Home Guard Battalion and had been awarded the O.B.E.[14] It was reported that the intrepid Aldwyn Rouse now a Flying Officer with the R.A.F. had officially been posted as missing as his fighter had been seen to crash land when on patrol over Holland.[15] There was no further news and later it was learned that this bright and successful Old Boy had been killed in action.

In 1943-44 Victor Stowers was Vice Captain of North House Football Team and Captain of its Cricket Team. He also played for the School Football Team gaining full colours and where many of the forwards' good goals were attributed to the dash and skilful dribbling of Stowers.[16] The School Play in 1944 was *Escort* a topical story of a British Ship on Convoy duty during the Second World War. J.B. Whitehead played the Captain, Richard Bolton later to be a partner in Yarmouth and East Anglian Chartered Accountants Lovewell Blake, the U Boat Captain and Ray Walpole mentioned for special praise as the Steward for his light hearted stewardship. Ray was subsequently a long term employee at Erie Electronics and a core member of the Great Yarmouth Chamber of Commerce.[17]

39. Victor Stowers in 1943

At Prize Day held in the Retford School Hall on March 16th 1944 one of the guests was The Mayor of Yarmouth Mr. F.W.Lawn. and in his Annual Report the Headmaster remarked that less than one pupil in

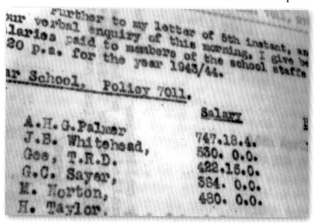

40. The Salaries paid to the Headmaster, Second Master and senior staff in 1943-1944

five now in the School had any knowledge, however small, of conditions and traditions of work at Yarmouth. He posed the question of whether the School could continue to live up to those traditions under the difficulties imposed by evacuation. He said that the years' record of academic successes with Fielding's open scholarship to Oxford and J. Wood's State Scholarship and Exhibition to London University gave rise too an optimism which was still left to the younger pupils who had never known the home traditions to justify.

The Debating Society lost its Chairman the Latin Master T.R. "Trigger" Gee who left to take up a post in St.Bee's School. The editor paid tribute to him for

[11] *Ibid*. pp.21-22
[12] *Ibid*. p.25
[13] Source Nick Pownall
[14] *Ibid*. p.28
[15] *Ibid*. P.27
[16] *Chronicle*, New Series No.25, July 1944 p.9
[17] *Ibid*. p.18

41. The School Cricket First Eleven at Retford in 1944

his enthusiasm in many causes from games to Societies and chess to golf. The Debating Society noted his ability to keep a debate going by speaking on both sides of the argument.[18] The editor of *The Chronicle* noted that of the pre-war staff only the Headmaster, Miss Roche, Mr. Sayer, Mr. Hare and Mr. Whitehead remained. Of the staff on war service Mr. Hillyer was still a prisoner in Japanese hands, Mr. Strafford was somewhere in the Mediterranean, Mr. Pereira in Italy whereabouts unknown where he might have met Mr. Rasmussen out there. Mr. Angwin (Captain Army Education Service) had been transferred to the Army Education Serviced and was second in command of a school for prospective Indian Army Clerks.[19]

The 1945 *Chronicle* recorded the return to Yarmouth from evacuation and Mr. Sayter's wood cut shows the shelters on the Salisbury Road field which the School was never compelled to use.

The School Buildings, so familiar in the past were now strange to many staff and boys alike. Stowers were one of those who had returned and he was now Second Boy and recorded an appreciation of Retford as one of the senior School members to return. He recorded the beauty of the surroundings of Retford noting the contrast with that surrounding Yarmouth and remarking on the greater interest in culture in Retford than that of the home town. He paid tribute to those in Retford who took the school members in and welcomed them and recorded that lasting friendships had been made been made and reflected that many of the evacuees would probably feel a call to return to Retford during the holidays.[20] News of the Old Boys at the end of the war brought news of how they were scattered across the world. Philip Papworth for many years a regular at the Old Boys Dinner was attached to the Indian Army near Bombay. R. A. Parker (Major) had been appointed the Headmaster of a special School founded by the Grand Lama of Tibet for sons of Court Officials being taught English and Jack

42. Gilbert Sayer Lino Cut Chronicle 1945 the School field with wartime shelters

18 *Ibid*. pp.22, 25-26
19 *Ibid*. p.26
20 *Chronicle*, New Series No.26 July 1945, pp.26-27

Dye now a Major and later to be awarded the Military Cross had been wounded twice in the drive to Berlin.[21] In December 1945 a meeting was held in the School Library to formally re-start the Old Boys Association while E.W. "Tusky" Foulser was dong the same in London for the Old Boys London Society.[22]

On the return from Retford in 1946 the formation of a Parents Association was thought to be of benefit to both the parents and the school.[23] Nearly 100 members joined the Association and the redoubtable Mrs Nellie Jordan, mother of the late Aleyn Jordan, a great attender at the Old Boys Dinner and a major force in classical music in the post war town, served on the first Committee.

At Prize Day 1945 the Headmaster reported that the distinction between scholars and fee payers had disappeared with the abolition of fees and the admission of scholars was now purely on merit with selection on merit at the age of 11. The Chairman of Governors Mr. H.T. Greenacre wished the School every success under the new Education Act and exhorted the boys to work since he felt that this would be the only way for the country to recover its stability after the war.

The Debating Society was reinvigorated in 1946 following the loss of all the School's good speakers, by the extra mathematics master Mr. "Charlie" Coldbeck a northerner as an extra mathematics master in January 1945. One of the subjects for Debate was the motion that "Co-Education in Secondary Schools was preferable to having separate schools for girls and boys". It was interesting to see that the "Co-eds" won the day by 10 votes to 3.[24]

The Chronicle noted the school sports records in its report of the School Athletic Sports in 1946 ands it was noted that the late A.G.H. Rouse had set records in 1939 before joining the services of 10.2 seconds for the 100 yards and 24 seconds for the 220 yards.[25] It was a tribute to Rouse's prowess that these fast times were to stand for many years before they were bettered by outstanding athletes.

The Deane brothers and Jimmy Masterson still managed to sweep all before them in post war Yarmouth as Old Grammarians. William Deane won the Ulph Cup with his brother Kenneth second and Jimmy Masterson third

in August 1946. The Ulph Cup is awarded to the victor of a sea swimming race between the Britannia and Wellington Piers and had been held since 1887.

In 1946 new staff posts were filled giving the school Biology and a Latin Master. The latter appointment brought Mr. J. "Tojo" "Jimmy" Morrow to the School and he was held in great affection by all the boys he taught. The first nickname was given as a note of a passing resemblance to a famous Japanese Genial in the late war.[27] The first issue of the Old Boys Roll of Honour and a list of Decorations and Awards were published. A copy of my researched version of these can be seen in the Appendices to this book. It was noted that information was still lacking to make the lists complete and the Editor appealed for any additional information or corrections or amendment to ensure that the most up to date details were available. Mr. Whitehead noted the assistance which Mr. Hillyer had given

43. Clean Sweep for Old Grammarians in Ulph Cup August 1946. From Left William H. Deane first , Kenneth Deane second, Jimmy Masterson third with coach "Tiny" Shreeve.[26]

[21] *Ibid*. p.24
[22] *Ibid*. p.35
[23] *Chronicle*, New Series No. 27, July 1946, p.1
[24] *Ibid*. p.8
[25] *Ibid*. pp. 20-21
[26] Source E. Barron
[27] *Ibid*. p.33

44. The Dramatic Society's production of
The Duke in Darkness, 1946

with the production of *The Chronicle* and in March 1947 he took over the editorship of the magazine. The March 1947 *Chronicle* records an intention to return to a termly Chronicle as in pre-war days as soon as possible. Mr. Whitehead had edited the magazine for eighteen years since it was restarted in 1929 providing a primary source for scholars and breaking the inter-regnum in the 1920's when no magazines were produced at all.[28]

The School Play of 1946 *The Duke in Darkness* by Patrick Hamilton was set in the French Civil Wars in the Sixteenth Century Mr. Whitehead played the captive Duke of Laterraine and had to sustain the main burden of the dialogue through the three Acts. It was noted that great ingenuity had been employed in scene making and lighting. Practical properties were also kept in use as the Dramatic Society notes record that keen members repaired the wind machine.[29]

Many School Clubs and Societies were active in 1946 and 1947 and the Chronicle gives notes for the Dramatic Society, the Art Guild, the Naturalists Society, the Historical and Geographical Society, the Stamp Club, the Debating Society, the Cercle Francais, the Science Society and the Recorded Music Circle.

The Cadet Corps visited the Royal Engineers Mine Clearance Unit at Weybourne and were shown the latest mine detecting equipment. This was to be a task on the Norfolk beaches for some time. *The Chronicle* of 1947 recorded a School visit took place in November 1946 with a party from the Cadet Corps travelling to Germany. The report for *The Chronicle* was written by C.S.M. Browne and he records the war scars of Hanover flattened and the coming to terms of enemies in a post war period.[30] The Football Team was rebuilding its strength and started to turn its results round at the end of the season. The Junior Eleven fared better winning four of their six matches and David Balfour the master who looked after the term recorded the hopes for the future for success in the Schools' league. Mr. Balfour arrived as Games and Mathematics Master in autumn 1946 and left the School to become the Headmaster of the Priority School some years later. Poetry and Articles from the pupils started to appear in the Chronicle and Mr. Whitehead in announcing his retirement as editor hoped that this would continue.

Early in June 1947 the Association Committee of the Old Boys invited the Headmaster of the School and the staff to supper at the Start Hotel. This was the first time that such a meeting had taken place and it offered an excellent opportunity for re-establishing contact with the School.[31] It was interesting to note how the Old Boys Committee survived the war in terms of continuity. Of several members who joined the forces prior to conscription Jack Boon, Johnny Green, Jack Guyton, Lenny Howes, Jimmy Masterson, Frank Nunn and Wally Phillips all served on the 1947 Committee.[32] 1947 was also the first year in which the Cross Country Race had been held as a separate event from the main Athletics Sports. The race took place on April 28th in a stiff westerly wind. E.R. Daniels forged to the front and held a lead of fifty yards but he could not increase his lead. The chasing group finished with a spread of eight seconds with Brian Fiddes of North coming fourth.[33] In the Athletic Sports Fiddes finished second in the mile and third in the half mile. After he left School Brian Fiddes played football for many years and especially for the Town Hall Team where he was in the Finance Department for all for his working career. He was also an active Tennis player and Coach playing at both the Ravine and Gorleston Clubs and still plays to-day.

Members of the School were issued each term with 'Preparation Books', commonly known as 'Prep Books', recalls Peter Woods They were used for listing the student's own homework for each day of the week. At the

28 *Chronicle*, New Series No. 1, p.2
29 *Chronicle*, New Series No.1, March 1947, pp.9-13
30 *Ibid*. pp.25-26
31 *Ibid*. p.43
32 *Ibid*. p.43
33 *Chronicle*, Second Series, July 1947, p.12

back of these books were pages for 'conduct' and 'work signatures'. If a boy misbehaved or did bad work the teacher (or prefect) concerned would put his signature, with the date, in the prep book (commonly known as 'getting a siggy'). If a boy collected three such signatures in a week, they were bracketed together and he lost his merit holiday (a half day's holiday awarded each term for those who had been good) and had to sit in a classroom with some unlucky teacher doing extra work. If a boy was unfortunate enough to collect two lots of bracketed threes within a term, then he was due for a visit to the Headmaster's study. Peter Woods recalls the punishment system of the 1940's and 1950's in a visit which he had to the Headmaster's Study in "A Visit by the School Secretary" to the classroom of B."Benny" Angwin, the Music Master.

Interrupting the afternoon lesson
In her quiet, demure, unhurried way,
Here comes Miss Fraser,
As we all knew she would.

A whispered message in old Benji's ear
Brings an amused smirk to his usually sombre features:
'Woods!.......Headmaster's Office!'
Thirty pairs of pitying eyes escort me from the room.

I join the queue of the ne'er-do-wells,
The runners in school, not-writing-to-the-marginers,
The cutters of fingers, looking-out-of-windowers -
The breachers of school rules.

A pall of doom hangs over the miscreant line,
White-faced, unsmiling, hang-dog, fearful, until
The portentous green light ushers in the first victim.
We hold our breath, then: THWACK! THWACK! THWACK!

Clean, crisp, like the angry snapping of a twig,
Only much louder and with cruelty and venom,
With something bendy and whistly in the air between.
We all flinch, and nurse our tender nether regions.

The green light shines for me
Alf, ghoulishly gowned, inspects my breaching record
And is clearly not impressed. He gives me his sternest
Glare, conveying centuries of adult condemnation.

'Take off your blazer, boy, and bend over that chair!'
The first cuts clean across like a sharpened sword.
The second whips a parallel trough of pain.
The third excoriates excruciating points of intersection.

I hobble out, lips tight, eyes twitching, bum aflame.
But by the time I arrive back at Benji's
It has become agreeably warm; and I am greeted by
Thirty pairs of hero-worshipping eyes. [34]

---

[34] Source Peter Woods 1945-1952

45. Junior members of the Cadet Force in 1948

Back R. Dyble, D Eales
Front George Smith, Ken Applegate

46. "Winter"
Gilbert Sayer woodcut 1948

Form Notes appeared in *The Chronicle* for the first time for some years. The Sixth Form notes recorded that eleven boys went up to the Sixth Form in the Science Sixth from the Fifth being later divided into the Mathematic and Biological sections. Geoff Bullent left the Science Group to continue a carrer as an assistant chemist at Grouts silk factory. Geoff also continued to play tennis locally for many years with Brian Fiddes at the Ravine Club in Gorleston.

The death was noted of John Backhouse who had joined the school in 1897 and had served as Second Master to W. G. Willliams until his retirement in 1932. J.B. Whitehead his successor as Second Master wrote a tribute of his service to the school having known him as a personal friend since 1924. He said that in the library were two oars presented by Mr. Backhouse to the School only a few months previously. His name appeared on each of them but it would be the memory of hundreds of Old Boys that his time of service to the school would remain.

The 1948 *Chronicle* recalls the severe winter of a year earlier when there were occasions when many boys and some members of the staff were unable to get into Yarmouth from the country districts with snow drifts up to ten feet deep in places. Mr. Sayer's opening wood cut of Winter recalls that time.

The Prize Day presentation took place at the Town Hall with prizes being distributed by Frank Stone in his first term as the Borough's Mayor. The subject prizes for the Fifth Form show that W.B. "Bill" Utting won prizes for Religious Instruction, English, Latin, Mathematics, Physics and Chemistry and gained distinctions in the Cambridge School Certificate in eight subjects. He was also secretary of the Debating Society. "Bill" Utting later Sir William was to go on to have a fascinating career as in the Civil Service as a Permanent Secretary in the Social Service and later as Chairman of the Rowntree Trust. He donated new prizes to the school in 2008 The Recorded Music Circle under the Chairmanship of Mr. Angwin met at School House with an average attendance of 25. The comment was made that the School House premises made the Society meetings much more intimate than any other society. The School House was unfortunately sold in post war years. The Recorded Music Circle continued to flourish and Peter Woods in 1948 also recalled the Headmaster's great love of teaching music.

"He introduced us to classical music in the second year, using a wind-up gramophone and the old breakable records, taking us through some of the popular pieces, coaching us on some of the intricacies and what to look for. He seemed to relax during these lessons. The Headteacher role had no place here – he was relating to us through the music. This is well illustrated by a particular incident. So taken was I by some things he played us, I stole back to the out-of-bounds classroom one lunchtime, wound up the gramophone and started playing them again. My listening position was leaning forward over the desk with my head on my hands. Then, horror of horrors! The door suddenly opened and in came Alf! I struggled to get to my feet, with an overwhelming sense of guilt that I was committing a great crime. But he waved me to sit down, tip-toed to the desk, quietly opened a drawer to take out some papers, and tip-toed out again."[35]

Mr. Palmer's School Secretary from 1945-1951 was Miss Fraser, now Rhoda Grimmer, and she records that Mr. Palmer was an accomplished pianist and a Fellow of the Royal College of Organists. The School had a fine Bechstein piano at this time and she remembers going to the Music Club Meetings held in School House.[36]

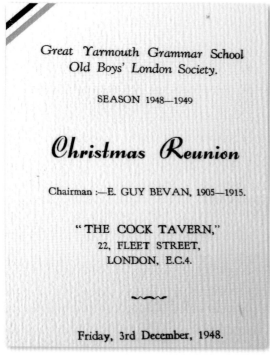

Great Yarmouth Grammar School
Old Boys' London Society.

SEASON 1948—1949

Christmas Reunion

Chairman :—E. GUY BEVAN, 1905—1915.

"THE COCK TAVERN,"
22, FLEET STREET,
LONDON, E.C.4.

Friday, 3rd December, 1948.

47. The Christmas Reunion of the Old Boys London Society was at the Cock Tavern in Fleet Street.

The London Old Boys' Association continued to welcome the Headmaster to its meetings and a Christmas Reunion was held at the *Rising Sun* at 46, Tottenham Court Road. The Association had presented a Cross Country Cup in memory of John Backhouse and congratulated Centre House as the holder for the first year in 1947.[37] In 1948 the Christmas Reunion way at the Cock Tavern in Fleet Street.

The Chronicle of July 1948 records that performances were good in the School's own sports with Buswell beating Blyth's recorded good times. into second place in both the 100 and 220 yards as they now competed against each other in the 13-15 age group. They were both later to return to the School successively as Sports Masters. Buswell won the Omnium Bowl and went on to 440 yards success in the Norfolk Schools Athletics Sports. In those sports held on the 19th June. John Blyth, although still under 14, in the under 15's was a creditable second in the 220 yards. Buswell won the under 15's 440 yards by 15 yards and was awarded the Thomas Cook Challenge Cup and Silver Medal for the boy with the best performance in any event over 13.

The Chronicle records that in three meetings of an active Parents Association the subjects of the meetings ranged between instructive talks on the school curriculum for parents to social events at which parents and staff participated.

48. Senior Football Team 1947-1948

1949 saw Mr. Whitehead awarded an OBE for his service to the Cadet Corps. was noted that during the evacuation at Retford he also served the School being also in command of the Air Training Corps at Retford. The School Hall was filled almost to capacity for the unveiling and dedication of the War Memorial on Sunday 28th June 1948. The names of the 56 Old Boys who fell in the 1939-1945 war were read by the Headmaster while the Vicar gave the address. The Annual Sports on the 30th May at the Wellesley Ground saw Ted Buswell become Victor Ludorum and John Blyth win the Omnium Bowl from Peter Woods in second place. The system of points always favoured the track successes over field sports so Blyth's success in the 100, 220 and 440 yards outweighed Woods' in the Long Jump, the Shot and the Discus.[38] Both Buswell and Blyth

---

35 Source Peter Woods 1945-1952
36 Source "Miss Fraser", Rhoda Grimmer
37 *Chronicle*, Second Series March 1948, p.57
38 *Ibid*. pp.18-19

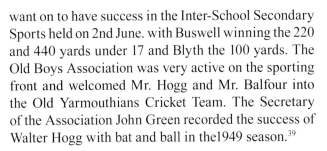

want on to have success in the Inter-School Secondary Sports held on 2nd June. with Buswell winning the 220 and 440 yards under 17 and Blyth the 100 yards. The Old Boys Association was very active on the sporting front and welcomed Mr. Hogg and Mr. Balfour into the Old Yarmouthians Cricket Team. The Secretary of the Association John Green recorded the success of Walter Hogg with bat and ball in the1949 season.[39]

The decade closed with the School, firmly back at Salisbury Road again after its period at Retford and having rebuilt its links in the town in the post war period.

49. Junior Football Team 1947-1948

50. Junior First XI Football Team 1948-1949

51. The Headmaster A.H,G. Palmer, Second Master C. Coldbeck and Senior Boys in July 1949

[39] *Chronicle*. Second Series No. 5, July 1949, p.40

Chapter 6
The 1950'S Anniversary and Consolidation

The Chronicle of 1950 records the events for the Academic year 1949-50 and the planning for the final changes of a staff complement to suit the new decade. The Biology Master since 1945 Mr Burns had left the school and the post had yet to be filled so the School had to appeal for assistance. Mrs Palmer, Mrs Pereira and Mr. Buddery answered the call.[1] Mrs Pereira having been a member of staff at Retford while Mr. Buddery was an Old Boy of the School. At the beginning of the School Year Mr." Ron" Teasdale had joined the staff as Chemistry Master and in the period immediately before his appointment Mrs Whitehead had assisted the staff. Masters' wives and relations had bridged a number of gaps in the last decade but Mr. Palmer had planned to complete a complement of largely Graduate Staff to carry the School further into a period of school expansion.

W.B. (later Sir William) Utting led the School as Head Boy into the new decade having been first in the Higher Certificate with distinctions in English and History. He also won the Edward Worledge Scholarship for outstanding merit; the Harrison Prize awarded on a General Paper, the Senior Reading Prize and was awarded a State Scholarship.[2] The Prize Day on November 1949 was noteworthy for the Headmaster's comment on the benefits of a good School Certificate when job opportunities were very limited in the town. "Boys who are obliged to stay in Yarmouth will have to limit their ambitions as the Town provides good openings, but only in a rather narrow range of occupations."[3] The speaker at the Prize Day was Sir Will Spens, Master of Corpus Christi College, (my own College half a century later) and High Steward of Yarmouth. His comment was that Grammar Schools were the particular glory of education in this country. He believed that the fact that there was only the one Grammar School in a town of Great Yarmouth's size was a real gain for the School's students.

The School Dramatic Society continued to be adventurous performing Gordon Daviot's *Valerius* a play set in Roman Britain and only performed once before by the Sunday Repertory Society of London.[4] The Society hoped to revive its evening play readings possibly in collaboration with the High School. A Junior Dramatic Society had been formed by Mr. Morrow, the Latin Master, to encourage boys from the First to Fourth Forms to be interested in reading and performing plays.

52. The light carrier USS Princeton burning soon after being hit by a Japanese bomb while operating off the Philippines on 24 October 1944. This view, taken from USS South Dakota (BB-57) at about 1001, shows the large smoke column passing aft following a heavy explosion in the carrier's hangar deck. [Official U.S. Navy Photograph]

[1] *Chronicle*, Second Series No.6, July 1950, p.3
[2] *Ibid*. p.5, pp.7-9
[3] *Ibid*. p.6
[4] A group who performed new plays

40

The Stamp Club had been reformed and the Chess Club was also in business having acquired a number of sets, three of which had been presented by the Parents' Association. The Cercle Francais was under the Presidency of M. le Principal, the Headmaster while Mr. Whitehead was Vice President of the Historical and Geographical Society with Walter Hogg the History Master now in the Chair. A noteworthy account for a Society Meeting was given by Aleyn Jordan, ever a maritime enthusiast, of the great Naval Battle of Leyte Gulf[5] which was recorded as excellently illustrated with pictures of the ships taking part.

The Science Society received a boost in membership and attendance with the arrival of Mr. George "Bushy" West the Physics Master who was also a Fellow of the Royal Astronomical Society, and later had his own observatory with a reflecting telescope at his house on Warren Lane in Gorleston where the skies were dark. The Music Club also had several meetings with Bill Utting as its Secretary. The Club had expeditions to orchestral concerts in Norwich and had the opportunity to send its members to the *Music for the Ordinary Man* Series of concerts arranged by Principal William Corrie at the College of Art and Design and also experienced its own live items. One of these involved Mr. Balfour, recorded by Peter Woods as having a "good" tenor voice[6] accompanied by the Headmaster on Piano performing Schumann's *Dicterlieber*, a very challenging and rewarding work for amateur performers. The 1950 *Chronicle* notes that at the end of the previous year, E.D.C. "Ted" Buswell and J. "Jonnie" Blyth, both later Masters at the School had been awarded full athletic colours while Blyth had also gained half colours at football.[7] The Annual Cross Country race took place on the 8th March 1950 in ideal conditions with only a gentle breeze blowing. However there was a slight haze which made the recognition of distant runners impossible thus thwarting an ambitious attempt to give a running commentary on the race progress. The race was marked with a thrilling neck and neck finish between Brewster and Shorten running level down the final straight with Brewster providing a shock when he tripped and fell heavily a few yards from the finish leaving F.R.B. Shorten, Company Sergeant Major of the School Cadet force, to win. Brewster recovered to finish second. At the Athletic Sports held on the Wellesley Recreation Ground on Tuesday 23rd May, Buswell was Victor Ludorum winning the 440, 220 and 100 yards with John Blyth runner up for each event and also runner up as Victor Ludorum. In the Annual Swimming Sports held in front of 1400 spectators at the open air pool on the sea front on the 29th June, D.Liffen who won the 440 yards open freestyle and was later to be associated with a prodigious swimming feat off the east coast.

The School was organising and participating in trips for its members of its organisations outside Great Yarmouth with the Cadet Force attending the Annual Summer Camp at Colchester while Mr. Whitehead led a mixed group of eleven Geographers, Marine Life Students and an Ornithologist to a week at the Field Study Centre at Melham Tarn near Settle in Yorkshire.[8] The Parents' Society was active. A large number of the boys who left the on the previous year had joined the Old Boys Association which had an active programme of events while the London Old Boys Society appealed for new blood from younger Old Boys who had moved to the London area. The School had opened the decade in determined fashion with a range of out of school activities and moved forward into the fifties in good heart.

1951 marked the 400th Anniversary of the School and an account of the celebrations was carried in the local press and the Times which reached many Old Boys, both at home and abroad, and brought many interesting letters to the school as J.B. Whitehead produced short history of the Grammar School covering the 400 year period with illustrations by Mr. Sayer.[9]

53. Retford Grammar School in 1941
Gilbert Sayer

5 A famous illustration from the Battle of Leyte Gulf which Aleyn Jordan would have sourced for his lecture
6 Peter Woods GYGS 1945-1952
7 *Chronicle*, Second Series No.6, July 1950, pp.21,23
8 *Ibid*. p.34
9 Whitehead J.B., *The History of the Great Yarmouth Grammar School*, Great Yarmouth , 1951

The School was subjected to a full Inspection in the first week in February 1951 by six Inspectors who had their headquarters in the old Dining Hall. Having studied all aspects of school work the report was very favourable Both Mr. Sayer and Mr. Buddery retired and Miss Fraser (now Mrs Grimmer) who had been Mr. Palmer's School Secretary for seven years left to be married to an Old Boy of the School.

GREAT YARMOUTH
GRAMMAR SCHOOL

Commemoration
Service

1551 — 1951

Ascension Day
Thursday, 3rd May, 1951

10.45 a.m.

AT

THE ACTING PARISH CHURCH
(ST. PETER)

54. The cover of the Order the School's
400th Anniversary Commemoration Service

The School celebrated its 400th Anniversary during the week 30th April to 5th May 1951 opening with a reception at the Town Hall on the Wednesday Evening given by the Mayor Mr. C.R.E. Matthews. On the following morning a Thanksgiving Service took place at St. Peter's, (the Town's acting Parish Church at this time) in the morning followed by the Annual Prize Giving.

On the Friday and Saturday evenings there was a performance of *"Macbeth"* directed by Mr. Whitehead who also played the lead at the Britannia Pier.

Other celebratory events included a social evening arranged between the Old Boys Association and the Parents' Association and a cricket match between the School and the Old Boys and a Mayoral Reception given by the Deputy Mayor Mr. Fred Kruber in the absence of the Mayor who was in London for the opening ceremony of the Festival of Britain. At the reception Mr. Whitehead, who had just completed a book on the History of the School to celebrate its Quarcentenary gave an illustrated lecture on the School's history illustrated by lantern slides.

The Thanksgiving Service to celebrate the Anniversary was held at St. Peter's Church, which was the acting Parish Church at that time, on the morning of Thursday 3rd May. The School assembled on St. George's Road and, led by the Headmaster and Staff, walked to the Church. Already assembled there were Parents, a contingent from the Hospital School where the School's Foundation took place in 1551 and the Girls High School who were under common Foundation Governance by the Grammar School. The Civic Party was led by the Deputy Mayor, the Service was conducted by an Old Boy of the School, the Reverend T.G. Platten, the Principal of the Saltley Training College in Birmingham, (later a Canon of Birmingham Cathedral),who noted that they were going through a period of change as great as any which had happened over last 400 years since the School's Foundation.

The Prize Day which took place in the afternoon was presided over by Alderman H.R. Greenacre, then Chairman of the Governors, while the principal guest was Sir Lawrence Bragg, Professor of Physics at the University of Cambridge. The Headmaster in giving his annual report said that he felt great satisfaction in the way that the School had responded to the increased opportunities for pupils who sought to go to a University. He remarked that the one or occasionally two Grammar School boys who went to University prior to the Second World War each year had now grown to six or seven and that there was every sign that this success would be maintained.[10] Sir Lawrence in speaking said that schools such as Great Yarmouth Grammar School taught boys to think clearly for themselves a factor which was very important for the nation.

---

[10] *Ibid.* p.10

In the Honours gained, boys whose interests were very different had success in their own chosen fields. Bill Utting gained an Open Exhibition Scholarship to New College Oxford to read Modern Studies while Aleyn Jordan was awarded the Marine Society's Bursary to H.H.S Worcester.[11] The variety in achievement also showed in Honours won by Old Boys, Richard Boulton who went with the School to Retford passed the final examinations of the Institute of Chartered Accountants, L.J. Brighton passed the Law Society's' final examainations, R. R. Gladden gained a BSc in Crop Husbandry from Durham, while John Woods, elder brother of Peter gained a PhD in Physics from London. Peter, the youngest of the three Grammarian Woods brothers was still at the School in this year having gained his Football Colours, played first X1 in the Cricket Team, won the over 15 shot, was second in the discus and third in the long jump in the annual sports. The School has a history of younger boys following their older brothers and both achieving in their own chosen fields.

Buswell the supreme athlete of his day won the cross country in February 1951 leading from start to finish in the creditable time of 2 minutes 40 seconds. He was for the third year in a row Victor Ludorum at the Athletics Sports on the 30th May winning again the 440, 220 and 100 yards with John Blyth once again runner up to him in all three events.[12]

In the Swimming Sports on the 28th June D.Liffen of West House again dominated winning the Overy Challenge Cup for success in the 440 yards, 100 and 50 yards open events.[13] Jimmy Masterson the successful school swimmer of pre-war days and veteran of the Ulph Cup for the race between the piers won the Old Boys Race at the School Swimming Gala.

The Old Boys Association was active. E.C.H. "Ted" Freeman as President attended the Remembrance Day Service on 10th November and placed the Association's Wreath on the School War Memorial.

At the Annual Dinner held at the Star Hotel on the 14th April there were sixty Old Boys and Masters present. John Whitehead proposed the health of the Old Boys Association with a response from Jack Boon. At the Old Boys Dinner held nearly 50 years after this in 2010, having proposed the health of the School, I was responded to by the serving Mayor, Councillor Tony Smith, himself an Old Boy who commented in responding to the toast of the School that I stood where my Father a fellow Old Boy had stood fifty years before.

EVENTS

1 100 Yards, 11–13

1 P. R. Crowe (N) 2 M. A. Anguish (N) 3 K. Harrison (C)
4 N. A. White (C) 5 D. C. Johnson (W) 6 I. T. W. Tosh (C)

1 Harrison 2 4 3 6 Time 14

2 100 Yards, 13–15

1 C. Valentine (W) 2 B. Mileham (C) 3 J. Severn (W)
4 R. F. Thompson (W) 5 J. G. Jary (C) 6 C. Cooper (W)

1 5 2 4 3 6 Time 12

3 100 Yards, 15+

1 J. H. Blyth (N) 2 J. Hendrickson (N) 3 M. J. Raby (C)
4 A. C. Martin (W) 5 E. D. C. Buswell (S) 6 B. W. Delf (W)
7 J. M. King (W)

1 5 2 1 3 3 Time 11·4 s

4 440 Yards, 13–15

1 W. G. Sendal (S) 2 R. L. Sunman (N) 3 T. P. Turrill (S)
4 R. Thompson (W) 5 B. E. Harbord (W) 6 N. C. Adams (C)

1 2 2 6 3 5 Time 68 s

5 440 Yards, 15+

1 M. J. Raby (C) 2 J. H. Blyth (N) 3 A. B. Mace (S)
4 V. W. Moore (N) 5 E. D. C. Buswell (S) 6 J. Hendrickson (N)

1 5 2 2 3 1 Time 52·7 s

55. An extract from the Athletics Sports Programme for 1951

Adrian Gardiner (1951-1958) the possessor of the programme has marked the results of the Buswell- Blyth duel

A retrospect of the year 1951 cannot be concluded without a consideration of the performance of *Macbeth* on the Britannia Pier on the 4th and 5th May. as part of the Quarcentenary Celebrations. Mr. Morrow in reviewing the production commented that the Dramatic Society's venture into Shakespeare had released the Bard from the cramping confines of the classroom and put Shakespeare firmly on to the Yarmouth stage.[14] It was an ambitious production and a herculean task by Mr. Whitehead, who supported by his colleagues took on the

[11] *Ibid*. p.11
[12] *Ibid*. p.30, 29
[13] *Ibid*. pp.31-32
[14] *Ibid*.

SCENES	DRAMATIS PERSONAE in order of their appearance :	

The Five Acts of Shakespeare's tragedy are played as Three Acts with the following Scenes :

ACT I.

Act 1.	Scene i.	A Desert Place
	Scene ii.	Duncan's Headquarters
	Scene iii.	A Heath near Forres
	Scene iv.	Duncan's Headquarters
	Scene v., vi, vii.	
Act 2.	Scene i.—iv.	Macbeth's Castle near Inverness

ACT II.

Act 3.	Scene i., ii.	Macbeth's Palace at Forres
	Scene iii.	A Park
	Scene v., vi.	
Act 4.	Scene i.	Macbeth's Palace

ACT III.

Act 4.	Scene ii.	A Room in Lady Macduff's Castle
	Scene iii.	An Anteroom in the English King's Palace
Act 5.	Scene i.	Macbeth's Castle of Dunsinane
	Scene ii.	Near Dunsinane
	Scene iii.	The Castle
	Scene iv.	Near Dunsinane
	Scene v.	The Castle
	Scene vi.	Near Dunsinane
	Scene vii., viii.	The Heath near Dunsinane

There will be a 10 Minutes Interval between each Act

Incidental Music, chosen by A. G. H. Palmer, is mainly from " Job, A Masque for Dancing " by Vaughan Williams, whose " Overture to The Wasps " is used as the Overture to the Play.

The Witches	T. H. Westgate, D. T. Read, J. Webster	
Duncan, King of Scotland ...	W. H. Coleman	
Malcolm, his Son ...	G. G. Frosdick	
Donalbain, another Son ...	B. A. Websdale	
Lennox, a Noble ...	A. R. Barber	
A Wounded Officer ...	J. H. Blyth	
Ross, a Noble	J. Gedge	
Macbeth, General of the King's Army	J. B. Whitehead	
Banquo, another General ...	R. Pashley	
Angus, a Noble	D. J. Ellett	
Lady Macbeth	H. F. G. Swanston	
Messenger	D. W. Thomas	
Macduff, a Noble ...	W. R. Pereira	
Fleance, Banquo's Son ...	G. Hewitt	
Porter in Macbeth's Castle ...	G. W. Giles	
The Murderers	B. C. Farrant, G. W. Giles, S. A. Dickinson	
Lady Macduff	W. G. Bain	
Her Son	P. W. Ralph	
Messenger	D. Liffen	
Doctor Attendant on Lady Macbeth	C. F. Martin	
Menteith | Nobles leagued	D. H. Higgins	
Caithness | against Macbeth	F. W. Symonds	
Seyton, Attendant on Macbeth	S. A. Dickinson	
Other Nobles	M. J. Raby, D. Liffen, C. F. Martin, J. H. Blyth	
Apparitions, Soldiers, Attendants	T. P. Turrell, M. F. Wood, R. A. Jones, P. F. Juby, D. W. Marshall, R. F. Thompson	
Drummers and Buglers ...	N. J. Cubitt, M. G. Harvey, S. R. Cooper, G. W. Giles	

The Play Produced by J. B. WHITEHEAD

56. Programme of Macbeth produced to celebrate the School's 400th Anniversary on the 4th and 5th May 1951. Profits were given to the Parish Church Restoration Fund.

role of the tragic hero. Mr. Pereira played Macduff, Mr Pashley, Banquo and Mr. Coleman, Duncan. The role of Lady Macbeth was taken by Hamish Swanston and Gordon Frosdick the Head Boy played Malcolm. Nearly 30 boys from the School, many of them from the Sixth Form took on all the other parts. This combination of Staff in the pivotal roles supported by the School Boys in mass was an ambitious venture and was, as Jimmy Morrow recorded, an occasion when all those who had taken part in this great business had a right to feel proud. He said that if the audience reaction was anything to go by the cast had succeeded in making Shakespeare truly popular. The year closed with School having successfully celebrated its past history and moving on purposefuly into the second decade of the century.

The Chronicle saw a change in 1952 as Mr. Sayer who had provided the wood cut illustrations for many years had retired and the new Art Master was Derek Excel who had previously taught at Eastbourne Grammar School. The frontispiece of the Chronicle showed a wood engraving of the old Suspension Bridge across the river Bure and was launched as the first of series of wood engravings depicting scenes of local interest.

The previous year's election fever had permeated the School where a 'mock' election was held. Speeches had been made by the three candidates Gedge (Conservative) Farrant (Labour) and McComas (Liberal) where opportunities presented themselves during the lunch break, after school and finally before the school assembled. The poll resulted in a win for Gedge the Conservative candidate.[15]

[15] *Chronicle*, Second Series No.8, July 1952 p.4

57. The Bure Bridge Woodcut Derek Excel.

At the Annual Prize Giving held at the Town Hall on December 9th 1951 the Head spoke of the changes in the examination for the General Certificate of Education. He paid special attention to the institution of gradings such as "good" and "distinction" at the Advanced and Scholarship levels. He commented that the two fifth forms had been the best for many years and had done really well.[16] Sir Edmund Bacon, the Lord Lieutenant of Norfolk, was the speaker and remarked on the value of tolerance after two World Wars, with the comment that never to allow anyone to have a point of view except one's own would inevitably lead to trouble. R.M. "Bob" Loynes won the Stanley Maxwell prize for Latin awarded by the Independent Schools Association to the candidate in the summer examination who passed highest at Latin at Ordinary Level, having offered the First Alternative Syllabus.[17]

At the School Concert held in the last week of the spring term the musical programme included an outstanding performance of Mozart's *Fantasia* in D Minor for piano played by R.A. Jones who in the previous year had won the Saxon Noble prize for the best performance in Norfolk in Grades 6, 7 and 8 of the Associated Board of the Royal College of Music. At the School Concert Jones also played a duet with Colin Bassett (violin) in the first movement of Mozart's *Sonata in B Flat K.378*. Both Jones and Bassett were to go on the Cambridge as music scholars.

58. A Husting in the Election.

[16] *Ibid*. p.7
[17] *Ibid* p.8

The Cercle Francais had gained well merited applause for a satisfying production of Moliere's *Le Bourgeois Gentilhomme* in French. Mr. Pereira had worked hard on directing the production while Gedge who had a good grounding in the Junior Dramatic Society played the named part. The rest of the actors were boys of the school, many of them juniors. R.A. Jones was noted in the review by Mr. Morrow for his flawless accent and unrivaled confidence.[18]

The Science Society's first meeting was marred by the realisation that the reflecting telescope mirror upon which much time had been spent in grinding was useless owing to strains in the glass. Howver there were many volunteers for the grinding of a replacement mirror. The meetings were popular including one held as a "Stump the Staff" quiz night. However the staff who formed the team were not to be stumped and Messrs. West, Teasdale and Morris answered all questions in a more or less satisfactory manner. The Art Guild undertook a variety of outings after mid March, when the weather improved, and trips were made to the Mansion House in Ipswich, to Colchester Castle, and closer to home to Hopton's ruined church, the quayside and to Burgh Castle. The aim was to provide enough pictures for the autumn exhibition.

59. *The Old Library.*

The Library was due to be opened in the first term of the following year having been out of bounds during the greater part of the school year. The Assistant Librarian, B.H. Dawson, reported that all the catalogues, fiction, non-fiction and reference had been thoroughly checked and the shelves clearly labelled. The Birds Egg collection in the museum had been labelled by two keen juniors; the shelves were stacked to capacity even after eliminating older books surplus to requirements by outdating and the liberty would be run by twelve liberty prefects to be appointed with authority in the Library and the Reading Room even over school prefects. The Reading Room, formerly the old Dining Room housed many magazines including *History To-day*, *Discovery*, the *Boys Own Paper* and *John O' London's Weekly*.[19] In the Library the monthly edition of the *Film Guide*, published by the British Film Institute, was available which had proved to be popular with all boys of the School.

A United Nations Society, formed only two terms previously, continued to grow with the viewing of films supplied by the United Nations Organisation. The Stamp Club held its second Annual Exhibition on Friday December 7th and about 60 boys went to see the 2000 stamps on show from Members, These included British Colonials (Long, Tosh and Wedon), Silver Weddings (Westgate), Two Penny Blacks and a Twopenny Blue) (Tosh). The layout of the Exhibition drew favourable comment from the Headmaster and the Staff.

John Blyth Captained the School football team in its best post war season being awarded new colours. While Peter Woods as his Vice Captain had his previous colours confirmed. Blyth scored 13 of the teams 51 goals in a season which saw 15 matches played eight won, two lost and two drawn. The Cross Country race was run on the 12th March in heavy going and yet spectators were kept interested throughout the race by means of wireless transmissions on the race progress by the Army Cadets based at various check points. The Athletic Sports took

18 *Ibid.* pp.13-14
19 *Ibid.* p.17

place in brilliant sunshine with a strong N.E. wind at the Wellesley Recreation Ground on Friday 4th July. With Buswell having left the School Blyth came into his own and was Victor Ludorum deadheading for first in the 440 yards with Shearing and winning the 220 and 100 yards outright. Peter Woods won the Aldwyn Rouse Memorial Prize for his performance in the Shot breaking the existing record with a put of 34 foot 11 inches. In the Swimming Sports held on the 27th June, D. Liffen once again carried off the Overy Challenge Cup with victories in the three open events of 440, 100 and 50 yards. Having performed prodigiously for West House in the School Swimming Sports Liffen then made history on the 21st July by making the first recorded swim from Yarmouth Beach to Scroby Sands and back in the time of 2 hours 8 minutes and 50 seconds.[20]

The Cadet Force had attended the Annual Camp at Lydd in Kent from July 29th to August 5th at the end of the previous year. The School Company had grown considerably since then with a growth from 50 cadets to 88 at the end of that year. The Second Cadet Battalion had again won the King's Cup and had made a good start to win it again with a 100% success record in Part I of Certificate "A". Congratulations was given to Major West on his appointment as Second in Command of the Battalion.

60. Operation Red Herring – the landing.

Mike Harvey has provided me with a couple of interesting photographs of a combined operation during which the Cadet Force had to land from the sea and advance up the north beach against defenders concealed in the dunes. It was called *Operation Red Herring.*

The Old Boys membership increased to 173 and at the Annual Dinner held in March the toast to the School was given by R.J. "Bob" Tooley, of the large local family fertiliser firm of J and H Bunn. Bob was a regular Dinner attendee until just before his death and I knew him well from the mid 1970's as he was my Harbour Chairman when I was Chief Executive of the Port and Haven Commissioners. It was noted by the Association that owing to the difficulties of obtaining the traditional red, white and black striped blazer for the Old Boys there would be would be an alternative version of a plain navy blazer with an Old Boys badge on the pocket. The Association specifically mentioned that the new alternative did not mean that the old striped blazer would not be forsaken altogether. The year was one of consolidation.

1953 was Coronation Year and to commemorate the occasion each boy was presented with a copy of the New Testament and a mug bearing a portrait of the Queen. The beginning of the year was marred by the east coast floods when the homes of many of the boys in the School were affected including that of Mr. Teasdale. Mr. John "Josh" Norris joined the staff as an English Master to replace Mr. Coleman as Assistant to Mr. Pashley the Senior English Master. John Norris was born in Caister, was a student at both London and Cambridge

[20] *Ibid*. p.5

61. Operation Red Herring- in the Dunes.

and apart from his English Degree he had qualifications enabling him to teach shorthand. His other interests included Cross Country Running and the Cadets. Another newcomer was Mr. S.J. "Sid" Hutchence who had previously covered for Mr. Whitehead following an unfortunate accident. He had studied Geography at Cambridge, which would be his main subject in the curriculum, and Economics at London.

Amongst the news of those passing was that of Alderman Greenacre aged 85 and Chairman of the Governors since 1940. Another name being a particular part of the School's history was that of Major H.P. Raven aged 77 son of the former Headmaster of the Grammar School. It was Major Raven who had presented the School with the portrait of his father which hung in the School Hall.

At the Annual Prizegiving on the 19th November 1952 the Headmaster had spoken of a change in the outlook of the whole scheme of education provided at the School following a School Inspection He said that in the past the aim was for a five years course of general education for all boys which led to the School Certificate followed by a two or three year course in the Sixth Form for the Higher Certificate for those who remained at school. He said that there was now a greater demand for boys with Sixth Form Higher Education in Industry, Engineering, the Armed Forces, the Civil Service and medicine and the other professions. It had been a minority of boys who had stayed on until they were 18 up to that time, but this had now grown in national importance. Therefore Mr. Palmer said that in future there would be two courses of equal importance, one of five years for those who wished to go no further than achieving Ordinary Level of the General Certificate of Education and one of seven years for those who chose to go forward to Advanced and Scholarship Level.[21]

He said with regard to choice between the Arts and Science a boy, if equally good at both, should consider

---

[21] *Chronicle*, Second Series No. 9, pp.6-7

that more jobs might be available for the Scientists than the Artists.[22] He placed emphasis on the fact that if a boy was considering going to University he could benefit from the advantages of a third year in the Sixth Form. These were very important statements of policy which governed the pattern of gearing of the school curriculum for many years to come. C.H Wilson the Principal of University College Leicester who was guest speaker told the boys not to be mere passengers in the School but to contribute which would be of advantage not only to themselves but to the School as well.

In the Honours R.M. Loynes won a Major Scholarship in Mathematics and Physics to Trinity College Cambridge as well as his State Scholarship. Liffen the successful swimmer won a Naval Cadetship in Engineering to the Royal Naval College in Dartmouth. Gerald Hawkins was awarded a PhD in Radio Astronomy at Manchester University in a field in which he became an international figure. Victor Stowers who was evacuated to Retford and returned with the School to Yarmouth gained a B.A degree in English and French at Nottingham. Peter Woods after winning the prize for being the best at Work and Games had received a Great Yarmouth Major Award to go to University while his elder brother Alan had been awarded a first class honours degree in Mathematics at Manchester University.[23]

The Dramatic Society and the Choir joined forces to launch an opera in March, *The Great Bell of Burley*. This venture was a challenging one with Mr. Angwin as Musical Director, Mr. Whitehead as Producer and Mr. Palmer as ballet master. The school hall stage was used for the production as well as areas of the floor to achieve a variety of angles and differing levels to enhance the effect of various groupings which meant that audience accommodation was challenging. A two piano background to the production was provided and "beautifully played", stated reviewer Mr. Pashley, by Mr. Balfour and R.A. Jones. It was generally recognised that this was a very important production for both the Dramatic Society and the Choir but one which they entire cast rose to the occasion and achieved something memorable.

In terms of sport the Football Team's season, as reported by Mr. K.H. "Streaky" Senior had not only one of its most successful seasons post war but one of the best seasons in the history of the School. The School Team was captained initially by Peter Woods until he left after the first term having had his colours confirmed yet again. The team played 18 matches winning 16 losing one and drawing one. The Cross Country Course which had been slightly modified now provides two water jumps near the start. Mr Pereira noted that it was a fine sight as the large field swept into Pump Lane and quickly spread out as the leaders set a very fast pace. Shearing who won the previous years race on the old course in 25 minutes 39 seconds led throughout and finished in the fast time of 21 minutes 48.4 seconds which was 51.6 seconds faster than the record for the old course.[24] Stuart Dickinson, another of the future tennis players who I subsequently played with 20 years later with the Ravine Club on the Cliffs at Gorleston, had challenged for the lead in the previous year coming third, came in second behind Shearing in the 1953 race.

The Art Guild continued to have outings throughout the summer at various local and venues further afield.

The Cricket X1 needed batting performances to support the bowling successes since in the 1953 season the team played 8 matches won 4 lost three and drew 1. Singled out for praise by Mr. Senior was R.A. Welshman who had batted admirably throughout the season, notably against Sir John Leman School in Beccles where he was repeatedly hit on an uneven wicket and Wilson Gooch who developed into a useful left arm spinner

On the Annual Sports Day R.A. Shearing dominated and was Victor Ludorum winning the mile in a new record winning time of 4 minutes 46.2 seconds, together with the 880 and the 440 yards. This Sports Meeting showed a move from previous meetings where the winners of the shorter distances held sway but with the common distance of the 440 yards now won by a distance man Shearing who used his stamina, strength and speed to win the longer distance races and was awarded the Aldwyn Rouse Memorial Prize for his performance in the Mile.

In the Swimming Sports so long dominated by Liffen who had now left the School Michael Temple of Centre came to the fore winning the Overy Challenge Cup for his victories in the 440, 100 and 50 yards freestyle open and also for the 50 yards open backstroke. Temple was a four event winner which was a first for many years.

[22] *Ibid*. p.7
[23] *Ibid*. pp.8-9
[24] *Ibid*. pp.26-27

B.A Mileham from the Fourth Form reported on how as a Sea Cadet he had been approached to act as a signaller on the Drifter *Ocean Sunlight* which attended the Spithead Review as one of the representatives of the Fishing Fleets.[25] He recalled the amazing sight as they moved into their positions off the Isle of Wight. In particular he noted two of the foreign representatives, the Russian cruiser *Sverdlov* and the great three masted Italian Training Ship *Amerigo Vespucci*. The Queen and the Duke of Edinburgh reviewed the fleet from *H.M.S. Surprise* and Mileham recalls *Amerigo Vespucci* passing with the sailors manning the masts and crosstrees. I saw *Amerigo Vespucci* in various ports during my own port career and a magnificent sight this giant is. Later in 1979 and 1981 when I managed to get two Tall Ships races to Great Yarmouth while Chief Executive of the Port I recall, the masts and rigging of the larger ships able to use the river such as *Georg Stag*, and the two British Schooners *Malcolm Miller* and *Winston Churchill* being similarly manned at Great Yarmouth to join the races.

Poetry from the boys started to appear in *The Chronicle* and a very evocative poem of its time was "Night Fighter" by M.J. Hayhoe of (6Ai)

Night Fighter

Twin jets screeching
Radar searching
In the midnight sky
Roams the hunter,
Ever seeking
Its unwary prey.
Radar blipping
'Plane side-slipping
Through the midnight sky
Dives the hunter.
Cannon spitting
At its hapless prey.

GLOSTER (ARMSTRONG WHITWORTH)
METEOR N.F.11

Country of Origin: Great Britain.
Type: Two-seat Night Fighter.
Power Plant: Two Rolls-Royce Derwent 8 engines rated at 3,600 lb. static thrust each.
Approximate Performance: Maximum speed, 590 m.p.h. at sea level; rate of climb, 7,000 ft./min.; range (normal tankage), 510 mls. at 30,000 feet.
Weights: Approximate loaded, 19,790 lb.
Armament: Four 20-mm. British Hispano Mk.5 cannon mounted in wing outer sections.
Development: The Meteor N.F.11 has been developed by Sir W. G. Armstrong Whitworth Aircraft Ltd., from the basic Meteor F.8 airframe. Distinctive features of this version are the two-seat cockpit, similar to that of the Meteor T.7, the long-span Meteor F.3 type wings, and the lengthened nose containing the radome. The prototype Meteor N.F.11 flew in May 1950, and the type is now in service with the R.A.F., and the Danish, French, and Belgian air forces.

48

GLOSTER (ARMSTRONG WHITWORTH)
METEOR N.F.11

Dimensions: Span, 43 ft.; length, 48 ft. 6 in.; height, 13 ft. 10 in.

D   49

62. Gloster Meteor NF 11 from the Observers Book of Aircraft 1953 (Source Michael Boon collection)

25 *Ibid.* pp.38-39

In the post war period this recalls the Meteor NF11 the nightfighter development from the Gloster Meteor F 8 both of which were detailed in the *Observer's Book of Aircraft* a book familiar to many boys of the School keen on aircraft recognition.

The Chronicle concludes with a sad notice on the 27th July 1953 recording the sudden death of Mr. Whitehead the Second Master in June, so long a pillar of so many activities in the School shocked all.

Mr. J. B. WHITEHEAD.

The sudden death of Mr. Whitehead on the 25th July has come as a great shock to the School and all associated with it. In this inadequate space we can but convey to Mrs. Whitehead and family our heartfelt sympathy in their grievous bereavement.

27th July, 1953.

63. The announcement of Mr. Whitehead's death in the July 1953 Chronicle.

64. The staff in 1953

The 1954 *Chronicle* opens with a tribute to Mr. Whitehead. "JBW" was a born Schoolmaster. He joined the School in 1924 and would be remembered as the editor of *The Chronicle*, the organiser of the Athletic Sports, the Cross Country Race and the Swimming Gala, the Chairman of the History and Geographical Society and of the Parents Association and the author of *The History of Great Yarmouth Grammar School*. He also gave his time to the production of plays and opera for the School and also for the Borough for which he was a talented actor and producer. His long service to the Cadet Movement was recognised in 1949 when he was awarded the O.B.E. and then again in 1953 when he received the Coronation Medal as the Senior Cadet Officer in the country. The funeral service was held at St. Andrews Parish Church Gorleston and attended by a full congregation in recognition of his service to the community. The School decided to establish a fund in his memory to be presented to the best Army Cadet of the year.

22 *Ibid*. p.7
23 *Ibid*. pp.8-9

In terms of staff departures and arrivals Mr. Balfour who had been with the School since 1946 left to take up an appointment at Chester City Grammar School. And Mr. "Rock" Thompson remembered by a number of us for his prodigious walking stride arrived to teach History and Geography.

Prize Day on the 12th November 1953 was marked with tributes to Mr. H.T. Greenacre and to Mr. Whitehead. The guest speaker was the Very Reverend W.E. Beck, Dean of Worcester one of the first two scholarship boys at Great Yarmouth Grammar School, while the other scholarship boy, Mr. G.J. Wroughton was in the audience. In his Annual Report Mr. Palmer spoke of the urgent need for extra rooms at the School to accommodate the increasing number of boys. He also expressed the equally urgent problem of playing fields since the moment building was started they would be taking away some of the little space the School had and it was already drawing heavily on the Beaconsfield Recreation Ground. He also reported that to bridge the gap in standards whereby boys who would have gained a School Certificate in the past, but were not able to reach the General Certificate of Education in more than one or two subjects, would now receive a formal statement of attainment naming the subjects in which they were considered to have reached a satisfactory level.[26]

65. Mr Morrow with a group of the players from She Stoops to Conquer

The Dramatic Society took on Oliver Goldsmith's *"She Stoops to Conquer"* at the end of the autumn term where the enthusiasm of the cast produced an undoubted success. The direction team of Mr. Morrow, Mr. Pashley and Mr. Pereira had the responsibility of transforming the play from text to stage. Notable amongst the cast in the review by John Norris were Latham Bewley as Tony Lumpkin, Wilson Gooch as Mr. Hardcastle and the triple female cast of Peter Hobbis, Ken Whiley and John English. Also mentoned in the simpler parts of "pastoral woolliness" were Mr. Hardcastle's servants in the shape of Tony Powles, Bill Thurtle, Mike Temple and David Minns.

House Notes were also a regular part of the Chronicles and North House had a most successful year in 1954 retaining the football cup for the fifth year in succession with the junior team at its strongest ever winning all its matches. The House photograph supplied by Tony Young shows the House Masters and various Captains of North House in 1954-55 with Walter Hogg in his final year before his departure as a Housemaster.

The success of the North House football team contributed to the strength of the school First X1. The juniors once again completed a season with the loss of a

66. Mr. Morrow explaining finer points of Latin to David Gunn, Alan Moyle and Adrian Gardiner

26 *Chronicle*, Second Series July 1954, No. 10, p.8

point in the local school league – the fourth year of topping the table in seven years. M. Borett, the left back and captain, received special praise from Mr. Belfour as he also Captained Yarmouth Town Boys Team throughout the season and was awarded Norfolk County Colours. Two other boys, Boast as centre forward and Wadsworth as Goalkeeper were also selected to play for the County while Thomason, Simpson and Ralphs played for Yarmouth Town Boys.[27]

In Easter 1956 John English told me that he and other members of 6(a)ii took advantage of an annual arrangement where a larger group of pupils from many schools could

67. North House with Housemasters and various Captains.

take part in a short visit to France. The photograph taken on top of the Arc de Triomphe shows from left to right (rear) Josephine Prior, Freda Bootman and Pat Curtis of the Great Yarmouth High School who also took advantage of the visit. In the front row from left to right is a stranger from another school and Grammar School pupils Terry Hurrell, John English and Latham Bewley.

68. A French visit at Easter.
On top of the Arc de Triomphe 1956.

Terry Hurrell taught at the Wroughton Junior and Styles Schools before emigrating with his wife to Canada in 1966. John English taught all his career at the Wroughton Junior School (1960-1994) retiring early in that year. Latham Bewley was ordained and had curacies at Wigan and Caister, subsequently becoming Rector of West Lynn and Vicar of Lakenham. He died a few years ago.[28]

In a field of 89 starters in the Cross Country many of the boys had trained before the race and improved performances markedly. The weather was ideal but the course distinctly muddy and Delf took the lead until Shearing, who had been troubled with his shoes, quickly overhauled him to hold a comfortable lead to win again. Shearing was again Victor Ludorum at the Athletics Sports on the 1st June holding both the Mile, 880 and 440 Yards titles. Brian Delf was runner up for the Victor Ludorum Prize.

The Swimming Sports, held on the 1st July, saw the beginnings of a great rivalry but a golden period for Centre House. Michael Temple once

[27] *Ibid*. p.25
[28] Source John English

69. School Army Cadet Force at Summer Camp in Folkestone 1954

again won the Overy Challenge Cup with "magnificent swimming" reported in the House Notes with victories in the 440, 100, and 50 yards open freestyles and the 50 yards backstroke. Rodney Clayton came second to him in three events and third in another and also won the diving event he had won in the previous three years making him runner upon for Overy Challenge Cup.

The Cadet force having lost Lt. Colonel Whitehead was now under the command of Major West. The Camp which took place at St. Martins Plain, Shornclife near Folkestone in Kent hosted by the Royal Inniskilling Fusiliers was recorded as one of the best camps which the Corps had ever attended. On a sombre note it was noted that the Fusiliers were then in Kenya at the time of the insurrection by the Mau Mau.[29]

The Old Boys continued their activities including an active Old Yarmouthians Cricket Season. Walter Hogg who now turned out for the Old Boys topped both the batting and bowling averages for the third successive year with the Association. Johnnie Green, now Headmaster of the Priory School coming second to him in both averages. The London Old Boys Association, held together by the efforts of E.W. "Tusky" Foulser, had decided that while membership was at a low level it would hold its Annual General Meeting at the same time as its Annual Dinner in an effort to see whether this brought a large number of Old Boys to London for the occasion. Membership at this juncture in London and around the Home Counties was 51 but as usual the Association presented books to the School Library and both the Senior and Junior Reading Prizes.

1955 opened with news of another death that of E.C.H. "Ted" Freeman President of the Old Boys Association and who had also been its Honorary Secretary. He had been appointed as Honorary Treasurer in 1946 and was interested in local dramatics having both directed for and acted with the Great Yarmouth Operatic and Dramatic Society since 1948 and had been the Society's Treasurer.[30] Johnnie Green the Association Chairman succeeded him as President with Charles Cooke from Oby moving up to be its Chairman.

Derek Excel's wood cut showed the ruins of St. Nicholas Church, a reminder of how far the town had still to go in post war recovery.

---

29 *Chronicle*, Second Series No.11, July 1955, p.3
30 *Ibid*. p.4

70. St. Nicholas in ruins 1955

In terms of Staff news Mr. R. "Ron" Tucker arrived from Loughborough College and Worcester Training College to assist with Physical Education, English and Geography. He also instituted the School Basketball League which had proved to be very popular.

It was a red letter day on Monday 14th February when the Rt. Reverend Ambrose Reeves, Bishop of Johannesburg and an Old Boy spoke to Assembly and afterwards to the Sixth Form about the policy of compulsory segregation being followed by the South Africa Government, a policy to which he bitterly opposed.[31] In recognition for his services to the Church of England and South Africa Dr. Reeves had had the honorary degree of Sacred Theology of New York conferred on him in the previous year. During the Easter Holidays a party of High School Girls and Grammar School Boys had visited France, made their headquarters at Tours under the guidance of Mr. Pereira and visited the Châteaux of the Loire. The trip was regarded as an unqualified success but Colin Bassett remarked wryly in his news item in the Chronicle that the school's rooms at the Paris Hotel in Tours were on the Fifth Floor and that seemed to dominate their lives. Another successful School trip was organised by Walter Hogg in the May. A party of 117 boys and six masters went on a day trip London and visited the Science Museum in South Kensington and the Zoo at Regents Park. The comment was made that all returned safely!

It was announced that Mr. Coldbeck who arrived at the Grammar School in 1946 as Mathematics Master and succeeded Mr. Whitehead as Second Master would be retiring to the north from whence he came.[32] He had had a teaching career of 52 years and had come to the School from the Henry Smith School in Hartlepool and had inspired attention with the warning whistle and the whispered "here comes Charlie" which were familiar to decades of schoolboys. His blunt comments delivered with northern pith brought many a boy back to his attention. "Ee lad thou't not learn Geometry by looking out of window – pay attention."

In terms of the Annual Prizegiving on the 16th November 1954 the Headmaster in his Annual Report had posed the question as to whether part time employment was a good thing for boys in a Grammar School. He said that he had serious doubts as to whether the one in four boys over the age of 13, who were working either before or after school hours could divide their loyalty equally between home, school and employer. Mr. Palmer concluded that his view was that the employment was not a good thing unless it was for a specific purpose such as to go to the Lake District for a week, to buy books or to assist the family income when times were hard. It is interesting to note that the Principal of the East Norfolk Sixth Form College, where all the students requiring "A" level training go to-day, has exactly the same problem with part time employment over half a century later. On the academic side Mr. Palmer said that the six places gained at the older Universities in a year was a very satisfying achievement and that to obtain two scholarships to Cambridge, R.A. Jones to Kings College for Music and J.R. Thompson to Trinity College for Mathematics was notable. He said that it was his ambition now to see an Old Boy of the School come down from Oxford or Cambridge with a First Class Degree.

The Cercle Francais staged Beaumarchais's famous comedy *Le Barber de Seville* in December 1954 before two large audiences in the School Hall. This second production in French following the success of Moliere's *Le Bourgeois Gentilhomme* three years previously, as again a success. Notable in the parts in the review by David Marshal of the third year sixth were John English, the rascally guardian who planned to wed his ward, Colin Bassett as Count Almaviva, David Minns as Figaro and Bob Boardley as Rosine, the young ward.[33] The assistance of Mr. Morrow behind the scenes was of great assistance to Mr. Pereira.

[31] *Ibid*. p.6
[32] *Ibid*. pp.11-12
[33] *Ibid*. p.15

On Friday May 20th virtually the whole school assembled to hear the result of the mock election which had sparked riotous behaviour during the previous fortnight. The placing of election addresses in hymn books at Assembly had been thwarted for the Socialists at the last minute by a change in hymn numbers. Posters were all over the windows of the school, difficult to remove from the Physics Laboratory afterwards, numerous hecklers during election addresses, a competition for flag flying at the top of the Raven Tower and worst of all, for the candidates having to field questions on which they had not been briefed had been the order or disorder of the day. The result showed a victory for Bob Barber the popular Independent candidate.

School Societies had an active year. The Natural History Society chaired by Mr. Morris held a very successful exhibition where the attendance topped the hundred mark which was close to a record for any society. The exhibits ranged from birds eggs to foreign birds and from fossils to fish. It was noted that the Society had great support from the middle forms of the school with, as always, a lack of support from the fifth and sixth forms and on this occasion, very few first formers.

It was interesting to note that the Science Society had two outings to the popular lectures series at the Norwich City College where firstly it heard Mr. Fred Hoyle give his view on the "Steady State" theory of the creation of galaxies whilst the second meeting was in March where the Astronomer Royal Sir Harold Spencer-Jones had provided the orthodox alternative view of the "Continuous Creation" theory. Mr West had explained the background to these opposing views before the lectures. The Grammar School was therefore at the cutting edge of this discussion of important astronomical ideas of the time.[34]

The Cross Country Race in 1955 had unpleasant conditions particularly for the spectators with a biting east wind bringing snow flurries to the course which itself was partly covered with ice and snow. However 82 runners turned out for the race, scrambled over the first water jump and disappeared up Pump Lane with J.P. "Terro" Brown well in the rear having lost a shoe at the first obstacle but then recovered well to finish 44th. Michael Temple won the race in a slow time with Russell Langham second and Alan Moyle third. Langham and Moyle came second and third in the Mile at the Athletic Sports held in Monday 6th June. The Victor Ludorum was Barry Boast who was successful in the 220 and 100 yards. Boast went on to improve his time by one tenth of a second when he was successful for the School again in the 220 yard at the Inter School Sports on the16th June.

Michael Temple again swept the board at the School Swimming Sports with the Centre man retaining the Overy Challenge Cup with victories in the 440, 100, 50 yards open freestyle events and the 50 years open backstroke repeating his success of the previous year. A youngster contended for honours when Mike Boice of South House was second in the open freestyle under 13 and won both the 50 yards breaststroke events for under 13 and under 14 being 13 at the time.

Swimming lessons and training in the pool took place after spring sessions of "land drill" in the gymnasium. Lessons given in the summer term on a form by form basis were at the 100 yard Open Air non-heated Swimming Pool on Marine Parade, regretfully no longer in existence. I can recall walking down Marine Parade from Salisbury Road for the weekly swimming session with the Form when the blackboard outside the pool showed no chalk figure for a temperature but early in the summer term it hovered around the 54-55 degrees Fahrenheit. Bracing times for learning to develop swimming skills. The instructor was "Bandsman" Jack Blake a former boxer with a career of some note. Mike Boice recalled that he owed a debt of gratitude to the School wall-eyed swimming coach "Bandsman" Jack Blake for getting him going in swimming. He remembered the land drill in the gymnasium and how the breast stroke became his only stroke of style and distance. As a result he won a number of School Medals over the years and the Overy Cup for breaking an old record. He also swam for Norfolk in the All England Championship. The pool on the sea front after he coped with mid March temperatures in the mid fifties became his summer home with a season ticket bought at 7s 6d.

Sixth Form Notes of the time spread a small sidelight onto out of hour's culture. No doubt the juniors would be surprised and shocked to learn that many Sixth Formers spent their one evening per week in Vetesse's Milk

---

[34] *Ibid.* p.31
[35] *Chronicle*, Second Series No. 12, July 1956, p.6

Bar, devouring numerous favoured ices, coffee and hot chocolates. For this riotous living had become even worse – the Prefects as well as members of Staff had been seen at a Gorleston Building known as the *Floral Hall*. Similar aspects of out of school activities are revealed by Colin "Dusty" Miller in his book of a country boy coming into the Grammar School from Rollesby in the 1950's. It is interesting to reflect that the bachelor Schoolmasters were often not much older than the older Sixth Formers and of course shared their social tastes.

71. The Sixth Form Common Room

The Cadet Corps welcomed Captain Norris who proved to be a very efficient and enthusiastic officer. The Company had grown to strength of 70 and was now a substantial part of the battalion. Colin Valentine the Staff Sergeant in his report said he looked forward to a time when the Friday morning parade in Tower Yard would be not only well-turned out but without a single case of "mufti"..

September 1955 had seen the beginning of a radical change to the School and now, in order to cope with the called "bulge" the school in 1956 was now a three stream school. Additional accommodation was now one the urgent needs and new buildings on the school site were bound to have an impact on the playing fields.

New Masters joined the staff. Brian Grimshaw to teach English, History and Art, Mr. Terence Tookey to teach English and French, Mr. Jones to teach Chemistry and Biology and Albert Pett to teach Mathematics and Physics. The two first named staff became two parts of the *Three Musketeers,* with Sam Sneyd later, marching across the playing field in a trio, since unmarried School Masters they had flats in the upper floors of School House. With arrivals came departures. Mr. Pashley Senior English Master for seven years retired to become mine host at Hills Marine View on the corner of the corner of Euston Road and North Drive. Mr. Tucker

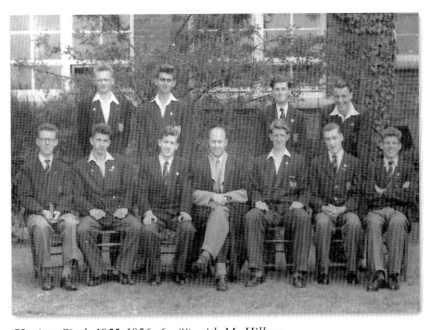

72. Arts Sixth 1955-1956. 6 a(ii) with Mr Hillyer

after a short first stay at the school took up an appointment as Master in charge of Malet High School in Hill a co-educational school which had the same number of pupils as Great Yarmouth Grammar School but which managed to put six football XI's into the field regularly. The popular Geography Master "Rock" Thompson also departed to teach Geography and Geology at Portsmouth Northern Grammar School for Boys.

73. Science Sixth 1955-1956. 6s (ii) with Mr West

It was noted that Sports Day in 1956 resulted in the setting up of nine new records with the improved performance of athletes resulting from an increased appetite for strict training due to the initiative of Russell Langham and the senior boys. Brian East of South House won the Aldwyn Rouse Memorial Prize for his performance in the High Jump clearing 5 foot five inches. Of the records set by Aldwyn Rouse himself before his wartime death that of the 100 years at 10.2 seconds in 1939 and the Long Jump at 21 feet 2 inches in 1940 still stood. Aldwyn Rouse's father, Aldwyn Rouse senior, a past Schoolmaster of the school was reported to be still looking forward to receiving his *Chronicle* with school news in retirement in York. He would be remembered as a fine cricketer and had established, in 1955 on the occasion of his 70th Birthday a fund out of which awards would be made annually for batting, bowling and fielding. Mr. Rouse put 2 shillings in the fund for every wicket he had taken, being a notable bowler for Yarmouth Cricket Club, the idea was novel and generous since the took over 1,000 wickets.[36] Mr. Stafford was one of the Trustees of the fund.

At the Annual Prize Day held on the previous 1st December the Headmaster in his annual report returned to his theme of being critical of part time employment. He said that it had come to his notice that some boys in 5B had started their jobs during the week prior to the examainations and continued them during the examination itself. He said that this had undoubtedly contributed to the fact that the result was significantly below the expectations for that form. He expressed the strong view that some blame must inevitably be attached to the parents of those boys who condoned their part-time employment and thus jeopardised their sons' future careers. The Headmaster referred to the school's academic worth and his wish to make Geography available to the Science as well as the Arts Sixth Forms. He said this would enable a combination such as Geography, Biology and Chemistry to be available. He was delighted to be able to report that the plans for the new buildings which had been produced would not only include new classrooms but also a new School Hall.[37]

In the Honours awarded Colin Bassett won a Choral Bursary to Queens College Oxford. The School play directed by Mr. Morrow and Mr. Pereira was the comedy thriller *Grumpy* in which John English and Latham Bewley, making their final appearances for the dramatic society, were the mainstays. English was particularly impressive in the role of the crusty old lawyer with all the mannerisms of old age. Bewley as Ernest had a part of dash particularly in his scenes with Virginia, a debut part for Richard Woodall of the Second Form. David "Ben" Gunn was a comical doctor while David Rich and Ron Eyre made the most of their parts as household servants.

The Football First X1 had a good season with Mr. Senior reporting that Tony Young had "handled his job as captain extremely well and was a happy inspiration to the rest of the team who responded to his sound leadership on the field." The team won 8 matches, lost 2 and drew one with Young, Moyle, Boast and Ralphs having their colours confirmed and with M. Gilder and R. "Dickie" Birds being awarded new colours. North led by Tony Young who was Football, Swimming and Athletics Captain won the House football competition for the seventh successive year.

---

[36] *Ibid.* p.8
[37] *Ibid.* p.25

In the Athletics Sports on Tuesday 5th June at the Wellesley it was the turn of the fast men again to become Victor Ludorum with Ralphs of Centre wining the 220, 100 and 120 yards hurdles. The beginnings of a rivalry in the 13-15 year group could be seen with Mike Eyre edging out Derek Farman for the Omnium Bowl. The Swimming Sports, with Michael Temple having left the School, saw his runner up of precious years Rodney Clayton carry off the Overy Challenge cup with victories in the 100 yards open freestyle and the

74. Football First XI 1954-1955 with Mr. Senior

diving and with second place in three other events and a third in another. Winning or being placed in six events was quite a feat. Mike Boice of South won the Rowe Memorial Cup for his performance in the 50 yards breaststroke under 14 in a time of 43.4 seconds where he beat the record set up by K. Chittleburgh in 1935.[38]

A short lived form publication as an internal newspaper the *IVA Grammarian* appeared and died during the year and disappeared in a welter of domestic strife amongst its authors. Changes had occurred in the organisation of the Cadet force with the alteration from a numbered described to a letter described company. The School Company thus became "A" Company instead of "1" Company. An attempt had been made to increase the activities and responsibilities of junior N.C.O.'s with the result that the Company had been organised into three platoons. As a result of this a need for the training of junior N.C.O.'s was noted.

75 The new Block of Classrooms 1958. (With acknowledgment to the Ivan and Les Gould Photographic Archive.)

[38] *Chronicle*, Second Series No. 13, July 1958, pp.11-12

The Chronicle reproduced the Roll of Honour and set out the intention of establishing a Memorial Book recording the death of Old Boys to be presented by the London Old Boys to the School Library. The London Old Boys Society was to meet the cost of this book and the first volume would have inscribed on its cover "Old Boys – London Society Memorial Book 1936-1956. It was the twenty- fifth anniversary of the establishment of the London Old Boys Society in 1936.

There was no *Chronicle* issued in 1957 so the 1958 Chronicle was a double issue recording the news over two years. The first stage of the new building project a block of nine new classrooms had been completed after being commenced in January 1957.

Four new Masters had arrived in September 1956. Mr. E.W. "Ted" Buswell, a former successful athlete at the School (1947-51) to teach Physical Education and General Science, Mr. Colin Cheshire to teach Geography and Music, Mr. W "Bill" Howell (French and Latin) and Mr. J. "Sam" Sneyd (Physics and Mathematics). Mrs. Sadler departed having been School Secretary from 1951 and was succeeded by Miss N. "Norah" Mobbs. Departures also occurred with Mr. Senior having arrived in 1946 departing after 12 years to take up an appointment as Head of English at Wincanton County Modern School in Somerset. He had organized both the Athletics and Swimming Sports, been responsible for the introduction of the Milocarian system of scoring at the Athletics Sports and had encouraged the development of field sports to go alongside track events. Mr. Buswell after a short stay left to become Head of Physical Education at the Henderson School Norwich, while Mr. Tookey departed to join the staff of Warwick School. However short their stays, staff members were always remembered by those boys who were taught by them. At the 1957 Prize Giving held on 20th November 1956 Mr. Palmer noted that the slowing down and eventual phasing out of National Service was a great blessing but would be creating some problems as with a greater demand for University Admission the gaining of places was becoming more difficult was leading to the advantage of spending a third year in the Sixth Form in order to secure the desired University place. The Headmaster referred to the fact that following the school building programme to take over the playing fields at Barnard Bridge vacated by the High School had provided the Grammar School with a sufficient playing field of its own for the first time in its long history.[39]

The School play was *The Hippolytus of Euripides* which was well staged, with excellent music and lighting and backed by Mr. Morrow's conviction that the language should be given full reign as the flesh and bones of the drama. Mr. Tookey reported that the Company served the producer at all times well and some times very well.[40] The holiday of Easter 1958 in Rambouillet was different from previous School visits to France because it was the first occasion on which party of school students had visited Rambouillet after the town of Yarmouth had been "twinned" with its French counterpart. A Reception was given in France by the newly formed Rotary Club which twinned with the Great Yarmouth Senior Rotary Club and still has a strong bilateral relationship to-day over 50 years later. The School Societies had a busy two years in 1957 and 1958 and the newly formed, in November 1956, Jazz Club under the chairmanship of Mr. Tookey had a paid up membership of 40 members as the only Society to demand a subscription. The scholars formed, as an offshoot, its own skiffle group led by Russell Langham. It was to be hoped that although the organizers had left the School in May 1958 others would come forward to keep the club alive. Skiffle at this time was an emerging offshoot of the British Jazz movement with home grown instruments such as a washboard and groups such as Lonnie Donegan's who headed Chris Barber's rhythm section in his jazz band formed his own offshoot Skiffle group in which Barber played . On the local front Beryl Bryden of Beccles achieved quite a reputation nationally as a washboard player.

The Dramatic Society followed *Hippolytus* with *H.M.S Pinafore* in 1958 which was great success. Three members of the Girls High School were "borrowed" to play the three female leads, Jancis Parkin as Josephine, Captain Corcoran's daughter, Penelope Evans as Little Buttercup and June Beck as Hebe, Sir Joseph Porter's cousin. Bob Boardley played the part of the lovelorn sailor Ralph Rackstraw with success while Mr. Pereira was an immensely proud and dignified Lord of the Admiralty as Sir Joseph Porter. Mr. Cheshire records this as a most successful production.

---

[39] *Ibid*. pp.15-16
[40] *Ibid*. P.32

The Cross Country now provided both a senior and junior race with Russell Langham winning the senior race in 1957 and J. Parry the junior race. In the following year in 1958, with a cold east wind sweeping the marshes, John Stafford won the Senior Race with Parry of West retaining the junior race in improving on his time of the previous year. In the Athletic Sports Barry Boast held on to the Victor Ludorum title with Derek Farman who won the Aldwyn Rouse Memorial Prize for his performance in Long Jump 13-15 having success in the Omnium Bowl. In 1958 conditions were perfect when the Athletics Sports were held on Tuesday 3rd June with ten records being broken. Farman was Victor Ludorum with a massive score of over 2000 points having won the Long Jump, the 220 yards and the 100 yards. The latter, I recall, was a tremendous performance when he recorded a time of 10.0 seconds beating Aldwyn Rouses' own time of 10.2 seconds

76. Ted Buswell winning the 440 yards at the Wellesley Recreation Ground. (With acknowledgment to the Ivan and Les Gould Photographic Archive.)

which had stood since 1939.[41] I watched this race and when Farman's winning time was announced by Walter Hogg there were cheers from the Wellesley Stand.

A previous Victor Ludorum Ted Buswell had joined the staff to teach Physical Education but had taken up a new appointment at the end of that academic year The picture shows him victorious in a 440 yard race on the 1st August in that year.

In the Swimming Sports of 1957 John Gibbs of South won the Overy Challenge Cup, a position which he retained in 1958 with victories in the 440 yards, 100 yards and 50 yards open freestyle the 50 yards freestyle under 15 and the 50 yards back stroke open being unbeaten in the five events he entered while still under 15.[42]

In the Sixth Form Notes there were always targets of the more eccentric members. David "Flick" Rich, a nickname required early in his school career as he read the part of a tall thin French detective who was also a "flic" came into the spotlight in 1957. "A Dark Horse indeed has been Flick, who after ten days of Riotous Living in Sinful Paris shares with his fellow 6A (ii) member Henry Hall the not unwelcome attentions of the Great Yarmouth High School Fourth Form. Having got into the note taker's sights in 1958 Flick's return to School, prior to going the Cullum Teachers' Church of England's Training College, was a member of 6A (iii), and it was recorded that he chanced his arm in crossing the threshold of 5 (B)'s form room. It was a sign of the times that Sixth formers, in bringing their vehicles to the school, competed for parking places with the staff in Tower Yard.

The Prize Days for 1958, One Junior and One Senior were held on consecutive days with the Senior first on 25th and 26th November 1958. The Headmaster pointed out that the growth in the size of the school, which commenced four years earlier, would begin to affect the Sixth Form. He expected to be able to divide the Science Sixth into sections which both catered for those seeking Scholarship Level and University and also to provide high level course to enable pupils to obtain two Levels and be able to advance by apprenticeships into major firms. Mr. Palmer made a significant comment noting that if there were a change of Government before the next Prize Giving it could see the introduction of Comprehensive Schools and the abolition of Modern, Technical and Grammar Schools.[43]

41 *Ibid*. p.38
42 *Chronicle*, Second Series No.14, July 1960, p.11
43 *Ibid*. p.14

The guest speaker R.W. Ketton-Cremer, the notable Norfolk Author and Historian made a very interesting historical address emphasizing the School's place in the history of Yarmouth and urged the boys to value the tradition of their school. He said that whatever they eventually achieved they were still "links in the chain of history" and linked with the earlier pupils of their Ancient School. Amongst the honours won by Old Boys was Peter Woods' B.A at London University in History. He was the third of the Old Boy Woods brothers to gain degrees.[44]

At the 1959 Prize Giving the Headmaster heralded the new Science Sixth which he proposed to establish in the following September and said he was pleased to note that Peter Hobbis of 6 (A iii) having stayed on for a third year in the Sixth Form to sit the Cambridge Entrance Examinations had gained an Open Exhibition for English at Selwyn College Cambridge. It was also interesting to note that John Stafford, son of the Mathematics Master Tommy Staffords gained an East Suffolk Major Award recording the fact that at the time, where the Staffords lived, on Warren Lane near Gorleston Golf Club, was on the Suffolk side of the County border. Later boundary changes have brought the area into the Great Yarmouth District Council Boundary.

77. A Midsummer Night's Dream Old School Hall 1959

I was pleased to note that having participated in Mr. Morrow's production of *A Midsummer Night's Dream* in December 1958 my first year in the Sixth Form with many of my friends that Mr. Whittaker gave it a rave review as a "delightful production".[45] Mr. Morrow was quite inspired in his casting. For the "Rude Mechanicals" after casting Michael Gough of the fourth Form as Bottom he went to a largely previously untapped source – the scientists. So Roy Fox, a large chap played Francis Flute the Bellows Mender. Bill Brugger was an imposing Theseus while Brian Joice took the female role of Hippolyta. John Bowles, Richard Harold and David Lilley all from the Fifth and Fourth forms took the parts of Puck, Oberon and Titania. The casting of the lovers was also unexpected, at least for me. Richard Woodall and Peter Davey, my fellow sixth-formers, were cast to play Lysander and Demetrius and I was approached to be offered a part by Mr. Morrow. To my surprise he offered me Hernia one of the female lovers something that with my subsequent experience with the Masquers would not now faze me at all. When I said "are you sure" he said "yes" and I was also surprised to find that he had asked Cliff "lugs" Cooper of the Fifth to play Helena. The female actors were made up by Mrs. Excel and the long photo taken by Derek the Stage Manager, Art Master and her husband shows the cast in a scene from Act V. I quite enjoyed playing the female role but was left with quizzical feelings on the last night when two female parents, leaving the front row were heard to say "I didn't know that they were using girls from the High School in this production.

John Blyth commented that the Senior Cross Country race held in depressing wet conditions on March 10th 1959 was poorly supported in terms of numbers of entries and also those who came to watch. I had been encouraged to

[44] *Ibid*. pp.19-21
[45] *Ibid*. P.32

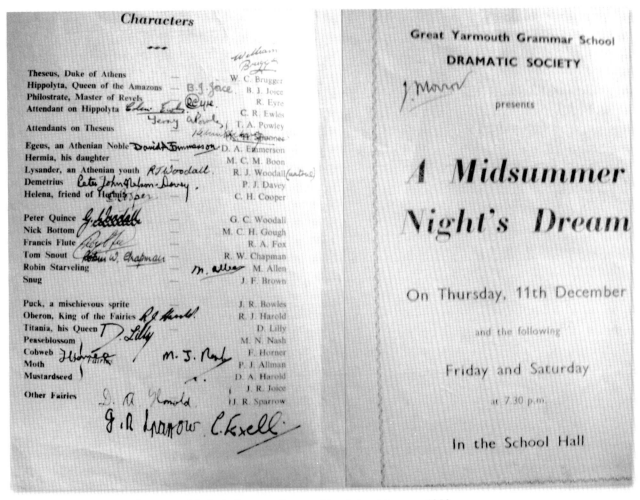

78. *Programme A Midsummer Night's Dream directed by John Morrow 1959*

run in the race by my keener athletic friends in the autumn and groups of us trained regularly running overtake circuits on the race course in each week in all weather. At the race itself this training paid off and Peter Davey, the keenest of the team won in the good time of 22 minutes 7 seconds. in dreadful conditions Brendon Byrne another of the autumn and winter training team also finished well and went on to be a very successful distance runner. I was very pleased to come in tenth thinking that training did pay off especially in stamina terms running east into the wind towards the finish over the dykes on the open marshes even if one did finish very cold and wet and a long way from a shower. In the Athletics Sports John Gibbs broke records in the (15+) Discus, Shot and Javelin. This was still not enough to bring him the Victor Ludorum as Derek Farman winning the three track events of the 440 220 and 100 yards outscored him on the Milocarian System. Gibbs was a determined competitor and swept the board at the Swimming Sports on July 6th at the Seafront Pool winning the 15+ 440, 100 and 50 yards Open Freestyle events and the Overy Challenge Cup for the third successive year.

The 1950's probably saw the greatest change in the School's size and character since its opening on the Salisbury Road site in 1910. The commentary on the decade left by Walter Hogg the Senior History Master in January 1962 records some of those changes by a Master who had lived through them Mr. Hogg having arrived at the School in 1948. He comments on that fact that the untimely death of John Whitehead, the Second Master, in 1953 meant that he had not seen the even greater changes in the school and town than when he closed his School History in 1951. Walter Hogg commented on the final decline of the herring industry in the period 1950- 1961, the alteration in the pattern of holidays taken in the town now relying greatly on motorized and caravan holidays and the development of light industries on the South Denes in the area once used for the drying of drift nets. As an historian Walter Hogg saw the disadvantage of a single river crossing of the Yare into the town and the vulnerability of the railways when the East Coast Flood of 1953 isolated Great Yarmouth. Post war educational rebuilding had seen the construction of two new Infant and Junior Schools, three new Secondary Modern Schools, two of them in new buildings, a new Technical High School, a new Girls High School and an extended Grammar School. He noted that whereas the population of Great Yarmouth in 1951 at 51,105 was less than that in the 1931 census (56,771), a greater proportion of the town's population was of school age. In 1961 the post war population was just reaching school leaving age and whereas this profile would pose economic problems for the town and it would also result in more prospective parents in the immediate future.

Mr. Hogg referred to Mr. Whitehead's analysis of the phases of Mr. Palmer's Headship. The period 1937-1940 after he had taken over from Mr. Seaborne was a settling in period while 1940- 1945 dealt with the war time evacuation. The School's reconstruction period of 1945-1951 was a precursor to the school reorganization period 1951-1960. The first changes began in 1953 and had involved far more that the acquisition of extra staff and additional classrooms. Education changes had also to be planned for with a more varied timetable much wider choice of subjects for the Fifth and Sixth Forms. The reintroduction of German and the introduction of the new Fifth Form Subject Technical Drawing were positive changes. Extra numbers in the Sixth Form and the addition of a second Science Sixth Form had to be also fully planned and the facilities necessary to cater for all the changes in terms of alterations and additions to the School, the provision of more laboratory space, the creation of a new Library, a new School Hall and Dining facilities were all part of the School's major expansion.

The pattern of School entrants had meant that more boys now from the county area around Great Yarmouth which had been a longstanding link and also more boys staying in the Sixth Form than ever before. The School's Athletics reputation and performance had improved markedly and there had been a great increase in boys going on to Higher Education after leaving School with many honours being won by Old Boys at University and elsewhere. Mr. Hogg commented on the value of the links which the School had with its Old Boy Association and its London offshoot and also with the Parents Association which Mr. Palmer inaugurated after the War. Mr. Hogg speculated on whether the School had reached its maximum six in numbers during the last ten yeas or whether it might have done when the rebuilding had been completed, commenting that the School's playing field, on which he had played as cricketer, had been greatly reduced.

Mr. Palmer had been left a problem in seeking more playing field space when he succeeded Mr. Seaborne in 1937. Mr. Palmer, Mr. Hogg remarked, will have left a similar problem to his own successor. Mr. Hogg concluded with the comment that ten years after its 400th Anniversary the School had been completely reshaped and would have to face the problems of the future under a new Headmaster and an enlarged staff.

Chapter 7
The Sixties and a New Headmaster

79. Mr. A.H. G. Palmer Headmaster 1937-1960

Mr. Palmer had given notice that he intended to resign at the end of the autumn term 1960 ending his reign which commenced in the spring of 1937. Mr. Pereira as his Deputy wrote an appreciation of the colleague with whom he had served for so long.

Mr. Palmer, Master of Arts (Senior Wrangler at Cambridge), Bachelor of Music and Fellow of the Royal College of Organists, had come to Great Yarmouth from the Whitgift School where he had been Senior Mathematics Master.

He had completed the East Wing at the School and the Gymnasium in a period when the School grew in numbers and more facilities were required. He had carried the School through evacuation at Retford and then dealt with staffing shortage in September 1944 when the School returned to Salisbury Road. *The Education Act of 1944* abolished protection which the Grammar Schools had had up to that time but instead he drew attention between those who would admit all pupils to the School and those who would abolish them altogether. He took advantage of changes and the School grew during his time to 500 boys as Walter Hogg recorded. He had also taken advantage of curriculum opportunities for change in the post war period and this saw the introduction of first Biology and the reintroduction of German and the institution of Technical Drawing. His interests were varied and many. He had written a new School song in the short period of his Headmastership prior to the Second World War and when he finally left Great Yarmouth Mr. Pereira forecasted that the variety of his musical connections in the town would miss his presence.[1]

The School Song

Praise be to God for those who set this town
Between the winding river and the silver sea
And ringed it round with towers and mighty walls
To give it strength to keep it's people free

Praise be to God for those who founded here
A school where truth might triumph and ambition shine
And those whose noble minds and loyal hearts
Strove year by year to keep its record fine

We will not cease to fight with heart and mind
Against a weak reliance on our past renown
Our school to heights more splendid we will raise
And bring new vigour to our ancient town

80. The Grammar School Song A.H. G. Palmer

Mr. Palmer took leave of the School at a Ceremony which followed at the end of the autumn term. He received tributes from Mr. Pereira, the Head Boy Richard Woodall, Mr. E.W. Foulser the Secretary of the London Old Boys Society and several gifts. In return Mr. Palmer presented the School with what he described as a wooden object six feet long. Relief was felt when it turned out to be a beautifully made seat' of Burmese Teak complete with a Commemorative Plaque. It was placed by the Poplar Tree on the South side of the School Buildings.

The illustration from *The Chronicle* shows the School with the new block and Library built on the left and the Dining Hall on the right. It would be the view that Mr. Palmer would remember from the School House looking towards the School.

[1] *Chronicle*, Second Series No.14, July 1960, pp.1-2

The School from the Headmaster's House

R. G. Cann

81. The School from the Headmaster's House

I am grateful to Bill Rayner for the following information on the cadet force and the Guard Mounting competition. A Company of the Second Battalion Royal Norfolk Regiment was based at Great Yarmouth Grammar School.

The photograph shows cadets practising for a Guard Mounting Competition in 1959 or 1960. Left to right John George, John Lambert, William Rayner, Monck, J Rodgers, Michael Curson and Bernard Ryder.

The Guard Mounting Competition was held every year at Head Quarters (HQ) Company of the Battalion based at the Drill Hall in Southtown Road which is now a Building Training College. The squad was trained by Bill Brugger, who took the photograph. Brugger went to Mons Officer Cadet College and later to the School of Oriental and African Studies at London University to Study Chinese. He wrote a book on life in a Chinese village but sadly died in the 1970's.

82. Rehearsal for a Guard Mounting Competition by the School Cadet Force.

Michael Curson, a good sportsman, also died at a comparatively young age at Soham in Cambridgeshire where he had captained the town Rugby team. John Lambert and John George became schoolteachers while Bernard Ryder worked in Sports Science in the University of East London and later carried out overseas project work. Monck went into business and "Jammy" Rodgers became a Veterinary Surgeon and treated racehorses at Newmarket before emigrating to Australia. William Rayner applied for Mons College but failed the entrance tests. "The only reason soldiers would follow this person would be out of curiosity" as one of the selecting officers said about a candidate.

The rifles shown are Short Magazine Lee Enfields, a number of which were kept in an armoury which was in the corridor facing the senior playground yard at the Grammar School. Cadets were also trained on Bren light Machine Guns. Occasional firing with live ammunition took place at a range in Pakefield just south of Lowestoft. From time to time manoeuvres with blank ammunition were held on the North Denes at the end of Salisbury Road. Thunderflashes – live explosive sticks activated by tearing of a strip of material and thrown like grenades were also used.

Cadets could elect to go to summer camp at various Army institutions in the Summer Holidays. They would be put through a programme of shooting rifles, Bren and Sten Guns. So preparatory courses were held at the Brittania Barracks in Norwich.

The Cadet Company at the School was commanded by Major G. F." Bushy" West, Captain F J. E. "Josh" Norris, Captain R "Ronny" Teasdale and Captain E. G. "Siggy" Sigston. Parades were held in the Tower Yard every Friday morning. Cadets could enter Certificate "A" examinations into military training and "A" Company had an excellent record in these.

Mr. Peter Marsden who studied at Kings College Cambridge with long experience as Housemaster and as Head of the Geography Department at the Ipswich School took up his appointment as the 41st Headmaster of the School on the 1st January 1961.[2]

School Notes recorded that the third and final phase of the reconstruction of the School buildings had been delayed until July 1961 and there had been no decision reached regarding the provision of adequate playing fields for the School.[3] However the new hall had been in very full use with activities which included a dramatic performance on the new stage from Mr. Trafford, a professional actor, who gave a solid performance of extracts from *Oliver Twist* to the Third and Fourths Forms on October 24th. The first Remembrance Day Service was also held before the tablet in its new position in the presence of John Green and Ray Packard, President and Secretary of the Old Boys Association together with Mr. A. J. Ovey who as an Old Boy had remembrances of those who fell in the 1914-18 War. The organ had been rebuilt at a cost of nearly £2,000 and was dedicated in a Service in March at the end of Term by the Vicar of Great Yarmouth followed by a recital given by John Inca Director of Music at the Ipswich School who played a programme which demonstrated the new Organ's capabilities. When Mr. J.A. Oddy who had been appointed in September to teach Scripture and History left at Christmas to engage in full time theological study, the teaching of scripture was undertaken by two local clergy the Reverend Dendle French and the Reverend Jackson. I am still in touch with Dendle French an old friend who served at St. Nicholas Church and had an interesting career thereafter being Chaplain at Glamis Castle to the late Queen Mother for many years.

Mr. P.E. Morris, "PEM", the Biology Master was appointed as Careers Master in February 1961 which was an important step for the School which up to then had not taken a lead in such matters.[4] An interesting sidelight in the School Notes was thrown upon Kenneth MacMillan the Choreographer at Covent Garden who left School at 15 in 1945 for ballet training having roomed with Victor Stowers in Retford. It was reported by the editor of *The Chronicle* that he was now a busy Choreographer with Royal Ballet and had recollected his wartime experiences vividly in a letter to the editor. The interesting comment was made by the editor that those who had no taste for ballet might be surprised to know that he was responsible for the choreography in *Expresso Bongo* the early British rock film which starred Cliff Richard and was based around the famous 2 I's coffee bar in London.[5] It was noted that Derek Farman, my own contemporary, who had broken many school records including the 100 yards established by RAF Pilot Officer Aldwyn Rouse 18 years before who soon afterwards had been killed in his Typhoon which was shot down in flames on a low level attack on the German HQ at the Hague.[6] It was noted that Rouse's Long Jump record remained unbroken.

The School sent congratulations to former Headmaster W.G. "Billy" Williams (1903-1933) on his 90th Birthday. Notable amongst sporting achievements was that of John Gibbs (6aii) in winning, at his first attempt, the

---

83. The Football First Eleven 1961 led by John Gibbs front row third left.

pier to pier race held in summer 1960 and organised by the Town Swimming Club.

I was reminded in a discussion with my contemporary, Mike Boice, who was Cricket and Football Captain in 1960, of a conversation he had had with Mr. Woodrow, the Sports Master. In a return coach trip from a School match, John Woodrow had discussed with Mike his idea for a coach trip to Moscow, on which he was very keen.

A fete was held on the school field in 1960 to raise funds at the end of the summer term for a trip to Moscow in 1961. The party would consist of 21 boys,

4 Masters and 2 Master's wives. The bus had been purchased and a practice camping run made to Southwold Common just before Whitsun. In the spring of 1961 a show put on by the boys to raise further funds took place on Thursday, Friday and Saturday, the 9th 10th and 11th of March. The show was a melange of music hall, goon show, slapstick with some genuine talent. Some of the acts were wonderfully deadpan. Girl Guide (Keith France) singing about the hole in her bucket, the Beverly Sisters singing with Philip Mortar looking like an expert teaser and the "School Orchestra" rendering Tchaikovsky's *1812 Overture* while wearing tin helmets which sounded like an interpretation of the battle of Borodino itself. Class was maintained by Ling on the tenor horn and Farman on the grand piano. Three guitarists, Brian Granger, John Gibbs and Roberts produced

some warm southern harmonies. The temperature was raised even higher by Mr Pereira who looked like he had just stepped off a Bombay troop ship and gave a polished performance as he sang *Mad Dogs and Englishman*. There was a mock musical hall including Mike Duncum singing *The Man who broke the bank at Monte Carlo*, which showed real mastery of gesture and singing technique. Mr Woodrow assisted by a generously endowed mammy "Mr. Teasdale" gave a first rate impression of Al Jolson, which almost alone deserved the vegetable bouquet so tenderly presented to him later by Mr. Pillar the School Caretaker. The vast band of performers and helpers and above all Mr. Sigston were congratulated on the fund raising event to assist the party who where going to Moscow.

84. Eric Sigston (left) in a sketch from The Moscow Follies March 1961

The event did take place in 1961 and I have the diary of the trip, which has been held by Roger Sandall, who was one of the participants, and also a recollection from Peter Phillips, another of the Grammar School Boy's on the trip.

Peter said that the trip was planned well in advance and a team of boys to go was selected early since there was plenty of fundraising and preparation required. He recalled spending several evenings, after School, collecting newspapers from the local households. The show *Moscow Follies* had been great fun and was well attended.[7] As a preparatory exercise the Coach was taken to Southwold Common for a couple of nights, both to try out the tents and allow the team to get to know each other.

Peter said that his first impression of the Coach was not very favourable as it was pretty old and had already seen better days. It was not quite a charabanc as there had been attempts at streaming lining and it had been painted in a dashing two tone colour scheme of red and cream. He said the interior reminding him of old railway carriages but at least the Coach started first time.

The great day finally arrived, and they departed from Salisbury Road on a bright sunny morning, waved off by parents and friends. The team comprised six Masters and Wives, two Drivers, and twenty one Pupils. The first night was spent outside Brussels, in the shadow of the Atomium, which was a futuristic structure built for the Brussels World Fair.

Peter said he did not recall much about crossing Belgium and Germany since the early start and endless miles spent on the road soon became an established pattern. The Autobahns were impressive and the Ausfahrt signs never failed to raise a smile. Berlin came and went without too much trouble, and then they were heading deeper into the sinister East. Poland had been a shock, appearing to be extremely poor, with children in ragged clothes, staring at the coach as they passed. On one occasion they threw stones, rather half heartedly at the Coach. The group was not allowed to camp in Poland, so a night was spent in the Grand Hotel in Central Warsaw. This splendid building had seen better days since it was dingy, rundown, and austere.

85. Working on the Bus for the Moscow Trip

Peter said it took a long time to traverse Russia, passing through Minsk and Smolensk with their Onion-Domed Cathedrals. The Team was not allowed to enter Moscow as planned, as a result of the celebrations of the 2nd Cosmonaut Titov who had just completed a successful flight. As the party toured the city on the next day, the streets were still draped in long red banners, with big portraits of Titov. This was in contrast to the general drabness in the Communist State. The absence of colour, posters, and advertising material was very noticeable. Peter remembers being approached in Red Square by some gentlemen, who wished to buy their blue jeans and exchange currency.

---

[7] *Ibid*. pp.54-55

86. East Berlin 3rd August 1961

87. Moscow Brochure 8th August 1961

He said that it was a relief to enter Czechoslovakia on the return journey, where the western influence made them feel much more comfortable. This feeling was further re-enforced on re-entering Germany at Frankfurt am Oder. By then the Berlin Wall had been erected and the Team had been totally unaware of this momentous event. Peter said that on one day on their return trip they had pulled up at a Service Station in Germany where another old coach was parked, probably with steam rising from the bonnet. It was another School trip to Moscow, organised by a Public School. He said that they were having a tough time since the Coach was constantly breaking down and they were considering abandoning the trip. The feeling of schadenfreude was irresistible amongst the boys from Great Yarmouth Grammar School. Peter said that in fact they were very lucky with their transport, since the worst thing to happen had been a small fire, which had been easily extinguished by their two excellent Drivers, resulting from an oily rag having been left in the engine compartment.

In reflecting on the journey, Peter said, it was remarkable how smoothly the trip had unfolded. In particular they had navigated their way through very foreign, often unfriendly cities, with no fluent Polish or Czech speakers amongst the group. The Russians had kindly solved this problem by providing us with a Lady Guide, who kept a very close eye on where we went and what we did in Moscow. Peter said that of course they were entirely free of risk assessments and worries about liabilities in those days. He said the final chapter was an appearance on local TV where four of the party had been able to give their brief impressions of the trip.[8]

A scrapbook of the Journey to Moscow and back has survived kept by Roger Sandall showing details of the routes taken and some of the cities visited on the journey.

88. Smolensk and Minsk Cathedrals

[8]   Source Peter Phillips

Michael Wood, my contemporary, reminded me that the School Christmas Auction was usually ably run by Ron Teasdale and "Bushy" West, both Science Teachers with the School in that era. They had a professional touch which was capable of extracting the last penny from your pocket. Michael Wood said he was unsure how many years the auction had run for, but that it was discontinued for an unknown reason during his time at School. Michael can remember the wide variety of goods, his memory is of the stage being absolutely packed with piles of comics, books, games, and every conceivable item that was of interest to pupils or more likely that parents wanted them out of the house. *Biggles* books abandoned, likewise *Just William* stories, and adventure stories by R. L. Stevenson etc. One particular memory was of a gramophone player standing proudly amongst the piles of lesser value items. He wondered how wealthy the parents must have been to be able to donate such an item. In his first year at School he remembered wanting to bid for a book but being far too timid to raise his bid in front of the whole School.[9]

A party of six formers visited Yarmouth police court last July accompanied by Mr. Howell and heard cases of shop-lifting, assault and traffic offences.

Three six form biologists spent a week at Flatford Mill, John Constable's home where they followed a course on fresh water biology. Mr Morris supervised such a course last year though he felt the boys were rather swamped by what he described as a "gaggle of females". In the Honours won by Old Boys, Colin Bassett gained a BA Honours Degree at Oxford and Keith "Jack" Harrison a former Head Boy a BSc. at Nottingham. In the current Honours W.E. "Bill" Rayner won a Foundation Scholarship and Mike Curson won the Whitehead Memorial Prize for the best Army Cadet. Richard Woodall, the School's Head Boy, won the Rotary Prize for Service, the Oral French Prize, the Senior Reading Prize, the best in Work and Games Prize, and the Senior Games Prize. With regard to the Cadet force Major West resigned despite many loud protests, and command of the battery fell to Captain Sigston.

The Jazz Appreciation Society was formed by a group of Sixth Formers and the meetings has been lively, the hall echoing to modern drum solos and the ever popular Acker. In the future the club hoped to hold more talks on records, and recording equipment and visit local Jazz concerts. Chris Barber and Lonnie Donnegan were favourites amongst the traditionists.

A new section of the Science Society, a radio group, held several good meetings during the spring term under the able guidance of Jack Fisher (G 3 OHO). Jack afterwards went to work in Canada and retired a few years ago. He moved to Canada in 1967 after obtaining his PhD and marrying. He carried out various research related jobs. He ran his own water quality consulting business until 2009. He retired from his main business after the Millennium and lives in Ottawa. His leisure activities in 2010 are travelling and oil painting.[10]

Mike Curson had pioneered the development of the "Comets" an unofficial Grammar School Basketball team which enjoyed a successful first season in the Great Yarmouth Basketball League. Prior to this School Basketball players had guested for other town clubs.

An interesting entry in the Chronicle refers to a journey undertaken by Ivor Davey of 6a (i) and Anthony Riches of 6s (ii). They left Southtown Station on a train journey that took them through France, Belgium, Austria, Germany and Yugoslavia to arrive at Salonika in Northern Greece. There they began a six week cycle tour of Greece, Italy and France returning by bicycle across the Apennines to reach Rome and cycling via the Italian and French Riviera, the Rhone valley and Rambouillet to arrive home just in time to begin the autumn term.[11] Davey's development of his leg muscles during that journey led to the fact that he won the School Cross Country Race in a time of 29 minutes and 29 seconds in 1961. The organized journeys from the School became more adventurous and on July 20th 1960 J.A. Ward (6sii) one of 25 British Air Cadets was selected under the international air cadet scheme to spend 22 days in July 1960 touring the eastern states of the U.S.A. The British Cadets were joined by 40 other Air Cadets from all over Europe and left R.A.F. Northolt in a Constellation aircraft of the Military Transport Service, to begin a 16 hour flight to Mitchell A.F.B.

[9] Source Michael Wood
[10] Source Jack Fisher
[11] *Chronicle*. Second Series No.15, July 1962, pp.30-34

89. *USAF transport plane in which J. Ward travelled the USA*

90. *Contemporary USAF fighter*

New York. J. Ward reported that they spent an afternoon at the Pentagon and was left stunned at its size and complexity. Over 40,000 people worked there, it had its own bus station, rail terminus, hospital, fire service and security guards. The Pentagon covered an area roughly the size of the Magdalen Estate in Gorleston and if its gardens and complex road system were added in it would easily cover the area of Great Yarmouth. John Ward reported the grand finale at the Officers' Club at Bolling Airforce Base when after a magnificent dinner with their escorts they were introduced to some of the country's leading dignitaries, and entertained as only the Americans could.

The sixth formers developed their own poetry magazine and in the spring of 1961 over 200 copies of the volume called *Fragments* were sold. Set out below is one of the poems from *Fragments* called *The Season* written by Bill Rayner of 6a (iii) which is a pastiche in the style of Alexander Pope.

THE SEASON

When in late August Phoebus beams,
On Yarmouth beach the sewage streams
With many a tanned and peeling face
There also streams the populace,
With dirt, ice-cream, kids, deckchair, flies
Fat bodies bulge towards the skies,
The brats scream in helpful glee
As they gladly sport in the cess and sea,
Their beach-balls bounce, spill cups of tea
That are balanced on a corpulent matron's knee.
Lovers love most blatantly and amorous looks
Fly on the promenade, where pornographic books
Entice the eager but enchanted readers.
Surrounded by their litters, those prolific breeders
Resembling women march, gorge candy floss.
The children bawl and cry, the mother now gets cross,
A spindly, thin-haired sullen man
Follows behind and if he can
Glances at postcards with old jokes inscribed
The spew of drunkards, on the night before imbibed
Lies on the dusty, tyre marked street
Nimbly avoided by the sockless feet,
Reminder of last night's good fun
Now drying in the rays of a chromatic sun.
Tasteless, gaudy, coarse, with pimples on each face,
The teenage youngsters slouch with grudging grace
Seek out the blaring juke box, coffee bars,
Edge weaker off the promenade, hold up cars.
Pout mouthed the girls return a sullen sneer
When these grease headed Don Juans leer-
They're after bigger game – the Navy's here.
Grin! Smile! Rejoice! Look cheerful!
This resort has everything-if you're not
Careful.

W. E. Rayner (6Aiii)

The Chronicle now carried both Science Sixth form notes and Arts Sixth form notes, which in some detail hammered the members of both Sixth forms. The Sixth form now had its own room on the other side of Tower Yard where for example discussion took place on the initiative of the band of stalwarts who were carrying the Great Yarmouth Grammar School banner across Europe to Moscow.

With the opening of the new hall the School Shop found itself a place in the kitchen of the old dining room and its lines were expanded to provide a wide variety of choice. Walter Hogg the History Master noted that the usual problems of litter existed but there was no problem obtaining service in the shop, theft had been eliminated, but the small amount of sharp practice remained including the passing at busy times of Swiss and French coins and Commonwealth currency. Although less than half a dozen incidents had been recorded an interesting one was the passing of an American commemorative coin of 1913 for an English penny. Surely this was of more value than the goods purchased.

THE OLD SCHOOL HALL SHORTLY TO BE RECONSTRUCTED

91. The Old School Hall as it was.

Finally with the construction of the new Hall the Old School Hall which had been in use since the School was built in 1910 was shortly to be reconstructed.

The School notes in the July 1962 *Chronicle* recorded the end of long negotiations for additional playing fields. The School had long hoped for additional facilities on the former railway land after the line had been closed as part of Dr. Beeching's grand plan. The outcome for the School, however, was rather disappointing in that only the former railway land to the west of the School between Salisbury and Beaconsfield Road with a piece the size of a football pitch to the south would become School property.

The Barnard Bridge ground where tenure in perpetuity had been confirmed could be transformed into a useful asset provided that it was suitably cared for, equipped with sufficient changing rooms and effectively fenced so that it no longer served as an unofficial children's playground. The land to the west of the School backing on to North Denes Road was largely covered with tarmac of the derelict Corporation Coach Park. All in all these long negotiations had not produced the equivalent of the School's original playing fields when the pupil level was much lower.

The third and final phase in the rebuilding and extension programme was timed to begin at the end of the summer term. The old School hall would be reduced size by the conversion of the bay to the north into classrooms and the building of a chair store. The existing staff block would become two stories and include a new staff room together with rooms for the Headmaster, his Deputy and the School Secretary. Other new features would include Biology and Junior Physics Labs, rooms for Pottery, Geography and Medical Inspections together with an enlarged Art Room and increased changing accommodation. It was calculated that this improved accommodation coupled with the reduced intake of the last 2 years and the child population of the Borough would make it unlikely that for at least the next 7 years the intake would exceed 75 a year with the result that there should be few classes larger than 25. It was noted however, that the 6th form was unlikely to diminish in size and the problems of large numbers particularly in the Science sixth would continue to need urgent attention.

The School Scout Troop was re-established after 22 years. Evacuation to Retford in 1940 had been instrumental in causing the School Orchestra to disband and it was confidently expected that a new School Orchestra would be formed in the autumn of 1962.

Various changes in School rules came into operation during the School year. Caps were now compulsory to wear for the first 3 years in the School. Distinctive ties had been introduced for Prefects and also games colours and gym vests in house colours made recognition for spectators easier at the athletic sports in 1962. Inkwells had disappeared and with them came the end of pen holders and nibs, which was surely the end of an era. Stiffer covered exercise books and preparation books (prep books) gave more space for writing down timetables homework requirements as well as containing the dreaded last 2 pages for work and conduct signatures.

The erection of palings, 20 foot square on the School playing field heralded the first stage of the school meteorological station. The space would house two Stevenson Screens containing a thermograph and a hydrograph to take continuous readings of temperature and humidity together with a rain gauge and ground thermometer. Although Mr. Morrow had retired at the end of the Christmas term, one achievement of which any Schoolmaster would be happy to emulate was since his appointment in 1945 he had not had a single day's absence. It was also pleasing to note that the School had the services of E. D. C. "Ted" Buswell who was a former member of staff, a star athlete while at School, who was hoping to follow advanced physical education studies at an American university in the following academic year.

Mr. E.A.C. Seaborne who was Headmaster from 1933 1937 and who was responsible for building the new block on the south side of Tower yard had retired as Headmaster of Bablake School Coventry at the end of the Summer Term. The editor noted that on his appointment at the age of 31 to succeed Mr. W. G. Williams, he must have been one of the youngest Grammar School Headmasters in the country.

Michael Woods one of the Chief Librarians and afterwards Rector of St.Nicholas Parish Church, Great Yarmouth, reported on the operation of the library during the academic year of 1962. One thousand additions had been taken into the library during the last 12 months. Fresh sections had been arranged but the library was badly in need of up to date books especially in the Science Section. He reported that a grant would enable more books to be purchased and recommendations from any members of the School would be welcomed by librarians.

92. Michael Woods after his retirement in 2010.

On Monday 24th July 1961 the Sixth formers used a fortnights vacation after their A levels examinations to present W.W. Jacobs macabre *The Monkeys Paw*. Which unfortunately, although a straight, play was received by a boisterous audience as a farce. *2 Gentlemen of Cobholm* adapted from Shakespeare, harmonized with the holiday mood and the audience had also especially enjoyed the part of the Duchess of Canterbury played by D.A. "Loon" Wombell who had also produced both plays

Russell Leggett has a copy of a football history extracted from *The Chronicle* between 1965-66 to 1971-72. It recorded the success of the various Grammar School teams during this period. For example during the season 1965-66 the School under thirteen X1 played 20 matches, won 19 lost 1 scored 150 goals and only conceded 24. The leading scorer Stiles the centre forward provided the thrust and skill which routed some opponents and always troubled opposing defences and his goal scoring feat of 69 goals in the season would, commented Walter Hogg, take some surpassing. When Russell Leggett himself captained the under thirteen's in the following season they played 23 won 17 drew 3 and lost 3 and scoring 117 goals and conceding 36.

When Russell Leggett went on to captain the under 15 X1 in the 1968-69 season, he played in the mid field and the team played 24 won 21, lost 3, scoring 98 goals against 27 conceded. Some of the comments on the team are interesting and Burgess is recorded as using his speed effectively on the right wing while Hazel had made the most of his "peculiar attributes" to mesmerize opposing defences and score some outstanding goals. Russell continued to captain the various sides including the under 15 and then the Schools first X1 in 1971-72. In that year the team had one of its most successful seasons. It retained the Cowles Cup for the fourth year in succession, won the Minor cup having appeared in the final for the third year running and travelled further than ever before in the English schools championship both in the competition itself and overland to the venues of the matches. The team lost in Torquay to Devon after defeating Suffolk and Essex. The team ran on a squad of 13 players, five of whom represented Norfolk at under 19 schoolboy level. They were Alan Fakes, Paul Breeze, John Palmer, Russell Leggett who captained the side, and Graham Parry.

A Headmaster's summary record of each Academic Year survives and gives an idea of how he had to spread himself across the many aspects of school life. For example in January 1969 on the day after term commenced the Head was having a meeting with Mr. Angwin the Music Master, while dealing with lunch records, and planning for the Prize Day and the School play on the same day. On the following day, he fulfilled his function as a prison visitor at Blundeston Prison and returned to the School for the election for the Committee of the Parents Association at 7.30. In February 1969 he attended the AGM of the Old Boys Association and had a meeting on the same day at the High School and then attended the Council Meeting in Norwich. On the 13th March he sat on the Blundeston Prison Review Board and on the same day dealt with Mathematics in Cambridge while on the following day he was interested in the inter Sixth Dance in the small hall between 7.30 and 10 pm. The months continued with similar demands on the Head's time. In December he was meeting Mr. West who had transferred to the Girls High School, seeing student teachers complete their practice while on the following day his attention was taken by seeing Mr. Stowers, then a pupil called Stenhouse, and finally attending the Sixth Form Fancy Dress Dance in the School Hall. This daily diary showed how varied the job of Headmaster had become.

The last phase in the reconstruction of the School Buildings began in mid November 1962 and the builders were unimpeded by the severe winter as these were internal works. These alterations meant closure of the old east entrance through the Raven Tower, with a new entrance to its immediate north. The panels listing prefects since 1909 have had to be removed. The editor comments that he hopes these worthies will not be forgotten. They have not and I have made certain that the panels which were in the School in my day are recorded in the Appendix to this book using a record prepared by the London Old Boys Society.[12] The gymnasium received additional changing rooms, the old dining hall was converted into 3 classrooms to remedy a shortage of space while Mr. Hogg's Sixth Form obtained some measure of privacy in the corner of the old hall by using barricades from the old cloakroom. The editor commented that it has not been uncommon to hear French conversation mingling with Sixth Form Mathematics since both old and new halls have been in use for group work and private study.

---

[12] NRO. London Old Boys Society Transcription of Prefects' List

The School acquired a sailing craft which was moored at Burgh Castle which became the HQ of the new Sailing Club. A School Orchestra was in existence again after 22 years and had already given two public performances. A swimming census of the School showed only a fifth of the School could swim, and the Headmaster appealed for the construction of a swimming pool that would ultimately be covered and heated. The Chairman of the Governors Mrs. K. Adlington suggested that the School set about the task itself and said that the Education Committee would be likely assist. It is interesting to note that the whole School was taught to swim by Bandsman Jack Blake in the old Great Yarmouth 100 yard pool now sadly missed, but the swimming pool on the School site had subsequently been completed. At the end of March Mr. Pillar the Caretaker for 26 years retired. He had seen many changes during his time at School but he did not fail in his duty and his forthright common sense, his ability to let a boy know his place as well has his colourful turn of phrase would be remembered with affection. In his retirement he lived in a flat opposite the School. R. Hedges, the son of the town librarian had decided to follow in the footsteps of Ivor Davey and Michael Woods and spend a year in voluntary service in the Solomon Islands. During his helicopter tour of East Anglia in May the Duke of Edinburgh, seeing how his Award Scheme was developing, met Mr. Sigston, Mr. Chapman and members of the Canoe Club. He said he had never seen any canoes resembling those designed by Mr. Chapman and seemed impressed. This is probably the only School society that can claim a royal visitor. David Cooke was the first student at the School to undertake the Duke of Edinburgh's Award Scheme and the picture shows him being presented with his Silver Award by the then Bishop of Norwich, Lancelot Fleming. David went on to achieve his Gold Award.

93. David Cooke receiving his Silver
Duke of Edinburgh's Award

The Chronicle records that R .M. Loynes who was still considered the most brilliant mathematician the School had produced had been awarded a PhD by Cambridge University for Research in Mathematical Statistics. He was a Fellow of the then recently founded Churchill College.

The School was sad to lose John Norris its Head of English when he moved after 10 years at the School to take up a post as Head of English at the Hewett Grammar School in Norwich, which was a large co-educational Grammar School. When John Norris arrived at the Grammar School, succeeding Roy Pashley in January 1956 he took charge of the English teaching in the School and planned and equipped a new library. As a Form Master and English teacher Mr. Norris was particularly concerned with those who found the O level hurdle formidable. His firm but just discipline and his unwillingness to accept second best in written work and his drive brought considerable success. He had many other talents playing the organ, piano, recorder and oboe. I remember his introduction of the English study group for Sixth Formers, which certainly assisted me to gain a good pass in A level English. His steady bowling for the staff cricket XI, his service with the Cadet Corp. where as a licensed Lay Reader he was Battalion Chaplain, his interest in cross country running and finally more recently his marathon walking feats would long be remembered. I knew him well for many years after he left the School and his unexpected and early death deprived many organisations of his talents.

Prize Day took place on the 12th November 1962 and the guest speaker was Professor R.W. Steel who was a pupil at the Grammar School from 1926-31. He cited his own experience as Professor of Geography at Liverpool and claimed that there were hundreds of suitably qualified applicants who could not be found University places. This was 47 years ago in the era of the Grammar School so the squeeze on University places continues. Professor Steel urged those who were anxious to enter University not only to work hard at their specialist studies but to widen their interests out of School. Such interests he felt could often win a boy a University place.

The School Dramatic Society was ambitious in producing James Elroy Flecker's *Hassan* in the School hall on the evenings of December 14th and 15th 1962. I saw this production and was most impressed by use of the large stage with new lighting equipment and the music of Frederic Delius. This piece is rarely produced and the directors Mr. R. J. Allen and Sam Rockinghorse Junior (Mr. Sigston) produced a memorable evening of spectacle.[13]

The editor recorded on prize day 50 years previously in 1913 the School produced what the local press called "a capital rendition of *The New Boy*" by Arthur Law a delightful little comedy simply abounding in ludicrous situations. The production was given at the Britannia Pier Pavilion with a staff taking a heavy share of the acting. It made a profit of £43 which in 1963 terms would be worth at least £200.[14]

School View   J. A. Dashwood (4th Form)

94. Woodcut John Dashwood

John Dashwood was in the 4th form of the Grammar School during 1964 and his woodcut of the School is in the front of the 1964 *Chronicle*. John was a talented artist and remains in the town having provided large murals, and a series of paintings representing Stations of the Cross in St. Nicholas Church, together with many other murals in the town on various walls.

There was considerable disquiet at the suggestions being made to abolish the Grammar School, not surprisingly these proposals involving staff buildings and pupils, received a frigid reception at Salisbury Road. Matters were complicated by the Boundary Commission's proposal to abolish the Town's County Borough status of Great Yarmouth which would mean that Norfolk County Council would have to approve abolition measures. The position was also complicated by the fact that the final arbiter would be the Minister of Education and that there was a General Election due to be held in the autumn 1964.

Rees Hedges had kept a detailed diary of his experiences teaching in the Solomon Islands during his voluntary service overseas. He said that his Christmas cruise with his Bishop visiting many islands was a memorable experience. His account of the excommunication of drunken communicants was quite unforgettable.

The number on the School roll in 1964 fell marginally from 520 to 512 but the sixth form increased in size from 83 to 94. Those studying Science fell from 57 to 56 but those following Arts courses increased from 26 to 38.

Brian Haylett who achieved a First Class Honours Degree at University College London, and gained an M.A. by his further work on the poetry of Robert Graves, returned to the School he had left as a pupil seven years before. He served in Cyprus with the R.A.F. during his National Service and had formed a junior debating society on his return to the Grammar School and had held meetings of the Sixth Form study group at his home.

The departure of Mr. E. Whittaker at the end of the summer term in 1964 was a loss to the School since he restarted German studies after an interval of 18 years. His pupils had managed to achieve distinction in German at advanced level, he had organised German trips and during his time at the Grammar School worked

---

[13] *Chronicle*, Second Series No.17, July 1967, pp.21-22
[14] *Ibid*. p.52

95. The Cricket First XI squad 1964

hard to keep the music club active. He was a talented pianist and an able critic of School productions for *The Chronicle*. He moved to Basildon Newtown where he became Head of the German Department in a large bilateral school.

At Prize Day on November 11th 1963 the guest speaker was Mr. J.J. Buddery an Old Boy of the School (1939 to 1946). He made amusing references to his School days during the evacuation to Retford, concerning his buying of an incendiary bomb fin for the high price of 5 shillings. During the night however, and air raid occurred, numerous incendiary bombs dropped around the School and the value of his fin dropped to three pence.

In December 1963 over 100 pupils and members of the staff took part in the four performances of the *Aqua-Follies* which raised over £200 for the school swimming pool fund "scout Sigston gave the show a fine start with his rendering of *Hello Muddah, Hello Faddah* which was just as well considering the quality of some the items immediately following. The most comical act, undoubtedly, was the four lads from the staff common room (Messrs Sigston, Allen, Teasdale and Morris) and their impersonation of the Beatles which was, on the final night greeted by loud applause and even a few screams. However the greatest blot on the show was the pathetic attempts of opening and final choruses and it was hard to believe that this was serious.

The Army Cadet Force had a successful annual camp at Brecon last summer gaining seven gold's and five silver awards under the Duke of Edinburgh's scheme. Senior cadets had tackled a gunnery course and 2 civil defence courses as part of the Duke of Edinburgh's Award Scheme. Battalion camps had been held last summer and during Whitsun week Cadets represented the battery at the Armistice Parade at London in November.

The Inter-Sixth Society formed by the sixth forms of the Grammar, High and Technical Schools had enjoyed the most successful year since its foundation four years previously Activities during the Christmas term included a trip to the Chinese restaurant where the society entertained Mr. and Mrs. Marsden and Miss Irvine the High School Headmistress.

The School Tower   A. Cadmore 6A(i)

96. The Raven Tower Woodcut Albert Cadmore.

The Raven Tower was 54 years old in 1964 and an imaginative woodcut by Albert Cadmore 6a(1) shows the tower.

Albert, one of twins with Reg, was subsequently ordained and is now priest in charge of Winterton and Somerton.

In the editor's article on the School 50 years ago reference is made to a illustrated talk on the 1912 Olympic Games held in Stockholm by Mr. Humphrey Lynde, a local solicitor, who had recently died in his 80's, which he attended as a spectator. Mr. Lynde had castigated local regional and national apathy towards systematic training for athletics and severely censured the lack of smartness of the British competitors, and any sense of pride in their appearance at the march past on the opening day.

E.J. Ovey one of the Old Boys of the School had compiled a list of members, which recorded, as far as possible, the careers adopted following their time at School. This list is in the Appendix.

The School Football First XI had a successful season playing 21 matches winning 13 drawing 2 and losing 6. The team had scored 66 goals and conceded 27, and was captained by Terry Pooley.

The Chronicle of 1965 recorded the approval given by the Town Council for the introduction of Comprehensive Education in Great Yarmouth, and this had brought the existing threat even closer. The Minister of Education representing a Government committed to the comprehensive principle has naturally welcomed "the Yarmouth plan", which had asked that its implementation be postponed until the fate of the Borough at the hands of the Boundary Commission had been decided. At this time the town was in grave danger of losing its County Borough status and with it full autonomy in matters of educational policy. During the year of protest, partition and propaganda a pointer to a future trend emerged. Difficulties in adequately staffing the Girls High School where already one third of the staff were men would according to the Chief Education Officer render the mixing of the Grammar and High Schools inevitable whether of not the comprehensive plan was carried out.

97. The Football First Eleven 1963-64.

R. Butcher of the Sixth Form was highly commended when he represented the School in the 1965 Norfolk School Shakespeare speaking festival held at Thorpe in Norwich and adjudicated by Marjorie Rawlings. He had also been offered a part by the National Youth Theatre based on the Old Vic which produced Shakespeare in London every summer. Butcher was like past competitors, trained by Mr. Morrow.

My own dramatic society The Masquers staged a production of the Schools O level set play *Macbeth* in the School Hall and this was seen by a large proportion of the fifth form. Boys from the School formed part of the stage crew and afterwards joined the society. I played Malcolm in the production and Arnold Budds another Old Boy played *Macbeth*.

The School also was taken to orchestral concerts organised at the Hippodrome by Aleyn Jordan in his position as Secretary of the Great Yarmouth Music Club. All the Schools except the fifth form attended the performance by the London Philharmonic Orchestra conducted by Anatol Fistoulari in the Hippodrome on Thursday morning 25th March. The programme was Glinka's overture *Ruslan and Ludmilla* Debussy's *L'apres- midi, d'une faune*, and most of the last movement of Sibilius's *Second Symphony*. The same programme was given in a public performance in the evening.

The School heard with pleasure of the marriage of M. Hantris French Assistant 1963-64 to Miss Linda Watts of Great Yarmouth in August last year. This was the first Great Yarmouth Rambouillet marriage and Linda Watts's father worked in the Town Hall, Borough Treasurer's Department.

Mr. W.G. Williams (Headmaster 1903-1933) who was living in retirement in Gorleston was then in his 95th year and was the oldest living member of Brasenose College Oxford. He had been elected an Honorary Member of the College which he attended between 1889 and 1892.

The Head Librarians Julian Senior and David Harrup reported that the combined Sixth Forms were in the process of reading more than 400 books which was the number recorded as being borrowed. Librarians were confident that this high rate of reading was due to the new labour-saving lending system which they put in place earlier in the year.

The Sixth Form had been producing annual magazines and in February 1964 the latest of these called *Spectrum* was produced by three members of 6a(1), Gray, Sherwin-White, and Johnson. The response to their call for contributions was to say the least limited. This resulted in a rather mixed bag of poetry and prose most of which seems to be included merely to fill up the pages. R.W. Hodds in reporting these items said that his contribution was rubbish, Browne's contemplation of suicide was very true to character and the most entertaining offerings were generally attributed to Bilyard. The magazine for the most part lacked fire, but nevertheless 200 of the 300 copies were sold and a percentage of the profits were given to charity.

The Debating Society had been at its most active for many years. A debating tournament had been initiated by Mr. Haylett and was originally composed of 10 teams of 2. This knock out competition was won by Rodney Edrich and Julian Senior who defended the idea "that ignorance is bliss".

David Harrup chaired the Geography Society and in addition to seeing a number of interesting films covering the control of locusts and the postal services in the Dutch Islands. David organised an interesting joint meeting with the Archaeological Society at which Alf Hedges the Borough Librarian gave the talk on ancient Yarmouth. Alf Hedges was the author of *Yarmouth is an Antient Town* which had been presented to all secondary school children in 1953. This was the book which Frank Meeres and I expanded and updated and presented to the secondary school children of the town as a Millennium Gift in the year 2000. David Harrup maintained his links with the Archaeological Society and after leaving School became an active member. He thanked Colin Cheshire and Mr. Richards for the time and help in assisting the Geography Society.

The Inter Sixth Society had well over 100 members and meetings were well attended. During the year the society had 6 meetings, 3 dances, a debate, a very successful film *Village of the Damned*, and the discussion on the motion "this house believes that coloured immigration from the Commonwealth should cease forthwith" – proposed by Mr. West from the Grammar School and opposed by Mr. Balls from the High School. The motion was carried by a considerable majority.

The London Old Boys Society was disturbed that the names of the prefects which were on view over the years on the wall in the east cloakroom corridor were no longer present. The Society therefore intended to present the School with a Prefect's Book which recorded the appointed prefects in each year. The Society expressed the view that this would show its interest in the School and its desire for its future well being in an age of change. I located this book in the Norfolk Record Office Archive and the names of the prefects were recorded in fine calligraphy down to the year 1971.

The School took part in a British Institute course in Paris in Easter 1965. The journey to New Haven was crowded and the atmosphere was one of joviality mixed with British Rail dust and the fumes of early indulgent drinkers. The channel crossing was calm and one member of the Grammar School party, through no fault of his own wearing dark glasses, found himself faced with females debating the possibility of his being Roy Orbison. The mornings were spent at the Lycee with lessons and lectures on set books. These proved particularly useful to the O level studies and the parties' accent improved slowly but surely. The trip was highly successful in advancing French studies in the Sixth Form.

The School sports teams continued to be successful and John Clare (Head Boy in 1968) played in both the Football and Cricket Teams.

98. A Football First Eleven 1965

The Chronicle recorded that the merging of the Grammar School and the High School in order to alleviate the staffing in the High School was now Educational Committee Policy. The editor recorded that such changes were easier to plan than to put into effect, but that the matter was of some urgency although it was acknowledged that combining the Schools would prove a very gradual process. The Committee's decision was viewed by the Grammar School with mixed feelings.

---

13 *Chronicle*, Second Series No.17, pp.21-22
14 *Ibid*. p.52

The Chronicle recorded the death early in the new year of former Headmaster Mr. W. G. "Billy" Williams, at the age of 95 in a life spent almost entirely in the service of the Grammar School. He was appointed as Second Master in 1896 and Headmaster in 1903 and on his retirement in 1933 had spent 37 years of his teaching career at Trafalgar Road and Salisbury Road. He was an extremely forceful personality commended as a disciplinarian and criticised as autocratic. He became a legend in his lifetime stamping his personality quite distinctly on the School in an important period of its history.

Ron Teasdale who had been in charge of Chemistry since his appointment in 1949 left the School in April to teach at Mangakina Museum. During his long stay Mr. Teasdale not only set high academic standards, but entered fully into many out of school activities.

Mr. Eric Sigston also left in April to teach in Fiji. He taught Biology at the Grammar School for over 6 years and did so much more, involving himself in Drama, Cadets, Duke of Edinburgh Award Scheme, Naturalists, Boxing, Football and Gymnastics. The editor commented that his energy and sense of fun would long be remembered. I am told that his talents in Fiji stretched to carrying that country's flag in the Olympic games.[15]

Mr. J. M. Woodrow who had been in charge of Physical Education for the last 8 years left the School for promotion to the Deputy Headship at the Secondary School Bingham, Nottingham. His contribution to School games and athletics will be remembered as will his organisation of the Moscow trip and his efforts to provide the School with a swimming pool. John Blyth his Deputy for the last 8 years would be taking over his duties as Head of P.E. in September 1956.

On December the 2nd, 3rd and 4th 1965 the Dramatic Society presented Bertold Brecht's the *Life of Galileo*. I saw this production at the School and was impressed by the School's venture into a Brecht play. This complex production owed much to the stage managers, and the lighting experts and the scenery constructers.

99. Programme of the School production of Brecht's Life of Galileo

On the 25th March 1966 Mr. and Mrs. Pereira shared the production of Moliere's *Le Bourgeois Gentihomme*. Mantrippe as the pretentious M. Jourdain provided a brilliant performance of buffoonery and many minor parts were played with distinction. The full house enjoyed the entertainment and this will be a worthy reminder that the twinning with Rambouillet had now lasted 10 years.

During 1966 John Clare was secretary of the games committee and also played in the junior cricket team.

In 1966 the School ran another mock election with conservative candidate Rodney Edrich, Labour candidate F. Hayhust and British Progressive party candidate GARR. Tennant. The opinion poll carried out a week before the election put the conservative candidate in the lead. The election was seriously carried out with candidate trying to secure votes of national policies, a change from the old promises of banning prefects and offering better School meals to obtain votes. The last meeting held by conservatives preceded polling day and Rodney Edrich's widely and loudly expressed political opinions made him the obvious conservative choice, and he carried his election speech with the assistance of his committee of body guards. Returning officer was the Headmaster and Rodney Edrich was elected with a 80 vote majority over labour with the British progressive candidate way behind in third place. I am certain that Rodney's widely expressed views enabled him to obtain the prestigious position of House Master at Wellington College. A very interesting position from which he retired after the Millennium.

---

[13] Information Colin Cheshire

The Chess Club had a very successful year in winning the eastern section of the Norfolk and Norwich Chess League, and in reaching the last 16 (out of nearly 800) of the Sunday Times National Tournament, there had been some outstanding individual successes. Robert Bellin age 13 was the under 18 Norfolk Champion. He won first prize at Hastings in a major tournament and was top of the Norfolk contingent in the southern counties under 18 congresses. He had represented Norfolk adults and juniors and Yarmouth.

The Senior Scout Troop had been very active in its second year. Its Easter camp was held in the Lake District and the seniors gathered valuable climbing experience under the guidance of Mr. R. Ward a former Grammar School pupil.

On a cool dismal morning in Easter 25 members of the Sixth Form together with 2 Masters departed to make a first hand study of the Isle of Purbeck around Swanage. P. Brianton of 6s(ii) reported that the work was hard but the enjoyment of the noble study of geography was brought home in exciting and beneficial ways. The group visited the Durdle Door which was exciting. The sight of Mr. Cheshire hanging to a tuft of grass on a terrifying slope and attempting to point out the geological sequence to A. T. Smith who was slowly disappearing over a 250 foot chalk cliff on his stomach would remain vivid in many memories forever. The field trip was a great success even if a visit to Chapman's pool was attempted on foot in arctic conditions and a force 9 gale. The view from the top of the 200 foot cliff was well worth seeing, even at great personal risk.

Restrictions of Government spending had resulted on building extensions for co-education being postponed for a year. It was anticipated that the High School merger with the Grammar School would be almost instantaneous except for those engaged on examination courses. This would mean that in the first year there would be girls in the lower Sixth but not in the upper. Meanwhile the former plans for comprehensive education had been scrapped and new proposals were being discussed but as every School in the Borough would be affected opposition to the scheme would be greater than the last time.

John Newman joined the Geography staff following a previous appointment at Oxford County School and Paul Gilbertson came from Swansea to take up a post in Biology. Colin McManus a name well known in Norfolk athletic circles arrived to assist with physical education. Victor Stowers the senior English master had spent 1967 teaching at York Community High School, Elmhurst, Illinois. By means of exchange from Elmhurst the Grammar School welcomed to the English staff Mr. R. Warner Brown. The editor comments that the School could not have wished for a more pleasant ambassador, and one of his achievements had been to serve as an antidote to the poisonous views of Americans so frequently dished up by their own television shows.

With the extension of senior school games to cover the whole afternoon, new sports were appearing. Sixth formers for example could not only be found on the School field but also playing rugby at Cobholm, sailing at Burgh Castle, skating at the Tower Tink and tenpin bowling at the local alley. Golf was also on offer but had not yet attracted much support.

The School Dramatic Society produced Robert Bolts *A Man for all Seasons*. Andrew Swanston gave a masterly controlled performance as Sir Thomas More while John Littlewood's Cromwell was nicely calculating. I saw this production and was impressed by its staging in the School Hall.

After 50 years (1916-1966) the second battalion of the Norfolk Army Cadet Corps. had severed its association with the School. Annual camp was held at Carnoustie in Angus Scotland, and the battery paraded every Friday night at Southtown Road Drill Hall at 7.30 pm. This ended the School parades, one of the reasons appearing to be that there were insufficient members of staff prepared to be officers in a School Cadet force.

In September the High and Grammar Schools were joint hosts to the second of the international conferences of which they were members. Visiting parties and staff have come from Holland, West Germany, Denmark and France. The event followed a similar conference in Copenhagen two years previously when a group of Sixth Formers from Yarmouth Grammar School participated. The programme arranged for the visitors included a coach tour of Great Yarmouth and Gorleston and Mayoral reception at the Town Hall, a discussion with the Bishop of Norwich, a visit to the Power Station, a day trip to Norwich, and visits to important buildings in Great Yarmouth including the Parish Church, the Library and the Elizabethan House at 4 South Quay. The Grammar School party at the conference was Roderick Bird, David Brown, Malcolm Calthorpe, Alan Dobbins, Richard Heard, Alan Hewitt, John Riseborough, Terence Rogers, Paul Timewell, David Turner, Philip Tye, Brian Windscheffel, Christopher Wright, John Chapman, John Clare, Graham Creasy, John Littlewood, Peter Banham, Victor Ecclestone, Patrick Hamilton, John Haverson and Richard Heyhoe.

The Comprehensive School Scheme for Great Yarmouth had been accepted by the Department of Education and Science with no alterations that concerned the Grammar School. However the merging of the Grammar School with the High School to form two educational establishments was more urgent because of the shortage of women staff and was scheduled to take place in 1970.

The Founders and Benefactors Commemoration Service took place on July 10th 1967. The speaker was the Dean of Kings College Cambridge, the Rev. D. L. Edwards who spoke of the necessity for pupils to complete their search for truth by determining the answer to the question left open by science: whether life was accidental or given a spiritual reality behind our material facts.

At the Annual Prize Giving on the 17th November 1967 new arrangements made this as far as possible an internal arrangement with parents being invited to a special open evening on the same day. The prizes were presented by an Old Boy of the School Mr. J. Elton, a Master of the Supreme Court Queen's Bench Division. He made very short but impressive speech Mr. Elton stressed the need to take time off from learning to do some thinking. The important objective for all of those he spoke to was to develop their own personalities amidst the conformity of present day life. A vote of thanks was proposed by the Head Boy John Clare.

100. The School Cricket First Eleven. Rear row John Clare (second right) Bill Chapman (far right)

Chapter 8
Further Expansion in the 1970's

The School Notes for 1970-71 record that the first year "mixing" had passed very smoothly. The Editor of *The Chronicle* recorded that it seemed difficult to remember the Grammar School as a monastic institution when only the second year sixth and fifth forms had remained male preserves.

The Editor noted in *The Chronicle* for 1971-1972 records the arrival of 118 first formers last September, the largest entry in the School history exceeding even that of the celebrated post war "bulge" year of 1959. Numbers were increased from the previous years 476 to 532 just under 200 were girls. There was an exchange between the Physics Teachers for the Grammar and High Schools with Mr West moving to the High School and Miss Brenda Westley transferring to the Grammar School with the additional post of Senior Mistress.

The retirements at the end of the summer term of 1971 of Mr. Hillyer and Mr. Angwin meant the departure of two really long serving Teachers. During the Second World War Mr. Angwin served with the Army in India while Mr. Hillyer endured a number of years of captivity having been made prisoner by the Japanese when serving with the RAF in the former Dutch East Indies. Apart from their war-time service these two Masters had spent the bulk of their working lives in the School and together had contributed over 60 years to the Grammar School.

Mr. Hillyer joined the School in January 1939 to teach French but he would also be remembered by one generation as a violinist in the pre-war School Orchestra and as the Editor of *The Chronicle*. He had the organisation of the Schools Meals Service for almost 20 years and during the last ten years had been best known as the first Housemaster of West House which at that time had enjoyed great sporting success. His classes would be remembered for his thorough teaching, his quiet manner and his unfailing appeal to gentlemanly instincts drew a warm response from many pupils as did his courtesy.[1]

Mr Angwin was appointed soon after Mr. Palmer became Headmaster in 1937 as the Head's enthusiasm for music led him to appoint a full-time music specialist. When Mr. Angwin left for the Tank Corps on war service Mr Palmer and Mr Hunn, on a part time basis, kept alive the choral work which Mr. Angwin enthusiastically took up on his return. He was a Fifth Form Master, an Officer in the Cadet Corps and the first Housemaster of Centre. His annual concerts will be recalled with performances ranging from *HMS Pinafore*, to Handel's *Sampson* to Britten's *Noyes Fludde*. Mr Angwin would be particularly glad that in his final year, two of his pupils, S. Lake and M. Freeman had gained admission to the Royal Academy and the Royal College of Music respectively.[2]

101. Noyes Fludde by Benjamin Britten in the School Hall

[1] *Chronicle*, 1970-1971, pp.13-14
[2] *Ibid*. p.14

The new Domestic Science block to the west of the south wing was described by Sixth Formers Gillian Bane and Jane Ditcham, as Jane recalled that a room divider cut off a dining area which had a fitted carpet and a dining suite. She said that the girls developed a programme for producing meals which needed "testing" by staff and senior members of the School and that the original sittings became oversubscribed so additional sessions had to be fitted in. She remembered the courtesy given to the girls with doors being opened for them and the attention by certain older members of staff who called in to see that all was well with them.

102. H.M.S. Pinafore (1969)

The Dramatic Society took a brave step into the realm of modern playwrights with a production of *Next Time I'll Sing to You* by James Saunders on December 5th and 6th 1970. Brian Haylett directed and the resulting performance showed that the staging of modern plays as an alternative to the classics was possible giving the pupils a wider view of the whole range of drama.

School Societies were wide in interest and the Campanological Society had an active year with the Headmaster assisting both with ringing and with transport to Halvergate where the bells were rung. The newly formed Cookery Club had, claimed Gillian Bane and Jane Ditcham of the Sixth, enabled girls to do something better than boys! It was noted that meetings after School had been well attended by boys of the second year sixth and members of staff. The boys had progressed beyond baked beans to chilli con carne, pork olives apple pie, upside down pudding and curry. The inspiration behind these activities was Miss Susan Windscheffel. Gillian Bane and Jane Ditcham had launched a Play Group for children under school age coping with up to 14 children. The Photographic Society had visited Lavenham, the Archery Club had a new lease of life from the first years while the Sailing Club had a waiting list owing to the combination of Grammar and High Schools. It was noted that some members of the Club, all female, had an irresistible urge to throw themselves fully clothed into the middle of Breydon Water and as a consequence one of the rescue fenders thrown in for practice has been affectionately renamed "Amanda."[4]

The Football First XI had a successful season wining the Cowles Cup which had virtually become Great Yarmouth Grammar School property. The team moved from a 4-3-3 system to a more successful one of 4-2-4 during the season. The back four gained the reputation of being fast and hard in the tackle while the attacking ability stemmed from the midfield success of Alan Fakes, John Palmer and Neil Hepworth. The spearhead of Russell Leggett, Graham Parry and Alan Apps coupled with the ability of Richard Fuller on the right wing brought a high goal tally. The team also had strength in depth from its reserves.

The School, continued to offer a range of visits for the pupils. Austria at Christmas for skiing led by Mr. Blyth and Miss Utting. Visits to Rambouillet and its twin town Kirchheim in South Germany with Mr. Pereira, Mr. Marsden for France and Mr David Ingall for Germany as escorts. Geographers visited geographical features in the vicinity and the geologists had an expedition. Historians visited Orford and Framingham Castles and there were parties to Norwich to see the latest film version of *Hamlet*. Other visits were to the Oxford Playhouse to see *The Merry Wives of Windsor* and to the Maddermarket in Norwich to see their versions of *Coriolanus* and Marlowe's *The Jew of Malta*. The Sixth Form Geographers spent a week on a field course at Swanage with D. Bowen of the Sixth Form commenting that Mr Cheshire's sophisticated interpretation of an invading warrior scaling the ramparts of Maiden Castle during the team's afternoon visit being worthy of a paragraph in any history book.

3 Source Jane Roberts (nee Ditcham)
4 *Ibid*. p.25

The Old Boys' Annual General Meeting held at the School in January saw long serving Committee members Sidney Goodrich, C. Newman and A. Ovey retire while a recent Old Boy David Harrup left for South Africa. The retirement of George Skipper after fifteen yeas as Secretary was notable and he received the Association's thanks. The noble trio of John Green, Clifford Cook and Ray Packard continued to serve as President, Chairman and Treasurer.

In 1973 the School and Town awaited in this year a Ministerial decision on the local scheme of comprehensive education. Even if such a scheme received a Ministers blessing it was very difficult, given the current boom in building and the severe shortage of construction workers to envisage a full 3 tier comprehensive system in operation in Yarmouth by September 1974. The editorial comment was that we must wait and see.

Meanwhile the School continued to grow with a record first year entry of 120 which increased School numbers to 556 of whom 230 were girls. The final merit half holiday was held in November 1973. This system of the award of two half holidays each term with those with a good conduct record had survived the ending of the School's independent status by almost 30 years. It had been replaced as a disciplinary measure by monthly detentions after Friday School and on the last afternoon of each term. Morning Assembly contained to be held as usual every Monday morning but the Sixth Form had met separately in the small hall for the rest of the week except for Fridays when there were House Meetings. The separate assemblies had resulted in more pupils reading lessons with the editor's comment that M. Trett of the Fifth Form had rivalled Bernard Miles with his version of the Bible.[5]

Amongst appointments of six new staff was the appointment of Miss S. Boon, my sister who was appointed to teach History. She had worked with Educational Administration in London with the Civil Service, taught at Lowestoft and also for two years at Oriel Grammar School and had obtained her Postgraduate Diploma in Education from Hughes Hall in Cambridge in the previous year. She was born in Wales and went to the High School, obtained her Degree from Birmingham University and would be marrying in late summer. The editorial notes that Miss Boon had family connections with the School where both her father and brother were former pupils and both had kept a close interest in the School and had helped it in many ways. A kind comment since I never expected my sister to teach at my former School.

The Chronicle has an interesting note on School authors commenting that Henry Manship was the earliest with his *History of Great Yarmouth 1619*. In his History he mentions, while a pupil at the School, how he helped to work on strengthening the Town Wall while a pupil in 1570 "being more willing to carry a basket of earth in my hand than a satchel of books on my shoulder.[6] Canon Raven Headmaster in late Victorian times and the Head after whom the Tower in Tower Yard was named wrote the standard book on Church Bells in England. Mr. A.H.G. Palmer, Headmaster 1937-1960 wrote a Mathematics text book while former Head Boy K.J. Fielding the Sainsbury Professor of English Literature at Edinburgh University had published editions of the Speeches and Letters of Charles Dickens as well as a critical edition to his novels. However the two best known of the Old Boys' books were undoubtedly as the editor comments *Stonehenge Decoded* by G.. S. Hawkins and Bishop Ambrose Reeves *Shooting at Sharpeville.*

Alphega a magazine of creative writing had appeared throughout the year and had attracted a wide range of contributions. It sought to publish challenging and controversial articles. The London Old Boys Society held its final meeting in February 1973 and I set out the reasons for its demise as given by its Secretary later in the book. Despite its distance from the School it had maintained firm links on an annual basis since its foundation in October 1936. The energy of the Society had principally come from its Secretary Mr E. W. "Tusky" Foulser whose efforts had been a tribute to the deep affection and sense of loyalty felt towards their School by many old pupils.

At the Leavers Assembly on July 5th 1972 Charles Wharton an Old Boy of the School and a local farmer presented the sports awards. He commented on the wide variety of sports played and suggested the addition

---

5 *Chronicle*, New Series No.27, July 1973, p.9
6 Manship Henry, *The History of Great Yarmouth*, Palmer Charles, ed., Yarmouth, 1854, p.46

of two squash courts. At the end of year Concert held on Monday 10th July 1972 Philip Gallaway played two violin sonatas by Suk and Monti and the quality of his performance augured well for his future at the Royal Academy of Music. Philip has since gone on to become a highly successful professional musician.

Prize Day was held on the 29th September 1972 and the prizes were presented by Professor G. Hawkins who had been at the Grammar School from 1940-1946 and who reminisced about his mathematical exercises at Retford in September 1944 in timing V2 rockets that been aimed at Norwich from Holland by trailing their vapour trails. He graduated from Nottingham University in Physics in 1949 and worked for his PhD in Radio Astronomy under Sir Bernard Lovell at Manchester. He later moved to the United States becoming Professor of Astronomy at Boston University. He had written a general survey of Astronomy called *Splendour in the Skies* but was more widely known for his controversial best seller *Stonehenge Decoded*.

Following previous productions of Gilbert and Sullivan, *The Pirates of Penzance* (1942) *Iolanthe* (1945), *HMS Pinafore* (1958) and the *Pirates of Penzance* (1969) the Dramatic Society under the direction of Brian Haylett and Chris Foy staged *HMS Pinafore* which was certainly the most ambitious production which the School had attempted. The previous production of *Pinafore* had been staged with an all boy cast and Mr. Pereira as Sir Joseph Porter. This production had the advantage of casting both boys and girls and I notice in the cast that Captain Corcoran was played by Andrew Fenton who had later acted with the Masquers. A chorus of over 50 added depth to the production.

The wide variety of School Societies continued to meet on a regular basis. The Archery Club was flourishing, the Model Railway Club was working on its layout for open night and the Gym Club had been well supported at Monday lunch time. Theatre visits had included a visit by the sixth form to the Prospect Theatre Company's production of *Richard III* at the Theatre Royal Norwich. Richard Briers who played Richard and the members of the Company spent the morning discussing the History Plays of Shakespeare with the schools audience in the morning before the afternoon performance.

The Chronicle carried an article from Mr. E. W. Foulser on the reasons for the closure of the London Old Boys Society. He said that the first London Old Boys Society was formed late in the 19th century and had not been re-formed until 1936 and had met regularly since that time. The Society had made annual gifts of books to the library and awarded the two Reading Prizes. The need to wind up the Society resulted from an age of change. In the past it was the payment of fees which allowed boys to attend the School, then fees or scholarship entry and subsequently the 11 plus examination. In the past Mr. Foulser said it had been a privilege to go to the School and perhaps now it had become an entitlement. Fewer Old Boys had settled in the London area making it more difficult to run social events with the result that the Society had been wound down. R. Foulser who had been its Secretary from 1936-1973 wished the School well and commented that few provincial schools had had a local students association based in the capital.

The final item in *The Chronicle* for the year was a note from Keith Peel, Old Boy and journalist with Eastern Counties Newspapers on the renamed Great Yarmouth Grammar School Past Students Association (formerly the Old Boys). Keith appeals for attendance at the Annual Dinner at the Imperial stating how much students enjoyed the occasion when they attended with School contemporaries. The same appeal which we on the Dinner Committee, some 37 years later, still make to the Old Students of the Grammar School.

The Chronicle for 1974 noted the loss of Great Yarmouth's County Borough Status, the resulting fact that education would now be controlled by the County Council from the County Hall in Norwich. Great Yarmouth Corporation had therefore relinquished control of its Grammar School founded 423 years previously, but its plans for comprehensive education in the Borough after 10 years of gestation had been rejected by the new Minister of Education and thus it would be up to Norfolk County Council to come up with a new plan. One reasonable certainty would be that the School would increase in size from its present level of 604 pupils (270 girls and 334 boys) to well over 700 in two years.

The classroom block at the end of the south wing opened in September 1973 and this had helped to accommodate the increase in numbers of pupils, then standing at 604 (270 girls and 334 boys). One room had been specifically designed for Needlework and equipped with changing and wardrobe areas and sewing machines, while another room had been fitted with desks for Technical Drawing.

The Prize Day speaker was Sir Arthur Hawkins Chairman of the Central Electricity Generating Board and Old Pupil (1925-32), known in his day, my Father who was his contemporary told me, as "Tubby" and the speaker generously gave £50 to the School. Two notable achievements gained by pupils were Philip Jeffrey's award of a place at St. Catherine's College, Cambridge and Joseph Oakley's who had gained grade 1 passes in all nine O level subjects and the grant of a place at Corpus Christi College, Oxford.

After 36 years Mr. Stafford having taught Mathematics at Salisbury Road finally retired. He had coached sports teams, as a violinist played in the School Orchestra and spent most of the war serving in the RAF. He taught a steady stream of able Mathematicians who left to pursue advanced studies, and he also had a talent for bringing on less gifted Mathematicians, as I remember well, by his patient approach. The editor noted that the staff would lose a quietly efficient colleague and those who taught Mathematics would loose a ready referee with the tricky problems.

This Chronicle recorded Mr. Stafford's early career in an article in which he recalled his early days of teaching in India with his brother before he joined the Grammar School at Salisbury Road. He taught Mathematics at the Diocesan Boys High School, Naimi Tal, United Provinces, India, in the foothills of the Himalayas at a Hill Station formerly used by the British Raj. Mr. Stafford recalled that his neighbour Major Jim Corbett, was probably the most famous tiger hunter in India, and he was surprised to learn that in later years in 1952, when Queen Elizabeth was told of the death of her father, she was with Major Corbett who was explaining to her the nightlife in the jungle from the Treetops house in Kenya. Mr Stafford concluded his valedictory article in wondering whether he was or might be the last of the staff who had been east of Suez.[7]

The editor noted the School minibus was a year old and had travelled over 4000 miles, including a field trip to Dover, theatre visits, picking up French students at Dover, visits to Ely and Cambridge, beside regular journeys with sports teams. The cost of the journeys had been calculated on petrol alone and it was noted that on this basis a return journey to Norwich for 10 people would cost 8p per person.

The wide variety of sports played by the School were highlighted on the last afternoon of the spring term, 5th April 1974, when Mr. Blyth introduced Mr. Bill Davy the last Mayor of the County Borough of Great Yarmouth, and the Mayoress, who were also his aunt and uncle to present the sports awards. The cricket first X1 had had a disappointing season in 1973 winning only 2 out of 8 matches. John Fuller, who captained the team, took 21 wickets and hit 110 runs, Andrew Giles hitting 114. The under 15 and under 13 first X1 both had successful seasons. Full and Half Colours were awarded for hockey, netball, gymnastics, soccer, basketball, cross country, and table tennis. Those who had been experienced and consistent in ability also received re-awards of colours previously gained. The under 14 Football First X1 in particular had a good season winning all but 5 of its 21 games. The team reached the local Schools' Cup final losing to Gorleston Grammar School and came 3rd in the league. E. Barr, N. Calver, and C Humphrey played in the towns boy's team.

The Sailing Club continued to operate from Burgh Castle, but Norfolk County Council site at Filby Broad had become available and 24 pupils and 6 cruising yachts took part in a combined cruise from Ludham with Gorleston Grammar School in the last week of the summer term. It was recorded that one teacher from Gorleston Grammar School did not manage to duck fast enough when passing under the notoriously low head-roomed Potter Heigham bridge and hurt his head badly but nobly returned heavily stitched to the cruise 24 hours later.

Once upon a time the Grammar School would have regarded a play with an all male cast as a Godsend. Brian Haylett in reviewing the *Thwarting of Baron Bolligrew* staged on February 19th-21st 1974, commented that it

---

[7] *Chronicle*, New Series No.28, July 1974, pp.12-13

seemed strange that Robert Bolt's all male play had been transposed for a mixed cast. It seemed that nobody minded as knights in tights seemed to be quite a welcome innovation.

The play stood midway between pantomime and straight farce. This suited the cast who stood midway between amateur actors and sixth formers enjoying private study in the library. This was quite a complement since the senior cast had rarely seen a stage before, and overcame that problem remarkably well.

Marcus Trett handled the part of Sir Oblong with a gusto that reminded individuals of Marcus Trett. At times he seemed to be taking two night run too literally and he finished the last performance with a large bump on the head, caused by sitting down on the stage too heavily. Gary Calver was an excellent foil but a rotten swordsman as he played Squire Blackheart, tall and stupid. Their sword fights bankrupted the woodwork department, but weas great fun. As Bolligrew, Craig Richardson, waxed villainous while wearing his moustache naturally. There was no room in the review for the cast of thousands but Mr. Haylett's only serious criticism was of the lighting plot, which to his great surprise the local paper praised. The mercifully short night scenes were played in a blue light that concealed so much that if realism was the criteria the light might have been put out altogether. It seemed that a great time was had by all producing a very enjoyable evening's entertainment.

103. The Thwarting of Baron Bolligrew – cast picture 1973

The main editorial written by Victor Stowers, noted that the mid 30s were a depressing time in England for those seeking employment since the huge number of graduates applying for a post in teaching French and Latin at the Grammar School in 1935 demonstrates. Even in that time Mr. Pereira fresh from College and doubtless pleased to be offered the appointment of French Master at the School was warned that if an expected increase in the numbers of pupils at the School did not materialize he would be sacked. In the event he stayed his entire teaching career of 40 years serving for the last 20 years as Deputy Headmaster. The editor comments that it was virtually certain that no teacher would ever equal the length or quality of his service to the School.

The sudden death of Mr. B. Angwin which took place in London on the 7th May after leaving a concert at the Festival Hall, feeling unwell was a profound shock to the School. Although he retired in 1971 Mr. Angwin returned to the Grammar School in the previous year to prepare O and A level music candidates and had been teaching and apparently in fine spirits only the day before his death. Mr. Stowers, commented that the School would miss Mr. Angwin very much.

Another ex member of staff had returned to teach part time during 1975. Mr Ron Tucker who had taught P.E. at the Grammar School in 1955 and 1956 and had also coached an unbeaten Under 12 Football XI. Mr. John Farmer had joined the staff in January after over 15 years teaching Music at both Fakenham and Lowestoft Grammar Schools, the latter now the Denes High School. Mr. Farmer was born in Skegness, graduated in music at Manchester University and was an associate of the Royal College of Organists. He gained his Teaching Diploma at Nottingham University. Mr. Farmer commenting on his appointment said he was interviewed by Mr. Marsden on his own and appointed on the spot and that during the whole time of his career at school Mr. Marsden was extremely supportive of all his musical undertakings.

The commemoration of Founders and Benefactors Service was held in St. Nicholas Parish Church on Wednesday July 3rd. 1974. In the absence of the Vicar through illness, the service was conducted by the Revered B. Spence, Curate of St. Pauls Newtown. The address was given by the Rev. Fr. Dominic Daly, Head of St. Augustine's College, Dungarven, near Waterford in Ireland, who said that the Grammar School and particularly the Sixth Form had a sound preparation for life. Lessons were read by past pupil Mr. Michael Boon, and the Head Boy. The guests included the first Mayor of the new District Council Mr. Jack Bishop past student of the School in the 1920s and his wife, and tea was given at the School. Unfortunately rain prevented the School versus Old Boys match from being played.

At the Prize Day on the 27th September 1974 E.W. Foulser who was my Father's contemporary at School from 1926-1933, the last Secretary of the London Old Boys Society, spoke to the assembled company. Mr. Foulser said that he felt his success in life was due to the School, and he hoped that the new Norfolk Authority would appreciate its value. The Headmaster received from Mr. Foulser all the documents and records of the London Old Boys Society. The Mayor, Mr. Jack Bishop, spoke of his happiness when at the School and his pride in it.

Mr. Pereira provided a brief valedictory note in *The Chronicle* of his 40 years at the School. The Grammar School needed a French and Latin Master who was also a scout. As a Londoner born within earshot of Whitehart Lane, he said that he felt he was coming to the ends of the earth and had he been told that he would still be there 40 years later he said he would have rushed screaming back to Southtown station with its large sign Garibaldi Hotel - men only.

He said it was through the Scouts that he acquired the name Pip, which was indeed helpful to one with a name like Pereira. He claimed the distinction of introducing the fierce game of "British Bulldog" to the local Scouts, and he enjoyed the field day when they appeared at School in shorts and also camps of the pre war era. He said he also enjoyed taking part in School plays, one of which was written by the then Headmaster and was entitled *Uneasy Head* which was quite a prophetic title. He said it had been asserted that he was the Master who said "Nonsense" when a pupil called out "sir, aren't those German planes?" and that his next dictated sentence was drowned by the crump of exploding bombs fortunately out to sea. He said that he naturally joined the RAF where knowledge of French proved useful in North Africa when negotiating such things as laundry prices with the local inhabitants. He said his journeys took him through North Africa, Sicily, Italy, Egypt, Southern France, Malta and Greece though only for an half an hour in the two latter. He had an audience with the Pope together with hundreds of other men in the services in 1944 and also gave lectures on radar to the units of the new French army in 1945 who were the most attentive pupils he had ever had. In 1956 he began his association with the twinning of Great Yarmouth and Rambouillet and he said that his life had been greatly enriched by the friendships made in this connection. His wife had been teaching French at the High School and her dynamism and resourcefulness produced tremendous support for twinning from beyond the river. He commented that the Grammar and High Schools had enjoyed a period of fruitful collaboration long before any question of co-education arose. He said of his last years of his time at the Grammar School had been under the threat/promise (striking out the word that did not apply) of comprehensive reorganisation. He said at first the battle was very fierce but after such a long period the supporters of both sides had almost ceased to argue through sheer weariness. Co-education was a different matter. He said that when it was mooted, he said to an Old Boys gathering, "the total sum of sin probably won't change, but there maybe more variety". So that he concluded what might be the future for the Great Yarmouth Grammar School, he felt that there were plenty of challenges to face and his best wishes went to the School where he had spent so much of his life. He wished to thank all ex pupils, present pupils and colleagues who had never made him regret (at least hardly ever), shades of his Sir Joseph Porter when he applied for the Grammar School post in 1935.

104. *Grammar School under 12 Football X!. Winners of the Yarmouth League Shield and Knock-Out Cup 1974-75.*

ın Ward, Gary Calver, Geoffrey Leavold, Graham Harris, David Kightley
Stephen Andrews, Peter Critoph and David Hurrell
School Basketball Team 1975

105. *Grammar School Basketball Team 1975*

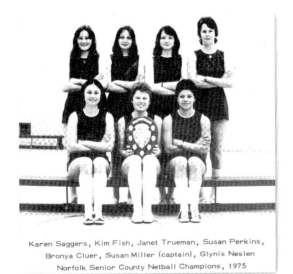

Karen Saggers, Kim Fish, Janet Trueman, Susan Perkins,
Bronya Cluer, Susan Miller (captain), Glynis Neslen
Norfolk Senior County Netball Champions, 1975

106. *Grammar School Netball Team, County Champions 1975*

At the Old Student Association Dinner Jane Ditcham was the sole female past student present. The Secretary Colin Tennant commented that he wished that she had more support from her contemporaries. The Mayor Mr. Jack Bishop proposed the toast to the School.

In September 1976 the School welcomed Mr. Mike Leigh on his appointment as Deputy Headmaster. Mr. Leigh had attended a small Grammar School in Somerset, then graduated in History from Leeds University and obtained his Teaching Diploma at the Oxford Department of Education. He had taught for 3 years at Havant in Hampshire and for 5 years in Uganda at an African Boys Boarding School and came to Great Yarmouth after a further 6 years at a Bradford direct grant Boys School.

Those who heard Mr. Leigh's talk to the Parents Association on his experiences in Uganda learnt of his skill as a negotiator. While he was visiting an African friend they were unexpectedly joined by a relative of his host who turned out to be General Idi Amin, then the commander of the Ugandan army. Unfortunately when Mr. Leigh was about to leave he found his path obstructed by the General's Mercedes. The diplomacy he mustered in rousing General Amin, now well fortified by drink, to move his car, should be well exercised at Salisbury Road where numbers for the first time had reached over 700 pupils with a record intake of 128 first formers and a Sixth Form of 108.

In Staff movements Mr. R.J. Parry teaching History replaced Mrs. S. Metters who had left at the end of the autumn term after 3 years at the School. Her daughter Katie was born in April 1976 and my sister tells me that she was the first member of staff to leave through pregnancy. She was then living in Norwich where her husband was a lecturer at the city college.

The programme of Sixth Form lectures given to the First Year Sixth with over 30 lectures given by members of staff. Apart from the obvious "subjects" the staff chose their own topics. Mr. Little spoke on "films and the supernatural", and "discovering America 1975", the legacy of his journey across the United States in the previous summer. Mr. Farmer spoke on "the ragtime revival", Mr. Gilbertson on "drugs", Mr. Cheshire on "pollution and conservation", and Mr. Loftin on the "History of A South Africa" The Second Year Sixth heard a variety of guest speakers which included talks from custom and excise, accountancy, probation and after care, independent television, problems of a store manager, health visitors, the public water supply, the National Health Service, the doctor in 1975 and the Samaritans. The Area Education Officer spoke on grants for further education which occupied the second half of the year. Other speakers presented topics as diverse as "drug dependence", "your prison service", "running a local newspaper", "John Citizen and a Lawyer" and "Nature Conservation."

The School Review was held on the 22nd and 23rd September 1975 and played to packed houses; this home spun entertainment had abundant comic fare. There was the incomparable Mr. Stowers who easily stole the show with his rendering of "one alone" ably assisted by continual interruptions by two passing Mexicans (Mr. Little and Mr. Wilcox) whose maracas were easily the best that Tina Morris had seen this year. They finally found Stephen Foster producing quite the nicest assortment of knickers that had been Tina Morris's pleasure to behold. Her review concluded by commenting that it was nearly one of the funniest shows she had seen for a long time.

In terms of drama there were junior house competitions and a variety of plays using the full resources of the stage were mounted.

Within a very few months of the death of Mr. Angwin in May 1975 a project was initiated to provide an appropriate memorial to his 32 years as Music Director of the School. It was the wish of the Worshipful Company of Musicians of the City of London, to mark Mr. Angwin's long membership and recent election as Master by making a gift to the School. This was coupled with Mr. Farmer's enthusiasm with more suitable teaching courses for Music which the raising of almost £5,000 facilitated the speedy conversion of the prefabricated buildings to the east of the School field. In January 1976 Mrs. Angwin received a Commemorative Scroll which was the work of Mr. Exell at the centres opening. This took place during the interval of a concert given by the Coull String Quartet which included Philip Gallaway (Violin) who was a former pupil of Mr. Angwin.

107. Opening of the Angwin Music School

The pupils continued to produce illustrations and drawings for *The Chronicle*. James Smart of the Sixth Form produced a very interesting drawing of the Marie Celeste in a Heath Robinson style which is very detailed. The illustration is reproduced below.

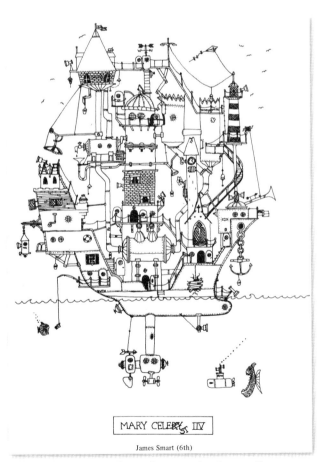

MARY CELESTE IIV

James Smart (6th)

108. The Marie Celeste drawing by James Smart

In addition sports teams continued to play successfully. In table tennis the under 19 team won all their games and were Norfolk Schools' team champions, and qualified for the English Schools' area championship at Wisbech where they won 2 of their 3 games and narrowly lost to the winners. This successful year, the report commented, should be repeated in the next year with young players of promise. The under 16 team lost only one match, to Attleburgh, to whom they lost the English Schools area tournament in the final.

In terms of football results, 11 teams played 164 games. The under 14 A XI lost only 2 of their 16 matches winning the rest, were league champions and runners up in the local cup. Kevin Boldra, the captain, Dean Hunniball, John Moore and Martin Moss all played for the Yarmouth Boys Team.

Over 30 lectures had been given by members of staff to the 1st year 6th. Apart from the staffs. These series of lectures for both the First and Second Year Sixth were intended to broaden their areas of interest as they moved forward either into employment or higher education.

League champions and runners up in the local Schools Cup, 1975-1976

109. The Under Fourteen School Football X1 League Champions and runners up in the Local Schools' Cup 1975-1976

Editorial for this year centres on the departure of Headmaster Peter Marsden after 16 years of leading the School. He inherited a boys' Grammar School of approximately 350 pupils already in the throes of change to a three streamed school and problems of building extension and limited playing field accommodation. In the year of his retirement numbers had increased to 730 and had begun to take in a much wider range of pupil abilities. A marked characteristic of Mr. Marsden's Headmastership had been his willingness to listen to other people's problems while no one in his position could be more approachable in all matters of School life. During Mr. Marsden's term of office there had been notable achievements in the School corporate life and additions to its facilities and playing fields had been developed at Barnard Bridge and Beaconsfield Road amongst additional useful buildings and sports facilities. A Sports Hall had been developed, cricket nets prepared and a sports pavilion at Barnard Road and a Swimming Pool on the Salisbury Road site had been built while additional School facilities saw domestic science rooms, metal work and woodworking centres and a new sixth form common room together with a new chemistry lab and new music centre. Also remembered as highlights during his Headmastership would be the coach trip to Moscow in 1961, an Annual Commemoration Service and School open evenings when work, hobbies and activities were on display to parents and friends of the School.

The School had a total of 721 pupils on the roll in September 1976, which was a small increase on the previous years 708 which included 362 boys and 359 girls. This meant that from the entry of the first girls in 1971 it had taken six years to balance the sexes. However of the staff of 38, 10 were female and the editor found it difficult to envisage greater expansion in numbers on the Salisbury Road site which was acquired in 1909 to cater for around 200 boys. The Norris prize presented by John Norris, Head of English, 1955-1962, which had previously been awarded for an essay, was now to be awarded for the best instrumentalist performing in the Inter House Competition. This reflected Mr. Norris's interest in teaching and performing music while at the Grammar School and the wide variety of instruments he played from recorders to harpsichord.

In terms of staff news there was a great sense of continuity in the appointment of Mr. Mike Leigh, who succeeded Mr. Marsden as Headmaster, after two years as his Deputy, and Mr. Bill Howell's promotion to Deputy Headmaster, after teaching Latin and French at Salisbury Road.

110. Patience 1977

Mr. K. Symonds having taught French and Physical Education for over 6 years had departed for Geelong Grammar School, Australia, where Prince Charles was once a pupil. He was succeeded as Head of French by Mr. Tom Harrison, who was also a former pupil of the Grammar School and who had left in 1962 to read French at Leicester University. Mr. Harrison had spent a year at Hagenau in Alsace as an English assistant and then had obtained a teaching diploma at Leicester. He had taught locally at St. Edmunds School and since 1970 at Gorleston Grammar School. He was closely involved with the Rambouillet twinning, and played football regularly in the local league where he ran two teams.

On the 16th-18th December 1976 John Farmer directed a performance of *Patience* by Gilbert and Sullivan. There was an interesting review in *The Chronicle* by John Harboard of the sixth form who commented that as a humble dragoon guard, he was unable to see the final result from amongst the audience, but had the advantage of seeing the characters develop the performances during rehearsals. He commented that particular praise was due to the three officers of the dragoon guard, who contrasted their ridiculous trio in Act II with their more military pieces. Mr. Pereira returned to take the role of the colonel supported by Mr. Mitchell and John Newman, and these three were supported by a colourful and hearty chorus of dragoons. The girls chorus was equally brilliant, perhaps more so as they did not have any staff support. The bulk of the praise was heaped on the heroine Patience, sung by Jayne Bull, who turned a good school performance into a masterful one. The production was a great success which would be remembered for a long time.

The School walk to raise money for charity, took place on Friday April 1st, 1977, along the beach to Winterton. Paul Gilbertson commenting said that the walk was probably easier to organise than its predecessors, because of the lessons learned from them. Thus the questions "is it on sir?!," 'I've lost my sponsor form ?!", "what happens if it rains?!" remained the same. The response of the School was magnificent both in terms of those who participated and also in the amount of money collected which was well over £2,000. Mr. Gilbertson commented that there had been no complaints from the public and only one serious injury resulting from a boy who tried to kick a buried stone and found it was larger than his big toe expected.

THE SCHOOL WALK TO WINTERTON, FRIDAY, APRIL 1st, 1977

Some weary walkers approaching Winterton.

111. The School Walk to Winterton 1977

On the 3rd June 1977 29 students and 3 adults set off from the Grammar School for an 8 day Dutch barge cruise. The group sailed from Sheerness to Vlissingen and travelled to Amsterdam by coach having a tour of the city by water bus in the evening. The barge then took the group to Utrecht and on to Schoonhoven on the river Lek, which was a very pretty town where the group went to see a silver factory. The barge continued down the river Lek into Rotterdam where it moored close to the Euromast which most of the party ascended to the revolving 180 metre observation platform. Mr. Laity commented that this was the high spot of the trip with spectacular views of Rotterdam. The group also travelled to Delft and saw the famous pottery factory to The Hague, where they visited the Maduradam a fascinating miniature village and to Haarlem where they saw an exhibition illustrating the recovery of the polder lands from the sea. On the way back to Vlissingen the ferry crossing, the group stopped at Scheveningen, the port where Norfolk Line sailed to Yarmouth, and then on to a night crossing returning to Yarmouth just after midnight.[8]

The School Clubs and Societies remained extremely active. There were moves afoot to inaugurate a group in Great Yarmouth of the British Association of Young Scientists. A Jewellery club for girls had met during the lunch hours attracting between 10 and 20 girls from the 1st and 2nd years to explore ring brooch and pendant making and the use of wire engraving and chasing.

Music at the Grammar School was wide ranging and following the production of *Patience*, the Yarmouth Schools' Carol Festival was again held at the Hippodrome in mid December. The Grammar School's bell ringing team provided an innovation in beginning the evening programme with carols played around the Christmas tree. This was extremely well received resulting in a suggestion that the hand bells be recorded in another year in the programme as an item in their own right. The choir rehearsed in two sections, with sopranos, altos and trebles meeting on a Monday with tenors and basses on a Tuesday, so that more attention could be given to individual parts. John Farmer commented that he remained grateful to his colleagues on the staff for their continued support in the choir with a special comment to the former Deputy Head, Mr. Pereira, who regularly cycled in twice a week to sing as a choir member.

BASKETBALL, 1977, THE RAVENS

The School Basketball Team, 1976-77

112. The Ravens The Grammar School Basketball Team 1976-1977

Sporting achievements continued to grow, and School Basketball Team for 1976-77 *The Ravens* finished only 3 points behind the eventual Yarmouth and District League winners. In the handicap cup they were successful defeating Shrublands, Gorleston Grammar and the *Eagles*, on their way to the final where they defeated the Americans 48-36 in a reasonable game.

The girls had equal success with the under 15 netball team winning the local tournament in a team composed of Fourth and Fifth formers.

The Chronicle for 1977 concluded by a fascinating article from Paul King of the Third Form, who won a national competition organised by a Airfix modelling firm, in which the first prize was a trip to Washington, in the United States, by Concorde. He said that he had never flown before and did not know what to expect, but when he looked at the Mach meter indicating Mach 2 the plane didn't seem to be moving. They flew mostly above the clouds between 50,000 and 60,000 feet, i.e. about 10 miles. He commented by the time they had champagne with caviar, smoked salmon and lots of other good things to eat it was almost time to land. The landing speed of the Concorde is about 450 miles an hour. The

8   *Chronicle*, 1977, pp.27-28

The Under 15 Netball team, winners of the local tournament.

113. The Grammar School Girls Under 15 Netball Team

group landed at Dulles Airport near Washington, stayed at the Washington Hilton (1000 rooms) and visited the Smithsonian Institute for Aerospace which exhibited space craft which had visited the Moon. He said he was excited to touch a piece of the Moon. The return journey turned out not to be so smooth as a fog diversion resulting in a landing at Manchester. Paul King commented that after travelling all night he arrived home very tired, but would never forget his wonderful journey and his stay in Washington.[9]

The editorial for that year's *Chronicle* noted that there was a Commemoration of Founders and Benefactors Service on the 6th July 1977. The Service was held at the School in brilliant sunshine with the address being given by the Reverend Michael Skinner Principal of Wesley House, Cambridge, The service was conducted by the Vicar of Great Yarmouth, Canon Donald Holt while prayers were said by the Park Baptist Church's Father John Hyland. Lessons were read by the Head Boy Peter Anderson and Mr. John Mobbs an Old Student a peal of bells had been rung before the service by Mr. Brown and his bell ringers. In addition, music given by the choir during the service the newly formed brass group valiantly attempted a jubilee tune arranged by Mr. Palmer. Guests and Old Boys were later entertained for tea in the School hall while a cricket match between the Old Boys and School which followed was drawn. The report was written by Barbara Brown of the sixth form.[10]

The editorial recorded that Mr. Palmer the Headmaster from 1937-60 who had died in February 1977 would be remembered for his fine mind, his absolute fairness and honesty and his love of music. His wife affectionately known to all as Dolly who gave great support to his work at the School died 3 months after her husband. They had spent their retirement at Eaton near Norwich. *The Chronicle* also records the death of Mr. Albert Pillar, the former School Caretaker, a week after Mr. Palmer's own death. Mr. Pillar had been appointed in the mid 1930s and with his wife prepared School Dinners in the days before the School meal service. He held the fort throughout the war while the School was evacuated to Retford. He had served Mr. Palmer as Caretaker of the School throughout his Headmastership and retired in 1963 to a flat opposite the School. During the Second World War he saw the School occupied by the Army and the R.A.F. and was in charge of an air raid post centred on the Headmasters study. The editor commented that Mr. Pillar's good humour and industry would be remembered by both staff and pupils. I certainly remember when Mr. Pillar told you to do anything you jumped.

D. Laley of the Second Year Sixth reviewed the revue the Salisbury Road show, which had taken place in July at the end of the previous academic year. He recorded that this was yet another roaring success and he was sorry to see the producers split up as the script utilized the talents of both staff and pupils in the material written. Victor Stowers was resplendent, as Leonard Sachs (or was it Frankie Howard), while John Harboard had looked like a cross between Sherpa Tensing and David Attenborough. These acts started the show, which had many fine sketches, including Mr. Willcock as the northern holiday maker and School Master. The reviewer said that the rest of the cast all put in more than creditable performances and they were in order of appearance:- Victor "Salacious Sugrubrious" Stowers, John "Ordinance Survey" Harboard, Tommy "The Throat" Harrison, and many others including Eddie "Fingers" Loftin. All the music was played by Andy Moll and to Robin Tubbutt who provided the electricals.[11]

9   *Ibid.* p.36
10 *Ibid.* pp.11-13
11 *Chronicle*, July 1978, p.4

There were many celebrations noting the retirement of Peter Marsden the Headmaster which were recorded in the 1978 Chronicle, which had taken place at the end of the previous academic year. A buffet dance had been organised on the 15th July at which 120 parents, pupils and staff marked Mr. Marsden's retirement. The music was provided by a larger than usual dance band *The Simon Miller Sound* who had included such old favourites as the Conga and the Hokey Cokey in their repertoire. The occasion was introduced by Mike Leigh, Mr. Marsden's successor as Headmaster, who expressed his confidence that the traditions and standards of the School which had been maintained by Mr. Marsden, would be continued. The Second Year Sixth form girls prepared a magnificent candlelit buffet and Mr. Marsden cut the iced retirement cake and served each guest with a portion. The evening had concluded with more dancing.

Four days later the Eisteddfod concert took place at which there were further presentations to Mr. Marsden. A well filled School hall heard the winners from the 68 entries from the inter-house music competition which had been judged during the course of the day by Mr. Geoffrey Lycock, the Principal Lecturer in Music at Keswick College of Education. Carol Jones (Violin) who played a Brahms Hungarian Dance and Robin Tubbutt (Trombone) with a performance of Gounod's *Lend me your Aid* where judged equal best instrumentalists and so shared the Norris prize. South House won the choir and overall competition and received the Pereira Cup.

Retirement presentations were then made to Mr. Marsden, the speakers were introduced by Bill Howell, the current Deputy Headmaster, who commented that he had been pleased to serve under Mr. Marsden, and referred particularly to the Headmaster's constant unpublished efforts to help local and national charities, both financially and practically.

Mr. Marsden in reply spoke of sauntering around the School for 17 years with the School's screwdriver in hand pouring oil on troubled waters. He had come from a very different sort of School and wondered if he might ruin the very School he had found. He said that he soon realised that it would take a far worse person than himself to do so, since Yarmouth, as he had been warned, was a place where people didn't change but which changed people. He said that he had been proud to work at the Grammar School and carry on its fine traditions which he was sure were in safe hands with Mr. Leigh and Mr. Howell, even when the future was so uncertain. He said that he had been a small cog in a big wheel and had wonderful support from his staff and his wife, and he wanted very much to keep in touch. The Chairman of the Old Students' Association, Mr. Clifford Cooke, spoke of Mr. Marsden's contribution to the work of the community as well as to the School. He said that Mr. Marsden was the latest of a long list of Headmasters of character who had both turned out not only outstanding pupils but also thousands of ordinary citizens who had been a credit to the community. He thanked Mr. Marsden for his constant support of the Association and presented him with a silver tea salver.[12]

The final assembly of the School and final presentations to Mr. Marsden took place on the last day of term on the 21st July 1977. Mrs. K. Adlington, Chairman of the Governors, said that Mr. Marsden had been a splendid Headmaster who had well maintained the Schools reputation for academic success and for turning out first class citizens. She said that Mr. Marsden like all his past Headmasters, had brought a different slant to the Grammar School, had shown sound judgement and above all as a truly Christian Headmaster had practiced what he had preached. The Governors had appreciated the happy School that Mr. Marsden had left for his successor, and he had demonstrated by his own industry the happiness that came from purposeful activity. In responding Mr. Marsden ended by presenting two pictures to the School who gave him three cheers, and the final prayer was begun by Mr. Marsden and completed by Mr. Leigh.[13]

At the Prize Giving on the 15th November 1977, the case for the retention of Sixth Forms in Schools which taught younger children was argued by Mr. Mike Leigh in his first speech as Headmaster. He said that the interaction between younger and older pupils was valuable as was the teaching of younger children by teachers who took advanced work in the sixth form.

---

[12] *Ibid*. pp.7-8
[13] *Ibid*. p.9

In March 1978 the Dramatic Society produced the *Government Inspector*, which was directed by Mr. Little. Brian Haylett, reviewing the production, said that it was heartening to see some younger actors emerging since the School was going to miss quite a few regulars when they left at the end of the summer. These included the two leading actors from the play, Dean Laley, and Philip Seago. Laley had brought his character, the manic extrovert, close to perfection, while Seago who had tended to specialise in languid characters, was equally effective. The two principal female parts had been most ably played by Sue Clarke, and Gabi Faerber, who had effectively portrayed the roles of mother and daughter. Over 600 people saw the two performances, which included attendance by the Mayor Mr. Harry Miller.

Andrew Moll, captain of the cricket 1st X1, noted of the 9 games played 3 were won and 5 were lost, and a fairly strong squad had been considerably weakened by those that had taken Saturday jobs. This was a problem that had marred what could have been a very good season. Stephen McMurrough had performed well with both bat and ball and had been awarded pads as the Governors' Prize.

School Societies remained active, and the Kart club had acquired two low powered single speed Karts for use on the Ellough circuit. The Karts had run very well, but one engine had blown up and put the club out of action for much of the spring term. The prospects looked good and the club hoped to be at full strength for practices on June 3rd and required all members to hold full licences in readiness for the National Schools Karting Championships which would take place in Barnsley in July. It was noted that the club would be open to new members from the present First year in the Autumn term of 1978 and present members were assisting the metal work club to build a competition Kart.

At the Prize Giving on Tuesday the 14th November 1978. 20 pupils spoke briefly on a range of subjects covering School activities varying from Sports to the School Council and the Library to the Karting Club. Mr. Leigh reports commented on the nemesis from the Grammar School and look forward to the way ahead. He said that teachers, parents, employers and members of the community had a duty to educate themselves and to look at the implications both good and bad of Sixth Form Colleges, 12-16 Schools and Middle Schools. He said that they must try to avoid a situation in 5 years time in which it could be said that the quality of education in the Schools was not as high as it was 5 years ago, and it was not as high as elsewhere in the area.[14] The Mayor Mr. George Scott made a humorous speech saying he was an ex Grammar School reject and that his father had been prepared to pay for him. He said that now that he had been invited back by the School to speak at prize day he wondered if everyone had made mistakes.

In terms of excursions that had taken place at the end of the previous summer holidays, ten members of the School including Mr. Loftin, Miss Lindsey, Miss Townsen joined other campers from the Greenacre and Gorleston Grammar Schools at the tiny settlement of Cefn Coch, in central Wales. Richard Green of the Sixth form reported that walking, sailing and pony trekking had left the team exhausted, wet and sore respectively. They had also visited Aberystwyth where he comments that Yarmouth knocked spots off its beach. Later on the same day the team had been most impressed by the magnificent falls at Devil's Bridge. Evening pastimes, had included the "pleasure" of the vocal strains from the boys trio from Birmingham, Football, Badminton, Orienteering and Archery. Richard Green commented that they would like to repeat the holiday if the staff could put up with them as it might give them a further chance to meet Miss Lindsey again.

During the autumn and spring terms of 1978-79 the Schools Football Teams, the under 16 First X1, had quite a good season consisting of friendlies, and Watney Mann and Yarmouth cup games. The team lost in the semi finals of the Watney Mann cup to the Hewett School of Norwich by 2 goals to 1 and shared the Yarmouth cup with Oriel Grammar after drawing 3-3.

The First X1 itself played 6 matches, won 3 and lost 3. M. Moss, G. Brown and R. Brown played for the county under 19 B team. The under 13 team also performed successfully.

---

[14] *Ibid.* p.13

The Christmas Concert took place on the 19th December 1978 and consisted of a sequence of Christmas music by pupils and staff which resulted, reported Alison Mobbs of the Sixth Form, in a varied and enjoyable programme. There were a series of carols, old and new, duets by Jacquie Farmer and Mark Donahue, and readings by Lucy Myatt, Nicholas Ball and Simon Hall. The brass ensemble had played their own arrangement of two numbers, and there had been polished performances from the School Orchestra, including a stirring rendition of the *Radetsky March*. Alison reported that the evening was a very happy Christmassy occasion and was much appreciated by a rather thin audience.[15]

The grim words of the editorial in this Chronicle recorded the acceptance by the Minister of Norfolk County Council's plan for comprehensive education in Yarmouth's Secondary Schools, bringing to an end of almost 20 years of speculation, discussion and protest the latter being led to the last by Grammar School Foundation Governors carrying out their duty such as Mr. Jack Boon. In 1982 the School would become a comprehensive High School for all Yarmouth children between 12 and 16 sweeping away its traditions of a Grammar School which had been in operation for 430 years. A Sixth Form College in Gorleston would cater for the A level study years.

In 1979 an Old Boy of the School Peter Woods gained his PhD and thereby became the third of three Grammar School brothers to achieve this honour. The brothers' years at the School are given below their pictures.

114. John Woods
1937-1943

115. Alan Woods
1940 -1947

116. Peter Woods
1946 -1952

John Woods
(1926- 1993)
1946 BSc Honours Physics (Queen Mary's College, London)
1950 PhD
1950-59 GEC (General Electric Company) Research Laboratories
1960 Department of Applied Physics, Durham University
1985 Dean of Science
1987 Professor of Applied Physics
1989 Emeritus Professor

Alan Woods
(1929-
1952 BSc Honours Mathematics (University of Manchester)
1955 PhD Mathematics (University of Manchester)
1955-57 Assistant Lecturer, Department of Mathematics, University of Manchester
1957-63 Associate Professor of Mathematics, Tulane University, New Orleans
1964-95 Professor of Mathematics, The Ohio State University
1995 Emeritus Professor

Peter Woods
(1934-
1958 BA Honours History, University College, London
1970 MSc (Ed) University of Bradford
1979 PhD (Open University)
1958-71 Teaching, mainly in grammar schools in Yorkshire
1972 Lecturer in Educational Studies, The Open University
1987 Professor in Education
1998-2005 Research Professor in Education, The University of Plymouth
2004 Emeritus Professor (Open University)

---

[15] *Chronicle*, July 1979, pp.8-9

This collective achievement marked the ability of Grammar School pupils to use their talents taught at School to gain success.

The School had opened in September 1979 with 681 pupils with a Sixth form of 107 members and significantly more girls (357) in the School than boys (324). The remorseless pace of change had already begun with alterations and extensions to the School buildings to enable them to cater for the 900 plus pupils who would arrive in a changed School. A greatly enlarged Library and new arts facilities would be two of many proposed changes.

A significant staff change took place with the retirement of I.E. "Bill" Chapman who had come to the School in 1958 to teach woodwork and technical drawing as O and A level subjects. At that time these subjects tended to be regarded as second choices by the less academically able students.

Technical Drawing was in fact only offered to those who were unable to progress in French studies. Facilities at that time were limited with a workshop only half the size of the Sixth Form Centre at that time. Although extensions were added, Technical Drawing lessons often took place on Library tables, and it was not until 1970 that Mr. Chapman could enjoy the more improved facilities. Bill Chapman had been at the School for 22 years and during that time excellent work had come from his workshops and high standards at O and A levels had been maintained. In addition his team provided assistance with stage sets and craft shops. His easy sense of humour probably puzzled French Assistantes at their first encounter, for he liked to practice his French learned in wartime days with the RAF in Canada. However the French Assistantes soon learnt to cope with his Canadian French to be able to pass the salt at table. Bill Chapman gave much time and energy coaching and umpiring the school Cricket First X1. His tact and humour had been essential to the task of supervising School dinners as well as being House Master at Centre for the previous 8 years. One of the high points of his time at the Grammar School was being one of the Leaders of the Moscow trip with the School party in 1961. He would be retiring to his home in Carlton Colville, where the large garden and bantam breeding would occupy a great deal of his time.

The Sixth Form General Studies programme had included a series of visits to the Cathedral and Museums in Norwich, the Sainsbury Centre at the University of East Anglia, the Yarmouth Power Station, the Toll House and Elizabethan House in Yarmouth. A series of outside speakers had talked to the Sixth form including representatives of the three main political parties, Sergeant Millican of the Police, who talked on violence, and Mr. Deakin of the community health service who gave presentation on drugs. In addition there were debates, films and lectures involving Mr. Loftin, Mr. Exell and Mr. Farmer.

The Chronicle recorded with regret the death in May, a few days short of his 97th birthday, of Mr. A.W. Rouse, who taught Music and Mathematics at the Grammar School from 1912 to the outbreak of was in 1939 when he became an RAF recruiting officer. Mr. Rouse's son Aldwyn Rouse had a very successful School career was Victor Ludorum and had a short spectacular and tragic career with the RAF when he died in a low level raid on the German headquarters in the Hague.

The Dramatic Society staged a double bill of one act plays on the 20th and 21st March 1980. This double bill attracted an audience of around 500. The *Dumb Waiter* by Harold Pinter was directed by Miss Rickwood and Malvin Peachy but Pinter's pauses were not appreciated by the young people in the audience. The sinister Ben and the bumbling Gus seemed to be involved in preparations for a professional hit job until Gus realised that he was the intended victim. The other half of the double bill was an Alan Ayckbourn one act called *Ernie's Incredible Illuminations*, in which Ernie's imaginary Walter Mitty like ego boasting causes him to act in frustrating Gestapo, becoming a fairground prize fighting challenger and being involved in international espionage in a public library. A large supporting cast was a background to Ernie's fantasies, and Victor Stowers in reviewing appreciated the use of the large resources in the two plays.

In the sports reports in *The Chronicle*, it was reported that the weekly meeting of the Gymnastics Club, held during the winter had resulted in the standard improving dramatically. It was noted that Gary Butler and Jason Statham had obtained Grade 1 B.A.G.A. standard.

The under 16 Netball Squad had had a very successful season. They were runners up to the old enemy "Oriel Grammar School" in the East Norfolk Schools' Tournament, which enabled them to progress to the next round in Norwich where they would reach the semi finals losing to Notre Dame. They won all their matches in their league and in the Yarmouth Schools Tournament losing only to Oriel Grammar in each. Joanne Seago and Julie Harris had been selected for the under 16 county squad with Joanne gaining her county colours.

The football teams in 1979-80 had a very successful season, the under 14 XI won 3 trophies in the local league by winning all their 8 matches, the local cup where they beat Gorleston 9-5, and the local six-a-side competition where they defeated St. Edmunds in the final. In the Norfolk six-a-side competition the under 14 XI came third after beating the eventual winners in an earlier match.

The under 15 XI had a season in which they only played friendly matches, but they won them all, and entered for the cup having a good run beating Oriel and Stalham (in a replay) before losing eventually to Dereham.

The under 12 XI started well with 3 wins, then drew twice equalizing in the last second against Oriel. The team beat Styles 18-0 in the cup but lost to Oriel in the semi final with the last 3 games against West Flegg, Alderman Leach, and Caister resulting in defeat.

117. Great Yarmouth Grammar School Football Under 14 XI

118. Great Yarmouth Grammar School Football Under 15 XI

The English Department's activities had included entering a team (Alison Mobbs, Linda-Jayne Dyble and Susan Tranfield), who spoke at a Public Speaking Competition at Gorleston Library. During the Christmas holidays Five Sixth formers had attended a Literature course at Manchester University and the *Albatross Literary Magazine* reappeared at the end of the spring term mainly through the efforts of Angela Rogers assisted by fellow First Year Sixth formers. Verse from Malvin Peachy and Teresa Wiltshire of the Sixth form and Jason Statham of the Second form was included amongst cartoons, humorous articles, a pop record review and a musical crossword. The publication sold well which would encourage further editions.

Normally *The Chronicle* information for 1981 would appear in the succeeding chapter which dealt with the 1980's. However, this year marked the end of the Grammar School which had been established 430 years ago in 1551 and which saw a successor School, The Great Yarmouth High School established itself to operate in the former Grammar School premises.

The transition obviously brought about many changes and upheavals with staff retiring, moving to the new Sixth Form College or opting to stay in the new Great Yarmouth High School. One of those who saw this year as an end of an era was Walter Hogg who retired at the end of the academic year which marked the ending of Great Yarmouth Grammar School. His comments from a view point of serving at the School since 1947 are very pertinent to the situation and I reproduce them in full.

> *"The last term of the school founded 430 years ago is an occasion provoking*
> *reflection. Egalitarians will regard its replacement by a comprehensive High School*
> *offering open access to higher education for all as the logical conclusion of a slow*

process of increased opportunity in English society. Elitists will, with equally strong feelings, lament the passing of a school where the best brains in the area could develop in an academic atmosphere.

The die has, however, now been cast, and we, who have shared in the Grammar School tradition, cannot let it pass away in Great Yarmouth without acknowledging the contribution it has made to the life of the town, particularly over the last 100 years. Not only has it sent our first class minds into the commercial world and the professions – many professors, two bishops and at least one General spring to mind – but the memorial tablet to those lost in the two world wars of this century tell their own story. The very heavy losses in the Second World War, high proportion being aircrew, reflect the quality of those who died.

Many generations of Yarmouthians were proud to have attended the Grammar School. Our hope must be that the new Yarmouth High School, on the same site, and with a high proportion of the same staff will begin an equally worthy tradition and gain similar loyalty".

Walter Hogg, History School Master, Great Yarmouth Grammar School, 1947-1981.

The Chronicle carries two valedictory reports on long serving School Masters, who had decided that they would end their teaching career with the end of the Grammar School. One of these was obviously Walter Hogg who had a University career at Durham, interrupted by five years wartime service with the RAF, with his appointment at the Grammar School in 1947 as History Master being his only teaching appointment. Both the School and Town had benefited not only by his incisive mind and skilled teaching of History, but also from his abilities as a fine cricketer and football player, when he coached School teams in both sports for well over 20 years. He worked closely with both the parents association and the old students association and spent morning breaks for many years in supervising the School tuck shop. He managed the business side of School productions and as South House Master, Head of year and a bass in the School choir, he had also given fine service. His personality and qualities ensured that his opinions commanded the attention and respect of his colleagues. The valedictory concluded by the comments that their would be few teachers of his quality prepared to throw in their lot with a School for so long, but certainly the Great Yarmouth Grammar School would have been a much poorer place without such sustained service.

The second valedictory records the death of Mr. John Morrow who died in December 1980 in Hornsea where he had been born 83 years before. John Morrow taught Latin at the School from 1945 to 1961 and for several years afterward part time. He served in the infantry throughout the First World War, and on demobilization graduated at London University. He had taught at a private school in Essex for many years prior to moving to Great Yarmouth Grammar School to restart Latin after its wartime lapse.

Mr. Morrow's love of drama and English Literature led him to produce several plays during his last decade of teaching, including one he had written himself. He was a bachelor who frequently said, he had not married because he could not as a younger man afford to do so. He was a staunch friend, to many pupils including myself and to members of staff. His funeral service was held in the parish church at Hornsea, where he had been a choir boy. He lived with his brother in retirement and I remember visiting him after his retirement in Hornsea and being touched at how pleased he was to see me.

The School Commemoration Service and Prize Giving was held on the 23rd September 1980. The address was given by the Bishop of Norwich, the Rt. Revd. Maurice Wood who emphasised the individuality of each student "from the highest of prefects to the smallest of first formers". He urged that the School should use his own recipe for inspiration "for the past, thank you, for the future, yes". The Chairman of the School Governors Mrs. Marjorie White welcomed the congregation and spoke of her hope of the future School would continue the traditions of the old. The Remembrance Day Service was held on Friday the 7th November 1980, when Old Boys killed in both World Wars were remembered in a short Service before School began. The Service was conducted by the Vicar of Great Yarmouth, wreaths were placed on the memorial tablets in the hall and the names of those who died were read by the Deputy Headmaster, Bill Howell.

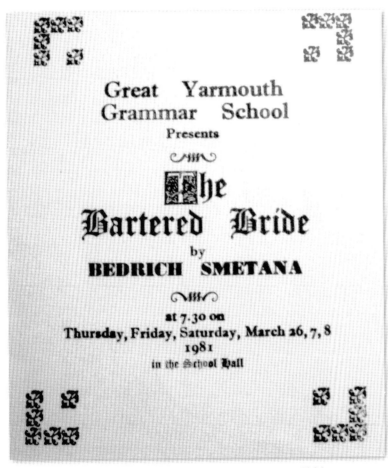

John Farmer excelled himself by producing the *Bartered Bride* by Smetana from the 26th to the 28th March 1981. Production had new lighting and the happy holiday mood of the opening scene was never dissipated. Set against the accompaniment of a well drilled chorus, who sang some sweet Slavonic melody, the principals accepted considerable challenge. They did not fall short and Mark Donahue, Jacqui Farmer, Jonathan Walsh, Pru Allington-Smith, Robin Tebbutt, David Felmingham and Susan Tranfield carried the production. Mr. Pereira, who first appeared in School productions some 45 years previously, would never have put in a more valuable performance. The chorus of 35 and the orchestra led by Peter Smith and conducted by John Farmer was well drilled and the back stage assistants were most effective. This was the last stage production by Great Yarmouth Grammar School, and the reviewer reflected on the many plays, operas and operettas performed during its history.

119. The Bartered Bride directed by John Farmer 1981

On Tuesday March 31st 1981 over 70 past pupils and staff met at the Imperial for the Old Student's Association Final Dinner. The guest speaker was Mr. David Harrup who had attended the School in the 1960s. Guests of honour were the Headmaster, Head Boy and Deputy Head Girl. An Annual General Meeting held at the Grammar School two weeks earlier had decided to wind up the Association because of the impending changes and the nature of the School. At a meeting later in the day, the Trustees of the Association decided to utilise the remaining society funds to assist with annual re-union dinners. Since that time I, David Rich as Dinner Secretary and firstly David Harrup and then after he died David Cooke, have been the Committee to organise the Great Yarmouth Grammar School Diners Club, for former Grammar School pupils. Thus the tradition of the Grammar School lives on annually when Old Students from the 1930s to 1981 meet together to maintain the traditions of the School.

Chapter 9
A New School and Sporting Achievements

The end of the Grammar School era and the commencement of a new School in the shape of the Great Yarmouth High School in the same premises on Salisbury Road, bought many challenges for Headmaster Mikel Leigh and his staff. Mike Leigh had been appointed as Headmaster to see the School through this sea change of the School's new age coverage of pupils and academic requirements to the age of 16. A new Sixth Form College, the East Norfolk Sixth Form College had been established in Gorleston in the former Alderman Leach Secondary School premises. Thus Sixth Form provision at the former Grammar School, now Great Yarmouth High, and the former girls High School now known as Lynn Grove High ceased. Any pupil leaving the Secondary Schools between the ages of 16 and 19 and wishing to pursue Further Education within the Town had the opportunity of applying to the East Norfolk Sixth Form College for A level study or the Great Yarmouth College of Further Education for A level study or Vocational Courses.

The School pupil numbers at Salisbury Road had expanded considerably in size between July 1981 and the September term when the new High School came into being. It was unfortunate that during the period of the 1980s when all efforts were being made to establish the new High School detailed records of dates and events are almost totally lacking as compared with the Grammar School era. Therefore until the establishment of first an internal magazine called *Inside Angle* in 1990 and then the new School magazine called the *High Standard* in 1994 my only dated records are such photographs as I have managed to glean from the School records of the period, coupled with a detailed Prospectus of the new High School prepared by Mike Leigh the new Headmaster. I do have a number of photographs of sporting achievements gained by the pupils during the 1980's across the new age range from 11 to 16. One of the characteristics of the make up of the new School was that the increased numbers of both boys and girls led to the ability to create successful sports teams in a variety of sports and to this end the new High School was remarkably successful in this decade.

I have managed to find a number of photographs of the staff who commenced teaching at the new School. When the change took place in 1981 some staff who preferred to teach at Sixth Form level, transferred to form the establishment of the new Sixth Form College. Other members of staff, who were in post as the Grammar School closed in July 1981, remained to serve under Mike Leigh in establishing the new High School. To assist him in establishing the new High School Bill Howell the long serving French and Latin Master became Deputy Headmaster and was placed in charge of Computer Studies and Latin. In addition to reflect the character of the now fully co-educational School Brenda Westley, who had a Bachelor of Science qualification from London University, joined the staff to become Senior Mistress and taught Physics. Mike Leigh's staff complement to teach the new School, included a few part timers dealing with the Greenacre School comprised of 45 members of staff. A new staff structure had been planned to cover the vastly increased number of pupils. There were five year Heads and in addition there were Heads of individual subjects. The old House system of Centre West, South and North Houses survived but became considerably more structured than in the period of lesser numbers in the Grammar School era. Thus the School had a Head Boy and a Head Girl and a Deputy Head Boy and a Deputy Head Girl. Under this structure each House had a House Master and an average of 15 House Tutors who were members of staff. Each House had its own Head Boy and Girl, and also its own House Prefects.

The Great Yarmouth High School changed from being an Independent Foundation School and now came under the control of the Norfolk County Council, as a Voluntary Controlled High School. Until 1983 the former Hospital School premises in the Market Place and the Greenacre School remained as annexes to the new High School. In 1982-3 there were 1142 on the High School roll of whom 150 were housed in the annexes. The County Council issued a document comprising information as to the minimum requirements expected for the High School to operate with regard to its funding control derived from the Norfolk County Council Education Committee.

Head Boy	: Stephen Bradnock.	Head Girl	: Karen Willimott
Deputy Head Boy	: Neil Platt.	Deputy Head Girl	: Joanne Blackwell.

Centre House.

House Master: Mr. T. C. Harrison.

House Tutors: Mr.J.Newman, Mrs.Heyhoe, Mr.D.Kightley, Mr.Pearson, Mrs. Simpson, Mr.E.Cobbold, Mr.D.Smith, Mr.E.Sharman Mr.R.Parry, Mrs. Adamson, Mrs. Nobbs, Miss Jones, Mrs. Symeou, Miss Brown, Mrs. Carr.

Head Boy : P. Ball.

Head Girl : J. Blackwell.

Prefects. : M. Futter, A. Karlson, S. McDonald, N. Platt, A. Rudd, J. Coleman, S. Dunnico, I. Emmerson, A. Hellingsworth, S. Howlett, J. Liddament, R. Martin, C. Palmer, R. Rush, N. Stanley, D. Tong, R. Winterburn, K. Wright.

West House.

House Master: Mr. V. A. Stowers.

House Tutors: Mr.J.Farmer, Mr.P.Baker, Mr.K.Davies, Mr.D.Exell, Mrs. Foster, Mrs. Grice, Miss Goodall, Mr. M. Mitchell, Mr. K. Rutland, Miss Way.

Head Boy : Mark Donaghue.
Head Girl : Jennifer Chinn.

Prefects : Janet Beck, Michael Caldon, Georgina Farrow, Marcus Galey, Nigel Hughes, Patrick Navarro, Antony Tate, Alison Turnbull, Suzanne Ziara.

South House.

House Master: Mr. D. R. Lever.

House Tutors: Mr.K.Brown, Mrs. Little, Mr.J.Laity, Mr.P.Peachey, Mrs. Day, Miss Smith, Mr. Harris, Mr. Maskell, Miss Grant, Mr. Bradnock, Mr. Hutchins, Mr. Patterson, Miss Webb.

Head Boy(Joint) S. Bradnock, G. Saggers.

Head Girl " K. Willimot, J. Seago.

Prefects : Rachael North, Sally-Anne Pegge, Christopher Platten, Debra Riches, Grant Saggers, Carole Sims, Amanda Smith, Jane Smith, Mark Barnet, Charles Blogg, Susan Jones, Rachel Banks, Benedict Barron, Sylvia Lenzen, Rachel Perkins, Andrew Platten, Samantha Skipper, Alison Starkings, Adrian Thompson, Robin Warrington.

North House.

House Master: Mr. E. Loftin.

House Tutors: Mr. J. Blyth, Mr.C.Cheshire, Mr.P.Gilbertson, Mr.B.Haylett, Mrs. Hutchin, Mr.A.McMinn, Mr. G. Oxborough, Miss Roby, Mr. Hacon, Miss Rose, Mrs. Taylor, Miss Jones, Miss Baldwin, Mr. Pack, Mr. Turner.

Head Boy	: Kelvin Burns.	Deputy H.B. : Darren Goodwin.
Head Girl	: Beverley Vos.	Deputy H.G. : Karen Gedge.

Prefects : P. Allen, M. Edwards, B. Mercer, S. Tyrell, R. Blyth, S. Hurren, A. Loveland, J. Shaw, M. Finch, S. Freeman, H. Leech.

(3)

120. New School and House Structure for Great Yarmouth High School 1981[1]

1 NRO., D/ED9/62

There was an attempt to run an internal School Magazine by the students and I have a surviving copy of the *Not the Yarmouth Mercury* No.2 from June 1982 which sold at 5p. It covered some of the topics which the old *Chronicle* covered such as visits but also was strongly orientated to comments by the students on their School life. Perhaps some of the views expressed have been there throughout the life of the School at Salisbury Road and unexpressed perhaps not but here are some. From a Second Form opinion a view that "Corporal punishment should be kept as it definitely puts people off doing bad things. Another Second Form view was that "when giving signatures for poor behaviour teachers should make sure that they give them to the right people". However different views on the area of study can already be seen. This is an extract from a Fourth Form comment "I think we get too many homework subjects in the 4th and 5th years we get 20 minutes for two to five subjects". Another comment was "The only homework that should be done is revision for exams and finishing the odd thing off from lessons, even if this means putting an extra period in the day. Pupils have to do enough work during the day and they should be allowed a lot more freedom after school. I'm sure, if they tried, the teachers could fit the work in somewhere. Isn't doing it at School a better idea?" In the days of the Grammar School homework was meant to extend or reinforce the knowledge gained at School and as such encourage individual study. The views may not be universal but it shows a changing culture. These views come of course from a School in transition where the students of the former Grammar School were working their way up the School to age 16, whereas below them a totally new wider intake of mixed abilities was following.

The magazine also shows the changing attitude of staff to meet pupils' aspirations as in the case of two sponsored discos organised to raise money for the School's own disco equipment. The discos on Friday 19th March and 26th March 1982 were organised in the Small Hall started at 4.00pm after School and went on through the night until 8.00 o'clock the next morning. Teacher Stuart King took the first watch from 4.00pm until midnight and then Headmaster Michael Leigh came in at midnight and relieved him until 4.30am when the participants collapsed and went to bed in sleeping bags with food, the boys in room 3 and the girls in room 4. At eight o' clock the group mainly of second, third and fourth years, were awakened by the Headmaster who brought in tea and coffee.

The photographs show the School's success in a variety of sports County wide.

121. Great Yarmouth High School Badminton 1981-1982

122. *Great Yarmouth High School Gymnasts 1981-1982*

123. *Great Yarmouth High School Tennis County Champions 1984-1985*

124. *Great Yarmouth High School successful Football Teams with Trophies and Trainers 1982-1982*

Rick Atkinson   John Pack ex-Head of PE   Dave Kightley   John Blyth ex-Head of PE

125. *Great Yarmouth High School staff holding trophies for all 4 County competitions won by the School in 1982-1983*

In 1984 Headmaster Michael Leigh retired. He was the last Headmaster link with the Grammar School having seen the School over the transition period. The press cutting records the gift he received from the School.

PRESENTATION AND TRIBUTES TO MIKE LEIGH

★ ALL lined up to say farewell to Mike Leigh.

Head's farewell to High School

★ CONSTANT reminder — Mike Leigh is presented with a picture of the school by Caroline Mercer.

HEAD Mike Leigh might have just retired from Yarmouth High School but he will not be allowed to forget it in a hurry.

For pupils presented him with a painting of the school to remind him of his 12 years there.

Mr Leigh, 47, who has been headmaster 10 years, is taking up a new post as the Norfolk County Co-ordinator for TVEI.

Fifth formers entertained staff, pupils and governors with a short skit at the presentation ceremony last Friday.

Then they presented Mr Leigh with a painting of the school by Sam Chilvers, head of art, from pupils and governors.

Mr Leigh told pupils he would treasure the picture. "It reminds me of 12 of the most fulfilled and happy years of my life at this school — it will be a constant reminder and I will love it.

"In this school there are the most alive and most tremendous pupils, I believe, anywhere in the country.

"I have worked and taught in several parts of this country and abroad and I can honestly say I have never met such a super bunch of people.

"It has been with immense pride that I have been associated with the school and a part of it."

Chairman of the Governors, Mrs Marjorie White, said after the farewell ceremony: "I think he will be very hard to replace.

"We are very sorry he is going, he has been the strength of this school."

Deputy head Mr Gordon Mason said: "I shall miss him he has been a great help here."

126. Headmaster Michael Leigh on his retirement from the Great Yarmouth High School with a gift of a painting of the School

Chapter 10
The High School Gains Momentum

In 1990 the Great Yarmouth High School launched an in house magazine called *Inside Angle*. The last Grammar School *Chronicle* had been in 1981 and there had been no School Magazine since that time.

Since 1988 the Great Yarmouth High School pupils had been involved in trying to improve the environment in town by assisting in a tree planting scheme. In 1989 pupils from Year 11 had assisted the Mayor of that year Derek Maddeys in planting trees on various sites around theTown. The School was ever conscious of the need to improve the environment and over 60 students took part in planting over 200 trees in Cobholm. The students appreciated that they would not see the immediate effects of their endeavours but would in future years hope to see well established trees and copses improving the local environment.

127. The Mayor with Elaine Powell and Sharlene Powels planting trees on the Beaconsfield Playing Field.

Photographs shows students Thomas Parry, Jane Hall and Sean Taylor receiving their award from Mr Michael Edwards the County Education Officer.

128. Students Thomas Parry, Jane Hall and Sean Taylor receiving student awards from Michael Edwards, the County Education Officer.

High School Teacher Mr. K. Deadman with colleague Mr. P. Ashby of the North Denes Middle School were lucky winners in the Great Egg Race which resulted in a visit to Lotus cars at Hethel, near Wymondham.

129. A variety of prize winners with two of the famous Lotus cars.

The School also tried to maintain links with students from other countries.

spent the last twelve months linking up with the students
Nagoya Commercial High School in Japan.

Photograph shows Emma Sherwood seated at the terminal, plus Sarah Norman and Andrea Gibson behind her and (front rig Sarah Hubbard

130. Emma Sherwood, Sarah Norman, Andrea Gibson and Sarah Hubbard had made links with students of Nagoya Commercial High School in Japan.

131. The clarinet quintet of Nina Richards, Gina Adams, Alison Powell, Alix Wright and Michelle Clark with Acker Bilk.

In 1991 Governors, Parents and Friends were invited to the official opening of the new music block. The new Music Suite consisted of two purpose built teaching rooms both equipped with hi-fi systems, pianos and new furniture. One room was fully equipped with key boards for each person and the suite also contained a large practice room which housed 2 computers together with another small practice room. The new Music Suite was established alongside the Drama Studio and provided an excellent Performing Arts area. The Great Yarmouth High School was very pleased to welcome Acker Bilk, the noted jazz clarinettist, to perform the opening ceremony which was performed by a School clarinet quintet of five girls.

Robert Brown had invented a device to prevent illegal parking in the School premises. Robert had produced a design to improve on the barrier system which was then in force, as part of his project study in his GCSE Technology Course. His improved design involved raised plates in the road, powered by compressed air which prevented cars passing, which could be lowered with a pass key. Rotary Club President, Roland Crighton presented Robert with a book on Astronomy and a Certificate for the design device which he had designed and built. Robert commented when he received the award that he was very pleased and although the prototype would be dismantled, the Certificate and Book would be a reminder of his help from the School which had provided all the assistance and material. Robert hoped to go on to the Sixth Form College to gain A levels after which he hoped to join the engineering section of the Navy.

ROTARY AWARD FOR ROBERT

From left: Mr. J. Newman, MR. R. Crighton (Rotary Club), Robert and Mr. K. Deadman Head of CDT

132. In 1992 Great Yarmouth Rotary Club President, Roland Crighton, presented a prize to High School student Robert Brown.

t edition of *Inside Angle*
r academic achievement
ne Graves achieved the
d marks in her GCSE for
evement was recognized
Board who awarded her
ine in coming top in her
,000 students in all other
rivate in the region. She
ptionally well in all her
grades in 9 subjects.

lication in 1993 and the
o issue a new in house
Yarmouth High School,
hronicle of the Grammar
of *The High Standard*
of 1994 as an 8 page

hown alongside a
he Head Teacher.

ial of the High Standard.

Ivan Pegg, headteacher

From The Head's Desk

I am, as always, delighted to be able to contribute to '*High Standard*'. Each issue is full of interesting and varied information which gives a flavour of school beyond just statistics. It is a sad reflection on our education system when we are only concerned with league tables and statistics. Young people are capable and skilled in so many areas of life and it is a pleasure to be able to celebrate their acheivements.

The school has established a growing reputation as a result of acheivements and changes over the last five years. I was proud to read the "work experience" reports from local employers. Our year 11 students had an excellent time at the end at the end of last term and clearly impressed their employers. As a result two companies have embarked on long term projects with us and are looking to sponsor our students through sixth form and university.

We are hosting a major conference on 'SuccessMaker' for all schools in Norfolk and have had visitors from as far away as Kent to look at the system. We are also featured in the 'SuccessMaker' guide published recently and circulated to all schools nationally.

'Positive Discipline' continues to attract attention. Mr. Mitchell has helped North Walsham High introduce it and I am leading workshops to schools in the Technology Trust network at their annual conference in Bradford, having recently addressed the Norfolk Psychological Service annual conference on the same topic.

We do value your support and are encouraged by the progress of our pupils.

Ivan J. Pegg

At this time the Great Yarmouth High School was considering whether it could acquire a Sixth Form to return to the original model so successfully pioneered by its predecessor the Grammar School. However the East Norfolk Sixth Form College was well established had a proven track record and resisted the initiative launched by the Great Yarmouth High School. The Head Teacher Mr. Pegg said if his initiative went ahead he would be happy as it would encourage his pupils to stay on at School. The tentative plan, if the Secretary of State for Education gave consent, would be to start a Sixth Form at the Salisbury Road premises in September 1995 with 90 plus students in a purpose built Sixth Form Block. The photograph shows

The School had decided to prepared its students for a Work Experience Programme so that they could get an insight in year 10 (age 15) of what their world would be like at the

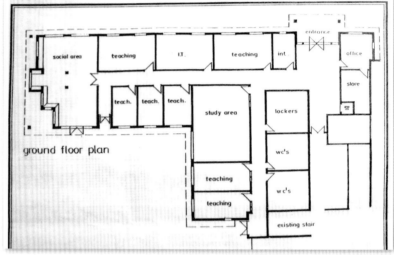

Sixth form education to return to Yarmouth High?

Sixth form education could be returning to the borough in September next year.

Schools in Gorleston and Great Yarmouth are seeking permission from the education secretary to bring back the sixth form for the first time in 12 years.

At present the grant-maintained schools only cater for pupils aged 12 and 16. When pupils reach 16, they face travelling miles to another college or leaving school to get a job.

The headteacher, Ivan Pegg, says, 'If it goes ahead I would be very happy. Pupils should be allowed more choice. It would encourage our pupils to stay on at school.'

At present none of the schools in the Great Yarmouth borough has a sixth-form.

If the system is put into action and is given the go-ahead by Christmas, the sixth-form could start in September 1995 with 90-plus students.

This should total to around 140 extras within two years. Sixth-form education at schools gives pupils and teachers an extra option, and that must be applauded, and may be able to offer much that is available at present at the East Norfolk Sixth Form College or at The Great Yarmouth College of Further Education or at colleges in Norwich.

135. A copy of the ground floor plan of the building which would accommodate a Sixth Form at Salisbury Road.

commencement of employment. James Nganga the School's Finance Officer, who had experience of a senior accounting role in a Great Yarmouth firm before joining the School, took a leading part in preparing students for work experience.

136. James Nganga interviewing a student.

Where are they now?

We look at the careers of past students of the Great Yarmouth High School

"I have good memories of my time at Great Yarmouth Grammar School, certainly the time I was in the sixth form. This is probably because the year I joined the sixth form was also the first year girls were allowed in the school!"

Nigel left the school with three A levels in English, history and geography and then went to Queen Mary College, University of London. There he studied for a BA (Hons) degree in geography, was president of the University Geographical Society, and left with an honours degree.

TRADE MAGAZINES

"When I left university, I decided that I wanted to go into publishing. I managed to get a job as an advertisement manager in a small publishing company in Wardor Street, Soho!

No, it wasn't that kind of publishing company; it produced trade magazines for the property market!". Hating selling, but having learnt a great deal about magazine production, Nigel left to join Associated Newspapers and became involved in Weekend magazine, the Daily Mail Motor Show Review and

> Nigel Fryatt, executive editor of Mini World, Cars and Car Conversions, Off Road and 4 Wheel Drive and Land Rover World.

Motor Show Review. This eventually led to the sub-editorship of Autocar magazine.

"I spent seven years at Autocar rising to the position of assistant news and sports editor. I gained a great deal of experience and drove a lot of exciting new cars!"

APPOINTED EDITOR

This experience and know how gained at

Autocar eventually led Nigel to become the editor of Link House Magazine's flagship publication, Cars and Car Conversions.

This is a major monthly publication with a very large annual turnover."

This magazine offered a great many opportunities and I am now the proud owner of a Caterham Seven sports racing car which I drive at a number of motor sporting events.

Link House is also responsible for publishing Miniworld, which is the magazine for the mini enthusiast."

(Editor: I have a Mini John Cooper Special and I think the magazine is brilliant).

I am very proud to say that Mini World was launched due to my initial instigation. After a meeting with a colleague from the advertising department, I presented the idea to the management and the rest, as they say, is history!"

CHALLENGES AHEAD

The big 40 is now looming for Nigel, and new challenges are beckoning. We thank him for all his help with this article and wish him all the best with his career, and say a special hello to Sue and cats J and H.

Nigel Fryatt.

137. The article shows; his success in becoming Executive Editor of Mini World, Cars and Car Conversation, Off Road and Four Wheel Drive and Land Rover World.

The High Standard also ran a series of articles on "Where are they now" in terms of former pupils. The 1994 edition of *The Standard* carries an article on the career of Nigel Fryatt a former Grammar School Pupil at Salisbury Road who joined the Sixth Form in 1981 which was the beginnings of the Co-Educational School.

138. His enthusiasm for driving is set out in the article and also shows in the picture where he drives his own Caterham 7.

The Great Yarmouth High School had expanded its range of sports in which pupils could participate.

By 1995 *The High Standard* had moved to 2 issues in an Academic Year in the Spring and Summer. The featured article in the Spring 1995 issue was the establishment of a Memorial Fund in memory of former Grammar School pupil and world famous Choreographer Sir Kenneth MacMillan. An appeal had been launched to raise £5000 in February 1995 in Great Yarmouth where Sir Kenneth trained as a boy. He had died from a heart attack back stage at Covent Garden in 1992 at the age of 62. The appeal had already raised £6,000 and Sir Kenneth's widow Lady MacMillan unveiled plaques at both St George's Theatre and the Great Yarmouth High School and commented on the value of the grant to enable talented dancers to be assisted with tuition fees. The plaque unveiled by Lady MacMillan who was an accomplished painter, at the Great Yarmouth High School, records Sir Kenneth's career at the Grammar School until he won a scholarship to Sadlers Wells Ballet School.

139. Liam Stanley's success in winning Gold in the finals of the British Judo National Championship in Oxford.

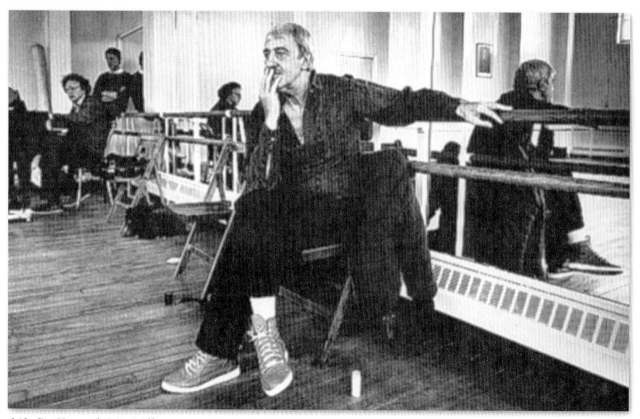

140. Sir Kenneth MacMillan.

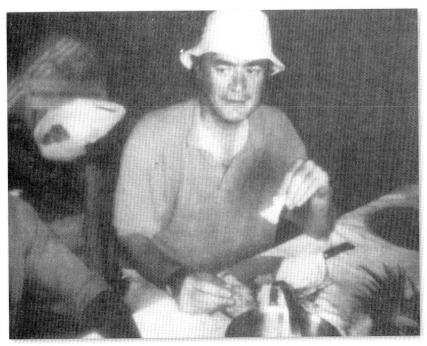

The other major article in this issue of *The High Standard* recorded a tribute to the former Yarmouth and then world famous campaigner on Green Issues Andrew Lees, son of Ted Lees the well known Yarmouth Hotelier and Rotarian. Andrew died tragically in the jungle of Madagascar and the Editor of *The Standard*, Brian Smith, who knew him well, recorded his achievements. I also knew Andrew well when I was running the Port, and though our view points were diametrically opposed I regarded him as a doughty opponent and our personal relationship was cordial.

141. *Andrew Lees in Madagascar before his tragic accident.*

The High Standard in the Summer of 1995 recorded the visit of the then Secretary of State for Education, the Rt. Hon. Gillian (now Lady) Shepherd to support a week in Great Yarmouth focusing on reading and story. The Great Yarmouth High School was involved in the project.

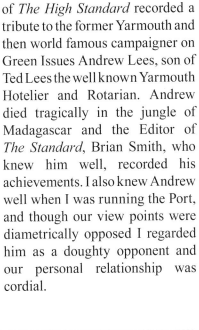

142. *The Secretary of State with Ivan Pegg Headmaster of the Great Yarmouth High School in background.*

143. *Ivan Pegg, the Minister and Michael Carttiss M.P. for Great Yarmouth during the book launch week.*

*144. Pupils from Great Yarmouth High School amongst the crew of the Excelsior
in the rigging of the ship as it enters Bremerhaven at the conclusion of the race.*

The High Standard then switched to an Autumn and Spring publication during each Academic Year. In Autumn 1995 a story recorded which recorded the participation of pupils from Great Yarmouth High School taking part on the *Excelsior* Sail Training Ship from Lowestoft in an International Tall Ships race from Leith in Scotland to Bremerhaven in North Germany.

*145. The girls of the Great Yarmouth High School also had considerable success in their
Netball matches. The picture shows the under 16 netball team with their Teacher Mrs. Gaze.*

In the Spring of 1996 a unique reunion took place with two of Ivan Pegg's predecessors as Heads of the Great Yarmouth Grammar School present at the Annual Prize Giving. Peter Marsden, the former Headmaster of the Great Yarmouth Grammar School, and Mike Leigh, Mr Marsden's successor and Head of the Great Yarmouth Grammar School in its time of major change and currently Principal of Southlands College, attended the evening. Mike Leigh presented the prizes and spoke warmly of his memories of the School. John Stephens, later Head boy and now Master of the Music and Organist of St. Nicholas Church, played the organ.

146. The three Heads of the School, Ivan Pegg, the present Head Teacher, Peter Marsden, the former Headmaster of the Great Yarmouth Boys Grammar School and Mike Leigh, Mr. Marsden's successor and the Head of the Grammar School in its time of major change.

147. Clive Needle Euro MP, Penny Patterson, High School Teacher and Maggie Wheeler.

The School had installed a new "success" maker Computer Suite which was a Computer Based Learning System which allowed pupils to make rapid progress particularly in Mathematics and English.

The Great Yarmouth High School was keen to let its younger pupils experience developments in other countries which would give them a broader vision of the world outside Great Yarmouth. In July 1996 30 pupils from years 8 and 9 went on a five day coach trip to the Futuroscope development near Poitiers in France. The return coach trip came through Paris and the Great Yarmouth contingent joined a long queue for their turn for the lift to the top of the Eiffel Tower for a breathtaking view of the city.

148. The Great Yarmouth High School group at the foot of the Eiffel Tower before ascending to the top.

A previous issue of *The High Standard* recorded former Great Yarmouth High School pupil Liam Stanley who wished to enter the Navy as an Engineer. The picture in 1997-98 shows him in his white tropics uniform after he had successfully completed his Royal Navy training and had been chosen to form part of the guard at his passing out parade at *HMS Raleigh*. He was then training to be a marine engineer mechanic artificer at *HMS Sultan*. His football prowess while at Great Yarmouth, where he was a founder member of the Yarmouth Boys team and also played for the Great Yarmouth Town Reserves before leaving to join the Navy, had stood him in good stead in his forces career. He had just been made Captain of the Football Team which had recently won the prestigious interforces Devril Games and his Navy Team had been successful against teams from both the Army and Air Force.

149. Liam Stanley in his white tropics uniform.

The School continued to produce successful athletes of all ages. Daniel Self of year 8 received the Foreman Trophy for being the most outstanding athlete in the Great Yarmouth area in 1998. Not only was he a class sprinter but his basic speed assisted him to produce a long jump distance of 5.62 meters which was an outstanding leap for a 13 year old. The Foreman Trophy was presented by the Newsagents' Federation and the competition had been organised by Ralph Childs for the past 18 years.

150. Daniel Self being presented with the Foreman Trophy.

The summer of 1998 recorded a remarkable chapter in the development of Great Yarmouth High School in its success in achieving recognised Government Status as a Technology College. In return for specialising in Mathematics, Science and Technology, the School would receive nearly half a million pounds in the subsequent 3 years. The Government had supported Technology Colleges as part of their strategy to drive up standards and the School would be required to meet regular targets and to demonstrate widespread use of Information Technology.

151. Headmaster Ivan Pegg with his colleagues celebrating.

John Clare spoke of the many fine memories he had of the Grammar School and of his Teachers. The Head Boy in 1996-97, John Stephens, presented John Clare with a picture of the Yarmouth Herring Fair in 1850, to mark the visit of a distinguished Old Boy at the Prize Giving.

Great Yarmouth High School was subject, as were all schools under Local Authority Control, to an Ofsted Inspection. The Inspection took place in the week which began 28th September 1997 and involved 12 Inspectors from the Norfolk County Council spending a week at the School. They had visited over 130 lessons, had attended tutor group time, assemblies, break time and lunch hours prior to completing their Report. They had talked to pupils and looked at their work and met with Governors and Parents. The Preliminary Report confirmed that the School had made progress over the last 4 years and recognized the hard work and effort that had been undertaken by Staff and Pupils.

152. At the Annual Prize Giving in 1996-97, John Clare, Head Boy of the Great Yarmouth Grammar School in 1968, and afterwards Managing Director of Dixons, the electrical retailers, presented the prizes.

153. Ivan Pegg, Head Teacher with Students and the Ofstead Report

At the beginning of June 1998 Head Teacher Ivan Pegg had an opportunity to meet the Prime Minister at Downing Street to celebrate the Great Yarmouth High School's achievements in the "Success in Schools and Colleges Programmes".

154. Prime Minister Tony Blair with Head Teacher Ivan Pegg at Downing Street.

155. Philip Scott with Marjorie White Chairman of the Great Yarmouth High School Governors.

Prize Day for 1998 gave the School an opportunity to reward many students for their hard work throughout the year both in their GCSE exam results and for normal class work. All the information for Prize Day was co-ordinated by Mrs. Gill Croft the School Secretary and the office staff. The arrangements involved sending out Letters of Invitation to the School Prize Winners and their families and guests in the wider community. The rehearsal for Prize Day took place to insure that all Prize Winners were sitting in the same order as the School had organized the prizes. The organisation was in the capable hands of Mr. Eddie Loftin. Head Teacher Ivan Pegg organised the Guest Speaker, Mr. Philip Scott, then the General Manager of Life and Pensions at Norwich Union and a former pupil of the Grammar School. Philip Scott is now a colleague of mine as an East Norfolk Sixth Form Governor and has recently retired as Finance Director of Aviva the successor company to Norwich Union.

The School of over one thousand students needed an efficient administration to enable it to function smoothly. An article in the Summer edition of the *High Standard* features three of the key members of the Administration Staff. Tracy Smith had worked for an offshore company and was responsible for inputting the timetable and records of achievements into the main computer. She also provided the information on the computer for the new students who commenced School in September. Jayne Willgress had been School Receptionist since 1996 having also worked previously for the Offshore Industry. Gill Croft came from an Education Office background, and had transferred to the new Great Yarmouth High School in 1982 as School Secretary, in which job she continues today.

156. The three administrators with Gill Croft centre.

The Millennium Edition of the *High Standard* in 1999-2000 featured two long serving members of the Finance Staff both of whom remain with the Great Yarmouth High School today. The article covering their career history's is shown below at the time when Eddie Loftin was Deputy Head of the School and James Nganga was the Finance and Administrative Officer.

Most students, and parents I suspect, think teachers come from some sort of privileged background.

This is not so; most, particularly the older ones, come from working class, council house backgrounds.

I came from a large poor family. (only in terms of money!) In the photograph, taken at Gorleston, I'm the well dressed one. Incidentally the reason my father is missing from the lineup is that he was in hospital at the time. Looking at the photograph again I only hope they allowed him to recover fully before they sent him home.

Ever since that time I've been very careful with money; not mean! Being careful with money and being mean with money are not the same.

Where ever I've been I've always ended being put in charge of money. Note; put in charge, I never volunteer.

I attended local schools, leaving what was then the Technical High School to study for a degree in Mathematics and Physics at Hull University; followed by a Post Graduate Certificate in Education.

My first teaching post was at Great Yarmouth Grammar School for Boys in 1964 teaching physics at "A" & GCE level! Great Yarmouth High VA School as it is known now. That is a long time in one school. Incidently despite poor health at times I've had less than ten days off in all that time!

I changed to teaching Mathematics, a shortage of teachers in Mathematics meaning there were more opportunities for promotion. I became Head of Mathematics in 1970 and a Deputy Head in 1982.

One of the things I find most frustrating in teaching is seeing students with talent wasting it; I know the vast majority will regret it later.

The last ten years in Education have seen tremendous changes, no more so than in the way schools are financed. The finance team have coped with all the changes and the school has always had a sound financial base. The organization of the school centres around

the Phoenix School Administration System. This was introduced six years when the school went Grant Maintained. All examination entries and results are posted using this system and the Internet. The system is now going to be used as the standard system for all of Norfolk so I feel my decision is fully justified. Norfolk have finally caught up with us.

In my leisure time, I don't seem to have much, I am the match secretary at Gorleston Lawn Tennis Club and play for them in the Lowestoft and Norwich Leagues. I rely on making my opponents play badly rather than playing well myself. I always enjoy the games even if my opponents don't!

For holidays I either go to Eastern Europe or stay with my daughter in France. I have a French grand daughter and at the moment I am struggling to learn French. All language students in the school have my sympathy; I'm too used to being able to use logic rather than rote learning; I'll keep at it though.

Eddie Loftin - Deputy Head

Ed's note:
Just in, is the news that Mr Loftin has been made Honorary Life member of the Norfolk Lawn Tennis Association

My career history is confined to oilfield based corporations where I spent some twenty four years of my past working life. Post training under the Institute of Company and Commercial Accountants, in 1970 I was appointed as Area Accountant by Decca Navigation at their Hydrographic Survey division, then situated in Main Cross Road Great Yarmouth. At the height of the North Sea oil boom, between 1970 and 1975, the Company was bought out by Racal Electronics PLC . The new Company must have liked the way I was doing something as they promoted me to the position of the Senior Financial Accountant responsible for finances in the UK, Holland and Norwegian Divisions. I left Racal at the end of 1986 because I was unable to relocate to Aberdeen as my son was then at a boarding school in Berkshire. I have very fond memories of Racal where apart from many friends I made there I feel a great sense of satisfaction in having

gained and contributed at lot over the seventeen years I was with the Company.

As a matter of interest, not many people know that Jayne Willgress, our receptionist, and I worked for Racal when she was a Miss (single). She was not my secretary! So much about Racal.

I joined another International Company immediately after Racal as a Group Financial Controller for some seven years, and again gained a lot of knowledge about International finances and trading as the Company had subsidiaries overseas under my financial control. By April 1994 I had really had enough of the oilfield companies as the industry remained depressed since 1986 and the 'hand to mouth' operating scenario of finances by companies in that industry became consistently stressful. I wanted to become self employed and operate as an Accountant and in parallel teach tennis at GM schools. I had

considered the considerable drop in salary and concluded that it did not matter. I sent a letter and CV to three local GM schools one of which was Gt Yarmouth High School - the rest as they say is history! I was appointed slap bang at the end of the school's first financial year end as a GM school - What an experience!! I have spent five very happy years at Gt Yarmouth High School and I particularly like the friendly caring atmosphere all round.

My main interest/hobby is simply Lawn Tennis for which I am qualified to teach and to which most of my out of work time is devoted. This always comes second to a regular get together in the woods with my best friend, Fritz, the dog! I also enjoy music generally, especially acoustic guitar music.

JAMES NGANGA
Finance & Administrative Officer

157. Eddie Loftin and James Nganga with their career history's.

In the summer of 2000 Ivan Pegg the Head Teacher moved to West Yorkshire to become Director of an Education Action Zone where he would have responsibility of raising standards in 19 schools in the area. Mr. Pegg had been Head Teacher at Great Yarmouth High School for twelve and a half years and was succeeded by the Deputy Head Teacher David Brunton who had taught at the school for 7 years. David said that as the School celebrated its 450th Anniversary he intended to build on its tradition and successes.

158. David Brunton in the refurbished Junior Entrance to the School.

Walter Hogg (1921-1999), School Master at Great Yarmouth Grammar School from 1947-1981 had died just before the Millennium.

Mr. WALTER HOGG 1921-1999
Teacher at Great Yarmouth Grammar School 1947-81

Walter Hogg, who taught History at Great Yarmouth Grammar School from 1947 to 1981, died on December 12th 1999 aged 78. Born in 1921 in West Hartlepool he entered Durham University in 1939 and was awarded an M.A. in History in 1947, after serving in the RAF during World War II.

Mr. Hogg, who for much of his time in school was Head of History and Head of South House, was also an accomplished footballer and cricketer. He spent many hours coaching, refereeing and umpiring school XIs, while also himself being a resolute batsman and bowler for many years with the Old Yarmouthian Cricket Club. In his final year of teaching he supervised the collection and transfer of the Grammar School Archive to the County Record Office.

Mr. Hogg died in Bury St. Edmunds after a long illness. His wife, Jean, died in September 1993. He leaves 2 daughters, Emily and Sally, and 6 grandchildren.

Walter will be warmly remembered by his many students, friends and former colleagues for his keen intellect, his dry sense of humour and his forthright, no-nonsense manner. He will also be fondly remembered

159. Mr. Peachey had produced an obituary for Walter which is recorded in the article above.

Chapter 11
After the Millennium

Head Master Peter Marsden who served the School in that capacity for 16 years died in the Millennium Year. The service was held at Hemsby Parish Church and was attended by many friends and Old Boys. His obituary is recorded in the article.

In November 2000 a spectacular event took place in Great Yarmouth organized by nationally recognized local man Bruno Peek Pageant Master. It was to commemorate the arrival of Nelson in Yarmouth returning to his home country after his great victory at the Battle of the Nile in Aboukir Bay just east of Alexandria. Nelson's victory cut off Napoleon and the whole of his army in Egypt. The re-enactment of his return in November 2000 was spectacular and Greg Catchpole of the Great Yarmouth High School joined the *Apollonian Volunteers* who were the Militia who played their parts in welcoming Nelson to Yarmouth in 1800.

I remember this event well having been cast in a speaking role as the Port Admiral of Great Yarmouth to welcome Nelson on his arrival.

OBITUARY
Peter Marsden
Headmaster 1961-1977

Peter Marsden's arrival at Salisbury Road, aged 44, was considered by many a somewhat surprising appointment. His experience of education as a pupil, as a student at Kings College, Cambridge, where he read Geography, and as a teacher at Ipswich School, had been entirely in the private sector.

But Great Yarmouth Grammar School itself had been a private school until 1945. Mr Marsden benefited from the residual effects of this tradition, enabling him to appoint or promote staff at his own discretion. He loathed paperwork and avoided it as much as possible, had a casual manner in dealing with education officials and showed a marked distrust of Inspectors who, curiously, steered clear of the school throughout his entire headship. His independent streak is further illustrated by his annual handing over of the school accounts to be audited overnight by two members of staff and by his quaint vocabulary. Idle pupils were 'scrimshankers' or 'hornswogglers' and school occasions were 'fandangles'.

In fact he settled in very speedily, joining a school of over 600 boys, larger than ever before. He achieved much, coping easily with the rapid University and Polytechnic expansion of the sixties when A Level students came to think almost automatically in terms of a degree course. He saw through the 'mixing' with the Girls High School in 1970 and opposed the distant thunder of the approach of a Comprehensive system of education at Great Yarmouth.

Peter's father had survived the trenches of France where he fought as an infantry officer and he was brought up to detest war. His pacifist convictions were part of his Quaker creed, as was his voluntary work as a prison visitor as Stokesby Bay Young Offender's Institution and Blundeston Prison. But his deep religious convictions were never paraded, nor did he seek to disturb those who held differing opinions.

Mr Marsden enjoyed a very happy home life with Constance and his three children. They were frequent and generous hosts, both at the School House and later at their 'cottage' in Hemsby. Under his brusque and rather blustering manner lay a generous nature and a sensitive and, in some ways, shy personality. Many will recall how, in the course of his final address to the school, his recollection of his mother as he mentioned her, caused him to be so overcome that the Deputy Head had to read the rest of his speech.

Happy in retirement he was, sadly, soon affected by ill health. But he was uncomplaining. The death of Constance in May of this year was a heavy blow. He survived her by only a few weeks, but long enough to spend time with his children and grandchildren at the Yorkshire family retreat. He will be remembered by many pupils and staff with considerable affection and respect.

Vic Stowers

160. Peter Marsden's Obituary.

161. Greg Catchpole among the Apollonian Volunteers

162. An actor playing Nelson toasting the town on his arrival at the South Quay.

Marjorie White long serving Chairman of the Great Yarmouth Grammar School Foundation Governors died in the Millennium Year.

MARJORIE WHITE

Chairman of Governors

Mrs Marjorie White was a remarkable lady and a very good friend and Governor to Great Yarmouth High School who carried out her role as Chairman of Governors efficiently, charmingly and cheerfully. Her dedication and loyalty were very much appreciated and staff and Governors alike sadly miss her regular visits.

Marjorie served both the school, town and County unstintingly. She was Conservative Constituency Chairman from 1977 to 1980 and again 1983 to 1985 - the only person since the War to have been elected for two separate terms. Marjorie served on the Education Committee for Great Yarmouth and for several years, she was a member of the new Norfolk County Council.

In the 70s Mrs White was well known and admired for her influential work for handicapped children, being deeply involved with special schools throughout the whole of Norfolk. The John Grant School at Caister is one of these schools where Marjorie devoted so much time as their Chairman of Governors. In the 80s she was a College Governor, Chairman of 3 High Schools and also Chairman of the Grammar School Foundation. In recent years she dedicated her time to the Foundation and especially to Great Yarmouth High School.

A dear friend of Marjorie's Michael Carttiss recalls:

"Modest and unassuming, Marjorie did not seek these positions for the sake of it, but for what she could do to help others." He goes on to say, she was 'honest with everyone - always diplomatic and even tempered - Marjorie could be firm in suggesting what ought to be done. Honest, yes, but she did tell one big lie. She added a year to her age so as to join the Women's Auxilary Air Force (the WAFFs) before the end of the War. In fact she was "a popsie in ops" working in the RAF Operations Room at North Weald, where one of her proudest memories was seeing the Prime Minister, Winston Churchill, on a war time visit there. She was attached to SHAEF headquarters for a while where she met General Eisenhower.

More important to Marjorie, however, was meeting the handsome R.A.F. pilot whom she married in August 1945. Together they had two children, Stephanie and Geraldine. Marjorie and Roy started in business with a restaurant in Regent Road, and later they purchased and ran the Ocean Edge Hotel, where her home-made apple pies were a particular speciality! She loved cooking and enjoyed teaching her granddaughter, Daniella, culinary skills. Everything else had to wait when they were baking cakes."

Michael also recalls Marjorie's visit to Parliament: "When I attended my first State Opening in 1983 Marjorie was my guest at Westminster." Marjorie was always punctual, but on this occasion she was delayed on the tube train, and for once was late. I had to be in the House of Commons, and Marjorie was supposed to be in her seat in the Royal Gallery by 10.15 a.m., 30 minutes before the Queen arrived. At the House of Lords entrance, beautifully dressed for the occasion, as always, she waved her invitation card to the nearest scarlet and gold encrusted personage, "Am I too late to get in?" she asked, apologetically and breathlessly. "No Madame" he said "We wouldn't dream of starting without you," and he escorted her to her seat. Some moments later, Marjorie, relieved she'd got there just in time, saw at the head of the Queen's procession through the Royal Gallery, the dignified Earl Marshall of England, the Duke of Norfolk - the same richly embroidered, uniformed gentleman to whom she'd showed her admissions card!"

This type of formal occasion was not unusual for Marjorie and she attended many such events countrywide and within Norfolk. In her later years her dedication and work for Gt Yarmouth High School was tremendous and her support for the Headteachers unstinting.

Marjorie will be greatly missed by all. May we take this opportunity to thank Michael Carttiss for his contributions to this obituary.

163. Marjorie White's Obituary.

In Spring 2001 Linda Fisher took over the Chairmanship of the Governors from the late Marjorie White. Both Linda's children went to the Great Yarmouth High School and she became a Parent Governor in 1989, then become a Governor appointed by the Foundation. She chaired the School Personnel Committee for several years and was involved with the appointment of staff. She worked as Business Development Manager for the Employment Service.

164. The pictures show the Lord Lieutenant of the County, Mr. Timothy Colman at the School.

The School Sports Teams went from strength to strength in 2000-2001 and after various trials a number of pupils gained representative honours in County and local teams. These included the Norfolk County under 14's and under 15's football teams. The Great Yarmouth School's under 14's and under 15's teams and the Norwich City Youth Team.

Left to right: Warren Nichols, Shannon Beare, Tiffany Tyler, Greg Crane, Kelly Hanley, James Long, Karl Crux

From various trials these pupils will be representing the following teams:

Norfolk County U14	Warren Nicholls James Long	Great Yarmouth Schools U14	Warren Nichols James Long Ben Kiki Karl Crux Ian Anjos
Norfolk County Under15	Ben Dixon	Norwich City Youth	Greg Crane
Great Yarmouth Schools U15	Ben Dixon Matt Allen		

The Under 14 Boys Football Team beat Benjamin Britten U14 in the first round of the English Schools U14 Cup - score: 8-1

165. various members of the High School Sports Teams.

The School celebrated its 450th Anniversary in 2001 and the Celebratory Events were recorded in the *High Standard* of 2002. As a physical reminder of the celebration the old School Junior Entrance was remodelled and renamed the Marsden Entrance after the late Peter Marsden Head Master.

166. The Grammar School Old Boys gather for the 450th Anniversary Dinner held at the School.

In July 2001 Great Yarmouth High School staged *A Night in New York* which was a medley of American Music, Drama and Dance featuring an abridged version of *West Side Story*. The acting and musical talent was obvious but the real achievement was in getting the boys to dance and dance well. The School made the production all the more exciting by providing a new PA system as well as lots of additional writing and these combined with a fine set and vibrant costumes made for a really stunning show.

167. The girls of the cast of A Night in New York

168. The cast of A Night in New York with Maria, Tony, and Officer Krupke.

In Autumn 2002 four longstanding members of the Staff retired or moved to other posts. A proper send off was arranged with the Staff receiving individual cakes at an event held in the School Hall which included dancing to a Ceilidh Band together with a presentation of Long Service Awards.

169. Iain MacDonald, Martin Keable, Jill Roberts and Bertie Patterson.

The Great Yarmouth High School had been playing tennis for many years and had its own tournament.

170. The two finalists in the Open Boys Singles.

Year 11 girls GCSE group had worked hard for 2 years and would be moving on to Further Education and work placements.

171. The girls in their last PE practical exam before the Rounders Assessment.

Shooting School

I have been shooting for about 18 months at mid-Norfolk Shooting Schools in Taverham. I got into the Norfolk team in the first year and went all over the country to shoot different disciplines. I use a 12-bore shotgun, shooting clays.
I have recently won the British Double Rise in the junior division and was only 2 clays off winning the whole British competition. I have submitted my scores for the England team.

Ross Jefferson

The range of sports undertaken by the Great Yarmouth High School pupils continued to expand and Ross Jefferson and Antony Antorkas had been keen enough to develop their shooting skills into County representation.

I have been shooting for about a year at Mid-Norfolks shooting school in Taverham. Within the first month of my shooting career, I was asked to represent the County.
Since being in the Norfolk team, I have travelled the country to compete in competitions. I specifically shoot 'Down the Line' (DTL). I really enjoy it and can recommend it as a good hobby to take up.

Antony Antorkas

172. Ross Jefferson and Antony Antorkas with their trophies.

The School Performing Arts Group continued to stretch the capabilities of the pupils by choosing demanding productions in which a large number of students and staff could be involved. The Great Yarmouth High School presented Grease on the 16th and 17th July 2002 which was a great success. The picture shows the principals, Kyriacos Kikis as Danny and Sandy was Cara-Marie Hawkins and the cast list of the production.

173. The Principles in Grease, Kyriacos Kikis as Danny and Cara-Marie Hawkins as Sandy.

CAST

Danny Zuko	Kyriacos Kikis
Sandy Dumbrowski	Cara-Marie Hawkins
Kenickie (T.Bird)	Anthony Antorkas
Sonny La Tierri (T.Bird)	James Clayton
Pudsie (T.Bird)	Thomas Allen
Doody (T.Bird)	Adam Wyer
T.Bird	Kenneth Lee
T.Bird	Abduramane Jalo
Betty Rizzo (Pink Lady)	Jenna Ferguson
Frenchy (Pink Lady)	Natalie Nelson
Marty (Pink Lady)	Maisie Leggett
Jan (Pink Lady)	Sally Dixon
Eugene	Thomas Rutherford
Patty Simcox	Marie Brierley
Miss Lynch	Heidi Judd
Scorpian Leader	Thomas Rowe
Coach Cahoon	Alex Massey
Kay Casino	Joseph Lightning
Cha Cha DiGregorio	Danielle Moore
Vince Fontaine/Teen Angel	Andrew Lyle

CHORUS

Leanne Arnold	Lauren Johnson
Emma Barwick	Amy O'Brien
Jade Berry	Nicole Palmer
Kerrie Davies	Hannah Reynolds
Liam Gates	Stephen Sipka
Jak Hume	Jack Smith
Brooke Humpherey	Kelly Tourle
Mamudo Jalo	Ashley Watson

174. The cast list of the production.

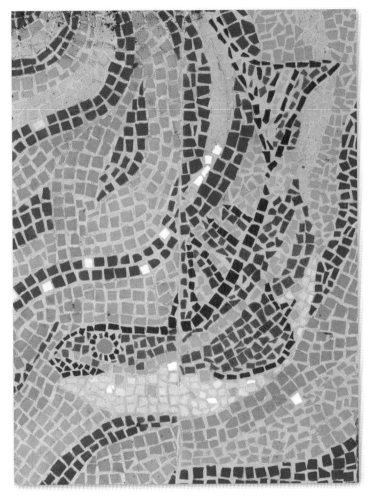

The School's Art students in year 11 Kelly Eastwood, Emma Wilcox, and Tara Galvin helped to design and make two Mosaic slabs which were placed in the garden designed as part of the Eden Project. The students were guided by Miss O'Leary and a local mosaic artist Miss Claire-Marie Hill and resulted in two beautiful fish designs linked to Yarmouth's fishing heritage.

Head Teacher David Brunton reported that Great Yarmouth High School's policy of entering some youngsters for GCSE exams early was paying dividends. These successes boosted the confidence of the whole year group and removed some of the pressure which they would come under during the examination season during the Summer term.

175. The picture shows the Mosaic, partly designed by Kelly Eastwood, Emma Wilcox, and Tara Galvin

176. Nearly half the year group had been successful in either their Mathematics or ICT examinations.

177. Cora Batley on her retirement from the Great Yarmouth High School Board.

Past Students

Sarah Bensley (nee Ferguson)

Sarah is a former pupil of Great Yarmouth Grammar School. She has been awarded a degree of Master of Law (in Employment Law) at the University of East Anglia. She is currently employed at Pasta Foods as an Human Resources Executive.

Cora Batley retired from the Governing Body of the Great Yarmouth High School in May 2004 after 46 years of loyal service. Cora gave much more to education than just her work with Great Yarmouth High School. She was a Governor at Greenacre School, a Grammar School Foundation Governor, a Borough and County Councillor and one of the first women to become a Great Yarmouth Port and Haven Commissioner.

The Winter 2004 issue of the *High Standard* records the success of past student Sarah Bensley (née Ferguson). Sarah was a former pupil at the Great Yarmouth Grammar School, and she had been awarded a Degree of Master of Law (specialising in Employment Law) at the University of East Anglia. She was employed at that time at Pasta Foods as a Human Resources Manager.

178. Sarah after she had been awarded her Master's Degree at the University of East Anglia.

179. Head Boy Brady Smith, Head Girl Hannah Reynolds, and Sports Captains, Ryan Seakings and Rebecca Grealy together with the Prefects for the year.

The School system of Head Boy, Head Girl, Sports Captains and the Prefects was an important one giving responsibility to and achieving the best from the senior students.

A new Head Teacher Jim Nixon who had been Deputy Head Teacher at Taverham High School in Norwich arrived to succeed David Brunton who was moving on to another post. Mr. Nixon took up his post after Christmas 2005. He had moved from Glasgow in 1974 down to Kent to train to be a teacher. His career started 3 years later at Chatham House School, Ramsgate in Kent. In 1982 he moved along the coast to work at Southlands Comprehensive School in New Romney. During this time he also worked as a part time tutor at Canterbury Christchurch College. He was appointed as Senior Teacher at St. Clements High School in Kings Lynn in 1994 before moving to Taverham High School in Norwich in September 2000.

180. Jim Nixon sitting at his desk.

The School continued its tradition in Cross Country with a variety of races for Boys and Girls of different ages. In addition the Girls under 14 Football Team had a great success in reaching the final of the County Cup for the second year running. The School also had the advantage in its Football Teams being able to use Norwich City's indoor training facility at Colney.

181. Various Sports Teams and High School teams training at Colney.

The Head Boy and Head Girl were appointments of responsibility and provided a link between the Students and the Staff. Their first task was to organise a duty roster for the Prefects and then to assemble a Student Council capable of expressing the views of the students. Their duties entailed meeting with the Head Teacher and members of Staff when required, looking after visiting Dignitaries to the School and ensuring that the Students enjoyed their time at Great Yarmouth High School.

A Day in the Life of ...
Head Boy and Head Girl

Since being appointed as Head Boy and Head Girl in September 2005, myself Thomas Allen and Victoria Kerry have had a busy yet exciting time. At the very beginning of our term we met with the newly appointed Head Mr. Nixon, and he explained what he expected of us and what our duties would include. He also informed us that we were the link between the students and the staff.

Our first task was to organise a duty roster for the prefects so they too would know what was expected of them, and to assemble a student council, capable of expressing the views of the students. This has been a big focus point of ours, as the student council have been given new powers which really affect the running of the school. Up till now we had felt that the amount of impact the student council had, was only limited to the type of toilet paper used in the loos!

A typical day for the Head Boy and Girl would entail the general overseeing of the prefects and their duties. In addition we will meet with the Head teacher and members of staff when required. Should there be any dignitaries visiting the school we are usually asked to meet and accompany them during their stay. At recent open and presentation evenings we have been asked to make a speech, explaining what life at our school is like. We are not however only here as a link to the staff, but more importantly to help the students enjoy their time spent at Great Yarmouth High School. On the rare occasions that a pupil feels that he is being bullied or is unhappy, then Victoria and I are friendly faces they can rely on and turn to.

Being Head Boy or Girl is a rewarding and enjoyable experience. Although the above may seem time consuming, we have not allowed it to affect our studies, as most of the meetings and tasks take place in free periods and out side of school hours. Finally should any of you be offered the opportunity of becoming a senior prefect then we recommend you jump at the chance. It is one of the few times during your school life that you really will feel that you have made a difference.

Thomas Allen and Victoria Kerry

182. Head Boy Thomas Allen and Head Girl Victoria Kelly.

The East Norfolk Militia are a re-enactment military group using the traditions and regulations from Nelson's period. They recently received authentic new uniforms. Mr. Patterson, a retired Maths Teacher from the Great Yarmouth High School is part of the group. Editor commented that presenting bayonets looked more fun than Mathematics.

In April 2006 two Year 9 students, 14 year old Sarah Carpenter and Zoe Threlfall, took part in a ceremony in St. Nicholas Parish Church to celebrate 50 years of links with Great Yarmouth's twin town of Rambouillet in France. The ceremony was attended by the Mayor of Great Yarmouth, the Mayor of Rambouillet, a French Government Minister, Civic Dignitaries and the Lord Lieutenant of Norfolk. Sarah and Zoe impressed all those attending by reciting a poem in French.

Nelson's Militia

Spotted in the EDP, one of the members of the East Norfolk Militia in their authentic new uniforms, has a familiar face! Second from the left is Mr Patterson, retired Maths teacher from GYHS. Looks more fun than Maths!

183. The East Norfolk Militia in their new uniforms with Mr. Patterson second from the left.

184. Sarah Carpenter and Zoe Threlfall at the front of the nave of St. Nicholas with the Reverend Michael Woods, Rector in his clergy pew on the far right.

The School continued to enhance its reputation for Cross Country top performances with successful teams of Boys and Girls. The year 10 boys (aged 15) won the Yarmouth District event with a team consisting of Max Moerkerk, James Comer and Jo Lees. Jo won his race and went on to represent the Yarmouth District in the Norfolk Championship. He produced a very successful top 10 performance in the Norfolk Championship and was subsequently chosen to represent Norfolk in the East Anglia Championship.

185. Max Moerkerk, James Comer and Jo Lees.

Head Teacher Jim Nixon when interviewed for his post in 2004 had emphasised the importance of standards including appearances. The result was new uniforms and new blazers for the Great Yarmouth High School pupils.

186. A group of students in their new uniforms outside the Marsden Entrance.

Students in all year groups including Year 8 either took their GCSE in Portuguese or Polish during May 2006. Each language GCSE is made up of oral, reading, writing and listening examinations. All 14 students passed and achieved A and B grades giving them a confident headstart on the qualifications ladder. Pictured are Cherno Bari, Diogo Da Silva, Marta Lazaro, Nair Martins, Diogo Sequeria, Tiago Sequeria, Anna Silver, Angela Louro and Adrian Kacica.

187. Year 8 Students who successfully took Portuguese and Polish GCSE Examinations early.

188. New College Oxford grounds and its Dining Hall set out for a Formal Dinner.

The School had developed regular trips to the Oxford and Cambridge Colleges. In the Summer of 2007 ten students visited New College Oxford.

The Designer of one of the most glamourous cars in the world, Malcolm Sayer, was a pupil at the Great Yarmouth Grammar School between 1927 and 1933. His Father Gilbert was a long serving School Master at the School where he was Head of Art. After leaving School Malcolm gained a Scholarship to Loughborough University where he studied Aeronautical and Automotive Engineering. He made his mark by being the designer of the "C type," "D type" and "E type" Jaguars.

Old Boy of the Grammar School Chris Wright recently donated a brand new Gretsch Drum Kit to the Performing Arts Department. When he was at School Chris played Timps, which were borrowed from the Caister Camp Orchestra to play in the old Grammar School Orchestra. The Head of Music at that time was Benjamin Angwin, a very strict task master.

Miss Fisher, head of performing arts with Chris Wright

She bangs the drums...

Old boy of the school, Chris Wright, has very generously donated a brand new GRETSCH drum kit to the performing arts department. He made contact with the school recently, to be put in touch with old school friends, which we were happy to help with.

When at school, Chris played timps (borrowed from the Caister Camp orchestra) in the old school orchestra. Head of Music at that time was Benjamin Angwin, a very strict taskmaster.

This is a wonderful new addition to our school orchestra. Many Thanks

189. Malcolm Sayer and an "E Type" Jaguar.

190. Chris Wright with Head of Performing Arts, Miss Fisher.

The Autumn Chronicle in 2007 recorded the success of past student Clair Jary. She attended the Great Yarmouth High School between 1999-2003 and continued her education at East Norfolk Sixth College in Gorleston. She then studied at Easton College (UEA) to gain a HND in Sports Science. At the time she was spending the year 2007 in studying for her Degree at Bedford University.

Clair Jary

Clair attended the Great Yarmouth High School between 1999 - 2003, continuing her education at the East Norfolk Sixth Form College, Gorleston. Her last two years have been spent at Easton College (UEA) achieving an HND in Sports Science. She is currently spending this year studying for her degree at Bedford University.

191. Clair Jary in Academic Dress.

192. The History Gifted and Talented group on their Study Tour of Colchester.

During the Summer of 2007 the History Gifted and Talented Students enjoyed a 3 day activity programme centred around the Roman Invasion. These Students visited the town of Colchester and its Castle Museum and discovered the rich history surrounding the Roman Invasion. Day 2 involved students working together creating various forms of Art with a Roman influence and these ranged from Mosaics to Shields. On the third day the students concentrated on Boudicca and examined in detail the evidence for her revolt against the Romans and the impact it had on Colchester and on Eastern Britain..

In March 2008 Seven Enterprise students from Great Yarmouth High School who had spent the previous year on the School Business Studies course, had formed their own Company Kenetic Productions, and had the opportunity to visit New York. With other Schools in the Norfolk area they stayed at the Pennsylvania Hotel located in the heart of mid-town Manhattan directly opposite Madison Square Gardens. The Great Yarmouth students attended an International Enterprise Conference at New York University's prestigious Kimmel Centre overlooking Washington Square Park in Greenwich Village where they heard from top experts what it took to make a successful business. Whilst in New

193. Great Yarmouth High School Students in New York.

York they had the opportunity to visit local attractions including a river boat cruise to see the Statue of Liberty, the Empire State Building, and Madame Tussauds' Business Study Workshop.

A few Great Yarmouth High School pupils were invited by Fiona Ford of Maritime Heritage East to model for a professional photo shoot at the Time and Tide Museum on Blackfriars Road. The students chosen were Michael Arnold, Leanne Bowen, Christopher Demetriou, Adam King, Ryan King, Hannah Oakley and Nathan Riches.

194. A group of Year 10 students at the Time and Tide Museum.

On the 24th May 2008 a Commemoration Day had been held to celebrate the work of designer Malcolm Sayer. It took the form of a Jaguar day in which a large number of Jaguars came together in Great Yarmouth and were exhibited in the School grounds. The work in organising the day was carried out by Eddie Loftin and a meal was organised by a group of students under the supervision of Mr. P. Jones for all the guests. A Plaque was unveiled in the main hall by Norman Dewis the test driver for Jaguar in the 1960's.

195. Eddie Loftin (right) with two of the distinguished guests and one of the participating Jaguars.

The major building programme had been completed and included a new Drama Studio and additional School Hall which were in full use. In the main buildings there were a new Art Room, Science Lab, Food Tech Room and Maths Rooms together with additional changing rooms for the Swimming Pool and new Lavatories.

196. The New Great Yarmouth High School Block.

197. Andy Toone.

The School had welcomed a new Head Andrew Toone who took over from Jim Nixon in 2009. It was Andrew Toone's aim to launch Great Yarmouth High School as a High Performing School with Humanities Status.

Emma Mason the History Teacher had organised a three day History Field Trip to Ypres in Belgian at Easter, The purpose of the trip was to experience the impact that the First World War had on so many lives and on so many differentnationalities.Despite Belgium remaining neutral during the First World War their country was devastated and the students gained a deep sense of recognition and the purpose of Remembrance during the trip. The picture shows the students in a re-constructed dugout.

Battlefields
History Field Trip 2009

Students across the year groups enjoyed a fantastic three day history field trip to Belgium - Ypres this Easter. The purpose of the trip was to experience the impact that World War One had on so many lives across so many different nationalities. Students learnt a variety of aspects relating to World War One which included a startling comparison between the German and British Soldiers in life and death at war. Students also gained an insight into how the Flemish people of Belgium coped with war. Despite Belgium remaining neutral during WW1 their country was devastated, and it is for these reasons and many more that students gained a deep sense of recognition and purpose of remembrance during the trip. It you are interested in taking part in next year's history field trip please see Miss Mason - WARNING places are limited!

King George V of England stated in 1922:
We truly say that the whole circuit of the earth is griddled with the graves of our dead. In the course of my pilgrimage, I have many times asked myself whether there can be more potent advocates of peace on earth through the years to come, than this massed multitude of silent witnesses to the desolation of war. King George V, Tyne Cot Cemetery 11th May 1922

What have I learnt?
The true impact of War can never truly be examined in the classroom alone. Remembrance is not just a community event but a world wide event that I am sure will continue for many, many years to come.

By Miss Mason

198. Students during their visit to Ypres.

199. *Daisy Middleton and Kiera O'Donoughoe in School uniform, with the wreath before the Service.*

On Remembrance Sunday in November 2009, Daisy Middleton and Kiera O'Donoughoe laid a wreath on behalf of the Great Yarmouth High School on the Cenotaph at the Remembrance Service in St. Georges Park.

200. *The picture shows non-uniformed students.*

On Friday 23rd October there was a Non-Uniform Day at the School in aid of the Prince's Trust Group which had raised £400. Great Yarmouth High School was the only School to take part in Non-Uniform Day.

201. *Ed Balls at Great Yarmouth High School.*

In the summer of 2010 Ed Balls then part of the Labour Government and a former Secretary of State for Education visited Great Yarmouth High School as part of his tour of selected schools in Norfolk and Suffolk.

For some years the Great Yarmouth High School Girls had taken part in football five-a-side teams. In January 2010 the under 13 girls team went to Carrow Road to play in a Tournament run by Football in the Community. A squad of 8 girls went to Norwich and they all played very well throughout the day narrowly missing proceeding to the last round.

202. *The Girls under 13 five-a-side team squad.*

Chapter 12
Great Yarmouth High School as a Humanities College

The Great Yarmouth High School now has over 1000 pupils and it is impossible to produce a whole school photograph in the same way as it was done in the years of the Great Yarmouth Grammar School. However at the end of the Summer Term of 2010 the Head Teacher organised a photograph of his Year 11 students (aged 16) before they left the School, either to move to Higher Education, to pursue specific careers or to seek employment. The photograph of the Year 11 group is reproduced at the end of this chapter.

Meanwhile the celebrations of the 100 years of the School on the Salisbury Road site focused on the Raven Tower which is the prominent landmark of the building. The Great Yarmouth High School Governors agreed that it would be a fitting memorial to celebrate the 100 Years Anniversary to refurbish the Clock on the South Face of the Tower and to re-activate the School Bell which for many decades had summoned pupils to School.

The Clock was subject to a site inspection on Monday 11th January, 2010, by S. Michlmair and Co. the Clock and Watchmakers from Norwich, who had been commissioned to quote for the re-furbishment work. The Inspection revealed that the time-piece movement was labelled as being by Aldred and Son of Great Yarmouth c.1911, with deadbeat escapement, and maintaining power. This Clock, although labelled Aldred and Son, was actually by Gilletts of London, as it was common practice, during this period to label the Clock with the local supplier's name. During the site inspection, it was found that the Clock mechanism was not functioning, since the gearing behind the dial had ceased to operate. The Specialist reported that the Clock was in need of a full overhaul and in its current condition no attempt should be made to run the Clock as it would cause severe damage.

203. The Clock repairers arrive from Norwich

The Clock repairers quoted for the overhaul, which would involve the Clock being removed in its entirety and taken to the Norwich workshop. A full overhaul would take place and the Clock would then be tested in the workshop before being stripped, cleaned, repainted and re-assembled and then re-installed on site, at a cost of £2650. The repairers also quoted for the dial restoration since the existing dial was very weathered and tired, although it did not impede the function of the Clock. A full restoration would take place in the Norwich workshop with the hands being removed and then primed and re-gold leafed, using 24 ct. double thickness gold leaf. The quotation for this work was £1,300. As part of the project it was felt that ease of operation at the School would be useful and on the current system, once the Clock had been overhauled, it would need winding once a week. The Clock repairers quoted for an electric re-wind system which would remove the need for anyone to wind the Clock. The system would include a Remontoire System, which meant that in the event of a power failure the Clock would continue to run for a minimum of two days. It was pointed out that the Clock would still be a mechanical Clock and that the hands might need to be set from time to time to compensate for the Clock gaining or losing time.

204. The Raven Tower before the repaired Clock was attached

205. Fixing the repaired Clock

This work took place during the summer holidays of 2010 and the Clock in pristine order with a newly refurbished face was in position to celebrate the exact day on which the School was opened.

206. The Clock with its refurbished face

In addition the High School Governors wished for the Bell to operate, to be able to indicate the beginning and the end of the School day. A further £3400 was expended to provide a control unit to enable the Bell to be operated on selected hours from ground level. This work was carried out and on Thursday the 22nd of July the restoration of the Clock was completed and the Bell was prepared to sound at 5pm, to launch the Humanities Activity Week.

On that day the Head Teacher Andy Toone, stood in Tower Yard in front of a group of Invited Guests, of which I was one, to celebrate the 100 years Anniversary and to hear the Bell strike as the Clock hands reached 5pm. Also present as Guests were members of the History Gifted and Talented Team who had done so much in the School to record the

History of the Raven Tower as a project, led and encouraged by their History Teacher, Emma Mason. A photograph of the Gifted and Talented Team is shown below.

Also displayed is an essay by Jessica Mason, daughter of Emma, from within the Group setting out what she and her fellow members of the Team had achieved during their project on the Raven Tower. The Head Teacher in acknowledging their work then went on to launch the Humanities College formally noting that it would swing into action in September 2010.

207. The Gifted and Talented team of Historians from the Great Yarmouth High School Carly Hughes, Daniel King, Jessica Mason, Daniel Beddoes and Daria Duglosiz who worked on the Raven Tower project in 2010

The Changing faces of GYHS

We, as a group have learnt a lot about the history of Great Yarmouth High School and how it has changed throughout the 100 years span. From 1910, when the school officially opened, to 2010 it has changed in both its ways of teaching and its appearance. In this essay I am going to write about the various changes of the school within 100 years and compare the school from 1910-20 to 2000-2010.

The school was founded not by the generosity of private benefactors but by the public spirit of the common council and its town's people. Our school was designed by two of the old boys named H. Olley and F. RIB Howard in 1909 but, due to the sad death of Edward VII the opening of the school postponed until 16th July 1910. Its foundation stone was laid on the 5th May 1909 but it was another year later that the new school was actually occupied.

The Clock Tower was built as a memorial to Dr. J. J. Raven who was a bell ringer and the Headmaster at the school in 1906 which was located on Trafalgar road. There were originally only around 400 students at the time in the school, and at this time only men were allowed to teach but in WW1 in 1914 the first women teachers had to fill in for men who had gone off to war. During the World War the school was evacuated to the countryside.

The school continued to change and became more modern as the years went by. Even the lessons they were taught were different to the lessons we have now. They had a limited curriculum but unlike today they learnt Latin and had to take part in class singing. Today's lessons are much more varied; we have a wide range of languages that are available to all students such as Spanish, German, French, Polish, Portuguese and many more. Our sports lessons are also very different; we have more sports that we do throughout the year which is due to the devotedness of sports around Norfolk. As well as the overall curriculum being different, assemblies were also different in a variety of ways. England back in the 1900's was much more religious, and the percentage of people who believed in both God and were devoted Christians was much more higher than today's, this led to prayers being read out in assemblies to show their love in God. Students also had to sing religious songs and god's prayer. In today's assemblies we don't sing songs, or say prayers and people still debate today - is that where our generation has gone wrong, should we have kept the traditional ways?

In the 1900's their prize day was similar but very different in comparison to ours. 60-70 years ago there would have been many songs sung by the school choir, then a scene from a famous play and many speeches from honoured guests and governors of the school and then of course the actual prize giving's. Even though there were many differences, both eras took the prize giving ceremony very seriously, and honour those chosen students greatly.

There are many things that could be argued, between the differences of the school and the schools everyday life. One thing that could most definitely be argued is the attitude of both teachers and students. I think it is safe to say that back in 1950, students cared more for school and that going to school was more of a want than a need. Students were more enthusiastic for school and preferred getting involved in extra curricular activities. There is evidence to back me up on this because as a group we have studied photos of students and read passages that the students themselves had written, and from just analysing these resources I can tell there was a high level of respect toward their teachers and peers. Teachers were more enthusiastic towards teaching students as well as learning themselves.

Behaviour was another thing that differs between the two time periods, because once again just from analysing resources, punishments weren't given as often however I personally think that the behaviour was better in 1920-60 because punishments were crueller and more harsh. In the 20th century, some of the punishments were getting caned, which was very common until it got banned in the UK and cleaning, such as scrubbing floors and cleaning toilets, these were much worse compared to today's punishments which are usually detentions which differ between ten minutes and two hours.

During our investigation to find out as much information as we can about Great Yarmouth High School, we went to the Norfolk Records Office which is situated in Norwich. Once we where there we searched through hundreds of photos and many written sources which contained important documents which helped us understand what school life was really like. This helped our research skills, and we learnt a lot, not just about Great Yarmouth high school and the surrounding community but something I think is much more important, how historians investigate. I really enjoyed going to the Norfolk Record Office because I learnt so much. I found it a really good lesson in history and how to properly research and I was surprised at how interesting it was. We took photos of the photos and the documents we were allowed to photograph which we then printed off and annotated so we could show our skills in our display.

We didn't just go to the Norfolk Record Office; we also worked at the local library and searched through the old issues of the Mercury which ranged from 1910-2000 on the microfilms. Although this wasn't as successful as the Norfolk Record Office we did find out information about the opening of the school which helped us greatly.

We have done many things to help us with our research like going to the NRO and the GEE library and meeting with Michael Boon who is a local historian who co-authored the book "Great Yarmouth is an ancient town." Being a local historian Mr Boon gave us tips on how to research and where to find out vital information.

As a whole, we have learnt so much and I will say on behalf of them that we all had amazing fun.

I didn't realise how many differences existed in our school between 1910- 2010, and although there were so many changes made, I personally think it was for the better. Today we are more skilled, advanced, and technologically aware which enables us to have better opportunities to what students did one hundred years ago.

208. Essay by Jessica L Mason - Age 13 years Student of Great Yarmouth High School

A High Performing Specialist School.

The School had issued a Brochure setting out for Parents what a Humanities College sought to achieve entitled *Great Yarmouth Voluntary Assisted High School Humanities College.*

Andy Toone, the Head Teacher, wrote a forward to Parents and Students in the Brochure which is set out below.

209. The High School Humanities Colour Brochure cover.

"This is a very important time for families having to make major decisions regarding a choice of school. I am all too aware of just how important it is to make sure that your children receive the very best education. I hope this brochure helps you to make your decision.

Great Yarmouth VA High is a very popular and successful school. We are very proud of the achievements of our pupils. We believe that each individual is very special and their time with us is very precious. Our aim is to enable all our young people to have confidence in their own abilities and to develop independence, initiative and self- discipline: to be prepared for lifelong learning. As a school we celebrate success whilst continually striving for improvement; high standards are central to all that we do.

We are actively involved with a wide range of external agencies so that our students can thrive in a safe and secure environment. We also work closely with parents and the local community We are a caring learning community that is continually aiming higher. If you would like further information about our school, please do not hesitate to contact us. I thank you for taking the time to read this brochure".

Andy Toone,

Head Teacher.

The colour Brochure outlines the School's aims as a Humanities College and is illustrated with appropriate photographs. One of the aims is to provide a high quality education in a calm and safe environment.

210. Pupil in the Great Yarmouth High School Library

211. Girl Gymnast vaulting on a Gymnastics Horse

The School Curriculum details opportunities and careers, the role of Physical Education and how Special Needs are dealt with in the Brochure and a detailed supporting document is also available.

A further section of the Brochure deals with how the team ethic at the School would work together to support the pupils. For example the whole School is divided into four teams named Blackfriars, Britannia, Tolhouse, and Wellington, these names reflecting key features in the Town. This grouping operates on an Inter House Competitive Basis extending that commenced by the old Grammar School Houses of North, South, West and Centre. The School is proud of its traditions based on those of the Great Yarmouth Grammar School and individual pupils have house ties, house badges and badges of office.

212. Great Yarmouth High School Head Students Badge

This continues the old Grammar School system of Prefects being given responsibility to regulate their fellow pupils in conjunction with the Staff. An innovation is that Junior Prefects have been created from those who show promise in the lower years of the School. The Humanities College in seeking an identity has centered on a Formal School Uniform for boys and girls of which the central feature is the School Blazer with the Great Yarmouth High School badge.

Thus Andy Toone launched the Humanities College, below the Raven Tower with its refurbished Clock, 100 years after the School's establishment on the Salisbury Road Site. He said that the present School, although very different from the Grammar School, which operated on the same site for 71 of the 100 years, had given the School purpose and the links with the Old Student's Association were greatly valued.

213. Headmaster Andy Toone launching the Humanities College

214. Great Yarmouth High School Year 11 Group 2010

Chapter 13
A Grammar School Retrospect

215. Dr. Raven Headmaster of the Great Yarmouth Grammar School 1866-1885

The Old Boys Association has been strong throughout the 100 years at Salisbury Road. Prior to the end of the 19th century the then Old Boys subscribed for a Silver Loving Cup which bears their names. The Cup was made in the year of Queen Victoria's Diamond Jubilee in 1887, and the Cup's base was presented by Dr. Raven, the legendary Headmaster of the Grammar School, in whose name the Tower built in 1910 was dedicated.

The Old Boys Association and its successor Diners' Club, has met regularly in each year of the 100 years in which the School has been at Salisbury Road. Initially during its Grammar School period which lasted up to 1981 and thereafter at the Annual Dinner, as a diminishing tontine of students ranging from those of great age to those now approaching 50. In the Appendices is an Old Boys' List of Subscribing Members in 1964, with their then addresses, the careers they pursued, and the years when they were at the School, where known.[1]

216. The front face of the Great Yarmouth Grammar School Loving Cup

217. The rear face of the Great Yarmouth Grammar School Loving Cup

[1] See Appendix 10

In 1982 Michael Boon, David Rich and the late David Harrup formed a Dinner Committee and since that time 29 Annual Dinners of the Great Yarmouth Grammar School Old Student's Diners' Club have been held with the last being on the 23rd March 2010. These Dinners continue to provide a forum for comradeship of students who passed their years together at the Grammar School and also an occasion on which the surviving Old Boys from the 1930's can meet with those from the post war period.

218. *Grammar School Diners Club Meeting c. 1990 with Arthur England centurion Old Boy presented with a Silver Salver by the Club*

219. *450th Anniversary Dinner of the Great Yarmouth Grammar School in 2001 organised by the Diners' Club and held at the Great Yarmouth High School, the Grammar Schools' successor School, with catering by the Imperial Hotel (see also illustration 166 on page 138).*

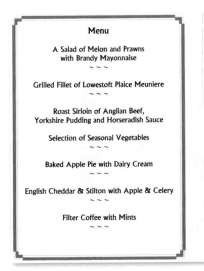
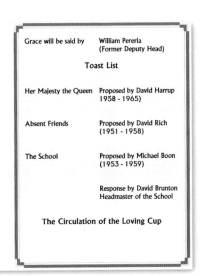

Menu

A Salad of Melon and Prawns
with Brandy Mayonnaise
~ ~ ~

Grilled Fillet of Lowestoft Plaice Meuniere
~ ~ ~

Roast Sirloin of Anglian Beef,
Yorkshire Pudding and Horseradish Sauce

Selection of Seasonal Vegetables
~ ~ ~

Baked Apple Pie with Dairy Cream
~ ~ ~

English Cheddar & Stilton with Apple & Celery
~ ~ ~

Filter Coffee with Mints
~ ~ ~

Grace will be said by   William Pereria
(Former Deputy Head)

Toast List

Her Majesty the Queen   Proposed by David Harrup
1958 - 1965)

Absent Friends   Proposed by David Rich
(1951 - 1958)

The School   Proposed by Michael Boon
(1953 - 1959)

Response by David Brunton
Headmaster of the School

The Circulation of the Loving Cup

220. Menu provided by the Imperial Hotel for the 450th Anniversary Dinner with Toast Lists.

Another related series of events has grown up based on Year Groups at the Grammar School, who have met together for their own Annual Dinners and also more ambitiously combing the world for classmates to come to Great Yarmouth for a convivial weekend on a key anniversary date.

The class of 1952 meets regularly for a Dinner at the Imperial Hotel in the Autumn.

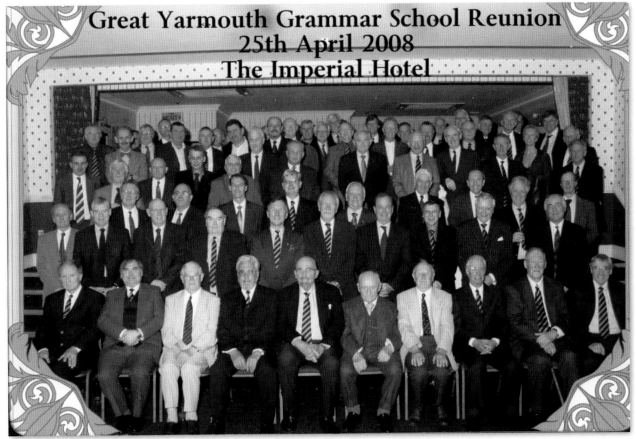

221. The Great Yarmouth Grammar School Diners Club 2008 Dinner at the Imperial Hotel

222. 50th Anniversary for the Class of 1953 after their tour of the School in Tower Yard in 2003

The Year Group of 1953, my own year, has had one weekend event in 2003 where a goodly proportion of the 66 entrants to the Grammar School in that year, came back to Great Yarmouth for a tour of the School, a dinner at the Imperial Hotel and a walk on the Sunday morning along the old Cross Country Course at Caister.

The third Year Group to attempt a year re-union was the class of 1958-65 who held a major event over a weekend in Great Yarmouth having contacted a large proportion of the over 107 entries to the Grammar School in that year.

223. Some of the Class of 1958 in their Reunion Weekend

224. Organisers Steve Carter, the late David Harrup and David Tubby in 2008.

Appendix 1
The Headmasters

The Headmasters of the Grammar School since the Foundation

1551-1552	Reverend.Walter Hall or Haugh	1661	Reverend Samuel Wilson
1553	Reverend. J. Emerson		
1554	Reverend Dent	1663	Reverend.Henry Fox
		1667	Reverend Thomas Bradford
1574	Reverend Wilcocke	1675	Reverend Richard Reynolds
1580	Reverend Daniels	1668	Reverend Henry Barington
1581	Reverend Evans	1692	Reverend Robert Pate
1584	Reverend John Ashley	1705	Reverend John Paul (short interval only)
1600	Reverend Hodgekins	1705	Reverend John Welham
1612	Reverend John Person or Pierson	1722	Reverend John Pitcairne
1613	Reverend Reeve	1730	Reverend John Mingay
1614	Reverend James	1744	Reverend Francis Turner (O.Y.) resigned 1757
1614	Reverend Robert Humfry	1863	Reverend Henry John Evans
1615	Reverend Isaac Rose	1866	Reverend John James Raven
1623	Reverend Thornton	1885	Reverend John G. Easton
1625	Reverend Robert Buxton	1888	Reverend W.H.Murray Ragg
1630	Reverend Thomas Falke	1898	Reverend Herbert Armstrong Watson
1640	Reverend Thomas Dove	1903	Walter George Williams
1646	Reverend John Hall	1933	Edward Alexander Seaborne
1647	Reverend Simon Wells	1937	Alan Henry Gill Palmer
1655	Reverend Daniel Locke	1964	Peter Marsden
1659	Reverend Robert Snelling	1976-1981	Michael Leigh

Head Teachers Great Yarmouth High School

1981	Michael Leigh
1986	Ivan Pegg
2000	David Brunton
2005	Jim Nixon
2009	Andy Toone

Sources
1. Whitehead J.B. *The History of Great Yarmouth Grammar School 1551- 1951*, Great Yarmouth, 1951
2. Great Yarmouth Grammar School *Chronicles*
3. Great Yarmouth *High Standard*

1911

Headmaster: W.G. WILLIAMS, M.A.

Second Master: J. BACKHOUSE, M.A. (Latin, Geography, English)

W.G. Bennett, B.Sc. (Science)
G.F. Cairns, M.A. (French)
F.M. Delbos, L.R.A.M. (Music, Art)
T.H. Rowe, B.A. (History, Latin, English)
Gomer Williams, B.A. (Latin)

Preparatory Dept: Miss P.Bracey, Miss M.Pratt

School Caretaker and Porter: F.Carter

1921

Headmaster: W.G. WILLIAMS, M.A.

Second Master: J. BACKHOUSE, M.A. (Latin, English)

D.B. Aubrey, B.Sc. (Science, Mathematics)
B.G. Brooks, B.A. (French, English)
R.P. Burwell, B.Sc., A.I.C., F.C.S. (Chemistry, Physics)
G.A. Graveling (Woodwork, Drawing)
Miss M.A. Moran (History, English, Latin)
Miss M.E. Rhind (German, French, English)
A.W. Rouse (Music, Mathematics)
T.H. Rowe, B.A. (History, Latin, English)

Preparatory Dept: Miss O.G. Beevor, Miss C.D. Smith.

Visiting Masters: Sgt.R.J. Boulton (Swedish Drill), W.A Green (Gymnastics).

School Caretaker and Porter: F.Carter

Note:
Miss M.A. Moran became Mrs. B.G. Brooks.

1931

Headmaster: W.G. WILLIAMS, M.A.

Second Master: J. BACKHOUSE, M.A. (Latin, English)

B.G. Brooks, B.A. (French, English)
R.P. Burwell, B.Sc., A.I.C., F.C.S. (Chemistry)
G.E. Fisher, B.Sc. (Physics)
G.A. Graveling (Woodwork, Drawing)
L.R. Manthorp, B.A. (French, English, Scripture, Geography)
A.W. Rouse (Music, Mathematics)
T.H. Rowe, B.A. (History, English)
W.H. Way, B.Sc. (Physics, Chemistry, Mathematics)
J.B. Whitehead, B.A. (History, Geography, English)

Preparatory Dept: Miss O.G. Beevor, Miss A.D. Roche

Visiting Masters: Sgt. R.J. Boulton (Swedish Drill), W.R. Gouge (Shorthand)

School Caretaker and Porter: F. Carter

Notes:

W.G. Williams, M.A., In retirement Marine Parade, Gorleston.

J. Backhouse, M.A. Died at Silloth in 1947

B.G. Brooks With Allied Control Commission, Germany, after service with Goldsmith's College.

R.P. Burwell In retirement in Fritton and Gt. Yarmouth. Second Master 1932-40

G.E. Fisher R.A.F. Education Officer.

G.A. Graveling Senior Assistant, Technical High School.

L.R. Manthorp. Ordained but now teaching in Lincoln.

T.H. Rowe In retirement, Earlham Road, Norwich.

Miss O.G. Beevor became Mrs. Duncan Saul. Lives at Gunton Drive, Lowestoft.

Miss A.D. Roche took place of sister, Miss E.H. Roche, who became Mrs. J.B. Whitehead, 1929

1941

Headmaster: A.H.G. PALMER, M.A., Mus.B., F.R.C.O.

Second Master: J.B. WHITEHEAD, B.A.(Geography, History)

Mrs.D.E. Corkill, B.Sc. (Physics)

J.C.G. Drennan, B.A. (History,Geography)

T.R. Gee, M.A. (Latin, English)

M.L. Hare, B.Sc., Diploma of Physical Education (Chemistry, Mathematics)

M. Norton, M.A. (English)

Miss H.M. Powell, B.A. (French)

Mrs.P.E. Pereira, B.A. (French)

Miss A.D. Roche (English)

G.C. Sayer, Art Masters' and City and Guilds Certificates (Art)

E.H.Taylor, M.A. (Chemistry, Physics)

W.H. Way, B.Sc. (Mathematics, Chemistry)

Visiting Master: W.R. Hunn, Mus.B., F.R.C.O., A.R.C.M.,L.R.A.M. (Music)

Staff on War Service:

A.A.P. Hillyer, B.A.

W.R. Pereira, B.A.

T. Stafford, M.Sc.

A.W. Rouse

E.A. Rasmussen, B.A.

School Caretaker and Porter: A.R. Pillar

Notes:

Mrs.D.E. Corkill with husband writes Nature Books under nom-de-plume of Harper Cory.

J.C.G. Drennan History Master, King's School, Grantham.

T.R. Gee Headmaster, St. Philip's School, Burley-in-Wharfedale.

M.L. Hare At Leeds Grammar School.

M. Norton Senior English Master, Ulverston Grammar School, Furness.

A.D. Roche Headmistress of Melton Lodge Orthopaedic Home School.

E.H. Taylor Chief Science Master at Leighton Buzzard. Succeeded by J.L. Foster. now
Headmaster of Yarmouth Grammar School.

W.H. Way Science Master at Devonport High School.

A.W. Rouse Recently in retirement in Leicester.

E.A. Rasmussen Regent St. Polytechnic. London

1951

Headmaster: A.H.G. PALMER, M.A., Mus.B., F.R.C.O.

Second Master: J.B. WHITEHEAD, O.B.E., B.A. (Geography, History)

B. Angwin, B.Mus., G.R.S.M., A.R.C.M. (Music, Scripture)
D.F. Balfour, B.Sc. (Games, Mathematics)
M.S. Coldbeck, B.Sc. (Mathematics)
W.H. Coleman, B.A. (English, Geography)
A.A.P. Hillyer, B.A. (French)
W. Hogg, M.A. (History)
J. Morrow, B.A. (Latin, English)
R. Pashley, M.A. (English)
W.R. Pereira, B.A. (French)
G.C. Sayer, Art Masters' and City and Guilds Certificates (Art, Woodwork)
K.H. Senior, Diploma of Physical Education (Gymnastics, Games)
T. Stafford, M.Sc. (Mathematics)
R. Teasdale, B.Sc. (Chemistry)
G.F. West, B.Sc., F.R.A.S. (Physics)
Note: H.M. Buddery has assisted the staff throughout 1950-51

School Caretaker and Porter: A.R. Pillar

Secretary: Miss R. Fraser

1961

Headmaster: P.T. MARSDEN, M.A., Cambridge

Assistant Headmaster: W.R. Pereira, B.A., (London) Senior Language Master.

Mr. R.J. Allen B.A., (Reading) English
Mr. B. Angwin B.Mus., G.R.S.M., A.R.C.M. Music
Mr.J. Blyth Diploma, (Loughborough College) Physical Education
Mr. R.C. Bryden B.A., (Cambridge) History and Religious Education
Mr. R.W. Caldwell Mathematics
Mr. R.G. Cann N.D.D.,A.T.D. Art
Mr. A.E. Chapman City & Guilds Woodwork and Metalwork
Mr. C.J. Cheshire M.A., (Birmingham) Senior Geography
Mr. J. Cullum B.Sc., (Bristol) Mathematics
 Mr. D.J. Exell N.D.D., A.T.D. Senior Art
Mr. A.P. Hillyer B.A., (London) French
Mr. W. Hogg M.A., (Durham) Senior History
Mr. W.R. Howell B.A., (Durham) Latin and French
Mr. D.R. Moreton B.A., (Cambridge) Physics
Mr. G.D. Martin B.A., (Oxford) English
Mr. P.E. Morris B.Sc., (Liverpool) Senior Biology
Mr. J. Morrow B.A., (London) Senior Latin
Mr. J.E. Norris B.A., (London) Senior English
Mr. A.B. Pett B.Sc., (Nottingham) Mathematics
Mr. D. Richards B.Sc., (Sheffield) Geography
Mr. E. Sigston   Biology
Mr. T. Stafford M.Sc., (Sheffield) Senior Mathematics
Mr. V.A. Stowers B.A., (Nottingham) English

Mr. R. Teasdale B.Sc., (Durham) Senior Chemistry

Mr. G.F. West B.Sc., (London) F.R.A.S., Senior Science and Physics

Mr. T.M. White B.Sc., (Wales) Chemistry

Mr. E.A. Whittaker B.A., (Nottingham) German

Mr. J.M. Woodrow Diploma, (Loughborough College) Senior Games and Physical Education

School Caretaker and Porter: A.R. Pillar

School Secretary: Miss N. Pitcher

1971

No available information.

1981

Headmaster: Mr. M.D. LEIGH B.A., (Leeds)

Deputy Headmaster: Mr. W.N. HOWELL B.A. (Durham)   i/c. Computer Studies, Latin
Senior Mistress: Miss E.M. WESTLEY B.Sc., (London) Physics.

Mrs. A. Adamson B.A. (London) English, R.E.,

Mrs. N. Allen-Semark. B.A. (Reading)   Art, French

Mr. J.R.A tkinson Cert. Ed., (Chester) Physical.Education., Geography, Mathematics

Mr. P.G. Baker B.Sc., (London) Head of Science, Head of Chemistry, Head of 2nd year

Miss. Baldwin (Part-time Greenacre)   Art

Mr. J.H. Blyth D.L.C. (Loughborough) Head of Lower School., Religious Ed., Physical Education

Mr. J. Bradcock Cert. Ed., (Avery Hill)   Support Education

Mr. K.L. Brown Cert. Ed., (St. Mark and St. John)   Mathematics

Miss K. Browne (part-time) Cert. Ed., (Leeds) Home Economics

Mrs. Carr (part-time) S.Sc., (Open University) Science

Mr. C.J. Cheshire M.A. (Birmingham) Head of Geography, Head of 5th Year.

Mr. E. Cobbold Cert. of Ed., (St. John's, York.) Head of Craft, Design and Technology

Mr. P. Cooper (part-time Greenacre) Cert. Ed. (Westminster College) History

Mr.K. Davies Cert. Ed. (Exeter.) Science, i/c. Combined Science Courses

Miss A. Day B.A. (Portsmouth) French, German

Mr. D.J. Exell N.D.D. (Eastbourne) ATD., (Brighton) Head of Art

Mrs. E.A. Foster, B.Sc., (Manchester)   Chemistry

Mr.P. Gilbertson B.Sc., (Wales) Head of Biology, Head of Third Year

Miss C. Goodall B.Ed., (East Anglia) Music, Drama

Mrs. A.M. Grant B.A. (Bristol) French, Italian, English

Mrs. M.D. Grice Cert.Ed., Adv. Cert. Ed. (Leeds)   Head of Home Economics

Mr. D. Hacon Cert. Ed (Newcastle)   English, History

Mr. E. Harris Cert. Ed. (Keswick Hall)   Mathematics, English, T.D.

Mr. T.C. Harrison B.A. (Leicester) Head of Modern Languages, French, House Master-Centre

Mr. B. Haylett. M.A. (London) English, Librarian

Mrs. V.A. Heyhoe B.Sc., (London)   Mathmatics

Mr. W. Hogg M.A (Durham) Part-time History, Head of Dept. Emeritus

Mrs. E. Holmes, B.Ed., (Sussex) Physical Education, English

Mrs. Hutchin B.A. (Exeter)   French Music

Mr. Hutchins (Part-time Greenacre) Cert. Ed. (Birmingham) C.D.T. i/c Woodwork

Miss H.C. Jones B.A. (Hull)   History, R.E.

Mrs. J.A. Jones Cert.Ed., (Keswick Hall)   Mathematics

Mr. D. Kightley Cert. Ed. (London)   P.E.

Mr. S.W.G. King part time Greenacre   Cert. Ed. (London)   Head of Religious Studies

Mr. J. Laity, Cert. Ed (Bolton)   Head of Careers, Science

Mr. D.R. Lever B.Sc., (Newcastle) Geography Mathematics, Geology, House Master South

Mrs. J.M. Little B.A. (East Anglia) French, English

Mr. E. Loftis, B.Sc. (Hull) Head of Mathematics, House Master North

Mr. N. Maskell. B.Sc., (London)   Mathematics

Mr. A.J. McMinn B.Sc. (Durham) Mathematics

Mr. M.D. Mitchell B.Sc., (Nottingham) Head of Physics, Head of Science Designate

Miss. A.V. Moore. Cert.Ed., (Sheffield) Physical Education, Biology

Mr.J.A. Newman. B.A. (London) Head of Sixth Form, Geography

Mrs. P.A. Nobbs B.Sc., (Aston)   Science

Mr. G.R. Oxborough B.Sc., (Liverpool) Biology

Mr. J. Pack part-time Greenacre. Cert.Ed., (Keele) Head of Physical.Education.Designate

Mr. R.J. Parry B.A. (Wales) History

Mr. S.F. Patterson Part-time Greenacre., Cert.Ed., (Worcester) Mathematics, T.D.

Mr. P.W. Peachey B.Ed., (U.E.A.) Geography, Mathematics.

Mr. C. Pearson Part-time Hospital Sch.,   Craft, Design, Technology

Miss. G. Roby B.Ed., (Leeds)   Textiles and Fashion

Miss L. Rose B.Ed., (Trent Poly.) H.E., Art, English, Physical Education

Mr. K.C. Rutland Cert.Ed. (St.Mary's Twickenham) Craft, Design, Tech., i/c Tech.Projects.

Mr. E. Sharman Cert.Ed., (Kesteven) Geography

Mrs. Simpson part-time Greenacre Cert.Ed., (Bedford) Support Education

Mr. D.B. Smith B.A. (Exeter) Head of German

Mr. F. Southgate part-time Greenacre B.Sc., (O.U.) Head of Biology Designate

Mr. V.A. Stovers B.A., Cert. Ed., (Nottingham) Head of English

Mrs. K. Symcou B.A. Cert. Ed. (London and Keswick)

Mrs. S. Taylor part-time Dom.Sc.Dip. (Edinburgh) Home Economics

Miss E.M. Townson B.Sc. (Aberystwyth) Head of Girls Physical Education

Mr. R. Rucker M.Ed., (Manchester) Head of Boys Physical Education

Mr. M.J. Turner part-time Hospital School B.A. (O.U.) Craft, Design, Technology

Mrs. Way B.Sc., M.Ed.Psych. Cert.Ed. (Avery Hill) Head of Support Educ.

Miss D. Webb part-time Greenacre Physical Education

Miss Wrightson part-time Cert.Ed., (London Inst.) Business Studies

Fraulein J. Hartmann   German Assistant

Mlle. I. Trublet   French Assistant

Mrs. P. Hudson   School Secretary

Mrs. N. Mobbs   Part-time School Secretary

Mrs. C. Reeder   Part-time School Secretary

Mr. G.J. Wheeler   Caretaker

Mr. W. King   Assistant Caretaker

Mr. A. Besford   Laboratory Technician

Mr. R. Canham   Workshop Technician

Mrs. Broome   Diningroom Supervisor

Mrs. Connor   Diningroom Supervisor

Mrs. Johnson   Diningroom Supervisor

Mrs. Clarke   Cook-in-charge

Mr. E. King   Groundsman

1991

No available information

2001

Headmaster: Mr. D.BRUNTON

Teaching Staff:

Mr. C. Allen	Music	Mr. K. Macdonald	English
Mr. P. Andrews	Physical Education	Ms. T. Martin	English
Mr. J. Barnard	Mathematics	Mr. M. Michell	Science
Mrs. D. Bushell	Science	Mrs. E. Morgan	Music
Mrs. C. Chaplin	English	Mrs. C. O'Leary	Art
Mr. A. Cooper	Student Teacher	Mr. G. Oxborough	Science
Miss J. Diver	Physical Education	Mr. J. Peck	Physical Education
Miss. J. Forster	French	Mr. J. Patchett	Art
Mr. J. Fox	History	Mr. B. Patterson	Mathematics
Mrs. J. Gandy	English	Mr. P. Peachey	Geography
Ms. P. Gase	Physical Education	Mr. G. Pickhaver	Religious Education
Miss L. Gibbs	Science	Mr. N. Pointer	English
Mr. T. Gray	French	Mrs. L. Postle-Knowles	Swimming
Mr. D. Hacon	History	Mrs. A. Roberts	Science
Mrs. K. Horrod	Art	Mrs. J. Shackleton	Mathematics
Mr. D. Hyde	French	Mr. M. Wigg	German
Mr. R. Jay	Science	Mrs. L. Williams	English
Mr. M. Keable	Science	Mrs. W. Woithe	French
Miss. A. Leggett	Science	Mr. K. Woodcock	History
Mr. D. Lever	Mathematics	Mrs. H. Wright	English
Mr. E. Leveroni	English		

Support Staff:

Mr. J.Atkinson	Careers	Mr. E. Loden	Administration
Mr. D. Bailey	Technology	Mrs. A. Mason	Special Needs
Miss C. Baldwin	Support	Mrs. A. Merridale	
Mrs. M. Beck	Technology	Mrs. T. Merridale	Secretary
Mrs. G. Bennison	Technology	Mr. A. Munday	ICT Testing
Miss C. Best	Librarian	Mr. J. Nganga	Burser
Mr. P. Bexfield	Technology	Mrs. L. Nicholas	Support
Miss D. Charlton	Secretary	Mrs. A. Ovenden	ICT
Mrs. T. Cook	Secretary	Mrs. A. Parson	Special Need
Mrs. M. Copp	Support	Mrs. P. Paterson	Technician
Mrs. N. R.Copping	Social Care	Mr. M. Philpot	Technology
Mrs. G. Croft	Secretary	Mr. M. Saunders	Technician
Mrs. S. Ellis	Finance	Mr. B. Smith	ICT
Miss K. Fisher	Support	Mr. D. Thorneycroft	Support
Mrs. J. Fortesque	Support	Mr. S. Tricker	Technician
Miss K. Howeth		Mr. L. Whiting-Smith	Technology
Mr. D. Knowles	Technician	Mrs. P. Wilson	Support
Mrs. S. Knowles	Technician		

Site Staff:

Mr. K. Blinko	Groundsman	Mr. B. Luterbacher	Groundsman
Mrs. L. Clark	Cleaner	Mrs. J. Moyse	Cleaner
Mr. P. Clark	Caretaker	Mrs. K. Patterson	Cleaner
Mrs. E. Collins	Cleaner	Ms. M. Robinson	Cleaner
Mrs. T. Cooper	Cleaner	Mrs. S. Thomas	Cleaner
Miss A. Dunn	Cleaner	Mrs. S. Underwood	Cleaner
Mrs. A. Horne	Cleaner	Mr. S. Young	Caretaker

2010

Head Teacher: MR. A. TOONE

Deputy Head	Mrs. C. Galloway
Assistant Head – Literacy	Mr. C. Allen
Assistant Head – National Initiatives	Mrs. G. Bennison
Curriculum Leader Science	Miss. A. Hampton
Assistant Head – Curriculum	Mrs. J. Wyatt

TEACHING STAFF:

Mr. P. Andrews	Curriculum Leader P.E.
Mrs. J. Appleby	Swimming Instructor
Mrs. R. Arya	Curriculum Leader English
Mr. J. Atkinson	Head of Citizenship
Mr. L. Betts	Teacher of P.E./ Team Leader
Mrs. D. Bushell	Teacher of Mathematics and Science
Mr. B. Butler	Coordinator of Additional Needs
Ms. D. Chastney	Teacher of MFL
Miss S. Daniels	Teacher of P.E. Deputy Team Leader
Mrs. M. Esherwood	Instructor
Mr. P. Fairman	Teacher of Science
Mr. D. Farr	Teacher of Technology
Mr. T. Fisher	Teacher of Mathematics
Mr. R. Fox	Teacher of ICT
Mrs. J. Gandy	Teacher of English
Mrs. C. Gowing	Teacher of Art/ Deputy Team Leader
Mr. D. Hacon	Teacher i/c History
Miss L Hall	Teacher of English
Mr. A. Jarrett	Teacher of Science
Mr. P. Jones	Teacher of Food Technology
Mr. E. Leveroni	No. 2 in English
Mrs. H. Lister	Teacher of Technology
Mrs. A. Martland	Teacher of Science
Ms. E. Mason	Teacher of History
Miss D. Mileham	Teacher of Science
Mrs. K. Nichols	Instructor
Mr. G. Oxborough	Teacher of Science
Ms. J. Pankhurst	Teacher of Mathematics
Ms. K. Pappadimitriou	Teacher of Technology
Mr. P. Peachey	Head of Humanities
Mr. S. Plume	Curriculum Leader Mathematics

Mr. N. Pointer	Teacher of Mathematics
Mrs. A. Pointon-Melville	Teacher of Religious Education
Mr. M. Rooke	School Sports Coordinator
Mr. J. Sanders	Head of PSRE/Citizenship
Mrs. E. Shailer	Teacher of Art
Mr. B. Smith	Curriculum Leader Information Technology
Mrs. N. Snell	Curriculum Leader Expressive Arts
Mrs. S. Steward	Teacher i/c Art
Mr. C. Vaudin	Teacher of Science
Mr. B. Walker	Teacher of MFL
Mrs. P. Walton	Curriculum Leader MFL
Miss K. Watson	Curriculum Leader Technology
Mr. I. Wells	Teacher of Mathematics
Mrs. M. Winney	Teacher of Geography

SUPPORT STAFF:

Mr. N. Alcock	Learning Support Assistant
Mrs. C. Barnes	Learning Support Assistant
Mrs. H. Bates	Receptionist
Miss T. Brewin	LSU Manager
Mrs. J. Bell	Cover Manager
Miss D. Charlton	Curriculum Data Manager
Mr. J. Cooper	Behaviour for Learning Manager
Mrs. T. Cooper	Senior Behaviour for Learning Manager
Mr. P. Crabtree	Skillforce
Mrs. G. Croft	Head Teacher's P.A.
Miss P. Davidson	Learning Support Assistant
Mrs. M. Davies	Learning Mentor
Ms. A. Dreimane	Learning Support Assistant – EAL
Ms. H. Esherwood	Senior Intervention Manager
Ms. E. Fisher-Cook	Learning Support Assistant
Ms. I. Hopwood	Learning Support Assistant
Mrs. T. Hunt	Behaviour for Learning Manager
Mrs. H. Hyde	Learning Support Assistant
Mr. M. Johnson	Learning Support Assistant
Mr. S. Jonas	ICT Technician/Web Designer (LRC)
Mrs. D. Jones	Learning Support Assistant
Mr. S. Knight	Skillforce
Miss R. Lawes	P.E. Technician
Mr. E. Loftin	Admin. Consultant
Mrs. C. Miller	Learning Support Assistant
Mrs. W. Miller	BIP Coordinator
Mrs. D. Myhill	Lab Technician
Mr. J. Nganga	Finance Manager
Mrs. L. Nicholas	Child Protection Coordinator
Mrs. A. Parsons	P.A. to Coordinator of Additional Needs
Mrs. P. Paterson	Network/LRC Manager
Mrs. Y. Pitt	Learning Support Assistant Mathematics
Mrs. D. Roddis	Community Learning Manager
Mrs. C. Simmons	School Support Manager

Mrs. S. Singleton	Clerical Assistant (Finance)
Mrs. C. Smith	General Clerical Assistant
Mrs. T. Smith	LRC Coordinator
Mrs. S. Thomas	Support Worker Behavioural/Cleaner
Mr. S. Tricker	D&T Technician
Mr. A. Turrell	Lab Technician
Mr. K. Webb	Learning Support Assistant
Mrs. J. Webster	Learning Support Assistant
Miss S. Williams	Attendance Manager
Mrs. P. Wilson	Cover Supervisor

SITE STAFF:

Mrs. G. Brown	Deputy Cleaning Supervisor and Midday Supervisor
Mr. P. Burton	Cleaner
Mrs. R. Charlton	Midday Supervisory Assistant
Mrs. H. Craig	Midday Supervisor
Mrs. P. Cuthbert	Cleaner
Miss A. Dunn	Cleaner/Midday Supervisor
Ms. L. Ford	Midday Supervisory Assistant
Mr. M. Kevern	Groundsman
Mrs. E. Locke	Midday Supervisory Assistant
Mrs. D. Moore	Midday Supervisor
Mrs. J. Moyse	Cleaner
Mr. A. Myhill	Site Manager
Mrs. E. Thompson	Cleaner
Mrs. S. Underwood	Cleaner
Mr. C. Volpe	Caretaking Assistant
Mr. S. Young	Caretaker

Source:
1. Whitehead J.B. *The History of Great Yarmouth Grammar School 1551- 1951*, Great Yarmouth, 1951
2. Hogg W., Supplement to Whitehead J.B. book
3. Author's Reseach Information and Great Yarmouth High School Records

Appendix 3
School Captains, Head Boys and Head Girls

1910	G.H.Jeary	1933	G.V.V.Squire
1911	A.V.Ames	1934	H.K.Taylor
1912	E.J.Bevan	1935	A.W.Avery
1913	E.J.Bevan	1936	J.E.E.Kirby
1914	E.J.Bevan	1937	A.V.Alcock
1915	E.G.Bevan	1938	D.E.Bailey
1916	K.G.Bevan	1939	D.E.Bailey
1917	K.G.Bevan	1940	D.A.Bayles
1918	T.G.Platten	1941	B.F.Waller
1919	C.G.R.Williams	1942	B.F.Waller
1920	C.G.R.Williams	1943	K.J.Fielding
1921	E.C.Hayden	1944	J.V.Bean
1922	F.J.Neale	1945	H.L.Jackson
1923	F.W.Thompson	1946	P.F.Bayles
1924	F.W.Thompson	1946	W.P.Goss
1925	H.J.H.Hare	1947	M.T.Brown
1926	A.W.Howard	1948	A.C.Woods
1927	A.W.Howard	1948	P.D.Bond
1928	R.H.Thompson	1949	R.J.Oxborough
1929	E.R.Oldman	1949	P.M.Read
1930	K.E.Lee	1950	W.B.Utting
1931	J.Gedge	1950	B.A.Nelson
1932	W.R.Keeler	1951	G.G.Frosdick

HEAD BOYS

1952	A.G.Carpenter	1960	R.J.Woodall
1953	J.M.Shipston	1961	R.J.Woodall
1953	M.H.Green	1962	I.C.Davy
1953	D.H.Higgins	1963	J.A.Rodger
1954	N.J.Cubit	1964	T.A.Powley
1954	A.B.Mace	1965	D.A.Anderson
1955	C.P.Bassett	1966	R.A.Barfield
1956	M.D.Murrell	1967	A.R.Swanston
1956	B.Caton	1968	J.Clare
1957	K.A.Harrison	1969	B.Howes
1958	D.E.Westgate	1970	D.Lavender
1959	B.W.East		

	HEAD BOY	HEAD GIRL
1971	P.Wiseman	Gillian M. Bane
1972	J.Burgess	Susan K. Smith
1973	Phillip Rivett	Juliet Rackham
1974	Peter Vettese	Jacqueline Courtman
1975	Gary Calver	Jacqueline Game
1976	Kevin Schofield	Susan Miller
1977	Peter Anderson	Wendy Bond
1978	Steven Harris	Jane Bryant
1979	Stephen Poole	Susan Pearse
1980	Philip Schofield	Gillian Hall
1981	Robin Tebbutt	Sally Larner

Source:
1. Whitehead J.B. *The History of Great Yarmouth Grammar School 1551- 1951*, Great Yarmouth, 1951
2. Great Yarmouth Grammar School *Chronicles*

Appendix 4
Prefects 1910-1981

SCHOOL CAPTAINS	PREFECTS		
1910			
G.H.Jeary	A.V.Ames	E.J.Bevan	W.H.Filbey
H.F.Johnson	S.W.LeGrice	P.A.Murrell	
	W.T.Nicholson	W.E.Sillis	H.E.Wilkinson
1911			
A.V.Ames	W.J.Bagge	E.J.Bevan	H.F.Johnson
	E.H.Jex	S.E.May	J.E.Plane
	A.Roberts		
1912			
E.J.Bevan	E.G.Bevan	W.J.Castell	H.F.Johnson
	S.E.May	R.C.Starkings	
1913			
E.J.Bevan	L.L.Beeching	E.G.Bevan	W.J.Castell
C.J.Galbraith	R.Lund	S.E.May	
	C.J.Ovey	H.F.Rushmer	R.C.Starkings
1914			
E.J.Bevan	O.H.Beevor	E.G.Bevan	H.J.D.Day
C.J.Ovey	R.H.Montgomery	R.C.Starkings	
1915			
E.G.Bevan	O.H.Beevor	K.G.Bevan	R.A.S.Castell
	H.J.D.Day	H.E.J.Huke	H.S.Matthes
	P.L.Starkings	W.F.Westney	
1916			
K.G.Bevan	G.B.Alcock	R.A.S.Castell	W.J.Lawn
R.E.Montgomery	A.J.Ovey	T.G.Platten	
	P.L.Starkings		
1917			
T.G.Platten	K.G.Bevan	C.R.Bradley	R.A.S.Castell
	E.A.Fisher	W.J.Lawn	N.D.G.Mackenzie
	R.E.Montgomery		
SCHOOL CAPTAINS	*PREFECTS*		
1918			
W.C.Bradshaw	H.W.Bambridge	T.H.Deary	E.A.Fisher
N.D..G.Mackenzie	R.E.Montgomery	M.H.Morgan	
	T.G.Platten	R.S.Playford	C.G.R.Williams
1919			
C.G.R.Williams	E.Beeching	G.E.Bevan	F.Boyden
E.A.J.Dyble	H.T.G.Tinkler	E.R.Westney	

SCHOOL CAPTAINS

PREFECTS

1920
C.G.R.Williams
E.C.Julier

G.E.Bevan	B.Bradshaw	W.G.Evans
E.C.Hayden	W.H.Mann	

1921
E.C.Hayden

R.R.Johnson	W.C.Moore	F.J.Neale
C.T.W.Newman	B.F.Robson	J.R.Webster

1922
F.J.Neale

C.G.Allen	C.T.Banham	L.W.Freeman
F.W.Thompson	B.G.R.Williams	

1923
F.W.Thompson

R.S.Bradley	H.W.Copeman	H.R.Guenin
R.J.Stone	B.G.R.Williams	

1924
F.W.Thompson
A.W.Howard

R.S.Bradley	H.R.Guenin	H.J.H.Hare
C.B.Staniforth		

1925
H.J.H.Hare

C.N.Elsey	M.B.Finkelstein	A.W.Howard
N.H.Tilsley	R.H.Thompson	

1926
A.W.Howard

W.C.Ellis	C.N.Elsey	M.B.Finkelstein
G.W.Miller	N.H.Tilsley	R.H.Thompson

1927
A.W.Howard

R.H.Thompson

C.V.Baxter	M.E.Claxton	T.Feather
J.W.E.Green	G.W.Rideout	A.W.Smith

1928
R.H.Thompson

J.M.Bishop	M.E.Claxton	L.E.England
T.Feather	J.W.E.Green	C.H.Mayes
E.R.Oldman	A.W.Smith	C.J.H.Ward

1929
E.R.Oldman

H.R.Blyth	M.E.Claxton	K.E.Lee
C.J.H.Ward		

1930
K.E.Lee
E.P.Land

B.L.Bell	J.Gedge	G.G.Jeary
E.R.Oldman	E.O.Skelton	
A.Smiter		

SCHOOL CAPTAINS	PREFECTS		
1931			
J.Gedge	B.L.Bell	J.Cossey	C.G.Harris
A.E.Hawkins	L.C.Howes	W.R.Keeler	
	E.P.Land	J.H.Roll	E.O.Skelton
1932			
W.R.Keeler	J.Cossey	A.E.Hawkins	L.C.Howes
G.G.Jeary	F.L.Nunn	J.H.Roll	
	H.P.Saunders	G.V.V.Squire	
1933			
G.V.V.Squire	O.C.Baker	E.W.Foulser	G.G.Jeary
F.L.Nunn	G.M.Plumbly	M.G.Sayer	
	R.A.Sayer	W.O.Waters	
1934			
H.K.Taylor	J.E.Baker	A.J.Brown	R.M.Mayes
A.A.G.McNaughton	R.A.Parker		
1935			
A.W.Avery	H.M.Docwra	G.A.Hogg	J.E.E.Kirby
H.D.Kite	W.B.LeGrys		
1936			
J.E.E.Kirby	A.V.Alcock	D.E.Bailey	A.D.Chaplin
	J.B.Dye	R.Fraser	G.A.Hogg
	A.W.Platford	L.D.Wooden	
1937			
A.V.Alcock (Captain)	J.Banks	I.M.Bell	J.B.Dye
D.E.Bailey (Captain)	P.G.Lincoln	A.W.Overy	M.E.Vickery
	L.D.Wooden	E.W.Wymer	
1938			
D.E.Bailey	R.H.Bird	S.W.J.Clements	F.H.Collins
E.W.J.Gant	P.G.Lincoln	W.E.Nicholson	
	P.J.Papworth	G.V.E.Thompson	H.J.Wroughton
1939			
D.E.Bailey	D.A.Bayles	R.H.Bird	B.J.Bland
	F.H.Collins	J.K.Jackson	E.J.Lewis
	P.G.Lincoln	P.J.Papworth	A.G.Rouse
	G.V.E.Thompson		

SCHOOL CAPTAINS	PREFECTS		
1940			
D.A.Bayles (Captain)	C.Banks	D.J.M.Buddery	K.Chittleburgh
A.G.H.Rouse (2nd Boy)	R.F.Dye	J.K.England	R.R.Gladden
	O.S.Harvey	A.G.Heron	J.H.Howard
	R.S.Kinns	P.E.Sillis	J.C.Squire
	G.M.Thornton	B.F.Waller	W.C.Whaites
1941			
B.F.Waller (Captain)	T.E.Darby	F.G.French	S.A.Goodrich
C.Banks (2nd Boy)	J.D.Hogg	J.H.Howard	M.J.Hull
	W.D.Parker	G.M.Thornton	
1942			
B.F.Waller	T.E.Darby	F.G.French	J.H.Garrett
	M.J.Hull	D.C.Joslin	N.F.Lowther
	A.Mays	W.D.Parker	G.M.Thornton
1943			
K.J.Fielding (Captain)	J.V.Bean	G.A.Gamlen	G.A.Griffiths
R.L.Eccles (Captain)	G.N.Lovegrove	T.N.Reynolds	
J.Woods (2nd Boy)			
1944			
J.V.Bean	N.B.H.Blake	P.W.P.Browne	H.L.Jackson
T.N.Reynolds	K.D.Mason	P.R.Starkings	V.A.F.Stowers
H.C.S.Garrett (2nd Boy)	R.G.J.Walpole		
1945			
H.L.Jackson	P.F.Bayles	G.L.Brown	W.P.Goss
V.A.F.Stowers (2nd Boy)	J.A.Mobbs	T.W.Read	F.G.Roll
	H.A.J.Scott	P.R.Starkings	
1946			
P.F.Bayles (School Captain)	M.T.Brown	E.R.Daniels	R.G.Edwards
W.P.Goss (School Captain)	G.S.Hawkins	R.G.Howlings	N.G.Hunter
J.H.Buddery 2nd Boy	E.F.N.Pownall	F.A.Rivett	B.K.Sykes
1947			
M.T.Browne (School Captain)	P.Beavon	P.D.Bond	G.Bullent
E.R.Daniels (2nd Boy)	R.G.Edwards	F.D.Gibson	N.J.Hunter
	R.J.Oxborough	M.L.Pratt	R.T.Severn
	G.E.D.Swann	E.A.Twelvetree	A.C.Woods
1948			
A.C.Woods (School Captain)	R.J.Balls	N.E.Bean	M.Browne
P.D.Bond (School Captain)	J.M.Flowerday	F.D.Gibson	R.J.Oxborough
P.Beavon (2nd Boy)	P.M.Read	G.E.D.Swann	W.B.Utting
	J.J.Ward		

SCHOOL CAPTAINS	PREFECTS		
1949			
R.J.Oxborough (Head Boy)	R.J.Balls	N.E.Bean	M.Browne
J.J.Ward (2nd Boy)	M.J.Chase	J.M.Flowerday	T.A.Fraser
P.M.Read (Head Boy)	F.D.Gibson	P.O.Johnson	B.A.Nelson
W.B.Utting (2nd Boy	G.E.Skipper		
1950			
W.B.Utting (Head Boy)	B.N.H.Blake	P.C.B.Boate	A.A.Budds
B.A.Nelson (Head Boy)	G.G.Frosdick	D.H.Kerridge	C. Martin
M.J.Chase (2nd boy)	S.C.Newman	J.L.Orton	P.J.C.Roll
F.R.C.Shorten			
1951			
G.G.Frosdick (Head Boy)	A.R.Barber	E.D.C.Buswell	M.J.Cooper
F.C.Newman (2nd boy)	G.Cullingford	P.F.Larrington	C.F.Martin
S.C.Newman	J.L.Orton	M.J.Raby	
	D.H.Sandall	H.F.G.Swanston	M.E.Thorpe
	B.A.Websdale		
1952			
A.J.Carpenter (Head Boy)	D.E.Bentley	J.H.Blyth	J.S.Coldbeck
B.S.Hurrell (2nd boy)	A.R.F.Dodd	D.J.Ellett	M.H.Green
	D..Liffen	R.M.Loynes	J.M.Shipston
	F.W.Symonds	P.E.Woods	
1953			
J.M.Shipston (Head Boy)	N.J.Cubitt	B.H.Dawson	S.A.Dickinson
M.H.Green (Head Boy)	D.H.Higgins	R.M.Loynes	A.B.Mace
D.E.Bentley (2nd boy)	R.H.Mobbs	G.O.Scott	R.P.Shreeve
	D.W.G.Thomas	P.E.Woods	
1954			
D.H.Higgins (Head Boy)	C.P.Bassett	B.W.Delf	C.R.M.Green
N.J.Cubitt (2nd Boy)	M.J.Hayhoe	R.A.Jones	P.F.Juby
N.J.Cubitt (Head Boy)	A.B.Mace	J.G.Parmenter	R.A.Shearing
A.B.Mace (2nd Boy)	D.J.Symonds	D.W.G.Thomas	W.R.S.Thurtle
A.B.Mace (Head Boy)	R.E.A.Welchman		
J.R.Thompson (2nd Boy)			
1955			
C.P.Bassett (Head Boy)	G.H.E.Barnard	R.W.Barber	K.G.Beales
D.J.Symonds (2nd boy)	I.G.Fox	N.G.Hunt	D.W.Marshall
	M.D.Murrell	D.L.Osborne	M.L.Temple
	C.Valentine		

SCHOOL CAPTAINS

1956
M.D.Murrell (Head Boy)
B.Caton (2nd Boy)
B.Caton (Head Boy)
A.S.W.Young (2nd Boy)

1957
K.A.Harrison (Head Boy)
D.I.Minns (2nd Boy)

1958
D.E.Westgate (Head Boy)
B.W.East (2nd Boy)

1959
B.W.East (Head Boy)
P.D.Hobbis (2nd Boy)

1960
R.J.Woodall (Head Boy)
B.J.Walker (2nd Boy)

1961
R.J.Woodall (Head Boy)
B.G.Granger (2nd Boy)

PREFECTS

J.C.E.Amos	H.C.Berg	R.M.Clayton
R.W.England	M.D.Fisher	K.A.Harrison
B.C.Haylett	T.Kitchener	M.W.Peck
K.J.Pitcher	G.H.Stables	
C.R.Barnes	J.K.Buckle	R.G.Carver
J.E.Clarke	M.J.Gilder	D.W.Gunn
A.V.Hall	L.G.Harbord	R.A.Langham
D.J.Ralfs	R.M.Sainty	I.T.W.Tosh
M.C.Allen	B.P.Boast	H.D.Cyprus
M.Dyball	L.P.E.Dye	D.W.Gunn
P.D.Hobbis	D.Lloyd	A.F.Moyle
R.L.Page	B.G.Powley	D.Rich
M.J.Roshier	J.H.Soanes	
R.F.Boardley	R.A.Brown	W.C.Brugger
A.B..Elliott	T.R.Fakes	R.A.Fox
D.A.Hewitt	A.Lloyd	C.R.Miller
B.G.Powley	M.Rudrum	D.J.Savory
J.A.T.Stafford	B.W.Teather	
M.J.Boice	J.A.Cadmore	D.R.Canham
M.G.Curson	P.J.Davey	R.A.Dowsing
D.A.Emmerson	M.Eyre	R.Eyre
D.T.Farman	G.P.Hobrough	R.D.Hurrell
B.J.Joice	H.R.Neave	J.K.Pereira
W.E.Rayner	D.E.Stone	
R.W.Chapman	P.J.Davey	J.E.Fisher
J.K.George	J.Gibbs	J.W.Grimmer
A.L.Hamilton	P.L.Harris	R.O.Hudson
D.C.Jolly	J.F.Lambert	N.M.Macmillan
J.K.Pereira	J.G.Plummer	E.L.Randolph
W.E.Rayner	B.R.Ryder	J.A.Ward
R.J.Wicks		

SCHOOL CAPTAINS	PREFECTS		
1962			
I.C.Davey (Head Boy)	M.Allen	R.Blount	N.Bonney
J.F.Pond (2nd Boy)	D.Brinded	P.Cooper	C.Ewles
	T.Fairhead	R.Farman	R.Greatrex
	R.Harold	P.Harris	T.Harrison
	F.Hinchcliffe	G.Howard	S.Larner
	D.Lilley	J.A.Rodger	C.Sherwood
	K.Spooner	R.Thompson	T.Trett
	M.Woods		
1963			
J.A.Rodger (Head Boy)	K.G,Allen	D.J.Appleyard	P.C.Bartram
R.L.Hedges (2nd Boy)	J.R.Bowles	G.H.Bradley	G.Burghall
	J.O.Burton	R.S.Cowell	R.E.Farman
	G.H.Futter	M.G.Green	A.Larner
	A.Lord	J.E.Morris	J.A.Owen
	T.A.Powley	C.D.W.Roberts	D.E.Stearne
	P.E.Whall	A.C.Wright	
1964			
T.A.Powley (Head Boy)	R.F.Calver	R.L.Gilbert	P.Hingley
K.G.Allen (2nd Boy)	P.J.Kirkby	I.E.Ling	R.E.Mattocks
	D.W.Nettleship	R.H.Osborne	P.D.Phillips
	D.W.Playford	J.R.Sparrow	A.M.Tucker
	I.J.Wallis	I.F.West	M.E.Wigg
	A.C.Wright	P.I.Wright	
1965			
D.J.Anderson (Head Boy)	P.M.Angwin	D.L.Bircham	D.W.Browne
R.A.Barfield (2nd Boy)	S.H.Carter	M.W.Duffield	R.G.Edrich
	D.B.George	D.J.Harrup	D.L.Kelf
	R.J.Masterson	T.J.Rice	C.J.Rudd
	J.H.Senior	A.C.Smith	T.J.Smith
	D.R.Stone	H.M.Swanston	C.G.Tennant
1966			
R.A.Barfield (Head Boy)	C.A.Angwin	P.Angwin	K.J.Baker
B.R.Philpott (2nd Boy)	S.J.Baker	R.Butcher	M.L.Clarke
	R.J.Davies	R.G.Edrich	D.C.Etheridge
	T.P.George	A.B.Hill	R.W.Hodds
	R.Howes	I.Jarvis	J.E.Leak
	P.R.Morris	J.H.Senior	D.M.T.Sherwin-White
	R.C.Sparham	D.C.Spooner	H.M.Swanston
	K.W.Symonds	R.P.Waller	J.F.Welton

SCHOOL CAPTAINS

PREFECTS

1967
A.R.Swanston (Head Boy)
P.R.Harold (Deputy)

C.Angwin	M.Bell	A.W.Bennett
M.J.Caston	R.J.Coward	J.F.Edwards
R.A.J.Emmerson	P.D.J.Forman	C.R.I.Friend
R.Fulcher	C.T.George	F.Hayhurst
D.Holland	R.H.Hunny	I.Jarvis
V.T.King	D.R.Lambert	R.J.Mantrippe
B.G.Norton	M.J.Sayer	E.J.Smith
R.C.Sparham	G.R.Tennant	N.Waller
N.C.Wiseman		

1968
J.Clare (Head Boy)
J.Chapman (Deputy)

R.Bird	M.Burgess	C.F.M.Creasy
A.Dobbins	V.A.Ecclestone	C.F.Elliott
P.E.Fryer	P.Hamilton	J.Haverson
R.Heard	A.Hewitt	R.W.Heyhoe
G.R.Johnson	I.D.Marsh	J.Riselborough
G.L.Roberts	D.Turner	P.Tye
B.L.Windschoffol	J.J.Wooton	C.I.Wright

1969
B.Howes (Head Boy)
RS.Farrow (Deputy)
P.Haverson (Deputy)

D.I.Clifton	T.J.Downing	C.J.Elliot
C.C.Harrison	G.R.Johnson	J.R.Lanham
P.J.Seal	J.Shreeve	D.A.Smith
P.Strachan	P.J.Thornton	S.C.Thorpe
J.A.Tubby	R.E.Welborn	I.C.Wells
C.V.Wright	D.Wright	

1970
D.Lavender (Head Boy)
C.R.Rauhl (Deputy)

R.Atkins	H.Bessey	John C.Blake
R.Chandler	Roland S.Crighton	Mark O.Duffield
Michael.J.Fenn	Steven.Hales	Jonathon.P.Hill
S.G.Knights	Stephen.R.Meale	P.Morley
N.J.Pendleton	Gordon C.Reed	M.C.Reynolds
C.J.Smith	Robert R.Swanston	David W.C.Thompson
H.Tubby	A.S.Thorley	S.L.Weiss
N.A.Willgress	D.Wright	Colin R.Young

1971
Paul R.Wiseman (Head Boy)
Alan K.Gates (Deputy)
Gillian M.Bane (Head Girl)
Jacqueline S.Boldra (Deputy)

Richard Algar	William S.Ball	Martin D.Berry
David I.Bowen	Jonathon P.Court	David H.Cracknell
Angela Drury	Stephen M.Fairweather	
Matthew P.G.Freeman	Richard J.Fuller	Graham R.Gall
Christine M.London	Phillip F.Myhill	Gary A.Palmer
Andrew M.Phillips	David S.Powell	John L. Roberts
Susan K.Smith	John A.Stead	Peter T.Walsh
Richard D.Wedon	Martin C.Wheller	Colin R.Young

SCHOOL CAPTAINS

1972
John Burgess (Head Boy)
Tim J.Chapman (Deputy)
Susan K.Smith (Head Girl)
Jacqueline Boldra (Deputy)

1973
Phillip G.Rivett (Head Boy)
Phillip A. S   y (Deputy)
Juliet Rackha   d Girl)
Judith Poole (De   )

1974
Peter Vettese (Head Boy)
David Isle (Deputy)
Jacqueline Courtman (Head Girl)
Nicole Favier (Deputy)

1975
Gary D.Calver (Head Boy)
Craig Richardson (Deputy)
Jacqueline Game (Head Girl)
Susan.Tubby (Deputy)

PREFECTS

Gillian M.Bane	Malcolm Bryant	Denise Ching
Stephen G.Church	Jane Ditcham	Angela Drury
Alan J.Fakes	Carolyne Fenton	Edgar A.Ferns
Phillip C.Gallaway	Marion Hare	Stewart K.Lewis
Christine London	John Parmer	Graham J.Parry
Felicity Pitts	Robert Read	Rodger G.Smith
David F.Springall	Christopher Simmonds	
Glenn Taylor		

Phillip J.Alison	Jeffery J.Bean	Claire Bloom
Peter Buchan	Susan Bull	Angela Grace
Andrew Eagle	Nigel Frytt	Penny Howell
Elizabeth Howes	Brian Jeffery	Stephen Jennis
Philip Kightley	Sheila Morton	S.W.Pearce
Susan Postle	G.Taylor	Nigel Tooke
David A. Turner	Rachel Warner	Colin G.Welborn
David C.Willliam	Linda A.Woods	

Ian Amato	Nigel Baldwin	Russell Bell
Philip R.A.Brown	Philip.Browne	Graham Dighton
Jacqueline Dommett	Barbara Fakes	Donald Ferns
John S.Fuller	Andrew P.Giles	Janet Goody
Denise Leeder	Pam McCullough	Colin McGuinness
Joseph P.Oakley	Kevin Oliver	Susan Reeve
Susan Richardson	John.D.Sayer	Heather Seaman
Jan Wozniak		

Jonathon Atkinson	Neal P.Bensley	William P.H.Calvert
Andrew J.Clarke	Ian Cox	Peter Critoph
Paul J. Dashwood	Glen Fiddy	Julian A.Fulcher
David A.Goodrum	Susan P.Hansell	Graham .Harris
Phillip Hatchett	David A.Kightley	Michael.Munday
John Osborne	David J.Poole	Jane Poole
Jane Sewell	Mark Skoyles	Gail Smith
Michael Tooke	Marcus Trett	Ian Ward
John Wiseman		

SCHOOL CAPTAINS

PREFECTS

1976
Kevin Schofield (Head Boy)
Ian Price (Deputy)
Susan Miller (Head Girl)
Christine Fellgett (Deputy)

Claire Amato	Stephen Andrews	Nigel Ashworth
Mary Bailey	Donna Baldwin	Neil Belden
Laurence Brookes	Malcolm Brown	Stephen Brown
Stuart Bushell	Ian Caspall	Bronya Cluer
Paul Cole	Susan Courtman	Andrew Fenton
Lesley Fraser	Keith Hammond	David Hurrell
Keith Jary	Mark Larner	Geoffery Leavold
Marlon Lodge	Denise Loomis	David Lusty
Paul Miller	David Newman	Deborah Nichols
Michael Oakley	Paul Page	Chris Racy
David Tess	Uma Thompson	Brian Wilkinson
David Wooden	Stephen Wright	

1977
Peter Anderson (Head Boy)
Martin Ecclestone (Deputy)
Wendy Bond (Head Girl)
Carol Jones (Deputy)

Anita Cimelli	Stephen Daniels	Kim Fish
Ian Fraser	Colin P.Goodrum	Lesley K.Jakes
Sandra J.Jones	George W Jurie	Thomas Jurie
Rosemary J.Lankester	Werner Mannes	John Mcdermott
Karen Metcalfe	Steven Mitchell	Glynis A.Neslen
Miranda Nichols	Paul Nichols	Michael Oakley
Susan R.Page	Stuart C.Partridge	Susan Perkins
Karen Saggers	Heather Trueman	Janet Trueman
Debra White		

1978
Steven Harris (Head Boy)
David Williams (Deputy)
Jane Bryant (Head Girl)
Nicola Warrington (Deputy)

Peter Anderson	Debbie Archer	Gillian Baer
Ian Baker	Martin Beckett	Nicholas Brothers
Barbara Brown	Jayne Bull	Nicholas Calver
Karen Colley	Kevin Cook	Heather Cunningham
Judy Fenn	April Fish	Richard Green
Amanda Hakes	John Harbord	Jonathon Hoar
Tim Hurst	Andrew Hilton	Dean Laley
Louise Leeder	Debbie Mallett	Stephen McMurrugh
Andrew Moll	Janet Nockolds	Mark Platten
Catherine Rae	Kathryn Rowell	Jenny Saunders
Phillip Seago	Anne Stuart	Ingmar Timmann
Paul Willis	Jeanette Wood	Carol Wright

SCHOOL CAPTAINS

1979
Stephen Poole (Head Boy)
Nicholas Pearson (Deputy)
Susan Pearce (Head Girl)
Anne Wright (Deputy)

1980
Philip Schofield (Head Boy)
Francis Navarro (Second Boy)
Gillian Hall (Head Girl)
Linda-Jayne Dyble (Second Girl)

1981
Robin Tebbutt (Head Boy)
David Felmingham (Deputy)
Sally Larner (Head Girl)
Susan Tranfield (Deputy)

PREFECTS

1979

David Anderson	Michael Archer	Gary Ball
Keith Batley	Graham Clarke	Susan Clarke
Josephine Coleman	David Cuffley	Kim Driver
Sarah Game	Louise Grace	Avril Grimmer
Linda Hambling	Beverley Hubbard	Caroline Ladmore
Heather Liddiment	Glyn Margeson	Neil Martins
Karen Mullins	Kevin Nolen	Wendy Read
Caroline Scarll	Simon Tribbett	Andrew Twitchell
Adrian Watling	Gary Wiseman	Jill Wooden

1980

Simon Anderson	Teresa Appleton	Nicholas Belden
Andrew Blyth	Kevin Boldra	Simon Bond
Caroline Branch	Kevin Brett	Robert Brodie
Sonya Brown	Andrew Cattee	James Cunnington
Paul Coffin	Michelle Dove	Gabrielle Faerber
Richard Green	Nicholas Kent	Andrew Lawrence
Sandra Liffen	David Luke	Priti Mather
John McNamara	Alison Mobbs	Simon Moore
Martin Moss	Carl Musson	Lucy Myatt
Michael Palmer	Simon Partridge	Malvin Peachey
Yvonne Plumley	Carol Randell	Debra Rodwell
Keith Roper	Stephen Rowe	Nicholas Starkings
Martina Sutton	Glen Tovell	Susanne Trip
Christopher Troise	Paul Trueman	Richard Walke
Wendy Walpole	Ian Ward	Ian Wills
Teresa Willsher	Roger Wilson	Fiona Wright
John Wright		

1981

Mark Abel	Pru Allington-Smith	Margaret Beck
Stephen Bowles	Peter Braidwood	Karl Clinton
Donna Cluer	Karen Collier	John Conway
Susan Driver	Jayne Edwards	Mandy Emerson
Jacqueline Farmer	Geoffrey Giles	Martin Greaves
Dawn Green	John Groome	Gail Hazell
Dominic Hellinsworth	Elizabeth Hepworth	Sharon Kendall
Paul King	Kevin Mace	Angela Medgrail
Christine Osborne	Joanna Parr	Andrew Price
Diane Read	Angela Rogers	Christine Sherman
Wendy Stuart	Dawn Symonds	Susan Taylor
Keith Tucker	Jacqueline Twitchell	Penelope Vardy
Jonathan Walsh	Susan Webster	Martin Woolsey

Source:
1. Whitehead J.B. *The History of Great Yarmouth Grammar School 1551- 1951*, Great Yarmouth, 1951
2. Great Yarmouth Grammar School *Chronicles*
3. The London Old Boys' Association record book. Held at the Norfolk Record Office. 1951

Appendix 5
Gloria Domus

1867	J.B. Lee	Exhibition. Sid. Suss. Cambridge
1875	A.T.S. Goodrick	Demy Magdalen College,.Oxford
1879	A.T.S. Goodrick.	1st Class Class. Mods. Oxford, Fellowship St. John's College. Oxford
1883	G.R. Thornton.	Sizar St.Johns's College. Cambridge.
1885	E.R. Frederick	Scholarship Magdalene College. Cambridge.
1886	F.A. Wright	Exhibition Magdalene College. Cambridge.
1888	E.L.M. Barry	1st Class Modern Languages. Tripos. Cambridge.
1889	C.O. Raven	Choral Scholarship. St. John's College, Cambridge.
1890	F.A. Wright	1st Class Class Tripos. Cambridge.
	F.H. George	Scholarship Jesus College. Cambridge.
1892	H.R. Yates	Scholarship. Jesus College. Cambridge.
	A.T. Goodrick	Sizar Corpus Christi College. Cambridge.
1894	A.D. Culley.	BA, Music. Bac. Cambridge.
1895	S.C. Moseley	Sizar St. John's College. Cambridge.
1898	E.P. Doughty	Scholarship Pembroke College. Cambridge.
1901	M.W. Flack	Exhibition. Keble College. Oxford.
1902	E.P. Doughty	1st Class Class Tripos. Cambridge.
1903	R.T. Dawson	Exhibition St. John's College Cambridge.
1905	H.M.S. Collier	Exhibition. Selwyn College Cambridge
	W.C. Bevan	Scholarship. University Dunelm.
1908	F.J. Woods	Sizar Trinity College. Cambridge
	W.E. Beck	1st Class Theology. University Dunelm.
1909	M.W. Flack	Radcliffe Fellowship Oxford
1912	E.J. Bevan	Exibition. St. John's College Cambridge
1914	E.J. Bevan	Sizar St. John's College Cambridge
1915	E.G. Bevan	Scholarship. University Dunelm.
1920	E.J. Bevan	1st Class Pt. 1 Class. Tripos. Cambridge
	E.J.Bevan	Scholarship. St. John's College. Cambridge
	T.G. Platten	Exhibition. St. John's College. Cambridge
1921	E.J. Bevan	1st Class Pt. 11 Class. Tripos. Cambridge
	T.G. Platten	1st Class Pt. 1 National Science Tripos. Cambridge
1922	T.G. Platten	1st Class Anthropology Tripos. Cambridge
		Scholarship. St. John's College. Cambridge
1943	J. Woods	State Scholarship. Exhibition. Queen Mary College. London
1944	H.L. Jackson	Norfolk Senior Scholarship.
	K.D. Mason	Exhibition. University College. London
	T.N. Reynolds	Scholarship. Sheffield University.
1945	P.F. Bayles	Norfolk Senior Scholarship.
	G.L. Brown	Norfolk Senior Scholarship.
	H.L. Jackson	Exhibition. King's College. Cambridge.
	V.A.F. Stowers	Great Yarmouth Major Award
1946	J.H. Buddery	Royal Scholarship. Imperial College. Science. Offered State Scholarship.
1946	G.S. Hawkins	Great Yarmouth Major Award
	W.P. Goss	Great Yarmouth Major Award
1947	M.T. Browne	Norfolk Senior Scholarship.
	N.J. Hunter	Royal Scholarship In Science.
	R.T. Severn	Royal Study In Science.
	A.C. Woods	State Scholarship.
	J.Woods	BSc., Physics, Queen Mary College, London.
1948	P. Beavon	Great Yarmouth Major Award
	P.D. Bond	State Scholarship.
	R.J. Oxborough	Great Yarmouth Major Award
	G.E.D. Swann	Great Yarmouth Major Award
	J.J. Ward	Great Yarmouth Major Award

1949	W.B.Utting	State Scholarship.
	D.H. Kerridge	Royal Study. In Science
	M. Browne.	Great Yarmouth Major Award
	A.A. Budds	Great Yarmouth Major Award
	P.O. Johnson	Great Yarmouth Major Award
	P.M. Read	Great Yarmouth Major Award
1950	W.B. Utting	Exhibition in Modern Studies, New College, Oxford
	D.H. Kerridge	State Scholarship.
	P.W. Brewster	Norfolk Major Award
	M.J. Chase	Norfolk Major Award
	G. Cullingford	Great Yarmouth Major Award
	S.C. Newman	Great Yarmouth Major Award
	J.L. Orton	Great Yarmouth Major Award
	G.G. Frosdick	Great Yarmouth Major Award
	A.R.Jordan	Marine Society's bursary to H.M.S. Worcester

HONOURS WON BY OLD BOYS

1950	R.Boulton	Institute of Chartered Accountants final examination
	L.J.Brighton	Law Society's final examination
	G.L.Brown	PhD, Physics (London)
	R.R.Gladden	BSc., Agriculture, 2nd class hons.in Crop Husbandry (Durham)
	D.Hender	Institute of Municipal Treasurers and Accountants final exam.
	P.O.Kleppe	BSc., Engineering (London, external)
	K.D.Mason	M.B., B.S. (London)
	D.B.Russell	BSc., 2nd class honours, Engineering (London, external)
	G.M.Thornton	English Tripos, part ii, class 2, division 1 (Cambridge)
	J.Woods	PhD., Physics Queen Mary's College, (London),

NEWS OF OLD BOYS

| 1950 | J.Woods (1937-43) | 1950-59 General Electric Company Research Laboratories |

BOYS PROCEEDING TO UNIVERSITY

1952	A.R.Barber	Great Yarmouth Major Award
	R.M.Loynes	Great Yarmouth Major Award
	H.F.G.Swanston	Great Yarmouth Major Award
	B.A.Websdale	Great Yarmouth Major Award
1952	M.F.Thorpe	Norfolk Major Award
	R.M.Loynes	The Stanley Maxwell Prize for Latin, awarded by the Independent Schools Association to the candidate in the summer examination who passed highest in Latin at Ordinary level, having offered the First Alternative Syllabus.

HONOURS WON BY OLD BOYS

1952	J.H.Buddery	PhD., Inorganic Chemistry (London)
	P.M.Read	Geography Tripos, part i, class 2 division 2 (Cambridge)
	H.F.J.Wroughton	BA.Architecture (London) A.R.I.B.A.
	J.A.G.Grimmer	Institute of Chartered Accountants final examination
	P.W.P.Browne	BSc., hons., class 2. Division 2. Mathematics (Nottingham)
	A.C.Woods	BSc., hons., class 1 Mathematics (Manchester)

BOYS PROCEEDING TO UNIVERSITY

1953	A.J. Carpenter	State Scholarship
	J.S.Coldbeck	State Scholarship
	J.Gedge	State Scholarship.
	A.J.McComas	State Scholarship
	J.M.Shipston	State Scholarship
	F.W.Symonds	State Scholarship.

	D. Liffen	Naval Cadetship, Engineering. Royal.Naval College, Dartmouth
	R.M. Loynes	State Scholarship in Maths and Physics, Trinity College. Cambridge
	P.E.Woods	Great Yarmouth Major Award

HONOURS WON BY OLD BOYS

1953	K.C.A.Y.Baldwin	MB., ChB., (Sheffield)
	P.D.Bond	English Tripos part 1 class 2 division 1 (Cambridge)
	R.P.Bradshaw	PhD, Physics (Cambridge)
	G.S.Hawkins	PhD, Radio-astronomy (Manchester)
	N.J.Hunter	BSc, hons., class 2 Chemistry (London)
	P.M.Read	Geography Tripos part ii.Class 2 division 2 (Cambridge)

HONOURS WON BY OLD BOYS

1953	R.T.Severn	BSc, hons., class 2 Mathematics (London), Ph.D., Mathematics (London)
	V.A.F.Stowers	BA. hons., class 2 division 1 English, French (Nottingham)

BOYS PROCEEDING TO UNIVERSITY

1954	D.E.Bentley	State Scholarship
	N.J.Cubitt	State Scholarship
	R.P.Shreeve	State Scholarship
	J.R.Thompson	State Scholarship
	B.H.Dawson	Great Yarmouth Major Award
	D.H.Higgins	Great Yarmouth Major Award
	R.D.Ibbett	Great Yarmouth Major Award
	A.B.Mace	Great Yarmouth Major Award
	R.H.Mobbs	Great Yarmouth Major Award
	G.O.Scott	Great Yarmouth Major Award
	W.R.S.Thurtle	Norfolk Major Scholarship

HONOURS WON BY OLD BOYS

1954	P.Beavon	MB. ChB, (Birmingham)
	N.B.H.Blake	BSc, special hons., class 3, Geology (Reading)
	A.L.Blakesley	Top in the Preliminary examinations of the Institute of Chartered Accountants of England and Wales
	P.D.Bond	English Tripos part ii class 2 (i) (Cambridge)
	P.W.Brewster	BSc, hons., class 1 Chemistry (external, London)
	R.G.Edwards	BA. hons., class 2 (i) Modern History (London)
	K.J.Fielding	D.Phil., English (Oxford)
	G.G.Frosdick	Classical Tripos part I. class 2 (i) (Cambridge), Senior Exhibition, Trinity College (Cambridge)
	J.D.Hender	Top in the Final examination, Society of Incorporated Accountants and Auditors.
	R.G.Howlings	Associate of the Chartered Insurance Institute
	D.H.Kerridge	BSc, hons., class 1 Chemistry (Nottingham)
	N.P.Toll	National Diploma in Design (pupil of the Great Yarmouth School of Arts and Crafts.)
	E.A.Twelvetree	Final examination, Institute of Municipal Treasurers and Accountants.

BOYS PROCEEDING TO UNIVERSITY

1955	R.A.Jones	Major Scholarship for Music, Kings College, (Cambridge)
	J.R.Thompson	Major Scholarship for Mathematics, Trinity College, (Cambridge)
	A.B.Mace	State Scholarship
	D.H.Higgins	Foundation Scholarship, 1953

BOYS PROCEEDING TO UNIVERSITY

1955	C.P.Bassett	Foundation Scholarship, 1954
	B.W.Delf	Great Yarmouth Major Award

P.F.Juby	Great Yarmouth Major Award
D.C.H.London	Great Yarmouth Major Award
D.W.Marshall	Great Yarmouth Major Award
J.G.Parmenter	Great Yarmouth Major Award
B.A.Shearing	Great Yarmouth Major Award
M.L.Temple	Great Yarmouth Major Award
M.J.Hayhoe	Norfolk Major Scholarship

HONOURS WON BY OLD BOYS

1955	M.Browne	BSc, General (London)
	M.J.Chase	BSc, hons., Chemistry (external London)
	G.G. Frosdick	Classical Tripos part ii, class 2 (ii) (Cambridge)
	I.Hargraves	BA.hons., class 2 Modern History (Oxford)
	M.D.R.Howlings	Associate, Chartered Insurance Institute
	P.O.Johnson	BSc, hons class 2 (i) Zoology (Nottingham)
	R.M.Loynes	Senior Scholarship for Mathematics, Trinity College (Cambridge)
	S.C.Newman	BSc. hons., class 3, Chemistry (external, London)
	R.J.Oxborough	BSc. hons., class 3 Chemistry (Nottingham)
	G.E.D.Swann (1953)	BSc. hons., class 2, Electronics (Birmingham)
	H.F.G.Swanston	BA. hons., class 2 (i) English (Durham)
	M.E.Thorpe	BA. hons., class 2 (i) English, (external, London)
	W.B.Utting (1942-50)	BA. hons., class 2 English (Oxford)
	B.A.Websdale	BA. hons., class 2 (ii) Geography (London)
	A.C.Woods (1940-47)	PhD. Mathematics, University of Manchester. 1955-57
		Assistant Lecturer, Department of Mathematics, University of Manchester

BOYS PROCEEDING TO UNIVERSITY

1956	C.P.Bassett	Choral Bursary, Queen's College, (Oxford)
	M.D.Murrell	State Scholarship
	R.M.Sainty	State Scholarship
	P.Mancini	Foundation Scholarship
	K.G.Beales	Great Yarmouth Major Award
	I.G.Fox	Great Yarmouth Major Award
	T.Kitchener	Great Yarmouth Major Award
	D.L.Osborne	Great Yarmouth Major Award
	D.J.Symonds	Great Yarmouth Major Award
	C.Valentine	Great Yarmouth Major Award
	R.W.Barber	Norfolk Major Scholarship
	C.H.E.Barnard	Norfolk Major Scholarship
	N.C.Hunt	Norfolk Major Scholarship

HONOURS WON BY OLD BOYS

1956	D.E.Bentley	Senior Scholarship, (Leeds 1954)
	A.A.Budds	BA, hons., class 2 (ii), Geography (London)
	D.B.Campbell	Higher National Certificate (Electrical Engineering), graduate membership of the Institute of Electrical Engineers.
	G.Cullingford	BSc, hons., class 2 (i) Engineering (Birmingham)
	R.F.Dye	BA. hons., class 3 History (London)
	R.M.Loynes (1946-53)	Mathematical Tripos part ii, class 1 (Cambridge)
	A.J.McComas	BSc, hons., class 1, Physiology (Durham)
	D.Nichols	A.R.C.O., (1954)
	B.S.Seabert	Higher National Certificate, Mechanical Engineering.
	J.R.Whitehead	Law Tripos part (i), class 2 (Cambridge)

NEWS OF OLD BOYS

1957	A.C.Woods (1940-47)	1957-63 Associate Professor Mathematics, Tulane University, New Orleans, U.S.A.

BOYS PROCEEDING TO UNIVERSITY

1958
J.K. Buckle	State Scholarship
K.A.Harrison	State Scholarship
P.D.Hobbis	State Scholarship
G.L.Whiterod	State Scholarship
M.J.Lacey	Foundation Scholarship
A.J.Gardiner	Great Yarmouth Major Award
D.W.Gunn	Great Yarmouth Major Award
R.A.Langham	Great Yarmouth Major Award
J.P.Loxton	Great Yarmouth Major Award
D.J.Ralfs	Great Yarmouth Major Award
D.E.Rich	Great Yarmouth Major Award
I.T.W.Tosh	Great Yarmouth Major Award
C.J.Barnes	Norfolk Major Scholarship
R.J.Carter	Norfolk Major Scholarship
R.G.Carver	Norfolk Major Scholarship

HONOURS WON BY OLD BOYS

1958
A.J.Carpenter	Natural Sciences Tripos par tii, class 2 (ii) Botany (Cambridge)
B.W.Delf	BSc, hons., class 2 (ii) Physics (Birmingham)
J.Gedge	Llb, hons., class 2 (ii) (London)
D.H.Higgins	Modern and Mediaeval Languages Tripos part (i), class 2 (i). Italian, class 2 (ii) French (Cambridge)
P.F.Juby	BSc, hons., class 1, Chemistry (Nottingham)
A.B.Mace	Mechanical Sciences Tripos part (i), class 2 (Cambridge)
R.H.Mobbs	BSc, hons., class 2 (i), Chemistry (Durham)

HONOURS WON BY OLD BOYS

1958
R.E.W.Murrell	BA. hons., class 3, Politics, Philosophy, Economics (Oxford)
D.Nichols	F.R.C.O.
R.A.Shearing	BA. hons., class 2 (i) History (Leeds)
H.F.G.Swanston	MA. (Durham)
F.W.Symonds	BSc, hons., class 2 (i) Electrical Engineering (Nottingham)
G.V.E.Thompson	BSc, hons., class 2 Chemical Engineering (London)
B.J.Thrower	Final Examination, Law Society.

NEWS OF OLD BOYS

1958
J.M. "Michael" Wood	Left School at 16 to develop his long cherished ambition to run his own Turf Accounting Business. He had an extremely successful career and his business was very prosperous. He retired in 2008.
P.E.Woods (1945-52)	Teaching, mainly in Grammar Schools in Yorkshire

BOYS PROCEEDING TO UNIVERSITY

1959
J.C.Bradley	State Scholarship
P.D.Hobbis	State Scholarship
G.L.Whiterod	State Scholarship
B.G.Powley	Foundation Scholarship
M.C.Allen	Great Yarmouth Major Award
A.L.Bewley	Great Yarmouth Major Award
R.W.H.Cooper	Great Yarmouth Major Award
N.A.Duffield	Great Yarmouth Major Award
B.W.East	Great Yarmouth Major Award
R.L.Page	Great Yarmouth Major Award
M.S.Smith	Great Yarmouth Major Award
J.H.Soanes	Great Yarmouth Major Award
C.C.Thorpe	Great Yarmouth Major Award

	D.E.Westgate	Great Yarmouth Major Award
	H.D.Cyprus	Norfolk Major Scholarship
	T.R.Fakes	Norfolk Major Scholarship

HONOURS WON BY OLD BOYS

1959	M.Atter	BSc., Fuel Science, Leeds
	B.A.Baldwin	B.Vet.,Med. Hons., M.R.C.V., Research Training Scholarship, Animal Health Trust.
	A.C.J.Chilvers	A.I.D.
	E.G.Hartley	M.R.C.V.S.
	M.J.Hayhoe	BA,Hons., class 2 (ii) English, Durham 1957
	P.O.Johnson	PhD., Zoology, Cambridge
	R.A.Jones	Music Tripos part I, class 2 (ii) Cambridge
	A.B.Mace	Mechanical Sciences Tripos part ii Cambridge

HONOURS WON BY OLD BOYS

1959	D.W.Marshall	BA, hons., class 2 (ii) French, London
	C.J.Martin	BCh.D, I.D.S., Leeds
	A.J.McComas	M.B.,B.S.,with hons, class 2 and distinction in Surgery, Goyder Scholarship in Clinical Medicine, Charlton Scholarship in Medicine, Ostterson-Wood prize in Psychiatry, Philgown Scholarship in Pathology (for being top in final examination) and the Dichinson Scholarship in Surgery.
	D.R.Read	BSc, Metallurgy (London)
	R.P.Shreeve	BSc, Hons, Class 2 (ii) Aeronautical Engineering, London. A.C.G.I., John Morris Legendre Fellowship, Princeton University. U.S.A.
	G.E.D.Swann	MSc., Physics, Birmingham 1954
	D.J.Symonds	BSc, Zoology, Liverpool.
	J.R.Thompson	Mathmatical Tripos part ii, class 1 Cambridge, Senior Scholarship, Trinity College.
	W.R.S.Thurtle	BA.hons., class 2 (ii) Modern History, London. 1957
	P.E.Woods (1945-52)	BA, hons., class 2 (ii) History, London

NEWS OF OLD BOYS

1959	C.Bowles (1953-58)	Joined R.A.F.Halton as apprentice

BOYS PROCEEDING TO UNIVERSITY

1960	P.D.Hobbis	Open Exhibition for English, Selwyn College, Cambridge.
	H.R.Neave	Foundation Scholarship
	J.F.Brown	Great Yarmouth Major Award
	R.A.Brown	Great Yarmouth Major Award
	A.B.Elliott	Great Yarmouth Major Award
	R.A.Fox	Great Yarmouth Major Award
	M.J.James	Great Yarmouth Major Award
	A.Lloyd	Great Yarmouth Major Award
	M.Rudrum	Great Yarmouth Major Award
	B.W.Teather	Great Yarmouth Major Award
	B.J.Walker	Great Yarmouth Major Award
	W.C.Brugger	Norfolk Major Scholarship
	C.R.Miller	Norfolk Major Scholarship
	D.C.Tennant	Norfolk Major Scholarship
	J.A.T.Stafford	East Suffolk Major Award

HONOURS WON BY OLD BOYS

1960	B.J.Aldrich	A.R.I.B.A

W.G.Bain	BSc, hons. Class 2 (i) Economics (London)
H.C.Berg	BA. hons., class 3 Modern History (Oxford)

HONOURS WON BY OLD BOYS

1960

B.N.H.Blake	L.R.A.M., L.G.S.M.
C.M.Cooper	Final examination, Institute of Chartered Auctioneers and Estate Agents
D.J.Green	Passed out from R.A.F.Halton as top aircraft apprentice
D.H.Higgins	Modern and Mediaeval Languages Tripos part ii, class 2 (ii) (Cambridge)
N.G.Hunt	BSc, hons. Class 2. Chemical Engineering (Leeds)
H.L.Jackson	L.R.A.M
K.J.Pitcher	BSc, hons, class 2 (ii), Chemistry (Birmingham)
R.M.Sainty	Natural Sciences Tripos part I, class 2 (ii) (Cambridge)
J.M.Shipston	BA, hons., class 2 (ii), History and Political Institutions (N.Staffs)
T.M.Smith	Passed out from R.A.F. Hereford as top boy entrant.
J.D.Temple	N.D.D.
M.L.Temple	English Tripos part I, class 2 (i) (Cambridge)
J.R. Thompson	Mathematical Tripos part iii, hons., (Cambridge)
M.D. Thompson	Des., R.C.A. hons., class 2 (i), School of Ceramics

NEWS OF OLD BOYS

1960

J.Woods (1937-43)	Department of Applied Physics, Durham University

BOYS PROCEEDING TO UNIVERSITY

1961

P.J.Davey	Great Yarmouth Major Award
R.D.Downing	Great Yarmouth Major Award
D.A.Emmerson	Great Yarmouth Major Award
R.Eyre	Great Yarmouth Major Award
J.E.Fisher	Great Yarmouth Major Award
T.E.Hunt	Great Yarmouth Major Award
J.F.Lambert	Great Yarmouth Major Award
W.E.Rayner	Great Yarmouth Major Award
D.E.Stone	Great Yarmouth Major Award
R.J.Woodall	Great Yarmouth Major Award
N.C.Haylett	Norfolk Major Scholarship
B.J.Joice	Norfolk Major Scholarship
J.K.Pereira	Norfolk Major Scholarship
H.R. Neave	State Scholarship
W.E.Rayner	Foundation Scholarship

HONOURS WON BY OLD BOYS

1961

G.H.E.Barnard	BA, hons., class 2 (ii), Theology (Leeds)
C.J.Barnes	BS., gen., div.i, Mathematics (Nottingham)
C.P.Bassett	BA, hons., class 2 English (Oxford)

HONOURS WON BY OLD BOYS

1961

R.G.Carver	BSc, gen., div.ii Mathematics and Physics (Nottingham)
P.H.Cushing	English Tripos part I, class 2 (i), (Cambridge)
J.G.Fox	B.D.S., (Durham)
J.Garrett	BSc, gen., class iii, (London)
W.E.Gooch	Final examination Institute of Chartered Accountants
K.A.Harrison	BSc, gen., Mathematics (Nottingham)
D.C.Joslin	Final examination Institute of Chartered Accountants
M.J.Lacey	BSc, hons., class 2 (ii) Chemistry (Hull)
R.M.Loynes (1946-53)	Diploma in Mathematical Statistics, with distinction, (Cambridge)
D.Osborne	BA, general class iii, (Durham)
D.J.Ralfs	BSc, div., ii, Mathematics, (Nottingham)
R.M.Sainty	Natural Sciences Tripos partii, class 3, Chemistry (Cambridge)

F.W.Symonds	MSc, Electrical Engineering, (Tennessee)
J.D.Temple	A.T.D.
M.L.Temple	English Tripos part ii, class 2 (i) (Cambridge)
C.Valentine	BSc, hons., class 2 (ii), Chemistry (Nottingham)
R.W.Walker	Loughborough College Diploma in Electrical Engineering, hons., class ii

BOYS PROCEEDING TO UNIVERSITY

1962	C. Stanyon	State Scholarship
	J.K. Pereira	Entrance Scholarship Imperial College of Science and Technology (London). Eastern Electricity Board Scholarship.
	D.C. Jolly	National Coal Board Scholarship.
	M.Allen	Great Yarmouth Major Award
	M.P.Blackwell	Great Yarmouth Major Award
	M.Cook	Great Yarmouth Major Award
	E.Cox	Great Yarmouth Major Award
	J.Grimmer	Great Yarmouth Major Award
	P.Harrington	Great Yarmouth Major Award
	P.Harris	Great Yarmouth Major Award
	D.Jolly	Great Yarmouth Major Award
	L.Riches	Great Yarmouth Major Award
	D.Wombell	Great Yarmouth Major Award
	J.W.Cunningham	Norfolk Major Scholarship
	N.Macmillan	Norfolk Major Scholarship
	J.Plummer	Norfolk Major Scholarship

NEWS OF OLD BOYS

| **1962** | C.Bowles (1953-58) | In R.A.F. passes ONC. In Mechanical Engineering. |

HONOURS WON BY OLD BOYS

1962	J.Amos	BSc., Pass and Diploma of Associateship of Royal School of Mines in Metallurgy, Imperial College of Science, (London)
	K.Beales	MB, ChB., (Edinburgh)
	A.Bewley	BA, hons., 11(i), General Studies (Leeds)
	J.C.Bradley	BA, hons., Geography 11 (i) (London)
	B.Caton	BA. hons., Geography 11 (i) (London)
	N.Duffield	BSc, Tech., Mechanical Engineering hons., 11 (ii) (Manchester)
	R.Fox	2nd M.B. Part I Physiology, Stephen Scott Scholarship, (Durham)
	B.Haylett	BA, hons., English 1, (London)
	B.Joice 1953-60	BSc, Chemistry 2nd class honours (i) University of Hull
	P.D.Long	Final Examination of Institute of Chartered Accountants
	R.H.Mobbs	PhD., (Durham)
	R.Page	BSc, Special Physics, Pass. Class 1
	M.Peck	BA, hons., History 11 (i) (London)
	R.A.Powley	Final Examination of Institute of Chartered Accountants
	M.Smith	BSc, hons., Economics 11 (ii), (London)
	J.G.Soanes	BSc, Ord. Div.11 (Manchester)
	M.Symonds	MSc, (Liverpool)
	R.W.Walker	Diploma in Technology (Loughborough)
	G.Whitehead	BSc, hons., Physics and Mathematics 11 (Birmingham)

BOYS PROCEEDING TO UNIVERSITY

1963	M.Allen	State Scholarship
	D.E.Gibbon	State Scholarship
	N.L.Bonney	Great Yarmouth Major Award
	J.R.Bowles	Great Yarmouth Major Award
	I.C.Davey	Great Yarmouth Major Award

R.I.Harald	Great Yarmouth Major Award
M.Harboard	Great Yarmouth Major Award
T.C.Harrison	Great Yarmouth Major Award
F.Hinchliffe	Great Yarmouth Major Award
J.Newberry	Great Yarmouth Major Award
A.Stolworthy	Great Yarmouth Major Award

BOYS PROCEEDING TO UNIVERSITY

| **1963** | M.Wood | Great Yarmouth Major Award |
| | N.R. Denver | Norfolk Major Award |

HONOURS WON BY OLD BOYS

1963	J.K.Buckle	BA, hons., Mathematics Junior, Optime, Cambridge
	R.Cooper	BA. hons., 11 (i) Geography (Birmingham)
	B.East	BSc, hons., 11 (i) Chemistry (Durham)
	D.Gunn	BA.Hons., 111 French (London)
	G.Jarvis	R.I.B.A, Northampton Polytechnic
	B.Joice (1953-60)	BSc, Chemistry 2nd class honours (i) University of Hull
	V.C.Kemp	Dip. Tech., (Loughborough)
	M.Lacey	MSc, (Hull)
	D.Minns	BA, hons., 11. Modern Language (Oxford)
	J.Parmenter	MB, Ch.B., (Bristol)
	K.J.Pitcher	MSc, (Birmingham)
	B.Powley	BA, hons., 11 Modern and Mediaeval Language and Literature (Oxford)
	M.Rudrum	BSc, hons. 11 (i) Chemistry (Liverpool)
	B.Teather	BSc, Physics. (Leeds)
	C.Thorpe	BA, hons., 11 (ii) Geography (Hull)
	K.Wedon	B.Tech., (Manchester)
	D.Westgate	BA, hons., 11 French (Nottingham)

BOYS PROCEEDING TO UNIVERSITY

1964	J.R.Bowles	Oxford
	G.H.Bradley	Hull
	J.O.Burton	Hull
	I.C.Davey	Newcastle
	M.G.Green	Nottingham
	A.Larner	London
	M.S.Woods	London
	J.A.Owen	Leeds
	J.A.Rodger	Glasgow
	D.E.Stearne	Manchester
	P.E.Whall	Durham

BOYS PROCEEDING TO TECHNICAL COLLEGE

1964	D.J.Appleyard	West Ham
	J.A.Feuell	Rugby
	C.H.Puxley	National College of Food Technology

BOYS PROCEEDING TO TRAINING COLLEGE

1964	C.D.W.Roberts	Sheffield
	P.Harrison	Sheffield
	A.Lord	Trent Park
	J.R.Thompson	Borough Road
	R.E.Farman	Winchester
	M.J.Byles	Birds Eye Scholarship

HONOURS WON BY OLD BOYS

1964	R.M.Loynes (1946-53)	PhD, Mathematics (Cambridge). Elected Fellow of Churchill College
	J.B.Brown	BSc, ordinary Div:11 Chemistry (Nottingham)
	D.R.Canham	H.N.D., Chemistry (Kingston Technical College)
	J.H.Dodsworth	BSc, General
	D.A.Emmerson	BA, hons., class 111 History (Nottingham)
	P.D.Hobbis	BA, hons., class 1 English and Philosophy (Cambridge)
	T.E.Hunt	BA, hons, class 111 Geography (Liverpool)
	M.P.Jordan	Hons., Diploma C.A.T., (Loughborough)
	H.R.Neave	BSc, hons., class 1 Mathematics (Nottingham)
	W.Rayner (1953-61)	MA. English 2nd Class honours (ii) Selwyn College, Cambridge.
	J.A.T.Stafford	BSc, class 1. Mechanical Engineering (Sheffield)
	B.J.Walker	BSc, hons., class 11 Div:1 Chemistry (Leicester)
	M.Boice	Dip.P.E.,Cert.Ed., Loughborough College
	C.Stanyon	BA, English. Keele University. (He was one of the first attendees on this new 4 year course) Subsequently he lectured in English at Monash University, Australia.
	A.C.Woods (1940-47)	1964-95 Professor of Mathematics, Ohio State University, U.S.A.

NEWS OF OLD BOYS

| 1965 | L.Bewley (1949-56) | Was ordained by the Bishop of Liverpool, and has begun his Ministry in Wigan. |
| | C.F.D.Brace (1956-61) | After three years study at the Yarmouth College of Art has been awarded a place at the Royal College of Art in the Faculty of Graphic and Interior Design. Having gained recognition for his ability in printmaking he will study this in a 3 year course leading to Associateship of the College. |

NEWS OF OLD BOYS

1965	G. Bradley (1956-63)	Now studying Mathematics at Hull, played regularly as left winger for the English Universities Soccer XI again this season. He played in a representative Great. Britain Universities XI against Holland and France in April.
	B.Byrne (1957-64)	At St.Mary's Training College, finished 20th in the Junior Section of the English Cross County Championships held in March this year.
	B.H.Dawson (1953-60)	Having gained a General B.A., degree in French, Spanish and Latin at Sheffield is a work study engineer at Birds Eye's Great Yarmouth factory.

NEWS OF OLD BOYS

1965	D.I.Green	Left in 1956 began as an apprentice and is now a Flying Officer.
	D.R.Ladbrooke (1953-58)	Also entered as an apprentice and recently received his wings and promotion to Flying Officer.
	K.MacMillan (1941-45)	Choreographer with the Royal Ballet, Covent Garden, gained his greatest success so far with his setting this year of Prokofiev's "Romeo and Juliet" which was danced by Fonteyn and Nureyev.
	Bernard Ryder (1953-60)	Cert.Ed., Keele University
	R.Sandall (1957-62)	Finished top of 63 Police Cadets after final training course held in Oxfordshire this April. A member of the Norfolk Constabulary he is stationed at North Walsham.
	W.B.Utting (1942-50)	Left School for New College Oxford in 1949, has been appointed Principal Probation Officer for Newcastle.
	J.A.Ward (1953-60)	Is a Flying Officer stationed at Wattisham and piloting Lightning's with 56 Squadron.

BOYS PROCEEDING TO UNIVERSITY AND UNIVERSITY COLLEGES

1966	P.J.Angus	Woolwich
	P.M.Angwin	Reading
	S.J.Beder	Birmingham

R.A.Barfield	Edinburgh
R.Burghall	Bradford
M.C.D.'Ath	Southampton
R.G.Edrich	Reading
D.C.Etheridge	Manchester
J.R.Farrow	Southampton
M.A.J.Furie	Rugby

BOYS PROCEEDING TO UNIVERSITY AND UNIVERSITY COLLEGES

1966	R.S.Howes	Aberystwyth
	J.E.C.Leak	Bristol
	B.Lloyd	Brunel
	D.M.Martin	Cardiff
	A.Medlock	Leeds
	C.B.Moreton	Southampton
	P.R.Morris	City
	B.R.Philpott	Imperial College
	D.Sherwin-White	Southampton
	J.A.Spinks	Rugby
	D.C.Spooner	Leeds
	D.J.Tyrell	City
	J.F.Welton	Leicester

BOYS PROCEEDING TO COLLEGES OF EDUCATION

1966	G.D.Brown	Walsall
	R.Butcher	Coventry
	M.D.Fiddes	Coventry
	A.B.Hill	Leicester
	R.W.Hodds	Loughborough
	J.G.Lidstone	Bede, Durham
	J.H.Senior	Brighton
	P.C.Taylor	Shoreditc

NEWS OF OLD BOYS

1966	R.G.Bailey	Trainee, May Gurney.
	R.A.Blount	Final year of Honours degree Sandwich Course in Electrical Engineering at Brunel College.
	N.L.Bonney	BSc, Economics (2i) London School of Economics. Obtained State Studentship and now reading for Master's degree in Sociology.
	D.C.Brinded	After completing 3 years Teacher Training Course at Leicester College of Education, now Assistant at the Lycee, Libourne, for one year.
	D.P.J.Brown	Serving in the R.A.F. at Hemswell, Lincolnshire
	I.Buchan	Assistant Controller, British Railways, Cambridge.
	P.D.Cooper	After completing 3 years at Westminster Training College, Oxford is now on the staff of Greenacre S.M.School.
	P.A.Corrie	Passed Intermediate Examination of Chartered Accountants. Studying for Final in 1967.

NEWS OF OLD BOYS

1966	N.R.Denyer	BSc, Electrical Engineering (2ii) Leeds University. Now working at Elliott Automation, Borehamwood to qualify for I.E.E.
	A.R.Ditcham	Second year of A.I.R.I. Course at National College of Rubber Technology. Will be taking H.N.C. finals in Applied Chemistry at John Dalton College of Technology
	C.Ewles	Four year Diploma of Technology Course at Brunel College of Advanced Technology, Acton.
	K.J.Fielding (1941-43)	Appointed to the newly instituted Saintsburys chair English Literature

		Edinburgh. Vice Principal College Education before his appointment. Dr. Fielding best known as an authority on Dickens.
R.Fox (1952-59)		Qualified Doctor Graduate M.B.Bs., Durham
T.W.Fairhead		Obtained H.N.D. Electrical Engineering, Cambridgeshire College of Arts and Technology. Now preparing for Part 111 exam of Institute of Electrical Engineering.
D.E.Gibbon		Final year of BA. Course, Longond University.
R.Greatrex		Gen., Deg., Hons., C1.2(ii) Physics and Chemistry. Now doing post-graduate research leading to M.Sc.,
A.Hall		Buyer's Clerk. Arnolds Ltd.
M.Harbord		BSc, hons., (3rd C1.). Final year for special degree in Cybernetics.
R.J.Harold		BSc, (2ii) Biochemistry, Sheffield University. Now research assistant in the Genetics Department of Glasgow University.
P.Harris		Obtained BSc., Gen., London, F.R.G.S. Employed as Executive Officer, Ministry of Agriculture and Fisheries.
P.Harrison		Final year at Sheffield College of Education.
T.Harrison		Graduated BA, hons., 2(i) in French at Leicester.
M.C.Hurrell		Town Planning Assistant/Building Inspector. Hitchin Urban District Council.
A.J.Kerrison		Apprenticed to Baker Perkins, Peterborough, and taking Mechanical Engineering Technicians Course at Peterborough Technical College
P.S.Killington		After obtaining the National Certificate in Agriculture, now farming near Oulton Broad.
M.King		Executive Grade Civil Service. Now working at the National Assistance Board, Wood Green.

NEWS OF OLD BOYS

1966	A.J.Lawson	Employed by B.P. Tanker Co., as Apprentice Navigating Officer. Obtained Second Mate's (Foreign Going) Certificate of Competency.
	D.Lilly	Received credits in Education and Advanced Physical Education at King Alfred's College. Now teaching in Oxfordshire.
	W.Rayner (1953-61)	School Teacher in English for two years at St.Joseph William Mathematical School, Rochester, Kent.
	N.R.Reynolds	At Leicester College of Art.
	R.J.Russell	Working for Photo Dealers' Examination
	G.K.Simmonds	Trainee Librarian at Great Yarmouth Public Libraries.
	W.Skinner	Civil Servant working at the R.A.F. Radar Station, Neatishead.
	A.J.Stolworthy	BSc., hons., (2i) Mathematics. Leicester University. Now employed as Computer Programmer, English Electric, Kidsgrove, Stoke-on-Trent.
	J.R.Thompson	Final year at Borough Road Training College.
	T.Trett	Passed Intermediate Examination, Institute of Chartered Accountants, Studying for Part 1 Finals.
	R.C.Ward	Final year, Royal Military College of Science.
	M.Woods	Final year of B.D., Course at King's College, London.

HONOURS WON BY OLD BOYS

1967	R.A.Blount	B.Tech., Class 11(i) Brunel
	J.R.Bowles	BA. Class 111., Philosophy, Politics, Economics. Oxford
	R.Brown	Diploma Architecture, Sheffield
	G.H.Bradley	BA, Hull
	J.O.Burton	BSc, Physics Hull.
	P.Davey	BD. Class 11 (ii) London
	T.R.Fakes	BSc, Institute of Chartered Accountants Manchester. First Prize.
	K.A.France	B Tech., Industrial Chemistry. Loughborough
	M.G.Green	BSc, Class 1 Physics. Nottingham

T.C.Harrison	BA, Class 11 (i) French Leicester
B.Joice	PhD,in Palladian Alloys, University of Hull
J.A.Owen	BSc, Class 11 (ii) Physics. Leeds
J.G.Plummer	B.D.S., L.D.S., R.C.S., English Dunelm
M.Rudrum	PhD, Chemistry
J.A.T.Stafford	PhD Engineering
D.E.Stearne	BSc, Class 1 Chemistry. Manchester
B.Walker	PhD, Chemistry
R.Ward	BSc,Special Physics. London

NEWS OF OLD BOYS

1967	Gerald S.Hawkins	Pride of place this year must go to Professor Gerald S.Hawkins, whose book STONEHENGE DECODED has created a considerable furore in Archaeological and Astronomical circles, both professional and amateur. His theory has been widely discussed in the national press.
	J.Atherton	Has obtained the Higher National Certificate and Endorsements in Chemical Engineering. He is at present working for the British Petroleum Company in Neath, Glamorgan.
	R.N.Bailey	Is on the staff of the British Bank of the Middle East and is now at Doha, Qatar, in the Arabian Gulf.

NEWS OF OLD BOYS

1967	R.W.Barber	Teaching in a school of 1,200 in Wolverhampton.
	P.C.Bartram	In his second year at the Leicester College of Art, Faculty of Architecture.
	N.L.Bonney	Spending one year reading sociology at Chicago University, having been awarded a fellow ship and Fulbright Travel Scholarship.
	G.Bradley	Doing a one year Diploma Course in Education at Loughborough College of Education.
	J.K.Buckle	In India for a year, helping to set up a computer department at the Indian Institute of Technology in Delhi. He is possibly the youngest Colombo Plan expert to work in India.
	B.Byrne	Has accepted a teaching post in Great Yarmouth.
	A.C.Cambridge	Is working for Tom Green Ltd.
	G.R.Dougal	Joined the East Suffolk Police as a Cadet in 1963, has now finished his training and is stationed at Lowestoft County Police Station.
	D.H.Gibbon	Obtained a Diploma in Estate Management in 1964 at the Royal Agricultural College, Cirencester, and is now working for the Agricultural Land Service Division of the Ministry of Agriculture in Yorkshire.
	R.B.Hogg	Is working in the Surveyor's and Engineer's Department of the Camborne-Redruth Urban District Council in Cornwall.
	T.R.Pratt	Has accepted a teaching post in Leicester.
	C.H.Puxley	Has obtained the Diploma in Food Technology of the National College of Food Technology, and is at present working in the Research Department of J. & J. Colman of Norwich.

NEWS OF OLD BOYS

1967	G.F.Roe	Reading Mathematics at University College, London, has been appearing for the College on television's "University Challenge". Incidentally, he is the third of our Old Boys to appear on the programme.
	D.Rogers	In training for the Roman Catholic priesthood.
	P.Shreeve	Has accepted a teaching post in East Suffolk.
	A.G.Sussams	Has completed three years of a five-year apprenticeship and has passed the first City and Guild examination in motor engineering.
	B.C.Swan	Has passed the first part of the Savings Bank Institute examinations, and is employed at the local East Anglian Trustee Savings Bank.
	M.E.Thorpe	Formerly working with Professor D.J.Enright at the University of

	Singapore, is now resident Lecturer at Leiden University. This year he has published an extremely useful specialist study of Siegfried Sassoon (Oxford. U.P.).
P.E.Whall	Congratulations on his marriage. He is now on the staff of Hellesdon Hospital and is also reading for an Honours Degree in English.
G.F.Wheatley	Is a trainee Quantity Surveyor with the firm of Sir Robert McAlpine & Sons Ltd.
R.J.Wooden	Is working for the Simon Community in London.
J.Would	Has passed the examination for the National Retail Distribution Certificate and has also obtained an Outward Bound Merit Award.

OLD BOYS NEWS

1968	M.Amos	BSc, in Electrical Engineering. Rugby College.
	D.J.Bray	Officer Cadet (Navigation), has taken a navigation course at Southampton, and also had an article published on "Sailing Wherries".
	B.L.Bell	Left the School in 1930, is teaching Chemistry at Bournemouth Grammar School.
	I.M.Bell	(1930-38) General Manager of an insurance company in Johannesburg.
	I.A.P.Bell	(1931-34) Manager of Barclays Bank at Norwich.
	D.T.Blockwell	Is a work study officer in the Branch Staff Planning Department of J.Sainsbury Ltd. In London. He is also reading for a B.Sc., in Economics at London University evening classes.
	I.Davey	Teaching at the Malosa Secondary School in Malawi.

OLD BOYS NEWS

1968	M.Farrant	Has been appointed to the Central Committee of the Metropolitan Police Traning College at Sunbury.
	Rev.J.Gedge	Rector of Mundesley.
	N.C.Haylett	Has obtained a graduateship of the Royal Institute of Chemistry at the Salford Royal College of Advanced Technology (now Salford University). He has joined the research department of the Ilford Photographic Company, following a period in the research department of Fisons at Ipswich.
	J.E.Ling	Has gone into Librarianship and is now in charge of an area group of libraries in Yorkshire.
	K.C.Moughton	After three years with Willsmore and Tibbenham where he was a Production Assistant, has now moved to Heatrae Ltd. (Norwich) where he is Assistant to the Publicity Manager.
	A.L.Oliver	Is on a five-year apprenticeship with Erie Electronics Ltd. He is working now for his H.N.C. in Electronics.
	R.J.Radmall	Is now working with a firm of consulting engineers in heating and ventilating.
	B.I.Scary	Has been forced by illness to retire early from his post as head master at Portsmouth.
	J.M.Smith (1945-50).	Has since leaving the School obtained the Diploma of College of Aeronautics, Associate Membership of the Institution of Production Engineers, become a chartered engineer and a graduate of the Institution of Mechanical Engineers. He is now Production Manager of the Components Division of the Telephone Manufacturing Company at Canterbury.
	A.Wright	Has joined the Geography Department at Chelmsford Grammar School.
	P.Wright	After obtaining 1st and 2nd class passes in Tele-communications Principles, is now working on outside broadcasts for the B.B.C.

NEWS OF OLD BOYS

1969	C.Alger	BSc, Aegrotat, Hull
	D.Anderson	B.Pharm. (II.ii) Nottingham..
	N.Bonney	MA. Sociology, Chicago.
	M.C.M.Boon (1953-59)	Associate of the Institute of Chartered Accountants. After taking articles at Lovewell Blake, Chartered Accountants.
	M.Cubitt	BSc, (II.ii). Linguistic and Regional Studies. Surrey

NEWS OF OLD BOYS

1969	P.Harrington	PhD, Birmingham
	G.M.Haylett	BA General, Languages. London
	T.Keeler	Dip.A.D., in Fine Art (II.i). Leeds College of Art.
	T.Rice	BSc, (III) Physics. Southampton.
	P.A.Rodgers	BSc, (II) Botany and Zoology. London
	J.Roger	B.V.M.S., Glasgow
	A.Hogarth-Smith	BA. General. Newcastle
	W.Rayner (1953-61)	MA. European Literature, French, German and Russian University of East Anglia. From 1969-73 worked for Central Asia Research Centr e (a little known Government Dept.) carrying out Russian translation.
	D.Stone	BSc, (II.ii), Electrical Engineering. Nottingham
	C.Tennant	BSc, Liverpool.
	A.Triggs (1957-64)	BA, (II.ii) English; Grad Cert Ed University of Leeds,
	A.Triggs (1957-64)	1969-71 Teaching in Primary Schools.
	D.E.Westgate	PhD., French. University of Western Ontario.

NEWS OF RECENT OLD BOYS

1969	D.Anderson	Has just been elected to the post of Information Officer for the British Pharmaceutical Students' Association.
	R.Bellin	Played chess for England in the International Junior Tournament at Le Mans.
	D.Browne	Is taking a degree course in Politics at Reading and hopes to go on to York in the autumn for Dip.Ed., Course
	S.H.Carter	Has just concluded a sandwich course in Mechanical Engineering spent at Rugby College and with George Wimpey & Co..
	M.W.Duffield	Is taking a medical course at Manchester
	G.Dye	Is Merchandise Manager with Debenhams at Bournemouth.
	D.B.George	Is working in the Norwich Trustee Department of Barclays Bank.
	Flt.Lt. K.A.Harrison	Has unofficially beaten the British United Kingdom gliding speed record for a 100-kilometre flight by 15 kilometres per hour.
	G.M.Haylett	Is completing a Cert.Ed., course at University College in Cardiff, before becoming a German teacher at Crown Woods Comprehensive.

NEWS OF RECENT OLD BOYS

1969	D.L.Kelf	Previously serving at meteorological stations in the British Isles, is now at Reading taking a degree course in Physics and Meteorology.
	C.J.Rudd	Is just completing a four-year sandwich course in Mathematics at Portsmouth College of Technology.
	D.G.Wain	Is with Maddison & Storey Ltd.

NEWS OF OLD BOYS

1969	J.B.Dye	Former Brigadier has been appointed General Officer Commanding Eastern Region and promoted to the rank of Major-General.
	B.W.East	PhD, has been appointed lecturer at the University of Strathclyde.
	R.G.Edwards	Is now Headmaster of King Henry VIII School, Abergavenny, Monmouthshire.
	J.F.Hovell	Has become sub-manager of the Midland Bank's branch at Mile Cross Lane in Norwich
	M.P.Jordan	Is Assistant Professor of Technical Publications and Publicity at Queen's University, Kingston, Ontario.
	R.M.Loynes (1946-53)	This summer becomes Professor in the Department of Probablity and

	Statistics at the University of Sheffield.
D.Stone	Takes up a Science Fellowship at Tennessee University.

NEWS OF OLD BOYS

1970	David Harrup	Associate of the Institute of Chartered Accountants.
	P.Woods (1946-52)	MSc. Education, University of Bradford

ACADEMIC HONOURS WON BY OLD BOYS

1971	D.Anderson	Has been awarded a Ph.D., Nottingham for work on the study of amines in the brain.
	P.Angwin	B.Mus., Reading
	D.Atherton	BSc, Agricultural Biochemistry 2 (i) Newcastle
	D.Buddery	A.R.C.S., B.Sc., Physics 2 (i) London
	M.Burgess	BSc, Chemistry 2 (i) Manchester
	D.Chapman	Dip. A.D. Graphic Design. Leicester Polytechnic
	G.Cutting	BSc, 2(ii) Civil Engineering, Nottingham
	A.Dobbins	LLB, Liverpool
	V.Ecclestone	BSc, (Ord.) Div. 1 Chemistry, Manchester
	K.Elsey	B.Tech., (Ord.) Div 1, Applied Chemistry, Brunel
	C.Friend	BSc, (Gen.) 2 (ii) Portsmouth Polytechnic
	M.Hacking	B.Pharm., Wales
	R.Hunn	BSc, Physics, Manchester

ACADEMIC HONOURS WON BY OLD BOYS

1971	T.James	Associated of the Institute of Chartered Accountants and later Master of Business Administration.
	D.L.Kelf	BSc, 2 (i) Meteorology, Reading
	D.Lambert	BSc, Microbiology, London
	J.Lidstone	BSc, II Economics, London
	J.Littlewood	BSc, 2 (ii) Physics and Mathematics, East Anglia
	B.Lloyd	B.Tech. 2 (ii), Psychology, Sociology and Economics, Brunel
	I.Marsh	BSc, 2 (ii) Biochemistry, Birmingham
	B.Norton	BSc, 2 (ii) Chemistry, Manchester
	T.Oxborough	BSc, Electrical Engineering, Lanchester
	G.Thompson	BA 2 (i) Fine Art, Nottingham
	N.Waller	BA. (iii) English, Lancaster

NEWS OF OLD BOYS

1971	Bernard Ryder (1953-60)	Lecturer in P.E. University of East London.

ACADEMIC HONOURS WON BY OLD BOYS

1972	S.Bone	BSc, Class 1 Chemistry, Leicester
	M.C.M.Boon	BA,Class II English and Law, Nottingham
	J.Chapman	BSc, Class 1 applied Physics, Hull
	J.Clare	BSc, Class II (i) Applied Mathematics, Edinburgh
	R.J.Coward	BSc, Engineering Metallurgy, Bath
	R.Downing	MA, (ii) Ecological Sciences, Edinburgh
	B.J.Dye	BSc, Class 1 Mathematics, Leicester
	G.J.Edwards	BSc, II Computer Science. N.Staffs. Polytechnic
	R.Farrow	BSc, Class II Electronics, Salford
	B.J.Haylett	BSc, Chemistry, Nottingham
	B.Howes	Master of Civic Design, Liverpool
	J.R. Lanham	BSc, Agriculture, Reading
	J.Shreeve	BSc, Chemistry, Nottingham
	P.Strachan	BSc, II (ii) Southampton
	B.A.Sturman	BA.Class II (ii) English, Swansea

A.Swanston	B.Tech., Brunel
P.R.Tye	BA. Class II (ii) German and French, Selwyn College, Cambridge
A.J.West	BSc, Marine Engineering, Newcastle
B.Windscheffel	B.Ed., Sheffield

NEWS OF OLD BOYS

1972 Michael Boon (1953-59)   Group Management Accountant for Caister Group, a Major Sub-Regional Holiday and Leisure Firm, operating Hotels, Garages, Broads Hire Fleets and Holiday Centres.

NEWS OF OLD BOYS

1972 Chris Bowles (1953-58)   Higher National Certificate in Mechanical Engineering, Sergeant, Air Frame Fitter, worked on Canberra's and Lightenings.

John Clare (1961-68)   Worked for Mars Ltd., in various Marketing positions in the U.K., Switzerland, Denmark, and Sweden.

Brian Joice (1953-60)   Works at York University in the Careers Advisory Service, advising students, until his retirement 30 years later in 2002.

A.Triggs (1957-64)   1972-79 Lecturer in Eglish, Bingley College, Yorkshire

Peter.E.Woods (1943-52)   Lecturer in Educational Studies, The Open University

ACADEMIC HONOURS WON BY OLD BOYS

1973	C.Angwin	BA. II (ii) Economics, Cambridge
	S.Baker	BSc, II (ii) Mech. Engineering, Birmingham
	A.Bennett	BA, II (i) Social Studies, East Anglia
	D.Brooks	BSc, II (ii) Economics, London
	R.Burghall	BSc, III Technology, Bradford
	B.Byles	II (ii) Biology, Sussex

ACADEMIC HONOURS WON BY OLD BOYS

1973	R.Chaplin	BSc, II (ii) Electronics, Manchester
	E.Cullum	BSc, II (ii) Civil Engineering, Newcastle
	J.Dashwood	Dip. Of Art and Design, Leicester Polytechnic.
	P.Davey	B.Ph. Prehistoric Archaeology, Liverpool
	M.De'Ath	BSc, II (ii) Electronics Engineering, Southampton
	B.Harbord	BSc, II Electrical Engineering, Manchester
	R.J.Harold	MSc, Bacterial Genetics, Glasgow
	M.Harvey	BSc, II (i) Economics, Hull
	D.Hayton	BA, I History, Leeds
	I.Jarvis	BSc, II (ii) Engineering, Imperial College
	V.T.King	BA, II (i) Geography and Sociology, Hull
	R.L.Mantrippe	BA, II (i) Modern and Medieval Languages, Cambridge
	B.Moreton	MA, German, Newcastle
	D.T. Sherwin-White	BA, II (i) English and French, Southampton
	B.Sloper	MSc, Operational Research, Hull
	E.J.Smith	BSc, I Geology and Physics, Aston
	A.Spooner	BSc, II (ii) Fuel Science, Leeds
	J.Welton	BSc, Mathematics, Lancaster
	J.F.West	MSc, Communications Systems Engineering, Essex
	N.Wiseman	BSc, I Economics, Leeds.

OLD BOYS NEWS

1973 D.L.Bircham (1959-66)   Is now in the second year of V.S.O. teaching at Balaka, Malawi

N.Bonney (1955-62)   Has been awarded a Ph.D. Sociology by the University of Chicago, for a study of race relations within the local steel industry. He has been appointed a lecturer at the University of Aberdeen.

I.Davey (1953-60)   And his wife are teaching in Malawi and spoke to the 6th form of

		their experiences.
W.B.Utting (1943-50)		Is now Director of Social Services for the Royal Borough of Kensington and Chelsea.

ACADEMIC HONOURS WON BY OLD BOYS

1974
R.Atkins	BA, II Accountancy, City of London Polytechnic.
R.Chandler	BSc, II (i) Physics, London
C.Creasy	BSc, I. Mathematics, Leicester
G.Cruickshank	BSc, II (ii) Estate Management, College of Estate Management.
C.Elliott	B.Tech. II (ii) Mechanical Engineering, Brunel
A.Haughey	BSc, III. Microbiology, London
A.Norton	BA, Geography, Cambridge College of Arts and Technology

ACADEMIC HONOURS WON BY OLD BOYS

1974
C.Rackham	BSc, II (i) Biochemistry, Bristol
M.Reynolds	BSc,, Ii (ii) Microbiology, Birmingham
D.Smith	BSc, I Chemistry, Liverpool
J.Tubby	BSc, II (ii) Mechanical Engineering, Southampton
D.Weiss	BSc, Engineering, Thames Polytechnic.
R.Welborn	BSc, II (ii). Chemical Engineering and Microbiology, Swansea
N.Willgress	III. Electrical and Electronic Engineering. Leeds
D.Hayton (1960-67)	Has been awarded a D.Phil. Oxford and a Junior Research Fellowship at the Institute of Irish Studies, Queen's University, Belfast.
M.T.O'Reilly (1957-62)	Teaching at Caister Primary School is among this year's graduates of the Open University.
Paul Seal	Associate of the Institute of Chartered Accountants.

NEWS OF OLD B OYS

1974
Michael Boon (1953-59)	Appointed Secretary of the Great Yarmouth Port and Haven Commissioners
William Rayner (1953-61)	From 1974-88 Took Welding courses, qualified as a Specialist in Non-Destructive Materials offshore. Worked at various oil platforms.

CAMBRIDGE GENERAL CERTIFICATE OF EDUCATION – A LEVELS
THREE PASSES

1975
Ian Amato	Geography, Plymouth Polytechnic
Philip Brown	2 Grade A passes, Physics, Imperial College London.
Richard Cooper	Queen Mary College, London
Jacqueline Courtman	1 Grade A Pass, Pathology, Norfolk & Norwich Hospital
Kevin Faerber	Frans Maas Shipping Co.,
Donald Ferms	Chemistry and Physics, University College London.
John Fuller	1 Grade A pass, Mathematics, Warwick University
Malcolm Grimson	Physics, University of East Anglia
David Hollowell	Lloyds Bank
Henry Kelf	Architecture, Kingston Polytechnic
Colin McGuiness	Aberdeen University
Trevor Mutton	Languages, Bangor University
Joseph Oakley	2 Grade A passes. History, Corpus Christi, Oxford
Kelvin Oliver	1 Grade A pass, Chemistry and Physics, University College, London
Graham Smith	Customs and Excise

TWO PASSES
Michael Baer	Accountancy, Birmingham Polytechnic
Nigel Baldwin	1 Grade A pass. Geography, Kingston Polytechnic
Nicole Favier	Keswick College of Education
David Isle	Architecture, Kingston Polytechnic
Susan Richardson	Keswick College of Education
John Sayer	Applied Biology, Ewell Technical College

Heather Seaman	Clacton College of Education
Anthony Seymour	Accountancy, Birmingham Polytechnic
Peter Vettese	1 Grade A pass, Geography, King's College, London

ONE PASS

Russell Bell	Yarmouth College of Further Education
Philip Browne	Amoco
Glen Bowie	Norwich Union
Graham Dighton	Physical Education, Dartford College of Education
Jacqueline Dommett	Cambridge College of Arts and Technology
Barbara Fakes	Nursing, Harold Wood, Essex
Terence Lelean	Oil Company, location.
Pamela McCullough	Keswick College of Education
Lennie Wescholuk	To Canada

NEWS OF FORMER STUDENTS

1975		
	D.J.Anderson	B.Pharmacy.M.P.S.,M.I Biology, PhD, District Pharmacy Officer, St.Luke's Hospital, Guildford.
	Martin Berry (1964-72)	BSc. (Honours) Geology, University of London. Worked for various company's' as a Geologist until 1984 when he went to work for Welltech International Pty.Ltd., (Australia)
	M.P.Blackwell	European Studies, University of East Anglia,
	C.Elliott	MSc, Operational and Management Studies, Imperial College, London
	M.Finley	Biochemistry, York
	A.Gates	Civil Engineering, Manchester
	N.Gilbert	Quantity Surveying, Trent Polytechnic,(Cleveland District Council)
	A.Grapes	Economic and Business Studies, Sheffield. (Probation Officer)
	C.Harrison	English, York
	R.Hazell	Already a graduate in Chemistry, is now a chartered Librarian and assistant reference Librarian at Peterborough.
	D.Helm	Geology, Bristol
	S.G.Knights	Building Economics and Management, Aston

NEWS OF FORMER STUDENTS

1975		
	S.G.Mather	Medicine and Surgery London.
	S.Meale	English, York (Research for MPhil, York).
	P.Myhill	Economics, City Polytechnic
	G.Palmer	Physics, Birmingham
	N.Pendleton	Chemistry, Manchester (MSc. Pollution control)
	S.Powell	Sussex
	B.Ryder (1953-60)	Having taught P.E. and History at the King's School Pontefract, gained advanced Dip. P.E., from Leeds University.
	M.Wheeler	Physics, Sussex
	C.Welborn	Has passed out of R.N.College, Dartmouth and is now serving on H.M.S.Wilton
	C.Young	Microbiology, Q.E.C. London (research for Ph.D.)

ACADEMIC SUCCESSES OF PAST STUDENTS
DOCTORATES

1976		
	Patrick Hamilton	Oxford, Geology, now research at Columbia U.S.A.
	David Hayton	Oxford, History of government in early 18th century Ireland
	E.J.Smith	Aston, Hydrogeology, now with Welland & Nene River Authority.
	Clark Friend	Geology, London
	Colin Creasy	MSc, Mathematics, University of East Anglia
	Richard Algar	1st class honours, Civil Engineering, Surrey, MSc, Imperial College, London
	Martin Berry (1964-72)	BSc, Hons.Geology , University of London
	Ian Brinklow	Physiology, Newcastle, PhD. St. Mary's Hospital.

Susan Brown	1st class honours, Mathematics, Sheffield
Malcolm Bryant	Anatomy, London
John Burgess	Geography, Liverpool, Wirral River Authority.
Robert Corrick	Physics, University of East Anglia, Ph.D. Manchester
Denise Ching	Biology, Birmingham
John Court	Applied Biology, Liverpool, Immunology.
Roland Crighton	Systems Management
Angela Drury	1st class honours Computer Science, Reading
Michael Furie	Education, Liverpool
David Grimson	Earth Sciences, Sheffield
Terence Hazell	Food science, top student, Nottingham, PhD.,
Derek Jarvis	Mathematics, Sheffield, M.Sc., University of East Anglia
Christine London	1st class honours, Mathematics & Statistics, Leeds Coal Board.
P.V.Pendleton	Chemistry, now MSc., Manchester Pest Control.
Graham Parry	Geography, London
Paul Roofe	Civil Engineering, Sheffield.
Susan K.Smith	1st class honours, Biochemistry, Q.M.C. London, Holzminden, Germany, perfumer chemist. (1st Head Girl of G.Y.G.S.

OTHER SUCCESSES

1976	A.Gee	Is an artistic assistant with the English National Opera
	Christopher Angus	Graduated at Southampton last year is studying Law at Chester Law College
	Stephen Gee	Pt.1 of Architecture Diploma, Plymouth Tech
	Stephen Sanderson	Diploma in Yacht and Boatyard Management, Southampton Tech.

OTHER PAST STUDENT NEWS

1976	Robert Bellin	Who was selected to compete in the January Grandmasters of Chess Premier Chess Tournament at Hastings was rarely defeated but was unable to make any wins.
	Donald Burton	Has appeared frequently on T.V. in the "Warship" series.

OTHER PAST STUDENT NEWS

1976	A.E.Hawkins	Chairman of the Central Electricity Board, who was chief guest at the 1973 Prize Day, has been created a Knight in the 1976 Queen's Birthday Honours List.
	Gerald Hawkins (1939-46)	Who presented prizes 3 years ago has been appointed Chief Scientific Advisor to the U.S.Bureau of Information.
	Michael Harvey (1945-52)	A Principal Lecturer at London Polytechnic produced (with his wife) the Ladybird book on knitting and has recently published a handbook on machine knitting, a field in which he was a pioneer. He has recently been made a Professor
	Kenneth MacMillan (1941-45)	Director of the Royal Ballet
	Dr.F.W.Symonds (1945-52)	Associate Professor of Electrical Engineering at the University of Tennessee has been elected a senior member of the American Institute of Electrical & Electronics Engineers.
	Philip Talbot	Is an assistant Stage Manager and actor at the Savoy Theatre, London.
	W.B.Utting (1942-50)	Director of Social Services for Kensington & Chelsea has been appointed Chief Social Work Officer at the Department of Health & Social Security with the rank of deputy-secretary.

OLD STUDENTS NEWS

1977	Father O.Baker	Of Downham Market is a Catholic Priest
	Michael Boon (1953-59)	The Chairman of the Port and Haven Commissioners announced that Mr.M.C.M.Boon, the Commissioners Secretary, had been appointed to the position of the Authorities First Chief Executive from an application list which contained a strong external field.
	Dr. Norman Bonney	Is a lecturer at Aberdeen University, is also a City Councillor and a parliamentary candidate for East Aberdeenshire
	D.J.Bray (1960-65)	Is Lecturer in Navigation at Lowestoft College. After 3 years in the Antarctic

	survey he gained his Master's certificate. He helps to run the Norfolk Wherry "Albion" in the summer months.
M.T.Browne (1941-48)	Lecturer in Physics at Queen Elizabeth's College, London University
P.K.Browne	Was working on his own account in computers after an R.A.F. career, was killed in the Zagreb air disaster in September last year, He was 40.
P.W.Browne (1937-44)	Was with the U.N.Statistics branch in Togo.

OLD STUDENT NEWS

1977	M.Dodman	Is Director of Studies at the Oxford School of English in Venice
	K.J.Fielding	Professor English Literature, Edinburgh
	Rev.D.W.Cleverley Ford (1924-29)	Is Domestic Chaplain to the Archbishop of Canterbury.
	Dr.G.Gamlen (1935-42)	Is now Professor of Chemistry at Salford.
	D.Jeffrey	Has moved from his reporting post with the local press to become a Parliamentary reporter at the House of Commons.
	R.M.Loynes	Professor Probability, Sheffield
	M.Harvey	Professor Commerce, London Poly.
	G.Hawkins	Professor Astronomy, Boston
	A.J.McComas	Professor Neurology, Ontario
	T.Nettleship	Recently passed out of Dartmouth R.N.College.
	R.Steele	Professor Geography, Liverpool
	Father Hamish Swanston	Lecturer at Kent, is a Catholic priest
	Peter Whall	Is principal of a school for autistic children at Southport

ACADEMIC HONOURS OF PAST STUDENTS

1977	Stephen Bone	PhD. Chemistry, Leicester (Research Chemist, Newcastle)
	Stephen Meale	B.Litt. English Literature, York (Consumer Protection, York C.C.)
	A.Triggs (1957-64)	MA in Linguistics while on secondment University of Leeds 1977-78

FIRST DEGREES

1977	Jeffrey Bean	Electrical & Electronic Engineering, Loughborough
	Nigel Fryatt	Geography, London (Production Engineer, Mullards)
	David Grimson	Physics, Leeds
	Roy Jennings	Electronic Engineering, Essex
	Andrian Lamb,	(Left to go City College, Norwich after O Level). M.B.B.Chir., Kings, Cambridge (House Surgeon, Harold Wood Hospital)
	Philip Kightly	Geology and Geography, London
	P.J.Osborn	Graphic Design, Lanchester Poly.
	Judith Poole	English, Reading
	Susan Postle	Geography, Cambridge College of Arts and Technology (M.Sc., Birmingham, Meteorology and Climatology, Birmingham)
	Keith Rose	Biochemistry, Manchester
	David Springall	French and German, Reading (Teaching)

FIRST DEGREES

1977	Nigel Tooke	Biochemistry, 1st class honours, Liverpool (PhD, Wales)
	Peter Welborn	Urban Surveying, Trent Polytechnic. (London, Surveying Coy.)

ACADEMIC HONOURS OF PAST STUDENTS

1978	Robert Steel	Is now Principal of University College, Swansea, and has been awarded an honorary degree by the University of Salford.
	Colin Crease	PhD. Mathematics, University of East Anglia
	Colin Young	PhD, Immunology, Fellow and Assistant Professor Microbiology and Immunology, California
	F.M.Cushing	M.Lit., York. For a thesis on the American Jewish Novel
	Derek Javis	MSc., Theoretical Mechanics, University of East Anglia. He is continuing with

Susan Postle	research at U.E.A. for a PhD, MSc, Birmingham in geography and climatology.
A.Triggs (1957-64)	Senior Lecturer in Linguistics, College of Ripon and York St.John (part time) 1978-80

FIRST DEGREES

1978

Philip Alison	Metallurgical engineering and management, Loughborough
Ian Amato	Geography, Plymouth Polytechnic
Steven Brown	Mechanical Engineering, Loughborough, (Ministry of Defence)
Philip Brown	Physics, Imperial College, London (M.Sc., research)
Nigel Baldwin	Geography, Kingston Polytechnic.
John Fuller	Mathematics and teaching, Warwick
Malcolm Grimson	Mathematics and Physics, University of East Anglia
Stephen Jennis	Engineering, Physics and Diploma in Industrial Studies, Loughborough.
Sheila Moreton	Sussex Education (Teaching music, Priory School)
Joseph Oakley	Modern History, Corpus Christi, Oxford
Philip Storey	1st class honours Electronics & Physics, Loughborough
Nigel Thorpe	1st class honours Petroleum Engineering, London.

ACADEMIC HONOURS OF PAST STUDENTS

1979

Michael Boon (1953-59)	Fellow of the Institute of Chartered Accountants
Russell Leggett	Associate of the Institute of Chartered Accountants.
Richard Morris	Associate of the Institute of Chartered Accountants
Peter Woods (1945-52)	PhD. Sociology of Education, The Open University.

ACADEMIC HONOURS OF PAST STUDENTS

1980

John Baer	1st Class honours Biochemistry, Manchester
Lawrence Brooks	Physics, Leicester
Jacqueline Dommett	English, Dundee
Lesley Fraser	Geography, Manchester
Philip Hatchett	1st class honours Applied Physics, Lancaster Poly. To study for Ph.D. in magneto-optic properties of metal.
Terence Hazell (1965-72)	PhD, Nottingham, Food science research.
David Harrup (1958-64)	Fellow of the Institute of Chartered Accountants. Afterwards worked as a Chartered Accountant in South Africa.
Deborah Martin	Zoology and Comparative Physiology, Q.M.C. London
Paul Miller	1st class honours Music, Huddersfield Poly.
Michael Munday	1st class honours Biochemistry, Chelsea College, London
David Newman	Physics, Manchester (Ph.D.)
Paul Page	Geochemistry, Leicester (M.Sc., in Mineral Process Design, Imperial College London)
Kevin Schofield	1st class honours Earth Sciences, Leeds
Stephen Wright	Electrical Engineering, Bangor

NEWS OF OLD BOYS

1980

Father Oswald Baker	Leader of the Tradentine Mass movement in the Catholic Church is now in Norwich.
Robert Bellin (1961-69)	Won the 1979 British Chess Championships title at Chester in August at his 7th attempt. Robert makes a living as a chess author and is an International Master.
Joe Bradley (1950-57)	Is a managing director of the Nationwide Building Society
Philip Galloway (1963-73)	Is a member of the Coull String Quartet as a violinist, they are musicians in residence at the University of Warwick. It broadcasts occasionally on 3rd programme.
A.Triggs (1957-64)	Educational author full-time 1980-96 part-time thereafter.
Dr. Colin Young (1963-71)	Is Sub-Professor at Surrey University researching into Immunological genetics.
Lt. Colin Welborn	Who left school in 1972 for Dartmouth Royal Naval College is Skipper of H.M.S. "Bronington" previously commanded by the Prince of Wales.

OLD BOYS NEWS

1981	Dr. K.J.Fielding (1955-65)	Saintsbury Professor of English Literature at Edinburgh University adds to his many publications with Volume 5 of an edition of Dickens Letters. It was described by one reviewer as a "model of scholarship".
	Mr. D.H.Higgins (1947-54)	Senior Lecturer in Italian at Bristol University has brought out an edition of Dante's Divine Comedy in translation.
	Nigel Ashworth (1971-77)	Pilot Officer has won the sword of honour as best officer cadet at his passing out parade at the R.A.F. College, Cranwell.
1981	Kenneth Macmillan (1941-45)	Principal choreographer of the Royal Ballet, produced his new ballet " Isadore" in April this year to commemorate the company's 50th anniversary.
1982	Russell Leggett	Made a Partner at Lovewell Blake, Chartered Accountants
1983	Bernard Ryder (1953-60)	Head of Recreation and Sports Science, University of East London. Teaching B.Sc., course in Applied Sports Science.
	John Clare (1961-68)	Worked as Marketing and Business Development Director for the Ladbrooke Group.
1984	Russell Leggett	Fellow of the Institute of Chartered Accountants.
	M Boice (1953-60)	B.A.Social Science, Open University.
	Michael Boon (1953-59)	Reformed the Old Port and Haven Commissioners Board and became the Senior Statutory Appointed Member of the Great Yarmouth Port Authority.
	Paul Seal	Fellow of the Institute of Chartered Accountants.
1985	Richard Morris	Partner Lovewell Blake, Chartered Accountants.
	Chris Bowles (1953-58)	Partner and Director in his own firm Eastern Windows.
1985	Martin Berry (1964-72)	Appointed Senior Geologist for Magellan Petroleum Australia Limited, Brisbane. 1985-2007
	John Clare (1961-68)	He joined the Dixons Group and after various posts became Group Managing Director in 1991 and Group Chief Executive.
	J.Woods (1937-43)	Dean of Science, Durham University
1987	J.Woods (1937-43)	Professor of Applied Physics, Durham University.
	P.E.Woods (1943-52)	Professor in Education
1988	Michael Boon (1953-59)	Chairman of the Medium Ports Committee of the British Ports Association.
	William Rayner (1953-61)	Principal Lecturer for the Welding Institute, Cambridge from 1988-97
1989	Richard Morris	Fellow of the Institute of Chartered Accountants.
	Richard Barfield (1958-64)	Formerly Head boy of the Grammar School became Head of International Standard Life. He retired to Scotland.
	J.Woods (1937-43)	Emeritus Professor, Durham University.
1990	Michael Boon (1953-59)	Served as National Federation Treasurer and the New British Ports Federation, the First Associations Successor Organisation.
1994	Michael. Boice (1953-60)	MA.Sussex University
1995	Michael.Boice (1953-60)	1995-2007 Visiting Resident Fellow Sussex University.
	A.C.Woods (1940-47)	Emeritus Professor, Ohio State University, U.S.A.
1996	Richard Burrage (1953-58)	BA.2nd Class honours (i)) in Fine Art, University of Central England. Then taught Fine Art in Rugby.
1996	Paul Seal	Fellow of the Chartered Institute of Taxation.
1997	William Rayner (1953-61)	1997-2007 Returned to the offshore platforms and then retired. Reads, French, German, Russian, Italian, Spanish, Portuguese, Norwegian, Dutch, Latin and Ancient Greek. (All self-taught).
	P.E.Woods (1943-52)	1998-2005 Research Professor in Education, The University of Plymouth.
1999	Michael Boon (1953-59)	Having served as National Treasurer in the Further Successor Organisation, the New British Ports Association, he then served as Deputy Chairman and finally as Acting Chairman at the B.P.A. Annual General Meeting.
	Michael Boon (1953-59)	Having completed all the paving work and being the architect of the Yarmouth Outer Harbour. Retired to return to his Academic Interests.
	Paul Seal	Member of the Society of Tax and Estate Practitioners.
2000	Ian Wells	Was Principal of Tees Valley University.

2001	Michael Boon (1953-59)	Advanced Diploma in Local History from Cambridge University in 18th and 19th Century Theatre Studies.
2002	Brian Joice (1953-60)	Retires from Careers Advisory Service after 30 years and now continues to play classical piano and assists his wife in promoting the Northern Branch of the Jane Austen Society.
	Bernard Ryder (1953-60)	Retired, set up own consultancy, Project work on European Social Funds Finance.
2004	John Clare (1961-68)	Group Chief Executive Officer of the Dixons Group was awarded the CBE.
2004	John Clare (1961-68)	Group Chief Executive Officer of the Dixons Group was awarded the CBE.
2004	Bernard Ryder (1953-60)	Project work in International Development Office, University of East London.
	P.E.Woods (1943-52)	Emeritus Professor, Open University
2005	Michael Boon (1953-59)	Diploma in Theatre History from Cambridge University in Shakespearean Performance in the Circuit Theatres of East Norfolk and North Suffolk, C. 1750-c.1830.
	Michael Boon (1953-59)	Master of Studies in Local History, Corpus Christie College, University of Cambridge and the Role of the Gentry in Yarmouth C.1450-C.1509.
	Roger Canwell (1953-58)	BA,2nd class honours (i) History, University of East Anglia. Roger Had worked as a Certified Accountant for 30 years at major Great Yarmouth firms such as Erie Resistor, and Johnson and Co., before returning to University.
2007	Michael.Boice (1953-60)	Retired – Honorary Visiting Resident Fellow to present day
	Martin Berry (1964-72)	Berry Energy Pty.Ltd. 2007-2008
	John Clare (1961-68)	He retired and holds a number of Non-Executive, and Chairman's positions on UK companies, and serves as a member of the Edinburgh University Advisory Board.
2007	Bernard Ryder (1953-60)	Project work for Anglia Ruskin University in India and Sri Lanka, and for Salford University in the Middle East, Nigeria, and West Africa.0
2008	Martin Berry (1964-72)	Chief Geologist for Celtique Energie Petroleum Limited 2008- present.
	Roger Canwell	Reached the Master Mind Final, after highly successful run in the competition, although he did not win, he put up a very creditable performance and was the first Grammar School boy to have achieved this success.
2010	Michael Boon (1953-59)	Is a current post-graduate 15th Century Research Historian at Royal Holloway, University of London, studying the Port and Town of Yarmouth. C.1450-c.1509. He is also the writer of Local History Books
	Russell Leggett	Senior Partner, Lovewell Blake, Chartered Accountants.

Sources:
1. Whitehead J.B. *The History of Great Yarmouth Grammar School 1551- 1951*, Great Yarmouth, 1951
2. Grammar School *Chronicles*
3. Author researched information

Appendix 6
Roll of Honour   1914-18

Arthur James Ames

Harrison Woodrow Arnott

William John Bagge

Kenneth James Mackenzie Baines

Gilbert Campbell Baird

Edward Leopold Milner Barry

Charles Edward Bond

Reginald Boydon Bray

Douglas Charles Brunning

Wallis John Castell

Geoffrey Rochfort Collins

Reginald Percy Cowles

Henry Julian Dunlop Day

Leslie George Deuce

Francis Cecil Cochrane Devlin

Leslie Harold Durrant

Vere Arthur Kelf Ellis

Lawrence Cecil Falcioni

Bernard John Glanfield

Gordon Glanfield

Hugh Stevenson Grand

Arthur Kidman Hewett

Gilbert Cecil High

Stanley Frederick Derry Hyde

Laurence Herbert Kay

Victor Reginald King

Charles Lawn

Stanley Walter Le Grice

Henry Lewis

Vernon Hatherden Littleboy

Frank Leslie Loftus

Robert Henry London

Alfred William Matthes

Stanley Ernest May

John Guilford Miles

William Irwin Nicholson

Henry Montgomery Scott Pillow

Harold Chadwick Porter

John Sleeman Reed

Percy George Edward Reeder

Thomas Ruddock

John Dakin Rushmer

John Henry Scarles

George Gibson Smith

Cecil Claude Frederick Staden

Ernest John Ballard Tacon

Bernard John Baptist Traynier

Richard Dacre Turton

Zouch Austin Turton

Francis Herbert Wade

Percy Gosden Ward

Henry Etridge Wilkinson

Herbert Wroughton

Source:
1. Whitehead J.B. *The History of Great Yarmouth Grammar School 1551- 1951*, Great Yarmouth, 1951
2. Memorial Plate in The Great Yarmouth High School

Adams C.E.	P/O	F.A.A		1927-33
Anderson C.C.R.	P/O	R.A.F.		1925-35
Balls W.R.	Sgt.	R.A.F.		1931-35
Barrett W.S.		R.A.F.		1931-36
Bird R.H.	F/Sgt.	R.A.F.		1932-39
Bland B.J.	F/O	R.A.F.		1932-39
Boulton D.	Lieut.	Commando		1929-36
Browne P.A.				
Butterworth A.N.	A.B.	H.M.S. Hood		1930-36
Campling J.N.	Lieut. (E.)	R.N.	M.B.E.	1928-34
Chittleborough K.T.	Lieut.	1st. Airborne		1932-40
Claydon R.A.	W/T	R.N.		1928-34
Cooke G.E.				1929-34
Cotton J.P.	Tpr.	R.A.C.		1936-41
Creek R.A.	F/Sgt.	R.A.F.		1932-37
Cremer T.	Lieut.	R.M.		1918-23
Crickmer P.M.		M.N.		1930-37
Dyball R.E.	Cpl.	R.A.F.		1933-37
Ellis A.G.	Major (Mentioned in Despatches)	R.Norfolk Regt.		1926-34
England J.K.	Lieut.	Parachute Regt.	M.B.E.	1933-40
Evans W.G.	R.S.M.			1918-20
Fraser R.	A.B.	R.N.		1932-36
Goward F.G.	Pte.	Essex Regt.		1935-41
Harvey E.L.				
Harvey O.S.	F/Sgt.	R.A.F.		1936-40
Harwood L.H.	F/Sgt.	R.A.F.		1936-40
Hatch R.L.G.	L/Cpl.	R.A.		1929-35
Heron A.G.	F/O	R.A.F.		1934-39
Jeary G.G.	P/O	R.A.F.		1918-32
Lane A.R.	F/Sgt.	R.A.F.		1933-38
Lansdell J.	Sgt.	R.A.F.		1924-34
Lawrence B.J.T.				
Lawson K.A				
Mack H.G.	Second Officer	M.N.		1925-30
Mayes N.W.	Second Officer	M.N.		1926-30
Mays B.D.		R.A.F.		1935-40
McAdam M.D.	Lieut.	R.A.		1918-28
Medcalf A.D.	Sgt./Navigator	R.A.F.		1930-39
Morgan G.E.	Major	Hampshire Regt.		1923-28
Page C.F.	P/O	R.A.F.		1929-35

Potter G.			
Richards C.T.			
Richards G.			
Roche R.M.J.	Capt.	Nigeria Regt.	1919-25
Rouse A.G.H.	F/O	R.A.F.	1928-40
Sadd N.			
Sayer R.A.	Lieut.	R.A.	1927-34
Sherman D.R.	Sgt.	R.A.F.	1932-35
Smith W.G.			
Tunbridge J.		R.A.S.C.	1917-25
Walpole H.W.	Sgt.	R.A.F.	1924-30
Websdale J.			
Welsted S.			
Wilson K.S.	F/Sgt. (Mentioned in Despatches)	R.A.F.	1929-35
Wiseman J.G.	Sgt.	R.A.F.	1934-40
Wood R.L.	P/O	R.A.F.	1935-39

Source:
1. Compiled from 1946 return
2. Whitehead J.B. *The History of Great Yarmouth Grammar School 1551- 1951*, Great Yarmouth, 1951
3. Memorial Plate in the Great Yarmouth Grammar School

Adams J.M.	Capt.	14th Army	1926-31
Adams L.	Major	Tank Corps	1922-27
Alcock. A.V.	Sgt.	R.A.F.	1929-36
Alcock E.G.	P/O	R.A.F.	1935-39
Allen V.J.		R.A.F.	1930-38
Appleby J.A.	Capt.	R.I.A.S.C.	1930-37
Applegate B.E.		M.N.	1933-41
Applegate J.		R.A.F.	1930-39
Archer E.J.		Tank Corps.	1934-36
Bacon R.A.M.		R.A.F.	1926-33
Bailey D.E.	L.A.C	R.A.F.	1931-39
Baker J.E.	Capt.	R.A.	1930-35
Baker N.	.	R.N.	1932-37
Balls L.R.	Lieut.	R.N.	1932-39
Barlow P		R.N.	1931-38
Barlow R.	Capt.	R.A.C.	1919-26
Base K..	F/O	R.A.F.	1929-37
Base M.	Cpl.	R.A.F.	1928-36
Baxter A.A.	Capt.	R.E.	1930-37
Bean J.V.	Sub/Lieut.	R.N.	1937-44
Beeching E.E.			1913-19
Beevor M.O.	Driver	R.A.S.C.	1933-40
Bell J.	Cpl.	R.A.F.	1921-26
Bellamy J.W.	Capt.	R.A.	1916-24
Bellamy R.L.G.	S/Sgt.	Intelligence Corps.	1919-30
Best L.D.	L/Cpl.		1938-43
Boon J.M	Major	R.A.	1927-30
Boon J.P.F.	Capt.	R.A.	1927-32
Bowring J.	F/O	R.A.F.	1935-38
Breeze R.D.			1924-34
Brighton L.J.	Sgt.	R.A.F.	1935-40
Broadhead H.F.	Major (Ass.Sup.Police, Palestine)	R.A.	1926-35
Brown A.J.	F/Lt.	R.A.F.	1923-34
Brown D.G.	Capt.	R.A.	1932-36
Brown D.R.	F/Sgt.	R.A.F.	1932-37
Carver F.	Sgt./Navigator	R.A.F.	
Chamberlain J.	F/Lt.	R.A.F.	1929-34
Chilvers F.W.		R.Norfolk Regt.	1938-43
Chittleburgh R.	F/Sgt.	R.A.F.	1925-31
Clements S.W.J.	Sgt.	R.A.F.	1931-37
Clutterham D.J.	Sub/Lt.	R.N.	1924-34
Coleman W.D.	Sgt.	R.A.F.	1932-37
Collett B.G.	Eng.Art.App.	F.A.A.	1940-44

Collins F.H.	W/OP.	Tanks	1932-39
Collis A.W.	F/O	R.A.F.	1924-33
Collis D.S.	L/Wr.	R.N.	1936-41
Cook J.S.			1931-37
Corkill A.	L.R.M.	R.M.	1941-41
Cory J.		R.A.F.	1935-40
Cossey J.	F/O	R.A.F.	1925-32
Cowl N.A.A.	Sgt.	R.A.F.	1929-36
Cox D.E.	L/Cpl.	Lincolnshire Regt.	1938-41
Crispy C.H.			1931-37
Crow E.W.	F/Lt.	R.A.F.	1921-25
Darby T.E.	Lieut.	R.E,.Indian Div.	1934-41
Dent A.L.	L/Bdr.	R.A.	1921-24
Drummond I.R.	Capt.	R.A.	1920-30
Dyball W.F.	Lieut.	R.A.P.C	1930-36
Dybell G.D.		R.A.F.	1935-40
Dye J	Major	R. Norfolk Regt..	1939-45
Dye R.F.			1932-39
Ellis W.C.	Cpl.	R.C.S.	1920-26
Elton J.B.	Lieut.	R.N.V.R.	1923-30
England L.E.	Capt.	Army	1921-28
Everett R.K.			1925-31
Fairclough N.H.	L.A.C.	R.A.F.	1937-39
Farrow G.E.		R.A.F.	1933-37
Fenn S.A.	S/Sgt.	R.E.M.E., B.L.A.	1916-18
Fielding K.J.			1932-42
Fielding T.B.			1929-38
Finch H.J.A.	S/Sgt.	A.P.T.S. (R.E.M.E.)	1927-35
Firman P.E.	Sgt.	Intellig.Cps., S.E.A.C.	1936-41
Fisher M..B.	Sgt.	R.A.F.	1929-38
Flemming J.G.	Bdr.	R.A.	1936-37
Forder J.			1929-38
Foulser E.W.	A.Ca.	R.A.F.	1926-33
Foulser H.R.		Pioneer Corps	1930-35
Fowler J.H.S.	P/O	R.N.	1934-37
Fox G.E.	Cadet	Indian Army	1938-44
French D.H.	L/Cpl.	R.A.O.C.	1942-44
Gant E.W.J.	P/O	R.A.F.	1931-38
Garrett H.C.S.	Sub/Lieut.	R.N.	1937-44
George R.H.	P/O		1917-21
Gibbs E.W.	Sgt.	R.A.F.	1928-34
Gillings A.	Lieut.	Army	1921-26
Gladden R.R.	L.A.C	R.A.F.	1935-40

Goodman E.	A.C.	R.A.F.	1931-37
Goodrich J.A.	Pte	R.A.S.C., B.L.A.	1937-41
Goodrich S.F.	P/O	R.A.F.	1935-41
Grice.J.	F/Sgt.	R.A.F.	1943-45
Griffiths G.A.	Sub/Lt.	R.N.	1938-43
Griffiths R.G.	Lieut.		1934-41
Grimmer J.A.G.	L.A.C.	R.A.F.	1936-40
Guyton H.J.	Capt.	R.A.	1929-34
Hadden B.R.		R.A.F.	1934-38
Hammond H.K.		R.A.F.	1933-37
Hammond T.F.		R.A.F.	1932-39
Harris C.G.	Capt	R.A.	1927-29
Harvey D.E.	Sgt.	R.A.F.	1931-36
Harvey J.A.W.	Major	R.C.S.	1927-35
Hemming G.B.	Supply Assist.	R.N.	1935-39
Heron R.F.	F/Lieut.	R.A.F.	1931-36
Hindes F.V.	F/Lt.	R.A.F.	1926-33
Hogg G.A.	Lieut.	R.C.S.	1928-36
Hogg J.		R.C.S.	1933-40
Holmes H.E.	S/Ldr.	R.A.F.	1926-35
Howard J.H.	Lieut.	R.E.	1938-40
Howard M.E.			1934-39
Howes L.C.	Lieut.	R.A.	1922-31
Hubbard M.	Cpl.	R.A.F.	1934-39
Hubbard R.		R.N.	1940-43
Hull M.J.	Sgt.	R.A.F.	1936-42
Hull O.M.		Canadian Merc. Marine	1936-40
Jackson G.B.		Friends Ambulance Unit	1933-41
Jeary H.	Capt.	M.N.	1918-24
Jeary H.G.	Lieut.	R.N.V.R.	1935-40
Jeary T.G.	Sgt.	R.A.	1923-30
Jermy A.J.	P/O	Fleet Air Arm	1937-42
Joice L.J.	F/Lt.	R.A.F.	1933-39
Jordan C.A.	S/Ldr.	R.A.F.	1910-15
Joslin E.G.P.	Lieut.	R.A.S.C.	1926-32
Kelf J.B.	Lieut.	R.Norfolk Regt.	1928-36
Kelf O.A.	Lieut.	Commando	1930-37
Kerry C.G.	Lieut.	Essex Regt.	1930-36
Kinns R.S.	P/O	R.A.F.	1933-40
Kirby J.E.E.	Lieut.	R.N.	1929-36
Kite H.D.J.	Cpl.	R.A.F.	1928-36
Kite L.N.		R.A.F.	1931-35
Lacey E.A.		Army	1931-36

Land E.P.	L.A.C.	R.A.F.	1922-30
Lane K.C.		R.E.	1933-42
Lewis E.J.	Lieut.	R.N.	1935-39
Lincoln P.G.	Dep.Cashier	R.N. Malta	1931-39
Lines W.E.		R.A.C.	1925-35
List R.W.			1919-26
Lodge B.A.		R.A.	1924-30
Lodge R.A.	Lieut.	5th H.L.I.	1924-36
Masterson J.C.	F/Sgt.	R.A.F.	1931-36
Mayes R.M.	Capt.	R.E.	1927-35
Mays A.			1935-42
Merrin E.H.		R.A.S.C.	1929-32
Milburn C.A.	Lieut.	Indian Navy	1929-39
Mobbs J.A.	Pte.	R.Norfolk Regt.	1937-44
Money D.E.		R.N.	1930-35
Montgomery R.A.	Capt.	R.A.	1908-13
Moore J.W.		R.A.F.	1933-40
Moore R.F.W.	S/Ldr.	R.A.F.	1911-13
Moore K.T.	L.A.C.	R.A.F.	1932-38
Morris S.R.	Cpl.	R.E.M.E.	1933-40
Moyle L.L.	Sgt.	R.A.F.	1920-25
Narborough S.G.		R.A.F.	1922-28
Neal E.P.	Sgt.	R.A.M.C.	1930-35
Neal T.A.	Cpl.	R.A.	1928-34
Neal W.	L.A.C.	R.A.F.	1934-38
Newby J.E.		Indian Army	1935-41
Newby S.B.F.	Lieut.		1933-38
Newman A.R.			1928-34
Newman E.E.D.		R.Norfolk Regt.	1929-37.
Newstead N.J.		R.A.F.	1938-44
Newstead P.G.W.	Cpl.	R.A.F.	1927-36
Nunn F.L.	A.C.	R.A.F.	1925-32
Overill A.G.	Cpl.	R.A.F.	1919-27
Overy A.W.	Cpl.	R.E.M.E.	1930-37
Overy J.H.		R.A.F.	1932-38
Pack N.A.W.			1930-38
Packard R.A.W.	F/Sgt.	R.A.F.	1932-38
Paddle M	S/Ldr.	R.A.F.	1931-37
Palmer C.J.	Sgt.	R.A.F.	1932-37
Palmer W.		Intelligence Corps	1931-36
Papworth C.A.	Capt.	R.A.	1925-31
Papworth P	Major	R.E.	1929-39
Parker R.A.	Major		1927-35

Pateman T.E.		R.A.F.	1933-38
Peck A.C.	Sgt./P.	R.A.F.	1926-32
Peck J.		R.A.F.	1928-36
Philips W.J.	Major	R.Norfolk Regt.	1927-32
Pipes E.J.	Lieut.		1930-34
Platford A.W.	Lieut.	Army Pay Corps.	1929-36
Platford R.H.	Cpl.	R.A.F.	1932-38
Playford W.J.		R.A.F.	1913-18
Plumbly G.M.	Capt.	R.E.M.E.	1926-35
Pope W.	F/O	R.A.F.	1931-36
Porter F.T.		R.A.M.C.	1925-33
Porter J.E.		R.A.O.C.	1928-36
Powley D.	P/O	Fleet Air Arm	1934-40
Pratt J.C.		Royal Signals	1927-34
Prouting N.A.	Lieut.	R.N.	1929-35
Randall R.H.	Sgt.	R.A.F.	1919-24
Rant L.G.	A.C.	R.A.F.	1938-40
Reilly J.M.		R.A.F.	1933-38
Reynolds R.F.	L.A.C.	R.A.F.	1930-39
Richardson D.M.	Sub/Lt.	R.N.	1936-41
Riches C.C.			1920-25
Rivett G.A.	D.R.		1933-39
Roberts H.Q.		R.N.	1938-45
Roche M.R.G.	Lieut.	R.N.	1919-26
Roll J.H.	P/O	R.A.F.	1928-32
Rook R.F.	Capt.	R.A.	1923-27
Rope A.S.R.		Fleet Air Arm	1936-42
Rule F.H.	Cpl	R.A.F.	1933-38
Sayer G.G.		R.A.F.	1932-37
Scott H.A.J.			1938-45
Sewell J.R.	F/Lt.	R.A.F.	1935-38
Smith A.W.	Lieut.	Army	1921-26
Smith E.G.	Lieut.	R.Dragoons	1933-38
Smith G.H.W.	C.Q.M.S.	R.Corps. Signals	1928-36
Smith M.L.	Capt.	R.E.M.E.	
Smith N.A.W.	Cpl.	R.A.O.C.	1925-30
Smowton K.F.	Eng./Artificer App.		1940-45
Southgate A.		Army	1933-36
Spalding W.F.	W/O	R.O.A.C.	1927-35
Spink B.J.	Capt.	R.A.	1921-27
Spiro H.J.	Cpl.	R.A.F.	1932-37
Squibb F.		R.A.F.	1936-40
Squire J.C.	Lieut.	R.Norfolk Regt.	1934-40

Starkings P.R.		R.A.F.	1938-45
Stannard H.R.	Major	R.A.	1925-31
St. John V.B.	F/O	R.A.F.	1923-30
Stone D.C.	Wing-Commander	R.A.F.	1914-19
Stone T.F.	P/O	R.A.F.	1926-33
Sutton E.E.		R.A.F.	1935-40
Swanston R.H.		R.A.F.	1932-40
Syder E.E.	A.C.	R.A.F.	1934-38
Sykes W.T.		Army Short Course	1938-44
Symonds V.W.	L/Bdr.		1934-39
Taylor G.	Sgt.	R.A.F.	1934-39
Thompson E.C.	Cpl.	R.A.S.C.	1920-27
Thornton G.M.	P/O	R.A.F.	1933-42
Thrower N.C.			1932-39
Turner A.H.		R.N.	1931-40
Turrell E.R.		R.A.F.	1934-40
Waller B.F.	P/O	R.A.F.	1933-42
Waller P.W.	Sgt.	R.A.	1924-30
Warner P.D.		R.A.F.	1937-44
Waters W.O.		R.A.P.C.	1927-33
Wells T.	Signalman	R.Signals	1938-43
Weston L.J.		R.N.	1933-39
Whall J.		R.M.	1936-41
Wheatley F.	Pte.	Suffolk Regt.	1927-33
Williams B.G.R.	S/Ldr.	R.A.F.	1913-23
Williams C.G.R.	Major	Allied Control Comm.	1909-20
Williams R.F.	F/Sgt.	R.A.F.	1933-37
Wilson W.F.		R.A.F.	1934-40
Wiseman W.P.	Sgt.	R.A.	1927-35
Withers J.P.	Sub/Lt.	R.N.	1939-40
Woods R.G.		R.E.	1937-40
Wright W.D.		R.A.S.C..	1919-23
Wroughton H.J.	F/Lt.	R.A.F.	1929-39
Wyness W.S.	Cpl.	R.A.F.	1923-28

Source:
1. Grammar School *Chronicles*.

Alcock P.F.G.	S/Ldr.	R.A.F.	D.F.C.	1931-37
Avery A.W.	S/Ldr.	R.A.F.	A.F.C., D.F.C.	1927-36
Bennett M.B.	F/Lt.	R.A.F.	D.F.C. and Bar	1934-37
Campling J.N.	Lieut. (E.)	R.N.	M.B.E.	1922-27
Claydon L.J.	P/O	R.A.F.	D.F.C.	1932-37
Crotch J.H.	S/Ldr.	R.A.F.	D.F.C.	1925-29
Dye J.B.	Major	R.Norfolks	M.C.	1930-36
Ellis A.G.	Major	R.Norfolks	Mention in Despatches	1926-34
England J.K.	Lieut.	Parachute Regt.	M.B.E.	1933-40
Freeman E.C.H	Report Centre	A.R.P.	B.E.M.	1914-19
French F.G.	Capt.	R.E.	M.C.	1934-42
Haylett G.M.	Sgt.	R.A.F.	D.F.M.	1930-36
Haward F.R.B.	Lt.Col.	Home Guard	O.B.E.	1894-97
Keeler F.H.	Sgt.	R.A.	B.E.M.	1929-34
Long A.	Capt.		M.C.	1930-33
MacDwyer P.H	Major	Indian Army	M.B.E.	1933-36
Mack L.J.	Capt.	M.N.	D.S.O.	1919-22
Munford D.S.	Major	Parachute Regt.	American Bronze Star	1919-29
Sayers L.A.	Lt/Com.	R.N.	Order of Red Star	1917-19
Skipper L.W.	F/O	R.A.F.	D.F.C.	1933-38
Whiteman W.E.	F/Lt.	R.A.F.	D.F.C.	1929-33
Wilson K.S.	F/Sgt.	R.A.F.	Mentioned in Despatches	1929-35

Source:
1. Whitehead J.B. *The History of Great Yarmouth Grammar School 1551- 1951*, Great Yarmouth, 1951

Allen C.G.		466 Earlham Rise,Norwich,……..	Banking 15/22
Amos J.C.E.		9 KittoeRoad,Four Oaks,Sutton Coldfield	Metallurgy 51/56
Bacon .D.F.		84 Rosebery Road, N.10	Music
Rev.C.Banks	M.A.	25 Dumbreck Road,Glasgow	Methodist Ministry
Rev.J.Banks	M.A.	16 Otley Road, Leeds.	Methodist Ministry 31/38
Barber R.W.		40 Pembridge Villas, W.11	48/55
Rev.R.Barlow	M.B.E	P.of Wales, Seaman's Club,Bombay	Church 20/25
Barnes C.J.	B.Sc.	2 Mill Road, Fleggburgh	Commerce 50/57
Barnes G.A.		172 Middleton Rd, Gorleston	
Bates B		4 York Rd, Grappenhall,Warrington	Engineering 44/49
Bayles D.A.		12 Crichton Ave,Chester-le-Street	33/40
Bayles P.F.		19 Bratby Lane,Burton-on-Trent	38/46
Rev.J.V.Bean	M.A.	Vicarage, St.Helens, I.O.W.	Church 36/44
Beaumont G.O.		66 Blackheath, Colchester	
Beckett A.E.		161 Burgh Road,Gorleston	Education 38/44
Bell BJ.R.		12 Welsford Road, Eaton Rise,Norwich	Banking 20/27
Bellamy J.W.		161 Edith's WurleBay, Cambridge	Banking 16/24
Rev.D.E.Bentley	B.A.	108 Gordon Road,Whitehall,Bristol	Church 46/53
Bessey G.E.	M.Sc.	91 Codicote Rd,Welwyn, Herts	Science 15/21
Rev.E.G.Bevan	M.A.	Vicarage, Tetsworth,Oxford	Church 05/15
Rev.E. J.Bevan	M.A.	32 Regent St. Stonehouse,Glos.	Education 02/14
Rev.G.E.Bevan		Abbotsham Vicarage,N.Devon	Church
Bevan H.G.L.	B.Sc.	24 Upper Park Rd, N.W.3	Education 23/32
Rev. H.W.Bevan	B.A.	1 Bruce Villas,Bruce Ave,Worthing	Church 99/02
Rev. J. S. Bevan		21 Forest Ave,Fishponds,Bristol	Church
Rev. K.G.Bevan		Woolhope Rectory, Nr.Hereford	Church
Blake B.N.H.	L.R.A.M	2 Gresham Cl.,Gorleston.	Education 42/47
Boice M.J.		14 St.Peter's Ave.,Gorleston	Education 53/60
Boon M.C.M.		"Lyndhurst",Burgh Rd,Gorleston	Accountancy 53/59
Bowman D.J.		"Sharrow" Upper Moulsham,Chelmsford	
Bradshaw H.J.		38 Brian Ave, Norwich	Commerce 13/16
Bradshaw W.C.	B.Sc.	63 Court Lane,Cosham,Portsmouth	Education 12/18
Brett R.W.		Pond House, Halvergate	Commerce 12/20
Brown R.A.		19 Crown Rd, Gt.Yarmouth	Architecture 52/59
Brugger W.		Commonwealth Hall,Cartwright Gdns.	52/59
Burley G.I		43 Lulworth Drive,Pinner	Insurance 29/34
Buswell E.D.C.		110 Wellesley Rd,	Education 47/51
Canham D.R.		133 Tennyson Ave, New Malden.	53/60
Carter R.J.		Caister Sands Est. Office, Caister	50/57
Caton B	M.A.	13 Greyfriars Way, Gt. Yarmouth	Education 49/56
Chapman A.W.	B.Sc.,	2 Queen's Rd, Dovercourt	Education
Clayton R.M.		Officers Mess, R.A.F,St.Mawgan	49/56
Cooke C		Glebe Farm, Oby	Farming 27/31
Cooper P		Westminster College, Oxford	54/62
Cory J.P.		Lords Lane, Bradwell	Commerce 35/40
Cushing P	B.A.	Worcester Training College	Education 38/41
Delf B.W.	Ph.D.	33 Heol Gabriel, Cardiff	Education 47/54
Diboll P.J		29 North Bar Without, Beverley	Banking 96/00

Drummond J.R.		8 Hillside Road, Radcliffe- on -Trent	20/30
Duffield N.A.	M.Sc.	72 Springfield Rd, Gorleston	Engineering 55/58
Durrant F.		Lichfield Rd, Gt. Yarmouth	19/23
Dye R	B.A	211 College St. Toronto, Canada	Education 31/39
East B.W.	B.Sc.,	14 Barnard Ave. Gt. Yarmouth	51/59
Edwards R.G.	M.A.	18 White Hall Lane,Llanfrechfa, Mon	Education 40/47
Ellis W.C.		11 Dudley Rd, Ashford,Mdx	Education 19/26
Emmerson D.A.	B.A.	36 Stanley Rd, Gt.Yarmouth	Advertising 53/60
England L.E.		46 Beccles Rd, Gorleston	Law 21/27
England R.W.		Lt. Osnabruck,B.F.P.O.36,Germany	Army 49/56
Felix E.F.T		17 Smithamdowns Rd,Purley,Surrey	Local Gov. 24/26
Fielding K.J.	D.Phil.	Manchester University	Education 32/43
Fisher J.E.		10 Salisbury House,Highbury Cr.N.5	53/61
Flaxman E.G.		Forest Lodge,Southwold,	Banking 14/17
Ford D.W.C.		4 Cambridge Pl.,W.8	24/29
Foulser E.W.	B.Sc.,	28 Greenhayes Ave,Banstead,Surrey	Education 26/33
Foulser H.R.		50 Hester's Way Rd, Cheltenham	Civil Service 29/34
Francis K.W.		Old Lane Cottage,Stansted Rd,Caterham	25/31
Gardiner A.J.		12 Regent St. Gt.Yarmouth	Commerce 50/57
Garrett H.C.S.	B.A.	1 Tyrolean Sq, Gt. Yarmouth	Education 37/44
Garrett J.	B.Sc.,	1 Tyrolean Sq, Gt. Yarmouth	35/42
Gedge D.G.	B.Sc.,	33 Willow Green,Ingatestone, Essex	35/41
Rev.J.Gedge	M.A.	The Rectory, Mundesley,	Church 19/31
Gedge J.	LL.B.,	23 South Terrace, S.W.7.	Law 45/52
George D.E.		"Dawnaway" Ormesby Rd, Caister	
Geeves E.W.		53 Cambridge Rd, Wigmore,Gillingham	16/20
Gibbs P.R.		19 Burgh Rd, Gorleston	Accountancy 50/56
Gillings R.A.		70 Smirrells Rd, Birmingham	
Gooch W.E.		134 Middleton Rd, Gorleston	Accountancy 49/54
Goodrich J		98 Denes Rd, Gt. Yarmouth	Engineering 37/42
Goodrich S.F		10 Harley Rd, Gt. Yarmouth	Education 35/41
Goss W.P.	M.Sc.,	90 Elborough St. S.W.18	Education 38/46
Grapes M.G.		591 Upper Nedwtonards Rd. Belfast	Engineering
Hartley E.G.	M.R.C.V.S	Medical Research Council, N.W.3	Medicine 46/49
Harvey J.A.W.		Queens Head Hotel, Maidstone	27/35
Hawkins A.E.		14 Coulsdon Rise, Coulsdon	25/32
Hawkins G.S.	Ph.D	Boston University, U.S.A.	Astronomy 40/44
Hayden A.E.		221 High Rd, Ilford	Optician 39/43
Hayden E.C.		6 Keswick Ave. Hornchurch	Education 39/43
Hayden H.W.		63 Downlands Rd, Purley	Optician 03/13
Haylett B.C.	M.A	67 Beatty Road, Gt.Yarmouth	Education 49/56
Higgins D.H.	B.A.	The University, Auckland, N.Z.	Education 46/53
Hogg G.L.		40 Woodland Rise, N.10	31/34
Hogg J.D.		22 Church Cres. N.10	33/40
Holmes J.L.		19 Linton Close, Leeds	Education 47/54
Canon G.W.Iveson		10 Fishpool St, St. Albans	Church 18/22
Jackson H.L.	M.A., L.R.A.M.	64 Quebec Rd, Blackburn	Education 37/45
Jackson R.A.		43 Sparrows Herne, Basildon	34/39

James P.J.		"Jasmine" Portland Dr. Stoke	Education 32/37
Jeary T..G.		13 High St. Caine, Wilts	Pharmacy 19/31
Johnson E.N.		14 Sunnyside Rd, W.5	28/32
Jones R.A.	B.A. A.R.M.C.	Holland Park, W.11	Music 46/54
Julier E.C.	B.A.	14 Paynes Lane, Maidstone.	Education 14/21
KempV.C.		C/o The Vicarage, Martham	54/58
Kerridge D.H.	Ph.D.	The University, Southampton.	Education 42/49
Leech W.F.		7 Connaught Ave. Gorleston	Banking 23/29
Lewis T		7 Ulundi Rd, S.E.3	25/31
Mackenzie N.O.G.		17 Victoria Rd, Horley, Surrey	Education 12/17
Macmillan K		12a Myddleton Sq.,E.C.1	Choreography 40/45
Maplesden R.J.A.		2 Selstead Close, Gillingham	44/48
Marshall D.W.	B.A.	1 Bendish Ave, Gorleston	Education 47/55
Marshall T.W.		29 Nelson Rd, North, Gt.Yarmouth	Civil Service 52/59
Mason K.D.	M.B., B.S	Medical Officer of Health, Nigeria	37/44
Matthes C.A.	F.C.A	Warren Lodge,Warren Lane, Hopton	Commerce 38/40
McComas A.	B.Sc., M.B.	12 Cavendish Pl, Jesmond,Newcastle	Medicine 44/51
McCord P.R.		46 Havering Rd, Romford	07/10
Miller G.W.		41 Oldfield Rd, Bexleyheath	Banking 20/26
Merrin E.H.		105/7 Southend Rd, Wickford	Commerce 28/33
Mobbs J.A.		3 Keyes Ave, Gt.Yarmouth	Engineering 37/44
Mobbs R.H.	Ph.D	14 Sutton St, Durham	Science 46/53
Moss E.P.		5/7 Station Lane, Hornchurch	Law 31/37
Murrell M.D.	B.A.	"Rusticana" Cantley	Engineering 48/56
Murrell P.A.		7 Perivale Ave, Ealing	Education 00/05
Murrell R.E.	M.A.	Mt.Ararat Rd, Richmond	Education 44/49
Narburgh S.G.		17 Blake Rd, Gt.Yarmouth	Education 22/28
Neal W		69 Canterbury Ave, Ilford	35/39
Newberry J		147 Edgwarebury Lane, Edgware	60/62
Nichols J.F.		"Aldea" Anstey, Herts	Education 07/11
Norton C.F.		33 Buxton Ave, Gorleston	Commerce 20/23
Nunn F.L.		32 Beatty Rd, Gt. Yarmouth	Education 25/32
Ovey A.J.	B.Comm	3 Seafield Cl., Gt. Yarmouth	Commerce 11/16
Ovey C.J.	M.B.E.	6 Westerfolds Cl, Woking	Civil Service 08/14
Packard R.W.		1 Downing Rd, Gorleston	Education 32/38
Page L.R.		192 Rydal Dr, Bexley Heath	23/32
Parmenter G.L.		23 Ridge Park, Purley	Local Govt. 16/19
Peck M.W.	B.A.	2 Northumberland House N.5	49/56
Pereira J.K.		205 Princes Gardens, West Acton	53/61
Platten G.E.	J.P	1 Osborne Ave, Gt.Yarmouth	Commerce 12/16
Platten T.G.		Saltey College, Birmingham	Church 11/16
Playford R.S.		"Redwyn", Station Rd, Potter Heigham	Education 12/18
Playford W.J		The Post Office, Potter Heigham	Commerce 13/18
Powley B.G.	B.A.	8 Admiralty Rd, Gt.Yarmouth	51/59
Pratt W		39 Davenport Rd, Witney,Oxon	Civil Service 97/00
Pumfrey J		23 Westbrook Ave, Gorleston	Pharmacy 49/54
Rayner W.		91 High Rd, Southtown,Gt.Yarmouth	53/61
Read D.J.	B.Sc.	125 Alderson Rd, Gt.Yarmouth	Engineering 46/53

Reeder L.J	B.Sc	2 Heathcote Ave, Ilford	Education 17/23
Reeder S.W.		43 Swallowbeck Ave, Lincoln	Pharmacy 20/24
Bishop Reeves R.A		3 Wilberforce House, S.W4	12/16
Reilly J		Holkham Hotel,	Hotelier
Roll F.G		28 Lynn Grove, Gorleston	Education 39/45
Roll J.H	B.Sc	81 Middleton Rd, Gorleston	Education 28/32
Rudrum M		102 Palgrave Rd, Gt.Yarmouth	
Scarles A.J		41 Park Grove, Edgware	16/20
Scott H.A.J.	B.Sc	8 Berberia Green, Gorleston	Commerce 38/44
Scott R.M.		48 Regent Rd, Gt.Yarmouth	Hotelier 31/41
Seary B.L.		22 Privett Rd, Gosport, Hants	Education 26/30
Sillis P.E.		79 Palmerston Rd, Buckhurst Hill, Essex	Education 29/40
Spinks B.J.		66 Canterbury Ave, Ilford	Education 21/27
Spinks G.E.		13 Sidegate Ave, Ipswich	Banking Hotelier 10/13
Stannard R.		"Rendezvous" Simonstown, S.Africa	
Starkings H.W.		30 Blake Rd, Gt. Yarmouth	
Stanniforth C.A.		188 Gilbert Rd, Cambridge	Industry 20/25
Steel R.W.		The University, Liverpool	Professor 26/31
St.John V.B.		2 Beulah Rd, Epping	21/29
Story W.E.		45 Lynton Rd, South Harrow	Accountancy 20/27
Stowers V.A.F.	B.A.	3 Waunci Cres, Gorleston	Education 37/45
Stuart F.C.		"Glendale", Salcombe Rd,Sidmouth	Banking 95/00
Swanston P.G.		53 Burgh Rd, Gorleston	Insurance 44/49
Symonds D.J.	M.Sc.,	Marine Laboratory, Aberdeen	47/55
Tammas E		17 Watson Ave, Chatham	24/34
Taylor H.K.	B.Sc., Eng.	4 Reed Buck Walk,Banecroft,Rhodesia	Mining 27/34
Thompson G.V.	B.Sc.,	1 Herbert Rd, Hornchurch	Astronautics 30/39
Thompson R.H.	B.A.,	13 Northumberland Ave, Newcastle	Civil Service 19/28
Thorpe A.C.		105 High St. Thornton Heath	31/36
Thorpe C.E.		6 Barkis Rd, Gt.Yarmouth	51/58
Thurtle P.R.		30 Balmoral Ave, South Harrow	16/20
Thurtle W.R.S		5 Woodside, Greenbank, Plymouth	49/54
Turner A.H.		16 Windsor Ave. Gt.Yarmouth	Education 31/40
Vickery M		10 2nd Clabon Close, Norwich	
Westgate D.E.		33 Lady Margaret Ave,Gorleston	Education 51/58
Westney W.F.		51 Roman Way, Caister	Civil Service 10/5
Whitehead F.	S.C.M.	Secretary, Lusaka, Northern Rhodesia	
Williams C.G.R.		7 Meadow Way, Rickmansworth	Law 09/21
Wiseman W.P.		28 Blake Rd, Gt.Yarmouth	Building 26/35
Woodfield W.P.		Waterval Boven, Transvaal	Archdeacon 04/07
Wright W.G.		Lowestoft Rd, Beccles	Pharmacy 19/24
Young A.S.		8 Hatfield St, Wakefield	Engineering 49/56

Source: Great Yarmouth Grammar School *Chronicle*.

Great Yarmouth High School Staff in 1983

MR. M.D. LEIGH
B.A.
HEADMASTER
Educated at Elmhurst Grammar
School, Leeds University and
Westminster College, Oxford.
After teaching posts in Hampshire
and Uganda, became Director
of Studies at Woodhouse Grove
School. Appointed Deputy
Headmaster and then Headmaster
of Gt.Yarmouth Grammar School
1975-81

MR. G.F.W. MASON
CERT.ED.
DEPUTY HEAD
Educated Downham Market
Grammar School and at Borough
Rd Training Coll. Isleworth.
Teaching experiences: Acland
Central Boys' School, Tufnell
Park, Burwell Village College,
Swaffham Secondary (Head of
Maths. and Science Department,)
Greenacre Secondary Dep.Head
1966-78, Head 1978-82.

MRS. B. TINGEY
B.Sc.
DEPUTY HEAD
Graduated from London U.,Asst.
Science Teacher at Durrants
Secondary Modern School,
Rickmansworth. Appt. Head of
Chem. Dept. when this school
re- Organised. Head of Science
Dept. at Grove Hill Comp.School.
Sr.Mistress At Gorleston Grammar
School,Deputy Head,Lynn Grove,
from Sept. 1981.

MR. B. LITTLEPROUD
Cert.Ed.
DEPUTY HEAD
Trained Wimpole Park Training
College. Taught At Greenacre,
Alderman Leach And Hospital
Secondary Schools. Head of
Science at Hospital School,
Subsequently Deputy Head
and Acting Headmaster from
September 1981.

MRS. A.C. ADAMSON
B.A.
ENGLISH
Educated Reigate County School
for Girls, London University and
Keswick Hall Norwich. Appointed
to Gt. Yarmouth Grammar School
in 1980

MR. J.R. ATKINSON
Cert.Ed.
PHYSICAL EDUCATION
Educated at Huddersfield New
College Grammar, Chester
College of Further Education.
Taught at Elfed High School
Buckley, N.Wales. Styles School
1977-79 And at Gt.Yarmouth
Grammar from 1979

MR. G. BARNES
Cert.Ed.,
HISTORY
Educated at Cheltenham Grammar
School and Matlock College
of Education. Wide teaching
experience In South Croyden, Gt.
Yarmouth Technical High School
and Styles School. Currently a
member of the National Executive
of NAS/UWT.

MR. J.B. BARNARD
Cert.Ed.
MATHEMATICS
Educated at Gt.Yarmouth
Grammar School And West
Midlands College of Education
Taught at Alderman Leach
Secondary School, Kabire, Zambia
(1970-80) and Claydon High
School (1980-82)

MRS. G. BENNISON
B.Ed.
HOME ECONOMICS, FABRIC
Educated at Tadcaster Grammar
School Bretton Hall College of
Education and Leeds University.
Taught at Gt.Yarmouth Grammar
School from 1976

MR. J.H. BLYTH
Head of Lower School
Educated at Gt.Yarmouth
Grammar School And
Loughborough College. Served in
the R.A.F. Taught at Bowthorpe
Secondary School and at
Gt.Yarmouth Grammar School as
Head of Physical Education and
Head of First Year.

MISS D. BROWN
Cert.Ed.
PHYSICAL EDUCATION
Year Leader, 5th Year. Educated
at Caister School, Norwich
City College And Keswick Hall
College of Education. Taught at
Styles Secondary School before
appointment to Gt. Yarmouth High
School.

MISS E.G. BROWNE
Cert.Ed.
HOME ECONOMICS
Educated at Gt.Yarmouth High
School For girls and Yorkshire
Training College Of Housecraft
(Leeds).Taught at Greenacre –
then Head Of Dept. of Home
Economics at Styles Secondary
School.

MR. A. CHILVERS
N.D.D.,A.T.D.
HEAD OF ART
Educated at Gt.Yarmouth
Grammar School 1946-51.
Studied at Gt.Yarmouth College
of Art and Hornsey College of
Art 1951-58.Taught at Fairlop
S.M. School,Ilford 1958-60.Since
then on Staff of Hospital School
Gt.Yarmouth. Head of Art Dept.
since 1969

MR. E. COBBOLD
Cert.Ed.City & Guilds.
HEAD OF RAFT,DESIGN,TECH.
Educated Pudsey Grammar School
and St.John's College,York. After
wide Teaching experience taught
at Tadcaster Grammar School,
Bermuda College, Dept Of Tech.,
and Penryn School. Appointed
As Head of Craft,Design,Tech., at
Gt. Yarmouth Grammar School in
1980

MRS B. COSSAR
N.D.D.,A.T.D. Cert. Ed..
ART AND HEAD OF FABRIC
Educated at Hull College of Art
and Leicester College of Art.
Lectured at Scarborough College
of Art and Head Of Dress Dept.
at Gt.Yarmouth College Of Art.
Taught Art and Needlework at The
Hospital School since 1974.

MR. K. DAVIES
Cert.Ed.,A.K.C.
HEAD OF COMBINED
SCIENCES
Year Leader 4th Year Trained
at St.Lukes' College, Exeter.
Taught Science in Doncaster-Then
County Supply in West Riding and
with British Families Education
Service in Lybia, Tobruk all age
school and in West Germany-
Comprehensive School. Claydon
School Head of Science 1976-81.

MRS. A. DAY
B.A.,
FRENCH/GERMAN Educated
Bude Grammar School,
Portsmouth Polytechnic,
and Christ- Church College,
Canterbury. Appointed To the
Modern Languages Dept. at Gt.
Yarmouth Grammar School in
1979.

MISS A.M. DOYLE
B.Sc.
GEOGRAPHY
Educated at St.Francis of
Assisi Comprehensive School,
Birmingham University and
Southampton University (P.G.C
.E.) Appointed to Gt.Yarmouth
High School in September 1982.

MR. K. ELLIS
Cert.Ed.,
PHYSICAL EDUCATION
Educated Earlham School and
C.F.Mott College of Education.
Taught at Wymondham College
and Styles School

MRS. A.M. GRANT
B.A.
FRENCH AND ITALIAN
Educated at Mountain Ash Comp.
Bristol University and Cambridge
University (P.G.C.E.) Bi-Lingual
Secretarial Cert. Editorial
Assistant in Italian Publishing
House 1978-80. Appointed to
Gt. Yarmouth High School in
September 1981.

MRS. M.D. GRICE
Cert. Ed.
HEAD OF HOME ECONOMICS
After wide experience in Norfolk
Schools,became Head of Catering
Section at G.Y.C.F.E.,Head of Home
Economics at Lawrence Weston &
Head Of Tech.Faculty at Hartcliffe
both C.S. In Bristol. Head of H.E.
at Oriel G.S. And then G.Y.G.S.
Involved nationally With Schools
Council Project and with 16+ Exam.
Organisation. 1981-82 a Member of
N.C.C. Advisory Team and Currently
Senior Vice President of the National
Assoc. Teachers of H. E.

MISS C. GOODALL
B.Ed.
MUSIC/DRAMA
Educated at Philip Morant
Comprehensive School and
Keswick Hall,Norwich. Main
Musical interests, Clarinet
and Singing. Appointed to
Gt.Yarmouth High School in 1981.

MR. S.J. GOUGH
B.Sc.
GEOGRAPHY
Educated St.Peter's and Merrow
Grange Comp.School and London
University (Enviromental Science)
University of Keele (P.G.C.E.)
Appointed to Gt. Yarmouth High
School September 1982

MR. D.V. HACON
Cert.Ed.
HISTORY
Educated at Northern Counties
College University of Newcastle-
on-Tyne. Taught At Duncan Hall
School and Styles School Before
appointed to Gt. Yarmouth High
School in September 1981

MR. E. HARRIS
Cert.Ed.
MATHEMATICS, TECHNICAL
DRAWING, SUPPORT
EDUCATION
Educated at Keswick
Hall,Norwich. Taught at Styles
Secondary School Since 1966
where responsible for T.D.
Throughout the school.

MR. T.C. HARRISON
B.A.
HEAD OF FRENCH HEAD
OF MODERN LANGUAGES
Educated at Gt.Yarmouth
Grammar School And Leicester
University. Taught at Gorleston
Grammar School from 1970-
76 When appointed as Head of
French and Modern Languages at
Gt.Yarmouth Grammar School.

MR. R. HEYHOE
B.Sc.
SCIENCE
HEAD OF CHEMISTRY
Educated at Gt. Yarmouth
Grammar School and Imperial
College, University Of London.
Trained at Chelsea College,
London and began teaching at
Weald Comprehensive School,
Billingshurst. Teacher of
Chemistry at Gorleston Grammar
School (Now Lynn Grove High
School) since 1973

MRS. C. HUTCHIN
B.A.
FRENCH/MUSIC
Educated at Thistley Hough
High School. City of Stoke Sixth
Form College, Exeter University
(Combined Honours Degree,
French and Music) and St.Luke's,
Exeter (P.G.C.E.). Appointed
to Gt.Yarmouth High School
September 1981.

MR. W. HUTCHINS
Cert. Ed
CRAFT DESIGN
TECHNOLOGY
In charge of Woodwork Educated
Saltley College,Birmingham
Many years experience as Cabinet
Maker, Wood Carver and in
teaching. Previously Head of
Technical Studies At Greenacre
School.

MR. R. JAY
A.S.D.C.
SCIENCE
Educated Alderman Newton's
Boys Grammar School, Leicester
Polytechnic (P.G.C.E.).Employed
in Textile Industry 1966-80
in technical and management
Capacities. After teacher training
appointed To Oriel High School
and then Gt. Yarmouth High
School September 1981

MRS. J.A. JONES
Cert.Ed.
MATHEMATICS
Educated at Hindley Grammar
School, Manchester Institute of
Technology and Keswick College.
Scientific Research Officer with
Atomic Energy Authority. Head
of Mathematics at Claydon School
School before appt. G.Y.H.S.in
1981.

MR. M. KEABLE
B.A.
HEAD OF UPPER SCHOOL
Educated at St. Luke's
College,Exeter followed in
teaching experience in Whitfield
Boys' School, Bristol. In charge
Of Science and second Teacher at
Styles School before joining the
staff at Gt. Yarmouth High School.

MR. D.A. KIGHTLEY
Cert.Ed.
PHYSICAL EDUCATION
Educated at Gt.Yarmouth
Grammar School and Borough
Road, College, (London
University) Taught at Hospital
County Secondary School 1980-81

MRS D.M. KING
B.A.
DIRECTOR OF MUSIC
Studied Music at King's
College,London And piano
at Guildhall School of Music.
Director of Music at Gorleston
Grammar School since September
1979.

MR. I.R.T. KING
B.Sc., (Econ)
HEAD OF GEOGRAPHY YEAR
LEADER 3rd YEAR
Trained at the College of St.Mark
and St John, London University.
Taught at South East London and
at the Hospital School, becoming
Deputy Head. Chief Examiner in
Geography for the East Anglian
Examination Board.

MR. S.W.G. KING
Cert.Ed
HEAD OF RELIGIOUS
EDUCATION
Educated at Oriel Grammar
School and Studied Religious
Education and Music at Borough
Road College (West London
Institute of Higher Ed.) Taught at
Nower Hill High School, Pinner,
Middx. Head of R.E./Music
Greenacre Secondary School
Since September 1978.

MR. J. LAITY
Cert.Ed.
HEAD OF CAREERS
Educated at Bridgend Grammar
School, Bridgend, and Neath
Technical College, Manchester
University. Faculty of Education
(Bolton T.T.T.C.).Two years R.A.F.
and 5 years as Scientific Technical
Officer with the N.C.B. Joined
staff of Gt.Yarmouth Grammar
School in 1962.

MR. B.H. LEARNER
B.Sc.C.Eng..M.I.E.E
MATHEMATICS
Educated at Lowestoft Grammar
School, Welbeck College, Royal
Military Academy Sandhurst,
Royal Military College of Science.
Served in the Regular Army for
19 years, Royal Electrical and
Mechanical Engineers. Retired
as Major in 1976. Taught at
Alderman Leach and Cliff Park.

MR. D.R. LEVER
B.Sc.
MATHEMATICS, YEAR
LEADER 5TH YEAR.
EXAMINATION OFFICER
Educated at Newcastle University
and Cheltenham College of
Education. Joined the staff of
Gt.Yarmouth Grammar School in
1975.

MR. E. LOFTIN
B.Sc.
HEAD OF MATHEMATICS
Educated at Alderman Leach,
Gt.Yarmouth Technical High
School and Hull University
Previously taught at Welton High
School (Hull). Appointed to
Gt.Yarmouth Grammar School in
1967. Head of Mathematics since
1974.

MISS M. LYNE
B.A.
HOME ECONOMICS
Educated at Hereward School and
Neale Wade School, Manchester.
Queen Margaret College and
Moray House College, Edinburgh.
Appointed to Gt. Yarmouth High
School September 1981

MRS. P. MACE
Dip. A.and D.
ART (Part-time)
Educated at Hendon County
Grammar School and Leeds
Polytechnic Dept. of Art
Education. Taught at Denes High
School, Styles School, Gorleston
Grammar School and as part-
time lecturer at the Gt.Yarmouth
College of Art.

MR. K.I. MacDONALD
B.A.
HEAD OF ENGLISH. SENIOR
TEACHER.
Trained at Central School of
Speech and Drama (London).
University of Ulster. P.G.C.E.,at
University of Durham. Taught as
assistant English Teacher at Selby
Grammar School,Leeds Grammar
School, then became Head of
English at Gorleston Grammar
School (Lynn Grove High School).

MR. M.D. MITCHELL
B.Sc.,Cert.Ed.
HEAD OF SCIENCE
Educated at the City of Norwich
School, Nottingham University
and Keswick Hall College
of Education. Appointed to
the Physics Department, Gt.
Yarmouth Grammar School in
1972 becoming Head Of Physics
in 1977.

MISS A.V. MOORE
Cert.Ed.
PHYSICAL EDUCATION
Educated at Notre Dame High
School Norwich, and Lady Mabel
P.E.College. Sheffield. Began in
1979 at Gt. Yarmouth Grammar
School teaching P.E., Geography
and Biology.

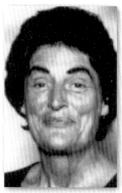

MRS. S. NEWTON
B.A.
ENGLISH, LIBRARIAN
Educated Ursuline Convent and
French Lycee, London.Worked
as a translator, Then in a Drama
School and finally the Library of
a College of Technology, before
Obtaining a degree in English at
Preston Polytechnic as a mature
student. Assoc. of The Drama
Board. Taught in Lancashire And
Wales, moving to Norfolk in 1980.

MRS. P. NOBBS
B.Sc.
SCIENCE
Studied Biology at the University
of Aston in Birmingham. P.G.C.E.
Birmingham University. One
year Teaching at Northgate High
School, East Dereham before
joining Gt. Yarmouth High School
in 1981

MR. G.R. OXBOROUGH
B.Sc.
SCIENCE/BIOLOGY
Educated at Northgate Grammar
School, Ipswich. Liverpool
University and Southampton
University. (P.G.C.E.) Appointed
to Gt.Yarmouth Grammar School
in 1977 to teach Biology.

MR. J.R. PACK
Cert.Ed.
HEAD OF PHYSICAL
EDUCATION
Educated at Madeley College and
University of Keele. Joined the
staff of Greenacre School in 1972
as Head of Physical Education
Dept. Widely Involved in the
coaching and Administration of
P.E. locally.

MR. B.F. PATTERSON
Cert.Ed.
MATHEMATICS.
Education at Alderman Leach
School, Gt. Yarmouth College of
Further Education And Worcester
College of Education. Previously
taught at Bungay County
Secondary School, Duncan Hall
School And Greenacre School.

MR. A. PAYNE
B.A., Cert.Ed
HEAD OF COMPUTER
STUDIES
Educated Lancaster University.
Taught Oriel Grammar School
1972-80. From 1980-82 worked
in the Research and Development
Department of the British Library
Service on Information Retrieval
Systsems. Appointed to Gt.
Yarmouth High School September
1982

MR. P.W. PEACHEY
B.Ed.
GEOGRAPHY
Educated at Soham Grammar
School. Trained at Keswick
Hall College of Education.
B.Ed., degree at University of
East Anglia. Joined Staff of
Gt.Yarmouth Grammar School in
1977.

MR. C.J. PEARSON
Cert.Ed.
CRAFT, DESIGN,
TECHNOLOGY
After a Mechanical Engineering
Apprenticeship at Rolls Royce,
Nottingham, became a Design
Engn. In the Dept.of Production
Engineering At the University
of Nottingham. Then At the
University of Loughborough
Dept. of Creation Design. On
Completion of Teacher Training
Course, College of Ripon and
York, St.John. Taught Metalwork
at Hospital School.

MR. K.C. RUTLAND
Cert.Ed.
CRAFT, DESIGN
TECHNOLOGY.
In Charge of Technology.
Educated at St.Mary's,
Chesterfield, St. Thomas More's
and St.Mary's College Strawberry
Hill. Worked in Solicitor's
Office before Teacher Training.
Appointed To Gt.Yarmouth
Grammar School 1974.

MRS. H. ALLEN-SEMARK
B.A.
ART
Educated Thorpe Grammar
School, Reading University and
Manchester Polytechnic. Taught
at Cranford Community School.
Appointed to Gt. Yarmouth
Grammar School in 1979

MRS. G. SCOTT
Cert. Ed.
MATHEMATICS
Educated at the Park School
for Girls, Preston and C.F.Mott
College of Education Subsequently
taught at Cliff Park High School.

MR. J. SCALES
M.A.
HISTORY
Educated in Norwich and at
Cambridge University. History
Master and Librarian in a
Liverpool Boys' Grammar School,
(Subsequently Comprehensive)
from 1959-79. Then Claydon High
School until 1982.

MRS. P.A. SIMPSON
Cert.Ed.
SUPPORT EDUCATION.
Educated at Queen Elizabeth's
Girls' Grammar School, Barnet
and Bedford College of Physical
Education. Taught At Greenacre
Secondary School, Gt. Yarmouth
and Clare Middle School. Suff.

MR. D.B. SMITH
B.A.
HEAD OF GERMAN
Educated at Wigan Grammar
School, Exeter University and
Leeds University (P.G.C.E.)
Taught at Wolsley Hall Grammar
School and the Head of German
at Bramhall High School 1969-78.
Appointed as Head of German At
Gt. Yarmouth Grammar School in
1978

MR. F.T. SOUTHGATE
Cert.Ed., B.A.
HEAD OF BIOLOGY
Educated at Rivington and
Blackrod Grammar School,
Sheffield City College And
Open University. Taught 9 years
at Stanground Comprehensive
School and 2 years at Greenacre
Secondary as Head of Science.

MR. E. STARKINGS
Cert. Ed.
HEAD OF RESOURCES.
In charge Of Greenacre Annexe.
Educated at Gt. Yarmouth
Grammar School and at
the College of St.Mark and
St.John,Chelsea Served in the
R.A.F. Taught at Styles School and
then Greenacre School as Second
Teacher until 1982

MRS. K.H. SYMEOU
B.A.
ENGLISH/RELIGIOUS
EDUCATION
Educated at Gt.Yarmouth
Grammar School And West
London Institute of Higher
Education. Previously taught
briefly at Claydon High School.
Appointed to Gt. Yarmouth High
School in 1981

MISS E.M. TOWNSON
B.Sc.
HEAD OF GIRLS PHYSICAL
EDUCATION
Educated at Plumstead Manor
Comp. (formerly Kings Warren
Grammar) S.E. London and
Aberystwyth University.
Appointed to G.Y.G.S.in 1973 for
Girls P.E. and Biology.

MRS. S.J. TOLLADAY
B.A.
ENGLISH
Educated at Kettering High
School, Leicester University
and Southlands College. Taught
at St.John's School, a Large
Comprehensive, in Epping from
1977-82.

MR. M.J. TURNER
B.A.
CRAFT DESIGN,
TECHNOLOGY
Educated in Norwich before
becoming an apprentice
boatbuilder. City and Guilds Silver
Medalist in 1979 and
Involved in the prototype
construction of Jack Powles
International Sailing And Cruising
Yachts. Gained B.A., Degree from
Open University in 1980.
Lecturer in Design in Further
Education.

MISS C.P. WAY
B.Sc., M.Ed.
HEAD OF SUPPORT
EDUCATION
Studied Psychology at North East
London Polytechnic, P.G.C.E.
at Avery Hill and Studied for a
Higher Degree in Psychology at
Sussex University. Taught in two
Comprehensive Schools in the
London Borough of Newham. Head
of Educational Therapy Unit. Moved
to Gt. Yarmouth High School after
work as a Adviser in a school for
Maladjusted Children and research
into needs of Gifted Children.

MISS S. WAYMENT
Cert.Ed., B.Ed.
ENGLISH
Educated at Haberdasher's Askes'
Hatcham Girls' School and Avery
Hill College, London. Worked
in a short stay Children's Home,
assessing children. Taught 4 years
in Sydenham Comp. School, 2
years at Cliff Park.

MR. K. WOODCOCK
B.A.
HEAD OF HISTORY
Educated at the Hospital School,
the Gt. Yarmouth College of
Further Education and Keele
University. Joined the staff of The
Hospital School in 1978 becoming
Head of History in 1980.

MRS. A. WOOLTORTON
Cert.Ed.
HOME ECONOMICS, SUPPORT
EDUCATION. YEAR LEADER
2nd YEAR.
Educated at Sir John Leman
School and College of All Saints,
Tottenham. Wide Teaching
experience at Harris Secondary
School and Harris Middle School.
Subsequently appointed to
Hospital Secondary School, where
Responsible for Home Economics
and Girls' welfare.

MR. E.J. BRADNOCK
Cert. Ed.
DIRECTOR OF SUPPORT UNIT
Educated at Eltham College and
Avery Hill College of Education.
Wide experience in teaching,
becoming Head of Art at Picardy
School, Belvedere and Ramsden
School, Orpington. Deputy Head
at western school, Mitcham before
moving to establish a Sailing
School in Norfolk.

MR. G. DARNELL
Cert. Ed.
SUPPORT UNIT
Educated at Carnegie School of
P.E., City of Leeds and Carnegie
College. Teaching experience at
Meole Brace School, Shrewsbury.
In charge of P.E. at Community
Home in Woking and at red House
Community Home.

MRS. C.P. HUDSON
SECRETARY
Previous experience includes
many years as the Principle's
Secretary at the College of Further
Education, and subsequently as
Clerical and Library Assistant
at Martham School. Appointed
as Secretary to Great Yarmouth
Grammar School in 1980.

MISS G.E. SMITH
SECRETARY
After six years secretarial work
in Great Yarmouth Town Hall and
Education department, became
Secretary at the Hospital school in
1977. Moved to Great Yarmouth
High School in 1982.

MRS. N. MOBBS
SECRETARY (Part-time)
Four years' service in the
W.R.A.C. were followed by ten
years as Secretary in the Great
Yarmouth Housing Department.
Appointed as Secretary to Great
Yarmouth Grammar School in
1958, has continued in the school
since then, first on a full-time
basis, and on a part-time basis for
the past 18 years.

MR. D. KNOWLES
Laboratory Technician
Educated at Ernest Bailey
Grammar School and North East
London Polytechnic, worked
as Laboratory Technician in
Industry and Schools. Appointed
to Great Yarmouth High school in
September, 1982.

MR. R. CANHAM
SENIOR TECHNICAIN, CRAFT
DESIGN TECHNOLOGY
Appointed to Great Yarmouth
Grammar School in 1981 after
many years of experience
in Industry. Interests and
Qualification in Engineering
and Art and allied with wide
Construction Industry experience.

MRS. C. HARRISON
LABORATORY/HOME
ECONOMICS TECHNICIAN
Previous experience includes
several years as Laboratory
Technician at Norfolk and
Norwich Hospital and as a
Technician at Fakenham Grammar
School. Apointed to Great
Yarmouth High School in 1982.

Source: Great Yarmouth High School

Notable Former Students

Great Yarmouth Grammar School

HENRY MANSHIP c.1550-1625 Historian, Merchant, Freeman of the Town and completed his formal education at the Town's Free Grammar School. Author of the first History of Great Yarmouth in 1619.

SIR WILLIAM GOOCH First Baronet 1681-1751. Army Officer and Politician in America. Born in Great Yarmouth attended the Town Grammar School. In 1727 commissioned Lieutenant Governor of Virginia and moved to America to serve in that post for 22 years. His term of office was marked by great amicability with the Americans. Boosted the Colony's economic trade.

AMBROSE REEVES 1899-1980 Attended the Great Yarmouth Grammar School in 1912 joined the West Kent Regiment in 1917. Poor eyesight prevented him from seeing active service in France. 1921 he entered Sidney Sussex College, Cambridge to read History and Moral Science. He graduated in 1924 (obtained his M.A. in 1943) and was an Anglican Ordinand at Mirfield College. Ordained Deacon in 1926 and was Priested 1927. After a curacy at St. Albans, Golders Green, he held incumbencies at St. Margaret Leven, Fife, St. James Haydock and St. Nicholas. Liverpool. In 1949 he was elevated to the Episcopate as the third Bishop of Johannesburg, a post which he held until 1961, as he was an opponent of Apartheid. He was deported for standing out against the South African Government following the Sharpeville Massacre. He then continued to serve the Church as an Assistant Bishop, firstly in the Diocese of London and then Chichester. He was Sub-Prelate of the Order of St. John of Jerusalem. He died on the 23rd December 1980.

SIR ARTHUR HAWKINS Born 1914. Attended Great Yarmouth Grammar School 1925-1932. Developed a career in the Electricity Industry in which he rose to the highest office. The Central Electricity Generating Board which was the overarching organisation which was responsible for the supply of Electricity for much of the country was formed in 1957. There were only 6 Chairman of the Board and Sir Arthur served from 1972-1977 taking an interest in his old town by visiting the former Oil-Fired Station on South Denes from time to time. Knighted in 1976.

PROFESSOR ROBERT STEEL CBE, 1915-1997. Educated at the Great Yarmouth Grammar School, and Cambridge and County High School for Boys, undergraduate at Jesus College, Cambridge. 1st Class Honours Degree 1937. A British Geographer who was John Rankin Professor of Geography at Liverpool University from 1957-1974, Principal of the University College of Swansea, 1974-1982 and vice-chancellor of Swansea from 1979-1981. Honorary Fellow 1982.

MALCOLM SAYER 1916-1970. Educated at the Great Yarmouth Grammar School where his father taught Mathematics and Art and later at the then Loughborough College. Worked for the Bristol Aeroplane Co. during the Second World War. Joined Jaguar in 1951 and was one of the first engineers to apply Principles of Aerodynamic to car design. His designs include: Jaguar C-type (based on the XK 120), Jaguar D-type, Jaguar E-type, Jaguar XJ 13 racing prototype. He also designed the Jaguar XJS although this was launched several years after his death.

JACK DYE Born in 1919. Educated at Great Yarmouth Grammar School 1930-37 Left School to become a Professional Soldier. Served in 1939-1945 War and was awarded the Military Cross in 1945. The Order of the British Empire in 1965, and became a Commander of the Order of the British Empire in 1968. Appointed Brigadier in 1966 and Commanded the South Arabian Army 1966-68. General Officer Commanding Eastern District of the Army 1969-71, Colonel Commandant The Queen's Division 1970-74, Deputy Colonel Royal Anglian Regiment 1974-76 and Colonel of Regiment 1976-82. Appointed Deputy Lord Lieutenant for the County of Suffolk 1979 and then the Vice Lord Lieutenant 1983-1994. Director Volunteers, Territorials and Cadets 1971-74. Major-General late Royal Norfolk Regiment.

PROFESSOR KENNETH FIELDING 1924-1994. Fielding began his long intellectual journey by being educated at the Great Yarmouth Grammar School. After University he became William Noble Fellow, College of Education, Kirkby, Liverpool 1954-56, Senior Lecturer 1956-57, Vice Principal at the City of Liverpool College. English Literature, Edinburgh University 1966-84. Emeritus Professor, Fellow 1984-2005. Major authority on the Letters and Novels of Charles Dickens.

WALTER GOSS (Died January 2008) Attended Great Yarmouth Grammar School and was evacuated to Retford, subsequently gained entrance to London University and gained a Diploma from University College. A lifetime of service to the Amateur Football Association. A life Vice-president of the Amateur Football Association in 1969 and having served that Association on the Football Association itself, a life member of the FA in 1987. Closely involved with the University of London Football Club, and a stalwart of the Amateur Football Alliance.

JOHN HENDER DL.,CBE, CFFA, FCA., 1927-2009. Chief Executive of the West Midlands Metropolitan County Council 1973-1986.

PROFESSOR G.S.HAWKINS Born in 1928-2003. Educated at the Great Yarmouth Grammar School from 1940-46, First at Retford and then on the School's return to Great Yarmouth. Graduated from Nottingham University in Physics in 1949 and then worked for his PhD in Radio Astronomy under Sir Bernard Lovell at Manchester University. He then emigrated to the U.S.A. where he worked for the prestigious Smithsonian Institute. He later became the Founding Professor of Astronomy at Boston University and achieved international fame with his book "Stonehenge Decoded" which sought to establish an astronomical significance to the placing of the Stonehenge Stones. He wrote a General Survey of Astronomy called "Splendour in the Skies" but was more widely known for his controversial best Seller "Stonehenge Decoded".

SIR KENNETH MACMILLAN 1929-1992. Won a scholarship at the age of 11 to Great Yarmouth Grammar School and evacuated to Retford, Nottinghamshire. Discovered Ballet, thanks to a local dance teacher Jean Thomas in Retford who taught him tap as well. Performed in Dance Concerts. Returned to Great Yarmouth in 1944, sought out a Ballet Teacher Phyllis Adams, who helped to ensure that he was accepted by the Sadler's Wells Ballet School in 1945 when he was 15. Major Choreographer with world wide reputation. Early professional career with Ninette De Valois's new Junior Company and then moved to Sadler's Wells Ballet School where he spent the rest of his career. Knighted in 1983, and died of a heart attack, back stage, during the first night of the Royal Ballet's revival of Mayerling in the Royal Opera House in 1992. The announcement of his death is made on stage at the end of the Ballet – an extraordinary, dramatic, public conclusion to a life in the theatre. Maintained his connections with the Great Yarmouth Grammar School through a foundation to train talented young dancers.

SIR WILLIAM UTTING CB. Born 1931 educated at Great Yarmouth Grammar School 1942-1950, evacuated to Retford as a first former and left the Grammar School as Head Boy in 1950. Gained an Exhibition Scholarship in Modern Studies at New College, Oxford. Obtained a B.A. Honours Degree in English from the University of Oxford. Became a career Civil Servant in the Social Services, holding Senior Posts in the Probation Service, Local Government and the Civil Service. He retired from the Department of Health in 1991 as the First Chief Inspector of Social Services for England. He engaged in voluntary work, being President of the Mental Health Foundation and Chaired the Joseph Rowntree Foundation, the Council of Goldsmiths, University of London and the National Institute for Social Work. He served on the Committee on Standards of Public Life (The Nolan Committee) from 1994-2001. For the Government he reviewed safeguards for children living away from home. Sir William is an honorary Fellow of New College Oxford, and of Goldsmiths University of London.

MICHAEL HARVEY was born 1934, educated at Great Yarmouth Grammar School 1945-51. His mother ran a Wool Shop in Great Yarmouth and he became greatly interested in the history of hand knitting. After National Service he joined the family business in 1955 opening the firms first post war branch. When he left 15 years later he was General Manager and the business operated from 10 shops. He left the firm toward the end of the 1960's went into academia where he became "Mike Harvey". He obtained a Bachelor's degree in Economics from the University of Hull and a Master's Degree in Accounting and Finance from the London School of Economics. He became professionally qualified and became a career Accountant and taught Accountancy at many Institutions. During his career he was President of the Association of Chartered Certified Accountants (ACCA) and Professor of Business Studies at the University of Westminster, London. He is currently a Freeman of the City of London and Professor Emeritus at London Metropolitan University. He has also served as president of a number of other professional organisations. Professor Mike Harvey serves as a Governor on the Great Yarmouth College of Further Education, Chairing its Audit Committee. He retains an encyclopaedic knowledge of hand knitting.

DAVID BENTLEY 1935 Educated at Great Yarmouth Grammar School 1946-53. Ordained in 1961 and began his Ministry with Curacies at St. Ambrose, Bristol and Holy Trinity with St. Mary, Guildford. Afterwards Rector of Headley, East Hampshire, and Rural Dean of Esher and Warden of the Community of All Hallows, Ditchingham. Bishop of Kings Lynn 1986-1993 and Bishop of Gloucester 1993-2003 in which year he retired.

ROBERT LOYNES Educated at Great Yarmouth Grammar School 1946-1953. Awarded the National Stanley Maxwell prize for being first in Latin at GCE Ordinary level nationally. Great Yarmouth Major Award in 1952. 1953 awarded State Scholarship and gained entry to Trinity College Cambridge and then awarded Senior Scholarship for Mathematics for Trinity College, Cambridge. 1956 awarded 1st class Honours in the Mathematical Tripos. In 1961 he obtained a Diploma in Mathematic Statistics with distinction from the University of Cambridge. 1964 PhD in Mathematics, University of Cambridge and elected Fellow of Churchill College. Professor in the Department of Probability and Statistics at the University of Sheffield.

WILLIAM "BILL" RAYNER Born 1942 educated at Great Yarmouth Grammar School 1953-61. 1960 Great Yarmouth Major Award, 1961 Foundation Scholarship to Selwyn College Cambridge. 1964 MA in English 2 (ii) Selwyn College, University of Cambridge. 1966-68 School Teacher of English, St. Joseph William Mathematical School, Rochester Kent. 1969 MA European Literature (French, German and Russian) University of East Anglia. 1969-73 worked for Central Asia Research Centre (a quasi Government organisation, carrying out Russian translations). 1974-1988 career change and took a Welding Course in Non-Destructive Materials Off-shore. Worked on Oil Platforms. 1988-1997 Principal Lecturer in the Welding Institute Cambridge. 1997-2007 continued to work Offshore as a Welding Specialist and then retired. Several languages self taught and reads both for pleasure and research, French, German, Russian, Italian, Spanish, Norwegian, Dutch, Latin and Ancient Greek. A true polymath.

RICHARD BARFIELD born in 1947 educated at Great Yarmouth Grammar School 1958-1966. Head Boy in 1965-66. Obtained a Bachelor of Science Degree from Edinburgh University and became Chief Investment Manager of the Standard Life Assurance Company, subsequently becoming a Director in 1997 and Chairman in 2008. He became a Director of the Merchants Trust PLC, the Edinburgh Investment Trust PLC, J. P .Morgan Fleming Overseas Investment Trust PLC, Standard Life Investments Property Income Trust Limited, and Coal Staff Trustees Limited.

JOHN CLARE Born in 1950. Educated at Great Yarmouth Grammar School 1961-68 Head Boy in 1967-8. Gained a place at Edinburgh University awarded a B.Sc., 2(i) in Applied Mathematics. Joined Mars Limited and worked for eleven years until 1983 in various sales and marketing positions in the UK, Switzerland, Denmark and Sweden. 1983-85 Marketing and Business Development Director of the Ladbrooke Group PLC. In 1985 he joined the Dixon Group where he worked until his retirement in 2007 holding several Directors' posts before becoming Group Chief Executive Officer in 1993. He was awarded the CBE in 2004. Following his retirement he remains as Chairman of a number of specialised PLC's and is a member of the Edinburgh University Advisory Board.

Sources:
1. *The Dictionary of National Biography*, Oxford, 2004
2. *Who's Who*, 2007
3. Author's Research

Bibliography

Primary Sources

i. Manuscripts:

Norfolk Record Office
Detailed records of the Great Yarmouth Grammar School and the
Great Yarmouth Grammar School Foundation.

NRO. D/ED/9/14,57,58,59,60,61,62,65a,70,71,72,75,76,77,78,83,87,89,102-203,204-224,
225,226,228, 282,283,284,311-332,333, 443,446,480.

Y/ED/ 163-164

ii. Printed Primary Sources

Journals

The Yare (1908-1915)
Chronicle (1930-1981) Great Yarmouth Grammar School
Inside Angle (1990-1993) Great Yarmouth High School
The High Standard (1994-2010) Great Yarmouth High School

Secondary Sources

Books

Boon M. and Meeres F., *Yarmouth is an Antient Town*, Great Yarmouth 2000.
Crisp W., *A Chronological Retrospect of the History of Great Yarmouth*, 1884
Ecclestone A.W., *Great Yarmouth 1886-1936*, Great Yarmouth, 1977.
Green W. and Pollinger G., *The Observer's Book of Aircraft*, 1953.
Hogg W., *Supplement to Great Yarmouth Grammar School History*, Great Yarmouth 1961.
Manship H., *History of Great Yarmouth 1619*, Palmer C, ed., Yarmouth, 1864.
Meeres F., *Norfolk in the First World War*, Chichester, 2004.
Palmer C., *The Perlustration of Great Yarmouth*, 3 Vols., Great Yarmouth, 1872-1875
Swinden H., *The History of Great Yarmouth*, Yarmouth, 1772-1778
Whitehead J. B., *The History of Great Yarmouth Grammar School 1551-1951*, Great Yarmouth, 1951.
The Dictionary of National Biography, Oxford, 2004
Who's Who, 2007